The Films of
Krzysztof Kieślowski

THE FILMS OF KRZYSZTOF KIEŚLOWSKI

The Liminal Image

Joseph G. Kickasola

continuum
NEW YORK • LONDON

2004

The Continuum International Publishing Group Inc
15 East 26 Street, New York, NY 10010

The Continuum International Publishing Group Ltd
The Tower Building, 11 York Road, London SE1 7NX

www.continuumbooks.com

Front cover image: Abstract close-up in *Decalogue II* (the resurrection scene) from
The Decalogue (DVD), © 1999 Facets Multimedia, Inc., used by permission.

Printed in the United States of America

Library of Congress Cataloging-in-Publication Data
Kickasola, Joseph G.
    The films of Krzysztof Kieślowski : the liminal image / Joseph G. Kickasola.
        p.   cm.
    Includes bibliographical references and index.
    ISBN 0-8264-1558-X (alk. paper) — ISBN 0-8264-1559-8 (pbk. : alk.
paper)
    1. Kieślowski, Krzysztof, 1941- – Criticism and interpretation.   I. Title.
PN1998.3.K54K53 2004
791.4302′33′092 – dc22
                                                                2004008974

Contents

Figures

To illustrate the points the author is making, some images from especially significant scenes in Kieślowski's films have been reproduced. Each image is a single frame taken from the full-length motion picture and is used here for educational purposes pursuant to the Fair Use Doctrine. This book is not endorsed by or affiliated with any of the performers, directors, producers, or screenwriters who created these films or by the entities that produced or distributed them, and the single frame images are used here for criticism and commentary only. Readers who are interested in seeing these motion pictures in their entirety are encouraged to buy or rent copies of the films from an authorized source.

Chapter 2 figures:

Figs. 1, 2, 5, 6, 38, 39, 40, 41 from *The Double Life of Véronique*, © 1991 Sideral Productions. Video release © 1992 Paramount Pictures.

Figs. 3, 12, 18, 19, 20, 21, 22, 23, 27, 28, 29, 30, 42 from *Red* (DVD), © 2003 Buena Vista Home Entertainment, Inc.

Figs. 4, 7, 10, 13, 14, 15, 16, 17, 34, 35, 36 from *Blue* (DVD), © 2003 Buena Vista Home Entertainment, Inc.

Figs. 8, 37 from *A Short Film about Killing* (DVD), © 2004 Kino International, Corporation

Figs. 9, 11, 24, 25, 26, 31, 32, 33, 43, 44, 45 from *The Decalogue* (DVD), © 1999 Facets Multimedia, Inc.

Chapter 3 figures:

Figs. 46, 47, 48 from *Blind Chance*, © 1981 Film Unit TOR

Figs. 49, 50 from *No End*, © 1984 Film Polski, Video release © 1994 New Yorker Films

Chapter 4 figures:

Fig. 51 from *The Decalogue* (DVD), © 1999 Facets Multimedia, Inc.

Chapter 5 figures:

Fig. 52 from *Blue* (DVD), © 2003 Buena Vista Home Entertainment, Inc.

Preface

But what is existence? Existence is the child that is born of the infinite and the finite, the eternal and the temporal, and is therefore a constant striving. . . . [1]

— Søren Kierkegaard

There I sat, typing away at Chapter 5, attempting to do justice to the kinship between Kieślowski's *No End* and *Blue*. As I began the paragraph, our phone rang, and my wife mercifully answered as I struggled to maintain my concentration. A dear friend from college called. She'd recently married and was announcing her new pregnancy. I smiled at my wife's enthusiastic reaction, passed on my congratulations, and set to work on the following sentence:

> *Blue* and *No End* both feature strong Kieślowskian visuals (e.g., close-ups on hands), blue as a thematic color, striking abstract compositions, a car accident, themes of grief and suicide, and a focused use of music.

Precisely at the time I was writing the words "a car accident," my wife interrupted me: an urgent call had come in on the second phone line. I left the sentence ominously dangling and picked up the phone, and my father, in faltering voice, informed me that his youngest brother (a dear uncle of mine) had been suddenly killed in a highway accident. New life mingled with new death, amid a sentence about a filmmaker deeply concerned with both. All stood in uncanny synchrony.

This was a Kieślowskian moment, not only because it might have been plucked from one of his films, but also because it serves as a nexus of human meaning. There is a strong sense of telos in the human person that makes us feel such things are not random, *could not* be random, and that meaning is not something we merely project onto the surface of things, but rather,

---

1. *Concluding Unscientific Postscript to the Philosophical Fragments,* trans. David F. Swenson (Princeton: Princeton University Press, 1941), 85.

especially at such moments, a message being delivered to us. Kieślowski never took a hard position on the truth of the matter. Rather, he was interested in the search. From whom is the message being delivered? we might ask. God? One's own coping mechanism? Something between? All interpretations may be fair game when approaching Kieślowski's films, but he does not permit avoidance of the issue. Metaphysics, real or imagined, *matter.*

Kieślowski's point seems to be that our desire for meaning makes us human and is worthy of exploration. This metaphysical quest runs consistently through Kieślowski's films. They almost never give us concrete answers to those questions, but function best as a sort of map, charting the tortuous, often bewildering topography of human experience. By calling his work "maplike," I do not mean Kieślowski's work can be seen as a complete, structuralist grammar. His approach is more elastic and phenomenologically focused than that. Giuliana Bruno uses the term *atlas* as she plots emotion's movements through the revelatory connections of architecture, film, and art.[2] In a similar way, Kieślowski charts the liminal spaces, demarcating the apparent thresholds of metaphysical and physical, transcendent and immanent, eternal and temporal. This is the same liminal ground that philosopher and critic George Steiner describes when he states that the arts are "rooted in substance . . . immanence," but "do not stop there." Art functions in "the continuum between temporality and eternity, between matter and spirit, between man and 'the other.' "[3]

Several books already have been written on Kieślowski. Annette Insdorf writes insightfully, even movingly, about her late friend Kieślowski in *Double Lives, Second Chances.*[4] Emma Wilson argues for a more rigorous theoretical approach to the Pole's French films, particularly in light of Gilles Deleuze's writing and other postmodern ideas.[5] The Lacanian theorist Slavoj Žižek has weighed in with his unique psychoanalytic perspective.[6] Among Kieślowski scholars, Paul Coates has published most extensively on Kieślowski, his

2. Giuliana Bruno, *Atlas of Emotion: Journeys in Art, Architecture, and Film* (New York: Verso, 2002).

3. George Steiner, *Real Presences* (Chicago: University of Chicago Press, 1989), 227.

4. Annette Insdorf, *Double Lives, Second Chances: The Cinema of Krzysztof Kieślowski* (New York: Hyperion, 1999).

5. Emma Wilson, *Memory and Survival: The French Cinema of Krzysztof Kieślowski* (Oxford: Legenda, 2000).

6. Slavoj Žižek, *The Fright of Real Tears: Krzysztof Kieślowski Between Theory and Post-Theory* (London: BFI Publishing, 2001).

edited anthology *Lucid Dreams*[7] and a continual stream of articles[8] being but a few prominent examples. There are many other sources: small books, articles, and theses, and Coates catalogs most of them at the end of *Lucid Dreams*. These authors each have their strengths, and our thanks is due them.

Even so, to my mind, no critic or theorist has fully explored the interplay between Kieślowski's cinematic style and his thematic concerns. During the last few decades, the film studies community has favored issues of representation (e.g., gender issues, racial issues, cultural representation and sexual orientation and representation) and politics (e.g., power, globalization, political "rhetoric," and economic issues) over formal concerns. Those who most vocally champion formal approaches have made an impact (e.g., David Bordwell and Kristin Thompson) but have not swayed the majority of the camp.

Of course, representational and political issues should have a strong presence in film studies, but I argue that too many film scholars have abandoned formal issues, to the detriment of the field. As Charles Eidsvik has remarked, it is no longer "fashionable" to talk about films in terms of how they are made,[9] but those of us who have worked in film production realize how important that factor is. Whereas Eidsvik pursued a point-by-point comparison of Kieślowskian script and final product, I will pursue a tendency in Kieślowskian style, with a focus on two key formal issues: immediacy and abstraction. I believe that writing about style deserves more theoretical rigor, and in Kieślowski's case, the style has direct bearing on how his films communicate. I will contend throughout that Kieślowski consistently pursues intangibles, metaphysical issues, and experiences that are "beyond words." He was always interested in these issues (even during his early, more "political" period), and his stylistic evolution can be seen as a quest for a clearer, more potent cinematic registration of them.

The danger in such a theoretical project is twofold: first, one can lapse into an anemic mysticism lacking any sort of theoretical rigor, and second, writing about things to which words do no justice seems self-defeating. I confront the first danger by rooting claims in several theoretical traditions

---

7. Paul Coates, *Lucid Dreams: The Films of Krzysztof Kieślowski* (Trowbridge, Wiltshire, England: Flicks Books, 1999).

8. Paul Coates, "Kieślowski and the Antipolitics of Color: A Reading of the 'Three Colors' Trilogy," *Cinema Journal* 41:2 (Winter 2002): 41–66.

9. Charles Eidsvik, "Decalogues 5 and 6 and the Two Short Films," in Coates, *Lucid Dreams,* 78.

(namely, a nuanced, contemporary phenomenology, combined with elements of cognitive psychology and contemporary neuroscience). The second danger I cannot completely avoid, but I hope my venture into epistemological mechanics will lend insight into the power of Kieślowski's work. My sincere desire is that more will see, rather, *experience*, the films. They are, without a doubt, more resonant than any book of criticism.

Classic phenomenology maintains that mere "signification" is a reductive way of approaching meaning in an image. In my judgment, this is particularly true in Kieślowski's case, as so much of his style hinges on the experience of seeing his stylistic devices employed within the narrative context. It is not simply that Kieślowski hopes to evoke feelings in the audience, but that the feelings are fundamental to the sort of meaning he is trying to express: the "unspeakable" (beyond words) and the metaphysical (beyond photographic indexicality). The reader will, no doubt, sense my struggle throughout the book to articulate that which is really inarticulable, but my description of the perceptive processes at work should lend some insight into Kieślowski's style and lend explanation as to why so many people around the world have found his films so deeply meaningful.

This is not to say I will avoid discussion of content (issues of representation, politics, or other "verbal" matters), but that form will not be treated as incidental to the overall "meaning" equation. I hope that this study will yield a double-sided view of Kieślowski's craft: a greater appreciation for his art making, as well as its capacity for meaning. I believe there is much more to be said about his mastery of abstract imagery, his innovative use of sound, and his deliberate circumvention of "standard" cinematic codes. Unlike other so-called art directors, who use similar techniques but often fail to rise above commentary on the medium itself, Kieślowski uses these stylistic liberties to explore his overarching philosophical concerns (i.e., human meaning, fate, God, human suffering, love, etc.). Whereas his documentaries and early films look considerably different from his later, more famous works, I assert that this stylistic metamorphosis is the natural result of his search for ultimate reality amid the bewildering uncertainties of postmodernity. For Kieślowski, the question of ultimate reality is not so much a scientific matter, but a humanistic one — an intentional question spanning human needs and the objective world.

Kieślowski's work goes beyond "telling" a story and, I maintain, even beyond "showing." In his foreword to the published volume of the *Decalogue* screenplays, the great filmmaker Stanley Kubrick observes:

... [I]n this book of screenplays by Krzysztof Kieślowski and his co-author, Krzysztof Piesiewicz, it should not be out of place to observe that they have the rare ability to *dramatize* their ideas rather than just talking about them. By making their points through the dramatic action of the story they gain the added power of allowing the audience to *discover* what's really going on rather than being told. They do this with such dazzling skill, you never see the ideas coming and don't realize until much later how profoundly they have reached your heart.[10]

Kubrick's observations form something of a foundation for this study, in that I am attempting to shed light on how Kieślowski accomplishes what he does. It is a rare gift indeed to communicate on this level, and the means by which Kieślowski accomplishes this task are a fertile field to harvest. Beyond "dazzling skill," a phrase worthy of explication, I believe there is a theoretical thrust to Kieślowski's work that informs his technique: a basic phenomenological commitment in Kieślowski's work directing his stylistic choices. What is fascinating about Kieślowski is his ability to grant experience a unique epistemological weight.

To talk about Kieślowski apart from style is to diminish his stature as an artist, not because technical skill is his paramount virtue, but because his technical, theoretical, and narrative concerns are so extraordinarily interwoven that to ignore one is to weaken them all. Others have provided strong "readings" of the films (a term betraying its literary bent, pertaining to themes, the interplay of symbols, dialogue, drama, characters, etc.), and I will do my share of "reading" and "reflection" as well. Yet I hope that this work will emerge as a distinctively cinematic study, highlighting cinematic experiences that often cannot be reduced to easy articulation or commonplace symbolic structures.

It was this stylistic thread of similarity that I perceived in Michelangelo Antonioni, Andrei Tarkovsky, and Kieślowski, which changed the way I thought about the value of the cinematic medium. The films themselves generated the theory, not the other way around (a virtue Dudley Andrew heralds in the introduction to the collection *Film in the Aura of Art*).[11] That thread initiated a long research project on abstraction in film, some

---

10. Krzysztof Kieślowski and Krzysztof Piesiewicz, *Decalogue: The Ten Commandments,* trans. Phil Cavendish and Susannah Bluh (London: Faber and Faber, 1991), vii.

11. Dudley Andrew, *Film in the Aura of Art* (Princeton, NJ: Princeton University Press, 1984), xi.

of which ends up in this volume. To me, this is neglected foundational material.

I feel the unique contribution of this book is a way of understanding how form might convey knowledge. While discussing Tarkovsky at the Society of Cinema Studies conference in 2002, a colleague confessed that he has never been able to teach Tarkovsky's style in a truly productive way. For instance, if there was a sumptuous visual of a tree-lined hill in a Tarkovsky film, he never felt able to articulate the full effect of the image. The key difference between these scenes and other, more common-yet-striking images is not the degree of visual flair, but rather the weight of epistemological significance created by the placement and execution of the visuals. We must get beyond the "wow" factor, lest we demean the filmmakers' efforts.

To accomplish this, we must first locate the themes — the ideas that are important to Kieślowski — and then articulate their stylistic manifestations. It will become clear that Kieślowski's active agnosticism (i.e., a searching out of his metaphysical instincts amid his many doubts and questions) manifests itself most often in that liminal space between the physical and metaphysical.

Annette Insdorf recalls a time, at the 1994 Cannes Film Festival, when Kieślowski refused the title "moralist," but, when presented with the follow-up suggestion "metaphysician," he shrugged and said, "If you wish."[12] This is a key quote for insight into Kieślowski's approach to life and films. It is probably a mistake to call him a Christian (at least in the dogmatic sense), yet to simply label him a humanist (as many have) is to understate his spiritual concerns. Paul Coates believes that Kieślowski should be seen as more atheistic than agnostic, yet still affords him the title "mystic," despite his distance from any organized religion.[13] It is certainly true that Kieślowski expressed distaste for Polish Catholicism on more than one occasion.[14] However, to take his flight from that church as an atheistic gesture strikes me as overreaching, and I will pursue this issue in Chapter 1.

On several occasions, he very clearly argues for a broader metaphysic:

---

12. Insdorf, *Double Lives,* 184.

13. Coates, *Lucid Dreams,* 2–3.

14. One such occasion is a public meeting in Ukraine, referenced by Polish film critic Tadeusz Sobolewski. Ibid., 20. Another is his agitated, irritated reaction to a comment by Piesiewicz that the *Decalogue* series might cause some people to turn to the Catholic Church. *The Ten Commandments of Krzysztof Kieślowski* (television documentary), prod. Adam Low, BBC, 1990.

> The world is not only bright lights, this hectic pace, the Coca-Cola with a straw, the new car. . . . Another truth exists . . . a hereafter? Yes, surely. Good or bad, I don't know, but . . . something else.[15]

It is within this context that we should interpret his comment that his approach to mystery has "no religious undertones," while, in nearly the same breath, stating:

> But I think that there is a point at which all these trifling matters, all these little mysteries, come together like droplets of mercury to form a larger question about the meaning of life, about our presence here, what in fact went before and what will come after, whether there is someone who controls all this, or whether it all depends on our own reason or on someone or something else. That mystery is there all the time. Of course it has certain religious connotations, but those connotations fundamentally arise out of the existential questions, rather than the other way around.[16]

In reading through the many interviews he gave, it becomes apparent that Kieślowski's discomfort with religion is actually a skepticism regarding dogmatic institutions, and not just those of a religious order. Kieślowski wanted his films to first be human dramas, not political tracts, moral lessons, or religious fables. It was in existential reality that Kieślowski personally confronted the metaphysical issues that haunted him, and it is that reality he hoped to portray on screen. So my use of the terms *spiritual* and *transcendent* throughout this book should be interpreted to mean "pertaining to metaphysics." Within this framework, I am able to legitimately apply a number of broad theological ideas to his work without overstating the measure of Kieślowski's beliefs. The metaphysical, including the spiritual, remained the object of his lifelong interrogation.

How to Read This Book

The purpose of the book is twofold: to provide a solid understanding of Kieślowski and his films and to advance a particular theory of his style. I hope this book will serve the general student of film as well as the Kieślowski admirer, and, for that reason, it consists of two parts. Part 1 (Chapters 1 and 2) provides background information and detailed theoretical discussion as a foundation for stylistic consideration of Kieślowski's corpus of fiction

---

15. Insdorf, *Double Lives*, xv. From an interview with *Télérama* (Paris: September 1993).
16. Interview with Coates, *Lucid Dreams*, 167–168.

films. Part 2 consists of detailed explication and analysis of each of the fiction films, with some time dedicated to the documentaries and shorter works.

As for Part 1, the first chapter discusses Kieślowski himself: his history, his country, and his themes. The second chapter builds a theoretical construct through which to view Kieślowski's films, focusing particularly on his stylistic transition in the 1980s. The second part of that chapter applies the theory to particular filmic instances.

In Part 2 (Chapters 3–5) I begin "reading" his feature films, but not as one reads a novel. I hope the reader will synthesize the theory of Part 1 with his or her experience of the films themselves. Only then can we properly begin interpreting Kieślowski's work. I do not mean to set up a false dichotomy between word and image, sense and meaning, or form and content. Rather, my aim is quite the opposite, as I see each of these pairs as inextricably linked and equally indispensable to the cinematic conveyance of meaning.

Also, I *assume the reader has seen the films*. As I explain in Part 1, suspense and "bracketed" information are essential factors in Kieślowski's aesthetic, and any discussion of the film before seeing it will effectively ruin something of what he wished to accomplish. The synopses before each film exist only to provide a foundation for the discussion to follow.

Throughout the book (and, in particular, Chapter 1), I will introduce smaller discussions on historical factors, cultural significance, and artistic influences as they seem relevant to the main discussions at hand. As for film theory, I will endeavor to blend it with the discussion, as it serves to elucidate the aesthetic issues. In terms of range, I will survey all Kieślowski's films, but I will focus on the feature-length fiction films (with the addition of the short film *Personnel* and the ten short *Decalogue* films), and emphasize his later, international efforts (*The Double Life of Véronique, Blue, White,* and *Red*). Other works (such as documentaries and short fictional pieces) will receive more condensed treatment.

A word about the auteur theory: although this debate has long ceased to be interesting, I should mention that I pragmatically treat Kieślowski as an auteur. It is absolutely true that his films were strongly influenced by other people, most notably his cowriter Krzysztof Piesiewicz, his cinematographers (particularly Sławomir Idziak), and his primary composer, Zbigniew Preisner. However, Kieślowski himself attested that all the final decisions for his films (i.e., what stays in, what stays out, what gets reshot or added, etc.)

rested on him, and I generally take him at his word.[17] We can never know all the multiple reasons that Kieślowski made a choice to have something "seen," but we do know he was extensively involved in the editing process of each of his films. I often phrase things in a manner that may suggest that Kieślowski receive credit for things that strike me as insightful, unique, or stylistically interesting. It is possible (even likely) that these things came about through circumstance or the suggestions of others (such as Piesiewicz or the cinematographers). Everything I say should be bracketed with this admission, and I hope I will not "undersell" the contributions of these others to this remarkable body of work. Essentially, Kieślowski is the organizing principle for this study in the same way that he was the central force in his films, but throughout, I will investigate his many influences.

---

17. Krzysztof Kieślowski, *Kieślowski on Kieślowski,* ed. Danusia Stok (London: Faber and Faber, 1995), 200.

Acknowledgments

I would like to thank my editor at Continuum, David Barker, for having such faith in me and continuing to encourage me in my ideas. I would also like to thank Dudley Andrew, Annette Insdorf, Carl Plantinga, Mark J. P. Wolf, Terry Lindvall, Michael Graves, Dennis Bounds, Brian Price, David Sterritt, and many others in the academic community who have given me invaluable help and inspiration through conversation and correspondence. Many thanks are due David Jeffrey, Wallace Daniel, and Michael Korpi at Baylor University, who all expressed solid support and gave me a much needed sabbatical to complete this project. Thanks to Mary Slaughter for steady encouragement and Elizabeth Belz Odegard for help with the manuscript. My parents, Dr. Joseph N. and Myrenna Kickasola, gave me everything I needed to arrive here, and my wife, Linnea, continues to sustain me. Her tireless assistance throughout this project has continually reminded me of that fact.

Part 1

History — Biography — Theory

WHICH KIEŚLOWSKI?

K rzysztof Wierzbicki's documentary *Krzysztof Kieślowski: I'm So-So* begins with perspectives on Kieślowski through the eyes of different people (a policeman, a medium, etc.). No two descriptions are alike. In film studies, the theoretical portraits remain no less varied. Some of these characterizations are more justified than others, I think, but my purpose here is not to debate the "real" Kieślowski. Indeed, Kieślowski himself could sometimes be as enigmatic and even contradictory as his films. His interviews often show his pessimistic (and occasionally cantankerous) side, as he might deny his desire to make films, deny the power of film to change anything, or express his hatred of being "stuck in a drawer and labeled" by anyone.[1] One needs to treat his comments with his personality in view. For instance, how seriously can we take his statement "I haven't got a great talent for films"?[2]

What I hope to do here is offer another dimension to the public portrait of this great artist, highlighting his stylistic virtues as they communicate the themes that mattered most to him. Every unique, artistic style emerges from the lifeworld (*lebenswelt*) of the artist, so it makes sense to begin here with Kieślowski's culture.

---

1. Nothing shows this better than the incredibly tense and strange interview featured on the 2003 release of *The Decalogue* (DVD) by Facets Video. In "Kieślowski Meets the Press," he skirmishes with a roomful of Polish journalists. By the end, he has labeled most of them incompetent and denied any of them the satisfaction of hearing romantic self-assessments of his art.

2. *Kieślowski on Kieślowski,* ed. Danusia Stok (London: Faber and Faber, 1993), 194.

Kieślowski's Poland

The following history of Poland illustrates that Kieślowski worked from a very specific historical and cultural position. This survey is not exhaustive, but condensed from several sources[3] and focused on themes that appear relevant to Kieślowski's work. The world in which he was raised and became an artist, the world with which he constantly dialogued in his films, was not stable, free, or economically successful like the United States or Western Europe. The sufferings of Kieślowski's early childhood mirror the sufferings of his country in many ways, and the fruits of that suffering — a philosophical outlook, a compassionate spirit, a certain constitutional rigor — emerge clearly in his work.

The history of Poland consistently bears the marks of upheaval, devastation, and, for lack of a better phrase, identity crisis. Throughout its history only a few constants have remained, including the Slavic heritage of the majority of Poles and the presence of the Catholic Church (both important sources of Polish identity and pride). The rest of Poland's history is a surging sea of instability and devastation, facing no less than three utterly destructive wars and hundreds of years of occupation in a constant tug and pull between covetous, invading powers. Only in recent times does Poland show signs of independence and stability, with hope of recovering something of a historical identity.

Scholars dispute the original dates of the Slavic settlement of Poland.[4] Some estimates place it as early as the sixth or seventh century and others as late as the tenth century. Regardless, a rich Slavic culture flourished there for centuries, and a national Christian identity was formed: "[Prince] Mieszko's baptism in A.D. 965 was the first step in the formation of the single most important element in modern Polish culture."[5]

The time of Nicholaus Copernicus (1473–1543), one of Poland's favorite sons, proved rich and fruitful, and, as historian Norman Davies points out,

---

3. Timothy Garton Ash, *The Uses of Adversity: Essays on the Fate of Central Europe* (New York: Vintage, 1990) and *History of the Present: Essays, Sketches and Dispatches from Europe in the 1990s* (New York: Vintage, 2001); M. B. Biskupski, *The History of Poland* (Westport, CT: Greenwood Press, 2000); Norman Davies, *The Heart of Europe: A Short History of Poland* (Oxford: Clarendon Press, 1984).

4. Davies, ibid., 283.

5. Ibid., 288.

religious tolerance was exemplary in this region.[6] However, in 1569, Poland and Lithuania united, with the ruler of the new kingdom elected by the Sejm, a type of parliament. Foreign candidates were acceptable to the Sejm, leading to the election of only four native Poles over 223 years (with seven foreigners ruling from 1572 to 1795). So begins a manic period in the nation, swinging from stability to foreign occupation, war, economic crisis, and governmental upheaval.

During this period, in the mid-seventeenth century, Poland was virtually destroyed.[7] A Cossack rebellion (one of several internal conflicts), numerous foreign invasions, famine, and the bubonic plague earned this period the name "The Deluge."[8] Jan III Sobieski revived the country for a while, but by the eighteenth century it was caught between Russia, Prussia, and Austria, each wanting Poland for itself. They divided the country among them through a series of negotiations called the Three Partitions of Poland (1764–1795). These partitions threw the country into tumult, and essentially Poland did not exist as a free union of all Poles for well over a hundred years, with only minor periods of reconstitution.[9] In this bitter period, the Russians and the Prussians were particularly brutal, attempting to eradicate all traces of Polish culture from their respective regions. Poverty was everywhere, provoking mass emigration.

During World War I, the occupying countries fought bitterly with each other. Again, the country was essentially leveled. This time it emerged from the conflict as an independent nation, devastated but hopeful. Unfortunately, this was not a restored Poland as much as a reinvented nation, with a completely different position in Europe.[10] Józef Piłsudski's army defeated the Russians in the Polish-Soviet War (1919–1920), and he emerged as a dictatorial, but stabilizing, political leader. In 1939, however, Russia and Prussia (now Germany) were at it again, agreeing to take back Poland. On September 1, Adolf Hitler invaded. Sixteen days later, Joseph Stalin did as well. Thus initiated one of the most bitter and evil periods in the history of the world. Russia and Germany spared little thought for the subjugated Poles. The atrocities of Vinnitsa on the Russian side (summary execution of

---

6. Ibid., 295–296.
7. Ibid., 304–305.
8. Biskupski, *The History of Poland,* 16.
9. Ibid., 158.
10. Ibid., 37.

prisoners) and Bydgoszcz on the German side (20,000 civilians executed) were only the beginning.[11] Germany's horrific eugenic and anti-Semitic efforts are well known. Lesser known are stories of Russian terror, such as the exile of two million Poles to Arctic Russia, Siberia and Kazakhstan. According to Davies, one million were dead within a year.[12]

Both occupiers aimed at eliminating Polish identity through executions of influential Poles, a ban on the teaching of Polish, the destruction of villages, and the replacement of Poles with non-Poles. The psychological effect of these efforts cannot be underestimated. It was this Poland into which Kieślowski was born: in Nazi-occupied Warsaw, June 27, 1941.

With Kieślowskian synchrony, in the very month of Kieślowski's birth, Hitler viciously betrayed Stalin. Within two weeks he had claimed all of Poland (and part of Russia) as his own. The Polish intelligentsia were summarily executed, and most of Poland's three million Jews died in the Holocaust. Native Polish soil became home to some of the worst Nazi experiments and death camps: Majdanek, Birkenau, and Oświęcim (Auschwitz). Resistance was heroic and, eventually, well organized,[13] but ultimately too weak in the face of Hitler's might.

It became clear to the Allies that they could not win without the Soviets, and Stalin was happy to cut a deal. All Poles greeted Hitler's ultimate defeat with joy, but victory came at a terrible price. The Yalta conference yielded Poland to Stalin, however reluctantly, and, in short, Polish rule was outmaneuvered by Stalin's machinations. The Allies had little ability to argue, and the Poles little strength to resist. By war's end, approximately 18 percent of Poland's prewar population was dead.[14]

Kieślowski only knew a Communist, Soviet-bloc Poland until the very last years of his tragically shortened life. He lived through what Davies has characterized as "The Legacy of Humiliation" for the Polish people.[15] Stalin crushed all resistance, Communist or non-Communist. After Stalin's death, Polish Communist authorities were granted some autonomy in matters of national policy (though general subservience to the Soviet Union was expected). Out of this arrangement, and as part of a governmental effort to

---

11. Davies, *The Heart of Europe,* 66.
12. Ibid., 67.
13. Ibid., 73.
14. Ibid., 64.
15. Ibid., 1.

pacify popular discontent, the Catholic Church remained intact. In 1921 Poland was 66 percent Catholic. After the Holocaust and postwar German and Ukrainian expulsions, the Poles left were 96 percent Catholic. This unifying element, however tragically born, proved a powerful force in Poland from the postwar era through the end of communism.

In 1956, when Kieślowski was a teenager, industrial strikes broke out in Poznań, with cries for "bread and freedom."[16] The strikes were viciously repressed by violence (a point alluded to in *Blind Chance*). Nikita Khrushchev massed armies on the border in October of that year, after a reformed government was elected without Moscow approval (an event known as the Polish October).[17] Soviet-style socialism was always an awkward fit for Poland. The country did gain some internal independence from the Soviet Union during the years 1956 through 1970, and the economy stabilized during this time. Kieślowski's film school experience, during which he was given extraordinary access to Western films (and ideas), exemplifies how some Poles could gain access to democratic points of view. These "holes" were sometimes difficult to find, and some of them were illegal; the *samizdat* (underground intellectual publications) and the underground "Flying University" ("uncensored lectures on historical, political, sociological, and cultural subjects in private flats")[18] both figure prominently in Kieślowski's *Blind Chance.*

Beginning in the late 1960s to 1989, however, the economy declined, and Kieślowski's films in this period — *The Scar, Personnel, Camera Buff, Blind Chance,* and *No End* — all reflect this desperate situation. *Blind Chance* takes place between 1977 and the summer of 1980, when strikes and riots lead to the birth of Solidarity, a political movement born of striking shipyard workers in Gdańsk guided by Lech Wałęsa.[19] In a cold war miracle, the government permitted the movement to unionize under a compromise

---

16. Ibid., 9.

17. Ibid., 9–10.

18. Sandor Szilagvi, "An Event in Hungary," *New York Review of Books,* March 13, 1986, http://www.nybooks.com/articles/5184 (accessed January 18, 2003). Szilagvi was one of the organizers of the Flying University, and this is his short description of the movement. He was also a coeditor of the *samizdat* review *Beszélő,* in Hungary.

19. The term *Solidarity* (known in Poland as Solidarność) does not refer only to the uniting of workers, but to the solidarity between classes, workers, and intellectuals, uniting their efforts for the first time.

agreement. The independent trade union soon boasted a staggering ten million members, representing nearly every family in the nation.[20]

One of the psychological catalysts to Solidarity was the 1978 election of the Pole Karol Wojtyła as pope (renamed John Paul II), the first non-Italian pope in nearly 500 years. He lent his power and influence to the cause of Solidarity, cheering them in the wake of martial law enacted in December 1981 to crush the popular movement. By 1982, Solidarity was formally dissolved (or, as *No End* depicts, driven underground), and the cost of living doubled. By 1983, however (when *No End* was being made), martial law was lifted. The pope's homecoming visit of 1983 is well chronicled, but a most moving account exists in Timothy Garton Ash's *The Uses of Adversity*.[21] He encouraged the Polish people to persist amid their discouragement. Ash claims church attendance during this time rose to an astonishing 90 to 95 percent.[22] The social restlessness continued, of course, and the people felt terribly fragmented, disillusioned, and socially burdened. Kieślowski's 1988 *Decalogue* articulates this pained existence, but the picture of the pope discussed in *Decalogue I* exemplifies a glimmer of hope for the Polish people. By 1989, Solidarity found new birth and Poland a new government. Polish communism was effectively finished.

However, the people's democratic inheritance proved terribly difficult. No economic miracles took place, political forces failed to stabilize, and the country faced many difficult transitional years. Poland is only now beginning to emerge from the chaos of sudden democracy. The political fratricide of the early 1990s gave way, in 1997, to a new, more stable government and a promising Polish economy.[23] Unfortunately, Kieślowski did not live to see the so-called Polish Miracle take place.

A Brief Biography

Kieślowski's early life experiences only amplified the rootless feeling pervading his country. As mentioned, Kieślowski's fascination with "coincidence" might be said to begin with his birth, the very month that Hitler betrayed Stalin. His characters often wonder about their own significance as they

---

20. Davies, *The Heart of Europe,* 19.
21. Ash, *The Uses of Adversity,* 47–60.
22. Ibid., 53.
23. Biskupski, *The History of Poland,* 180–184.

intersect with history. Witek, the main character of *Blind Chance,* for in-stance, ponders the irony of his 1956 birth date, the very night of the violent Poznań suppression, the arrest of his father, and the death of his twin brother. Witek also mirrors Kieślowski's own birthdate: June 27.[24]

Kieślowski's father, stricken with tuberculosis, constantly moved the fam-ily around the country, from one sanatorium to another. According to Annette Insdorf, Kieślowski had moved an astonishing forty times by the time he was fourteen years old.[25] The specter of death and the lack of a social anchor — a home — surely proved formative in young Krzysztof's life. As he jumped on yet another train, he must have wondered what would be different if he had missed the train or taken it to a different place. When one does not have a home, the world looks mutable and restless.

Kieślowski's father died at the age of forty-seven. His mother died in a tragic car accident at the age of sixty-seven, with a family friend driving the car.[26] But Kieślowski has told us all of this already. These themes form the foundation for all his work.

Insdorf tells the story of a young Krzysztof, too poor for a movie ticket, maneuvering to a vent on the theater roof to watch a small visible portion of the movie screen;[27] Kieślowski's own account to Danusia Stok adds the mischievous detail of spitting on the audience through the vent.[28] This childhood motif of peeking, a species of the more general Kieślowskian concern of the hidden being revealed, recurs several times in Kieślowski's films (e.g., Paweł's partial view of his father's university lecture in *Decalogue I* and Karol's view through his comb in *White*).

Young Kieślowski's health was also weak ("bad lungs" in danger of tu-berculosis). As a by-product of convalescence, he read a lot. He claims his reading, both of "good" literature (Dostoevsky and Camus) and "bad" ("some third-rate American writer who wrote cowboy adventures"), was formative.[29] Kieślowski esteemed the powers of literature throughout his

---

24. Assuming Witek's mother gave birth after midnight. Tadeusz Lubelski's article "From *Personnel* to *No End*" first pointed this out to me (in *Lucid Dreams,* ed. Paul Coates [Trowbridge, Wiltshire, England: Flicks Books, 1999]).

25. Annette Insdorf, *Double Lives, Second Chances: The Cinema of Krzysztof Kieślowski* (New York: Hyperion, 1999), 7.

26. Stok, *Kieślowski on Kieślowski,* 20.

27. Insdorf, *Double Lives,* 5–6.

28. Stok, *Kieślowski on Kieślowski,* 15–16.

29. Ibid., 5.

entire life. In a telling comment, he asserts that the world of books was "equally real" to him as his own material, existential reality.[30] Kieślowski clearly had a strong imagination as a child, and his anecdote about the malleability of memory exemplifies this:

> ...When I was five or six...I was going to infant school and clearly remember walking with my mum. An elephant appeared. It passed us by and walked on. Mum claimed she'd never been with me when an elephant walked by. There's no reason why, in 1946, after the war, an elephant should appear in Poland, where it was hard even to get potatoes. Nevertheless, I can remember the scene perfectly well and I clearly remember the expression of the elephant's face.[31]

It is no coincidence that an unpublished screenplay of Kieślowski's *The Big Animal (Duże Zwierze)* features an equally curious sight: that of a camel, abandoned by a traveling circus, wandering through a Polish town. One of his favorite actors, Jerzy Stuhr, made this script into a charming film in 2000.

One might think that Kieślowski felt an early artistic call and followed his instincts into his career. As Kieślowski describes it, however, the whole business came about through coincidence more than anything else. He tried a firefighter's training college and hated it (a resistance to regimen and uniforms).[32] He then entered the College for Theater Technicians, largely because he had a connection through an uncle in the theater[33] (his experiences there, working in the costume department, strongly inform his most biographical film, *Personnel).* While in school, his father finally succumbed to tuberculosis. After graduation and a brief time working, Kieślowski spent a year studying drawing, pretending he wanted to be an art teacher. His real object, however, was to gain partial exemption through his student status from mandatory service in the Polish military.[34] He eventually achieved full exemption through a hilarious bit of fakery. The amusing story is fully told in his interview with Stok, but the short of it is this: Kieślowski knew that if the examiners at the military conscription office thought he was crazy, they'd mark him unfit for military service. He played the part

---

30. Ibid.

31. Ibid., 6.

32. Ibid., 25.

33. Insdorf quotes him: "If I'd had an uncle in banking, I might have become a banker." Insdorf, *Double Lives,* 7.

34. Stok, *Kieślowski on Kieślowski,* 24.

(exemplifying obvious neurotic fixations), and, after very extensive tests and observations, they did just that.[35]

According to Kieślowski, he thought he would like to be a theatrical director, and film directing might be an avenue toward that ambition. He had applied earlier to the prestigious Lódź School and failed to gain acceptance. He applied a second time and failed again. The day he had to tell his mother this bad news, he met her outside in the rain. He could not tell if the water on her cheeks was simply rain or rain mixed with tears (a potent ambiguity that will show up in his films),[36] but he knew she was terribly disappointed. "Maybe you're not cut out for it," she said. At that point, he was determined to get in.[37] A few days after his drama with the military conscription office, he took the exam for film school yet again. The third attempt was successful.

Film school provided certain privileges not enjoyed by ordinary Poles. Kieślowski had access to American and Western European films, just as the European "art film" was enjoying its heyday. The films he witnessed during his film school years forever changed him. Likewise, he had the opportunity to study with some of Poland's greatest filmmakers, including the documentarian Kazimierz Karabasz.

It should be helpful, at this point, to say a few words about Polish film history and the creative milieu in which Kieślowski found himself. Many of the ideas that would drive his career emerged here at the Lódź Film School. Coming out of the Polish October of 1956, several filmmakers broke with so-called socialist realism (a Communist aesthetic designed to exalt Communist ideals) and pursued the direction established by Italian neorealism.[38] The result was the "Polish school" of filmmaking, featuring names like Kazimierz Kutz, Andrzej Munk, Andrzej Wajda, Wojciech Has, and Jerzy Kawalerowicz. Many of these filmmakers represented the best of Polish cinema at the time Kieślowski was beginning his documentary career. All of them, in a general way, proved inspirational to Kieślowski's generation, providing the first steps away from Stalinist aesthetics and toward a more

---

35. Ibid., 24–29.

36. For example, the script for *Decalogue I* calls for an ambiguity between melted ice and tears. Krzysztof Kieślowski and Krzysztof Piesiewicz, *Decalogue: The Ten Commandments,* trans. Phil Cavendish and Susannah Bluh (London: Faber and Faber, 1990), 30. *The Double Life of Véronique* features Weronika looking up into the rain in joy, wiping away "tears."

37. Stok, *Kieślowski on Kieślowski,* 2.

38. Marek Haltof, *Polish National Cinema* (New York: Berghahn, 2002), 64.

subversive, existential, and socially relevant cinema. There is not space to detail all the individual filmmakers here, so I hope the reader will forgive the following oversimplified continuum: the films in this period (1950s and 60s) range from the "romantic-expressive" tendency in filmmakers like Wajda to the "rationalistic" (and even ironic/cynical) tendency in Munk and others. In an interview with Paul Coates, Kieślowski resisted any easy parallelisms or efforts to peg him in a tradition, but acknowledged he might be closer to the intellectual tradition than national romanticism (despite self-admitted personal romantic traits in his work).[39]

Some of these filmmakers taught at the Łódź School (Kazimierz Karabasz was among Kieślowski's favorite teachers[40]), and all became peers of the younger generation of filmmakers. Kieślowski's fellow students included some important names in Polish cinema: Jerzy Skolimowski graduated while Kieślowski was at Łódź; Roman Polanski finished a few years before. Other famous Polish filmmakers, such as Krzysztof Zanussi and Agnieszka Holland, began their careers around the same time as Kieślowski (mid-to-late 1960s).

While not visibly active in politics, Kieślowski documented a reality the Polish people longed to see: their own. In subtle ways, Kieślowski exposed the weaknesses of a totalitarian regime, and audiences became adept at looking for the political critique (what amounted to a "conspiracy" between filmmaker and audience, according to Agnieszka Holland[41]).

As a result of his documentary work and some early ventures into features, Kieślowski and his friends became known as the "Cinema of Moral Concern." There has been much debate about this title, and various alternatives have been proposed: the "Cinema of Moral Anxiety" (the term Kieślowski used, though he didn't much care for it[42]), and "Cinema of Distrust" (a term proposed by Mariola Jankun-Dopartowa and embraced by Marek Haltof[43]). The titles refer to a general anxiety or unrest over Poland's loss of its cultural, moral, and philosophical foundation. They should not be taken to mean any dogmatic or overtly clerical call for a codified morality, but rather a concern for a more general, unifying philosophical

---

39. Coates, *Lucid Dreams,* 160.
40. Stok, *Kieślowski on Kieślowski,* 40.
41. Quoted in "A Discussion of Kieślowski's Early Years," *Blue* (DVD), Miramax, 2003.
42. Stok, *Kieślowski on Kieślowski,* 41.
43. Haltof, in *Polish National Cinema* (p. 147), discusses this term and cites Jankun-Dopartowa. *Człowiek z ekranu: Z antropologii postaci filmowej,* ed. Mariola Jankun-Dopartowa and Mirosław Przylipiak (Kraców: Aracana, 1996), 108.

and moral vision among the Polish people, largely lost to the totalitarian state. Kieślowski listed himself as a member of this movement, as well as Zanussi, Edek Żebrowski, Holland, and Wajda, among others.[44] Other critics list additional filmmakers and slightly different dates (all centering on the late 1970s to 1981), depending on who they include in the movement.[45] Polish film historians Bolesław Michałek and Frank Turaj characterize the movement this way:

> While the official media organs were bragging about triumph in society, and art, and economic progress, these films were showing things people were talking about at home.... Indeed, at base there was a longing for elementary values like truth, loyalty, and tolerance. Things were often placed in a harsh light, but it was light, not darkness....These films were not "literary" in style, nor subtly psychological, nor extremely artistic. The style of the films of the movement was derived from the documentary tradition, thus the approach was quite direct.... [T]he hero of a film of moral concern faces his problems, fights them head on.[46]

Some films of this movement may have demonstrated clearer ethical choices, but Kieślowski nearly always portrayed the contemporary situation as terribly vexing. His heroes most often *do not know what to do;* hence the high anxiety level and axiological focus of Kieślowski's films. His fiction films of this period are *Curriculum Vitae* (1975), *Personnel* (1975), *The Scar* (1976), *Peace* (a.k.a. *The Calm,* 1976), and *Camera Buff* (1979); because of government censorship, *Peace* was not seen until the late 1980s. Of these films, all of which could be included in the movement, *Camera Buff,* released in 1979 (one of the most remarkable years in the history of Polish cinema[47]), is the most archetypal of the movement. Kieślowski's reflexive turn in that film (a story about a filmmaker) adds a personal dimension to the political milieu that is critiqued. *Camera Buff* takes on the Communist bureaucracy directly, but the central focus of the film shifts to the moral struggles of the character, Filip Mosz. After this film, Kieślowski would continue to focus less and less on the government per se, and more and more on the

---

44. Stok, *Kieślowski on Kieślowski,* 104.

45. See Haltof's list in *Polish National Cinema* (p. 147) and that of Bolesław Michałek and Frank Turaj, in *The Modern Cinema of Poland* (Bloomington: Indiana University Press, 1988), 59–79. In short, Haltof argues for a more narrow definition of the movement and films included. Michałek and Turaj see the title as a label applied to a general impulse in Polish cinema stretching back into the early 1970s. Either position is equally defensible.

46. Michałek and Turaj, ibid., 73.

47. Ibid., 70.

individual, trying to make his or her way in the world. *Blind Chance* (1981) and *No End* (1984) feature Polish politics as background for more universal questions. Beyond *No End,* the Polish government is rarely addressed, even though the entire *Decalogue* series (1988) was written and shot before the fall of communism.

The Decalogue gave Kieślowski's career a boost internationally. He had received acclaim abroad with his earlier films, but it was around this time that Kieślowski began to emerge as one of Europe's most popular and respected directors. His retreat from politics cost him the love of many of his countrymen, however, who felt he had abandoned the nation.[48]

In Kieślowski's defense, life after communism in Poland was hardly ideal. Politics in post-Communist Poland were anything but tame, even among former friends in the Solidarity movement. While observing a rancorous meeting of Lech Wałęsa's Citizens' Committee, Ash says Wajda (who worked in politics for a time) leaned over to him and said, "You see all they need is sabers and they'd be fighting each other outside."[49]

Kieślowski was looking to transcend petty differences and pursue the broader universal issues that so consumed him. All the same, near the end of his life Kieślowski said:

> My love for Poland is a bit like love in an old marriage where the couple know everything about each other and are a bit bored with each other, but when one of them dies, the other follows immediately. I can't imagine life without Poland. . . . I still feel a Pole. In fact, everything that affects Poland, affects me directly: I don't feel so distanced from the country as to feel no concern. I'm no longer interested in all the political games, but I am interested in Poland itself. It's my world. It's the world I've come from and, no doubt, the world where I'll die. . . . Everyone ought to have a place to which they return. I have a place; it's in Poland. . . . I come to Paris. But I come back to Poland.[50]

His last four films (*The Double Life of Véronique* [1991], *Blue* [1993], *White* [1993], and *Red* [1994]), the ones that secured him international status, were primarily made in countries outside of his native land (only parts of *Véronique* and *White* take place in Poland). He declared *Red* (a film made in Switzerland, financed by a French company) his final film. Many received news of his retirement in 1994 with disbelief. Those closest to him, however,

---

48. Stok, *Kieślowski on Kieślowski,* xiv.
49. Ash, *History of the Present,* 36.
50. Stok, *Kieślowski on Kieślowski,* 1–2.

like Agnieszka Holland, knew that he was utterly exhausted. His shooting schedule for *The Decalogue* was incredibly difficult, with little rest afterward. *Véronique, Blue, White,* and *Red* all followed in quick succession. During the shooting of the trilogy, Kieślowski would routinely shoot all day, then edit and write all night. Holland still maintains that the breakneck pace ultimately killed him.[51]

Even after his supposed retirement, he continued to work on screenplays. *Heaven* (2002), the first of these, was planned for Florence, moved to Turin and the surrounding area, and filmed by the German director Tom Tykwer. Kieślowski never saw his treatment realized.[52]

In 1996, Kieślowski, a lifelong smoker, needed bypass surgery, as he'd barely survived a recent heart attack. According to Insdorf, he had been offered the chance to have surgery in some very fine hospitals in New York and Paris, but he declared his confidence in his local Warsaw hospital.[53] He never woke up from the anesthesia. Rumor had it, the staff was not sufficiently familiar with the newly imported operating equipment. The date was May 13. The specter of heart failure, haunting his films (e.g., *The Scar* and *No End*), had finally claimed him. Kieślowski was fifty-four years old.

Kieślowski's Career: Beginning a Dramatic Outline

At the 2003 Society of Cinema and Media Studies conference, a presenter somewhat sheepishly stated, "I know it's not fashionable to quote André Bazín these days, but...," then proceeded to quote him. In his response, Tom Gunning (of the University of Chicago and preeminent film theorist) said: "I believe the most oft-quoted line at this conference is 'I know it's not fashionable to quote André Bazín these days, but....'" Everyone laughed because, whatever one's opinion of Bazín, he can no longer be

---

51. "Discussion of Kieślowski's Later Years," *White* (DVD), Miramax, 2003, as well as an interview with Holland by the Facets Video organization, http://www.facets.org/decalogue/holland.html (accessed September 13, 2003).

52. The film was cowritten with Solidarity-era lawyer Krzysztof Piesiewicz and finished by him. Piesiewicz also finished the second screenplay, *Hell,* but it has not yet been filmed as of the time of this writing.

53. Insdorf, *Double Lives,* 1.

written off as a naive realist (much as some have tried). As a theorist, he delivered extraordinary insight into the functions of the cinema that, in many ways, define what we mean when we say cinematic "realism" or "formalism." Surely, the debate has matured (few believe the photograph is unmediated reality, for instance), but the fact remains: the cinema carries a strong indexical trait that is tightly bound up with its expressive, formal capacity. The debate now centers around the theoretical weight one should grant indexicality (or form, for that matter). Kieślowski's career reflects this debate very clearly.

Before I launch into a discussion of this reflection, I should make some comments on contemporary film theory's approach to the issue. The gist of the matter is that discussion of "ontological" cinematic realism dealing with real-life existents and film's purported reflection of them has been utterly critiqued. These days it is much more common to refer to cinema as a type of speech act, a convention that refers only to other conventions.[54] After all, we are prisoners of our own subjectivities and have no access to the "real" world in any ontological sense (or so say many contemporary thinkers), so there is very little reason to discuss film as a touchstone to the "real" world. Rather, it is a type of discourse that is fraught with subjectivities and may be deconstructed like any other "text."

Kieślowski's work bears some of the marks of his time — elements that might be aligned with any number of contemporary theories: dialectical/dialogical approaches to truth (Marxism), indeterminate endings (like Roland Barthes' concept of "jamming" in S/Z), and the poverty of representational efforts (not far from Jacques Derrida). However, all of these ideas can be understood as a shift in attitude away from a nihilism that abandons any hope of absolutes and toward a more hopeful searching for solid axiological ground. In that light, these elements have religious corollaries: dialogical theology (not unlike Martin Buber's concept of the "I-Thou" relation), indeterminate endings (not unlike certain ideas in religious existentialism), and the Unrepresentable as tangible spiritual mystery. I do not wish to suggest Kieślowski took any of these positions, but only to make that point that all who would like to make Kieślowski into a postmodern (e.g., Emma Wilson) must also acknowledge that he can be recast as a more traditional romantic or modernist figure. The truth is most likely in

---

54. Robert Stam, Robert Burgoyne, and Sandy Flitterman-Lewis, *New Vocabularies in Film Semiotics* (London: Routledge, 1992), 184.

the middle, but my approach here is to pursue Kieślowski's position as accurately as possible. Implicit in all his conversations was the idea that truth was "out there," and however poor an instrument for attaining it, the filmic medium remained his tool of choice. Where the truth seems impenetrable, Kieślowski's interest was in the human struggle with that problem. In his 1981 manifesto, he said, "Today the truth about the world, which for me continues to be a basic precondition, is not enough. One has to search out more dramatic situations, postulates that reach beyond everyday experience, diagnoses that are wiser and more universal."[55]

Realism

Kieślowski's career began in documentaries under the Communist regime in Poland.

> At that time, I was interested in everything that could be described by the documentary film camera. There was a necessity, a need — which was very exciting for us — to describe the world. The Communist world had described how it should be and not how it really was.... It's a feeling of bringing something to life, because it is a bit like that. If something hasn't been described, then it doesn't officially exist. So that if we start describing it, we bring it to life.[56]

In his interviews with Danusia Stok, Kieślowski tells of numerous occasions when he was forced to "edit" some of the reality he had recorded, particularly if the reality on film did not coincide with the image of reality that the government wanted to project. He often found ways around this censorship by "tricking" the censors through various deceptive methods in order to preserve the "truth." The paradox inherent in this statement reflects a more general paradox: that of "objective" documentary shot by an inherently subjective auteur. Kieślowski developed a theory about this in graduate school:

> The documentary film-maker has to have the right to his own views of reality, to represent it as it appears to him. He has to have the right to a subjective point of view and it's a great mistake to demand that every, even the shortest, documentary film portray an objective synthesis of reality.... Film industry, which guarantees the right to subjectivity and bears in mind the different

55. Translated by Paul Coates, "Kieślowski and the Antipolitics of Color: A Reading of the 'Three Colors' Trilogy," *Cinema Journal* 41:2 (Winter 2002): 45. Originally from Krzysztof Kieślowski, "Głęboko zamiast szeroko," *Dialog* no. 1 (1981): 111.

56. Stok, *Kieślowski on Kieślowski,* 54–55.

temperaments and views of directors, has a great chance: it can, as a whole, become an image of reality close to truth and portray its bad and good attributes proportionally.[57]

Kieślowski's realist rhetoric grows more intense later in the thesis:

> We have to get to what has constituted the essence of art from the beginning of the world — the life of human beings. Life itself has to become, simultaneously, the pretext and the essence of film. How it looks, how long it takes, the course it takes. With all this entails.[58]

Kieślowski never believed in "objective truth in art," and explicitly says so,[59] but he did feel a cinema with a significant "depth of reflection" could give us enough of the truth to discuss it, come to an opinion, and, above all, *feel* the experiences of the world in a focused way.[60]

It is interesting that the very quality of film that drew Kieślowski to the documentary, its capacity for truth, became a liability for the form in his mind, and Kieślowski never returned to the documentary again. He describes an incident to Stok in which he had spent an evening clandestinely documenting people in Warsaw's Central Railway station. That evening his footage was confiscated. It turned out that a girl had murdered her mother, cut her up, and packed her in suitcases, which she carried to the station that night. The police thought Kieślowski might have some evidence for them (he did not, they found). The incident shook him badly; the issue was not whether a murderer should or shouldn't be caught, but that the police were going to arbitrarily use him and his craft for their own ends. He believed in the truth of the cinema, but he did not trust what the state would do with that truth.[61]

Kieślowski thus moved to fictional forms, bringing to them a criterion of authenticity. His first professional fictional effort, *Pedestrian Subway*, is a case in point:

> [O]n the ninth night [of shooting] I realized I was shooting something idiotic, some nonsense which didn't mean anything to me. The plot didn't mean

---

57. Kieślowski's graduate thesis, "Author, Film, Reality," in *Krzysztof Kieślowski: We Are What We've Absorbed* (Lódź: Camerimage, 2000), 61.

58. Ibid., 69.

59. "The Functions of Contemporary Film," ibid., 86.

60. Ibid., 88.

61. Stok, *Kieślowski on Kieślowski,* 79–81.

much to me. We would put the camera somewhere. The actors said some lines. And I had the impression we were making a complete lie.[62]

Kieślowski elected to shoot the whole film again on the final night with a documentary camera, "which you could carry on your shoulders." His approach to the actors: "I said to them, 'Listen, act it all out. Do it all the way you feel best. And I'll shoot it.'" Kieślowski felt the result of this "rather desperate operation" was that the film "took on a life of its own" and became much more authentic: "This was terribly important to me at the time, and still is, in fact — to make films authentic in reactions, and details."[63]

Such loose, improvisational techniques were, for Kieślowski, a step in a new direction. By the end of his career, Kieślowski had gained a reputation for knowing precisely what he wanted from his actors. Before casting, he would meet with a potential actor and discuss life, particularly his or her philosophical approach to life (says Juliette Binoche, lead actress in *Blue*[64]). In an interview with Erik Lint, Kieślowski remarked that casting is the most important part of the production cycle, because actors generate many of the ideas that arise on the set.[65] Kieślowski, in the same interview, states that the film "comes into being" during editing, and everything beforehand is simply "gathering material." This description of filmmaking as something like discovery would appear to contradict Julie Delpy's comment that he was giving her very precise instructions on gestures and reactions.[66] Binoche says that, at times, he asked her to "express less" and stay silent. Yet even this dynamic was a process of discovery, as she testifies, because at one point Kieślowski asked her, with no explanation, to repeat an action. She did so, then asked him the difference (seeing he was satisfied). "You breathed differently," he said.[67] Although there is not space to go into all the details here, this approach to acting bears the marks of both Robert Bresson and Tarkovsky, who were famous for their exacting direction of actors and propensity toward less expression. However, Kieślowski's aim in these

---

62. Ibid., 94.

63. Ibid., 94–95.

64. "A Conversation with Juliette Binoche on Kieślowski," *Blue* (DVD), Miramax, 2003.

65. Lint, a workshop given in the summer of 1994 during the Amsterdam Summer University and European Film Academy workshop. *Krzysztof Kieślowski: A Masterclass for Young Directors* (VHS, Erik Lint, dir., Editions a Voir/Espace Video Européen, 1995).

66. "Conversations with Julie Delpy on Kieślowski," *White* (DVD), Miramax, 2003.

67. *Blue* (DVD), ibid.

techniques was not toward the asceticism of Bresson or the higher stylistic vision of Tarkovsky. Rather, he was trying to provoke authentic emotion that did not reek of "acting." There are some key expressive moments from his actors, and this sparing use of emotion serves to amplify the power of those moments. Kieślowski strenuously avoided sentimentality, but he refused to discard emotion completely.

In Kieślowski's film *Personnel*, he made another step toward "authentic" cinema. Again, he was well into the project when he was convinced that the film was "inauthentic." His quest for authenticity drove him to drop production for about a month, turn to an outline script (for improvised dialogue), and, in the tradition of the Italian neorealists, utilize nonactors for the majority of the roles. In describing this film to Stok, he emphasized how the characters are "true" because they contradict the conventions of filmic stereotype. For instance, the tailors in his film are real tailors, and none of them "wear tape measures around their necks,"[68] because tailors, in reality, don't do so. In this film, he used only one professional actor, "and he's terrible." "Imagine . . . if I'd taken actors like him to play the tailors. Not only would you have tape measures around everyone's necks, but you'd have a clash of inauthenticity in the manner of speech and thought because an actor like that would naturally like to stand out."[69]

Kieślowski's quest for authenticity was fruitful. In his *Film Quarterly* discussion of *A Short Film about Killing* and *A Short Film about Love*, film scholar Charles Eidsvik speaks of Kieślowski's sensitivity in presenting "the clutter of reality." Things often block the camera's view, and the cameraman "continually reframes, refocuses, and then cuts to a new, better vantage point."[70] In summary:

> . . . Kieślowski has found a form to make the struggle for spiritual survival in such a land exciting. That struggle can be filmed by treating stories as if they were real, by treating characters as if they were people, by treating film as if it were always a document.[71]

This "spontaneous" camerawork evidences the influence of the French New Wave cinema of the 1950s and 1960s. Yet it is clear from Kieślowski's

---

68. Stok, *Kieślowski on Kieślowski,* 98.

69. Ibid.

70. Charles Eidsvik, "Decalogues 5 and 6 and the Two Short Films," in Coates, *Lucid Dreams,* 54.

71. Ibid., 55.

story that the scenes were carefully staged,[72] theoretically (but not practically, perhaps) diminishing its legitimacy as "realist" feature.

Formalism

In the shift to feature films, it is clear that Kieślowski was becoming somewhat disillusioned with the whole realistic aesthetic altogether. He was beginning to see the limits of the realist aesthetic, and there was still much in life to be explored:

> Not everything can be described. That's the documentary's great problem. It catches itself as if in its own trap. The closer it wants to get to somebody, the more that person shuts him or herself off from it. And that's perfectly natural. It can't be helped. If I'm making a film about love, I can't go into a bedroom if real people are making love there. If I'm making a film about death, I can't film somebody who's dying because it's such an intimate experience that the person shouldn't be disturbed.[73]

However, the fact that the camera changes the ecosystem it is filming can have ramifications in more positive directions as well. One example Kieślowski gave is a documentary he was making about the courts during Polish martial law in the early 1980s. He received permission from the activist lawyer Krzysztof Piesiewicz (who later became his co-scriptwriter) to film a number of cases, with the understanding that the film would expose the brutal and unfair sentences the Polish judges were passing on Piesiewicz's worker clients: "The moment I started shooting . . . the judges didn't sentence the accused. That is, they passed some sort of deferred sentences which weren't, in fact, at all painful."[74] The judges clearly did not want to be recorded on film passing unjust sentences. They shot for a month and a half. No sentences were passed during that time, Kieślowski's film was wrecked (though he certainly didn't mind), and every lawyer in town was begging him to film their cases.[75] Kieślowski even rigged up dummy cameras without film in some courtrooms.[76]

With false visions of an unvarnished recorded reality behind him, Kieślowski began to pursue other modes of reality:

---

72. Stok, *Kieślowski on Kieślowski,* 172.
73. Ibid., 86.
74. Ibid., 127.
75. Ibid., 128.
76. Ibid.

The realm of superstitions, fortune-telling, presentiments, intuition, dreams ... [a]ll this is the inner life of a human being, and all this is the hardest thing to film. Even though I know that it can't be filmed however hard I try, the simple fact is that I'm taking this direction to get as close to this as my skill allows. That's why I don't think *Véronique* betrays anything I've done before. In *Camera Buff,* for example, you also have a heroine who knows that something bad is going to happen to her husband. She knows it. She feels it. Just like Véronique feels things. I don't see any difference. I've been trying to get there from the beginning. I'm somebody who doesn't know, somebody who's searching.[77]

André Bazín's optimism about film's abilities to capture the inner life (or, at least, its outward reflection)[78] is verbally countered by Kieślowski's pessimism on the matter.[79] However, this pessimism (an aspect of his personality, he admitted) initiated a Sisyphean struggle in his mind to transcend these limitations. For instance, Kieślowski insisted his remarkable shot of a bottle of milk spilling in *A Short Film about Love* is nothing more than its physical description:

[W]hen it spills, it means milk's been spilt. Nothing more. It doesn't mean the world's fallen apart or that the milk symbolizes a mother's milk which her child couldn't drink because the mother died early, for example. . . . And that's cinema. Unfortunately it doesn't mean anything else.[80]

It is not that Kieślowski completely disregarded cinema's metaphorical ability; he even encouraged metaphorical interpretation of his films.[81] He simply found it more difficult for cinema than, say, the novelist, to capture the inner life (contrary to Bazín's equivocation).[82] Kieślowski acknowledged the "literal nature" of film (thus agreeing with Siegfried Kracauer),[83] yet, at

---

77. Ibid., 194.

78. In his celebrated essay on Robert Bresson's *Diary of a Country Priest,* Bazín states: "What we are asked to look for on their faces is not for some fleeting reflection of the words but for an uninterrupted condition of the soul, the outward revelation of an interior destiny." *What is Cinema?* trans. Hugh Gray (Berkeley: University of California Press, 1967), 133.

79. Stok, *Kieślowski on Kieślowski,* 194.

80. Ibid., 195.

81. "I don't film metaphors. People only read them as metaphors, which is very good. That's what I want." Ibid., 193.

82. Ibid., 40.

83. Siegfried Kracauer, in *Theory of Film* (Oxford: Oxford University Press, 1960), 60, discusses the "affinity" of film for "nature in the raw," in keeping with Kracauer's realist commitments.

the same time, he stated: "If I have a goal, then it is to escape from this literalism. I'll never achieve it; in the same way that I'll never manage to describe what really dwells within my hero, although I keep on trying."[84]

But even this judgment is not absolute. Kieślowski acknowledged that "a few times" in history a filmmaker has moved beyond the literal, into the metaphorical, and into true art:

> [Orson] Welles achieved that miracle once [in *Citizen Kane*]. Only one director in the world has managed to achieve that miracle in the last few years and that's Tarkovsky. [Ingar] Bergman achieved this miracle a few times. [Federico] Fellini achieved it a few times . . . Ken Loach, too, in *Kes*.[85]

The combination of these two realities, internal and external, provides a means of articulating human experience. This was the guiding force in Kieślowski's career, as he clearly stated in *Sight and Sound* magazine.[86] He believed that a sign of quality was realizing that an artist had formulated something that he had experienced or thought: "exactly the same thing but with the help of a better sentence or better visual arrangement or better composition of sounds than I could ever have imagined."[87] Imagine the pleasure of receiving, as Kieślowski testified, numerous notes from people over the years saying, "You've plagiarized my life. Where do you know me from?"[88]

Kieślowski thus moved from being a committed realist documentarian to an anxious, probing formalist. He no longer shied away from formal conventions, because he saw the cinema as a storytelling medium, and he could find truth "contained within a convention."[89] However, to say that he completely abandoned his realist roots is a mistake, as it is clear from his films that "authenticity" (however subjectively judged) was still the touchstone by which he tested his chosen conventions: Do they mirror real-life? Are they convincing? Do they reveal truth about the inner life of the characters? These were the pertinent questions to Kieślowski.

According to Stok, Kieślowski claimed to make his films on documentary principles right up to the end of his career. However, those principles

---

84. Stok, *Kieślowski on Kieślowski,* 195.

85. Ibid.

86. "No Heroics, Please: Krzysztof Kieślowski," *Sight and Sound* (Spring 1981): 90–91.

87. Stok, *Kieślowski on Kieślowski,* 193.

88. Ibid., 210.

89. Ibid., 170.

reflected not "unmediated truth" (a documentary ideal Kieślowski had long abandoned as impossible), but the premise that films "evolve through ideas and not action."[90] In short, Kieślowski still believed human experience (i.e., "reality") to be his primary artistic territory, but, over his career, he moved away from a social and political focus to universal metaphysical ideas (less tangible, but no less real). In Kieślowski's words, he always pursued "the big questions."[91] That is, "What is the true meaning of life? Why get up in the morning? Politics don't answer that."[92]

The elements Kieślowski preserved from his documentary period proved rather radical in the fictional cinematic arena. His editing pace was often more phenomenologically driven, with a high regard for reactions and absorption of "the inner life" rather than action or plot (as with the classical Hollywood cinema form). This editing style also highlights his fascination with everyday detail. The long shot of Valentine drinking water in *Red* is similar to the quotidian "trivialities" of Bresson's attention.[93] There are many pedestrian details that mark Kieślowski's work. Often they are significant, other times they are merely interesting, and most often they are visual traces of another story that is yet to be told. For instance, in *White*, Karol enters a phone booth. Upon the directory sits a smoldering cigarette. He simply puts it out and moves on with his business. The question is, why this cigarette? Anyone who has ever shot a film knows that such details must be planned and carefully worked into the image (props supplied, focus measurements calculated, camera positions adjusted, and numerous other details accounted for), leaving no doubt that this detail was very deliberately included. The answer to the question is uncertain, but Kieślowski feels these details are important traces of other narratives that constantly cross our path every day, unfairly dismissed. On the other hand, there is plenty of other expository information Kieślowski cuts very quickly, counterintuitive to the standard Hollywood mind that prizes clarity of action over interior pause.

---

90. Ibid., xiii.

91. Coates, *Lucid Dreams,* 12.

92. Stok, *Kieślowski on Kieślowski,* 144.

93. Stam et al. parallel this fascination with Christian Metz's concept of *vraisemblable* (the "true-seeming" or "verisimilar"). *New Vocabularies in Film Semiotics,* 194. That is, these directors expand the territory of what counts for reality on film, including everyday things not previously "worthy" of film, like Jean-Luc Godard deliberately shooting his characters using the bathroom.

His approach to "the clutter of reality" and use of the handheld camera (though not an exclusive use) persisted through the end of his career. At the same time, these instruments of "authenticity," borrowed from the documentary aesthetic, were turned toward the task of metaphysical exploration and found their fulfillment when coupled with more formalist techniques. Among these techniques, largely avoided by the documentarian, are highly manipulated color schemes (both in cinematographic color effects and manipulated art direction), distorted lenses, lighting effects, and the creative use of sonic elements.

Kieślowski's late period most explicitly pursued the universal issues that were, by definition, metaphysical. Within these films it is quite obvious that the universal issues are not simply questions of morality, but also ontological probes with heavy theological resonance. Although Kieślowski never settled on a "god" of any specific sort, and his films became more resistant to any particular creed, his musings on the possibility of spiritual reality became increasingly positive. In this sense, he pursued the Transcendent, though it might be more accurate to say that he did not divide the Immanent and Transcendent so neatly. Kieślowski's films suggest that the temporal may intersect the spiritual through mystery. We simply haven't plumbed the depths of our reality enough. Kieślowski pursued the goal of his 1981 personal manifesto through the end of his life: "Deeper, rather than broader. . . . "[94]

Kieślowski's career stands as a critique of the contemporary empirical paradigm, precisely because of his deep belief that the empirical real is insufficient. In his 1981 manifesto, he wrote:

> Today the truth about the world, which for me continues to be a basic precondition, is not enough. One has to search out more dramatic situations, postulates that reach beyond everyday experience, diagnoses that are wiser and more universal.[95]

The stylistic shift is merely a shift in emphasis, synchronous with the shift from sociohistorical issues to what Slavoj Žižek has called "ethico-religious" issues.[96] The dialectic remains in the later films; representation creates the "realist" context, the immanent boundaries of which are challenged by form,

---

94. Coates, *Lucid Dreams,* 34.

95. Coates, "Kieślowski and the Antipolitics of Color," 45.

96. Slavoj Žižek, *The Fright of Real Tears: Krzysztof Kieślowski Between Theory and Post-Theory* (London: British Film Institute, 2001), 8.

THE FILMS OF KRZYSZTOF KIEŚLOWSKI

mediating the "unrepresentable." This mediation is a phenomenological incarnation of nonrational knowledge and is often seen as bleeding over into supernatural experience (or providing an index of such). Whether it actually does so is a matter of faith, and Kieślowski encourages us to examine where our faith lies.

Kieślowski's Influences

Kieślowski listed the following as the ten films that most "affected" him, asserting they were in no particular order:

La Strada, by Federico Fellini

Kes, by Ken Loach

Un condamné à mort s'est echappé (*A Man Escaped*), by Robert Bresson

The Pram, by Bo Widerberg

Intimate Lighting, by Ivan Passer

The Sunday Musicians, by Kazimierz Karabasz

Ivan's Childhood, by Andrei Tarkovsky

Les Quatre Cents Coups (*The 400 Blows*), by François Truffaut

Citizen Kane, by Orson Welles

The Kid, by Charlie Chaplin

Kieślowski named Ingmar Bergman as the director who affected him the most, Giulietta Masina his "greatest" actress, and Chaplin his "greatest" actor.[97]

I could spend an enormous amount of time postulating why any given film was among Kieślowski's favorites, and traces of most of the directors above may be found in his work. However, Kieślowski himself did discuss a few filmmakers in more detail, and those comments reveal something about his cinematic preferences. His account of Karabasz's ten-minute documentary shows how his former teacher taught him to look with a compassionate and loving eye upon his documentary subjects and find the universal quality inherent in the film (in this case, the "something that can give a meaning to life, and elevate it").[98] That same humanistic impulse might be said to thrive in Chaplin and Truffaut as well as in Kieślowski's films themselves.

---

97. *Projections 4 1/2,* ed. John Boorman and Walter Donohue (London: Faber and Faber, 1995), 102–104.

98. Ibid.

Kieślowski also remarked several times on Bergman and his influence. For example, in Erik Lint's documentary of Kieślowski's masterclass for young directors,[99] Kieślowski chose to work with Bergman's script for *Scenes from a Marriage*. Why Bergman? Because the script and the man were "dear" to him:

> I can identify with what Bergman says about life, about what he says about love. I identify more or less with his attitude towards the world . . . towards men and women and what we do in everyday life . . . forgetting about what is most important.[100]

Bergman's constant concern for the issues of "God, death, art, and love" (as Robert Lauder has summarized)[101] created a metaphysical thrust to all his films, and Kieślowski clearly walked in his footsteps. His essay on Bergman's *Silence* makes it clear that Bergman's "portrayal of feelings" and ability to present "human nature" affected him most.[102]

Although Kieślowski's later style was clearly more baroque than the spare, antidramatic asceticism of Bresson, the metaphysical themes are clearly similar, and there are some important stylistic parallels: a strong concern for rhythm, the everyday "trivial" item and/or gesture, the sufficiency of silence, and the calculated use of the close-up (the hands in *A Man Escaped* reappear in nearly every Kieślowski film). Other influences may be traced: Insdorf, for example, makes an argument for the influence of Wojciech Has.[103] For the focus of this study, however, I place more emphasis on the influence of Krzysztof Zanussi and, particularly, Andrei Tarkovsky.

Zanussi's influence was primarily thematic (i.e., a consonance between them as to which questions in life were worth pursuing in film). In the Cinema Militans lecture of 1993, Zanussi's description of his influences might have been spoken by Kieślowski: "I have learned to watch a detail watching Bresson, and a mask watching Fellini. I was watching some very peculiar moods that only Antonioni was able to describe."[104] The influence

---

99. Lint, *Krzysztof Kieślowski: A Masterclass for Young Directors* (VHS).

100. Ibid.

101. Robert Lauder, *God, Death, Art, and Love: The Philosophical Vision of Ingmar Bergman* (Mahwah, NJ: Paulist Press, 1989).

102. "Bergman's Silence," in Kieślowski, *Krzysztof Kieślowski: We Are What We've Absorbed*, 89, 91.

103. Insdorf, *Double Lives*, 49–52.

104. Krzysztof Zanussi, "Is There Progress?" Cinema Militans lecture, delivered September 26, 1993, St. Pieters Church, Utrecht, the Netherlands, http://www.filmfestival.nl/hfm/Holland_film_meeting_militans_93.html (accessed July 7, 2003).

is not so much a stylistic mimesis as it is an attitude, an inspiring search, on the part of each artist, to find the most appropriate cinematic language for his particular expression of life. Kieślowski and Zanussi were very close friends, and, although their cinematic languages grew to be quite distinct, they always pursued similar ideals in their work. In that same speech Zanussi describes the writing of a screenplay, in which the protagonist is miraculously spared a grenade attack:

> He went out to make a telephone call to his wife in the States and, at this very moment, a grenade exploded and another man with whom he had been speaking was dead. I started to rewrite the script and I thought it is a crucial turning part in the life of the young man. His first thought when he ran back to call his wife again would be: Why did it happen, why did I decide to call you this very moment and this saved my life? And my intention was to express the fact that he is looking for something metaphysical. Maybe for God. Is there a God who intervenes? Or is it a blind chance? At least this was a problem for the protagonist as I saw it.[105]

To anyone familiar with Kieślowski's films, the parallel themes and motifs are quite obvious (e.g., *Blind Chance* and *Red*). A survey of Zanussi's films shows remarkable thematic parallels with many of the stories in Kieślowski's career, and Kieślowski placed many of the same actors in similar roles as in the films of his friend. Tadeusz Lubelski observes that the idea for *Blind Chance* was first sown in the Zanussi film of 1972 called *Hypothesis,* asking what would have happened had the protagonist's later life followed a completely different course, simply by chance.[106]

Most of Kieślowski's films investigate philosophical and existential questions such as those mentioned above. *Illumination* (1973) bears the same critique of empiricism and science that pervaded much of Kieślowski's work. *Camouflage* (1974) proved a very important film in its day, in large part for the political critique many viewers pulled from the subtext. In truth, however, the film may be read as a battle between two worldviews (that of a Machiavellian pragmatism vs. a romantic idealism). Not only does this universal moral strain appear in Kieślowski's films, but he features Zanussi's *Camouflage* itself in his film *Camera Buff* (1979). The death and subsequent dream sequence at the end of *Spiral* (1978) bears some resemblance to the conclusion of Kieślowski's *No End* (1984). The tension between physics

---

105. Ibid.
106. Coates, *Lucid Dreams,* 67. Lubelski's article in this anthology is on Kieślowski's political features.

and the brutal unpredictability of fate (culminating in a child's death) connects *The Constant Factor* (1981) and Kieślowski's *Decalogue I* (1988). Clearly, Kieślowski and Zanussi shared similar values in the world and asked many of the same questions. As the head of the Tor film unit, Zanussi approved many of Kieślowski's projects.

As for Tarkovsky, I will detail stylistic parallels between him and Kieślowski in Chapter 2. Tarkovsky pursued similar metaphysical themes to Zanussi but spent less time in philosophical debate or existential questions and more time in the "mystic" realm, an arena of truth that he believed transcended words. In his Transcendent pursuit, Tarkovsky also employed a unique formal style that clearly impressed Kieślowski, as he often mentioned his reverence for the Russian artist:

> Andrei Tarkovsky was one of the greatest directors of recent years. He's dead, like most of them. That is, most of them are dead or have stopped making films. Or else, somewhere along the line, they've irretrievably lost something, some individual sort of imagination, intelligence or way of narrating a story. Tarkovsky was certainly one of those who hadn't lost this.[107]

Many of the filmmakers in Kieślowski's list were also influences on Tarkovsky, strengthening their solidarity of style. What Kieślowski and Tarkovsky had most in common, however, was a metaphysical goal and a similar aesthetic vehicle as a means of attaining it. Both men tailored their cinematic styles toward abstraction as a means of venturing into that realm.

Kieślowski's embrace of both Zanussi and Tarkovsky is instructive. Zanussi is the realist — the man who explores the everyday man or woman and the crises he or she faces. Tarkovsky is the formalist, coaxing extraordinary expressivity out of every shot. Both strain toward a certain aspect of authenticity: something greater, a higher metaphysical ground.

Kieślowski's Motifs

Before we focus on style and visual aesthetics, specific thematic elements ought to be discussed as groundwork for the close reads in Chapters 3 through 5. Many motifs alluded to here receive more detailed treatment in those later chapters. To list these thematic elements and motifs is not to say that each (or any) exists in every film, only that they are commonly found.

---

107. Stok, *Kieślowski on Kieślowski,* 33–34.

The Immanent and the Transcendent

Kieślowski's childhood feeling of rootlessness inevitably led to foundational questions. Throughout Kieślowski's films there are continual dialectics playing out: home versus exploration, interior versus exterior, the personal versus the social, the immanent versus the transcendent, the particular moment versus universal time and space. Philosophically, to group these binaries all together under the heading Immanence and Transcendence is to be imprecise. However, in aesthetic discussions, neat categorizations rarely exist, and similarities often link particular issues into a whole, particular concern, especially when that concern has a root in the artist's own formative experience. After watching Kieślowski's films straight through, the pattern emerges: Kieślowski's question centers on existence, at any given time and place, as partial knowledge, thrown into relief against the ultimate reality, perhaps unknowable, but ever complete. What can we, as humans in an existential position, truly *know,* and, should our knowledge be more full, would it really change the way we live? Because our own "knowledge" (the epistemological question) is an amalgam of our social construction (the home we lived in, for instance), our existential position, and our ability to perceive any given moment, the quest for knowledge is always personally invested yet paradoxically straining outward. Edmund Husserl believed that real meaning resided not in the mind alone, nor in the world alone, but in the intentional relation between the two.[108] Kieślowski's films are, at root, about the joys and perils of intentionality while living in the "between" Søren Kierkegaard describes (in the quote that opens the Preface of this book).

The Problem of Evil and Personal Anguish

It is telling that these two concepts are nearly always yoked in Kieślowski. That is, characters face not mere disappointment, but a true existential angst, usually centered around the meaning of existence, reasons for living, grief over the loss of a loved one, struggles with belief in God and/or His providence, and so on. Evil, for Kieślowski, is a very real entity. In his 1981 manifesto, he spoke of fighting evil.[109] In his interviews with

---

108. Edmund Husserl, *Logical Investigations,* trans. J. N. Findlay (London: Routledge & Keegan Paul, 1970), 690–692.

109. Christopher Garbowski, *Krzysztof Kieślowski's Decalogue Series: The Problem of the Protagonists and Their Self-Transcendence* (Boulder, CO: East European Monographs, 1996), 4.

Danusia Stok, he expressed contempt for those who would not own up to their own evil acts under communism. ("Evil's in others. Always," he joked, darkly.) Even so, he maintained that evil comes from basically good people unable "to bring about the good."[110] So, while holding a belief in real evil, human freedom, and responsibility, he maintained a sympathetic, compassionate stance toward humanity. For Kieślowski, ethical decisions were often terribly difficult, as we are bound by our biology, passions, and a host of other sociohistorical factors.[111]

Kieślowski often articulated these themes through nonverbal strategies. For example, Japanese journalist and film critic Hiroshi Takahashi mentions meeting a Serbian woman (of suspected ill-repute), whose feelings about the film *No End* "were stronger than about the war" in her own country. She "reflected with unease on the scene where the woman makes a hole in her stocking, and then tears it . . . ," a visual gesture pregnant with connotation and phenomenological power that speaks volumes and finds multiple variations throughout Kieślowski's films. Recalling Stanley Kubrick's quote, there are times when words won't suffice, and one needs a moving image, a vehicle for experience. Urszula's moment with the stocking finds reincarnation in Weronika's taught string (mimicking a flatline electrocardiogram) in *The Double Life of Véronique,* in Dorota's crushing of the plant stem in *Decalogue II,* and in Julie's inexorable push of the piano lid support in *Blue.* These images carry phenomenological power, not simply because they articulate internal struggle, but because they visually render the tension in the chosen item as a metaphor for that struggle, and allow the audience to feel that tension through the viewing of the film. A literary critic may stop there, at the level of metaphor, but I believe it is important to move beyond that, to ask why it is that the image the Serbian woman remembered from the film was *that moment,* as opposed to a line of dialogue. The tension resonance is part of it, but, as I will discuss in detail later in this chapter and thread throughout the book, Kieślowski makes powerful use of abstract imagery in his films. Abstraction has a unique epistemological power that

---

Garbowski translates the quote from the original Polish publication of the manifesto (Krzysztof Kieślowski, "Głęboko zamiast szeroko," *Dialog* 26:1 [1981]: 110).

110. Stok, *Kieślowski on Kieślowski,* 118, 135.

111. Ibid., 150, "But often, even when we know what is honest and the right thing to do, we can't choose it. . . ." A discussion of the complexities of human freedom follows this quote.

is underdiscussed in film studies, but impossible to ignore in the oeuvre of certain filmmakers, particularly that of Kieślowski.

Divine Existence

Given Kieślowski's struggle with the problem of evil, it is unsurprising that he was not a moral relativist.[112] His conception of God was often harsh and demanding, but that harshness also creates a standard of responsibility in human life. We often fall short of that standard, however, and he suggested God does not always give justice on earth.[113]

Providence and divine existence are not the same issue, but they are connected in that the former is not possible without the latter (in some form). Kieślowski was constantly musing on the idea of circumstance and choice out of an existentialist position, but there is often a religious dimension to his depiction of those issues. The question, constantly circling in so many of Kieślowski's films, is whether an event is caused by "blind chance" or is a part of a preordained plan. Sometimes the synchronies of life appear too meaningful to ignore, and Kieślowski highlights them. Along these same lines, characters are continually thinking about their dreams and intuitions, many of which appear to be premonitions or prophetic thoughts. Are they coincidence, self-fulfilling prophecy, or a message from someone beyond? It is not always clear.

Lest we think Kieślowski too deterministic, he often posits a related (but philosophically converse) question, the conditional: could things have been different? In some cases, the difference would spell life; in some it would be death. There are many images in Kieślowski's films that make this clear, but none more than the double-edged final scene of *Red*. Hundreds die, and some of them are shown as corpses on the screen. The lead characters of the trilogy live. Some may call this overly fortuitous and convenient. As Irène Jacob, the lead actress in *Red*, admits, some find the ending "outrageous." She prefers to see it all as an allegory of "what we know."[114] They survive because someone survives, and Kieślowski believes everyone has a story worth telling. Work backwards through the films,

---

112. "I believe in Right and Wrong," he said to Phil Cavendish, in "Kieślowski's Decalogue," *Sight and Sound* (Summer 1990): 164. Similar admissions are found in Stok, ibid., 119, 149, and "No Heroics, Please: Krzysztof Kieślowski," *Sight and Sound* (Spring 1981): 91.

113. Stok, ibid., 149–150.

114. "A Conversation with Irène Jacob on Kieślowski," *Red* (DVD).

and it seems more reasonable; why shouldn't the survivors have interesting stories?

Paul Coates claims that, in what is supposedly his final interview, Kieślowski's personal verdict on the issue of God's existence was negative: "I think that if someone like a God above exists, someone who made everything around us, and made us too, then we very much slip out of his grasp."[115] Paired with his other comments on God (as listed in the foreword of this book), a portrait of a spiritually searching, vacillating soul emerges. Kieślowski's final film, *Red,* suggests that seven out of hundreds of people on a sinking ferry did not slip from His grasp (perhaps), and their stories ought to give us pause. A more recent book by Coates turns up a little known interview with a Polish Catholic weekly. In this article, Kieślowski stated, quite flatly, that he was "not a nonbeliever." Coates pairs this with an interview with Tadeusz Sobolewski, where Kieślowski clearly affirmed a belief in God but rejected any need for "intermediaries" (such as the church).[116] In the documentary *I'm So-So,* he spoke of his "private ties" to God, asking Him for *jasnosc* (which Insdorf says translates closer to "illumination" or "lucidity," rather than the subtitled translation "intellectual overview").[117] It is precisely this door to theism, sometimes cracked, sometimes wide, that keeps me from fully embracing Žižek's materialist conception of Kieślowski's style or Emma Wilson's characterization of Kieślowski's work as "a cinema of optical illusion and mental trauma."[118]

This is not to suggest that Kieślowski's films move closer and closer to some sort of metaphysical resolution. Rather, his whole career might be seen as dialogical — a sort of dialectic between metaphysical positions (the presence vs. absence of God). Kieślowski never arrived at an answer

---

115. Coates, *Lucid Dreams,* 114. Originally from an interview with Jacek Błach and Agata Otrębska, "Ponieważ są ciągle ci ludzie . . . " ["Since there are always these people . . . "], *Incipit* 2 (April 1996), reprinted in Tadeusz Lubelski, ed., *Kino Krzysztofa Kieślowskiego* (Kraków: Universitas, 1997): 296.

116. Paul Coates, *Cinema, Religion, and the Romantic Legacy* (Aldershot, Hants, England: Ashgate, 2003), 60. The original sources are Tadeusz Szyma, "Pomóc samemu sobie" [Interview with Kieślowski], *Tygodnik powszechny,* November 12, 1989, 6, and Tadeusz Sobolewski, "Normalna chwila" (Interview with Kieślowski), *Kino,* 24:6 [June 1990]: 20–22.

117. Insdorf, *Double Lives,* 81.

118. Emma Wilson, *Memory and Survival: The French Cinema of Krzysztof Kieślowski* (Oxford: Legenda, 2000), xvi.

and never pretended such answers were easy, but neither did he abandon any possibilities. I believe Kieślowski may be best described as a "hopeful agnostic" who vacillated on the issue of God's existence throughout his life but philosophically believed, for the most part, that "an absolute reference point does exist."[119] In his interviews, he tended to be pessimistic as to God's benevolent character, but his films are often more hopeful. Agnieszka Holland has said:

> I think that Krzysztof is somebody who had an incredibly deep need to believe in something transcendental. He did believe, but at the same time he wasn't really the member of any church, and his relationships toward the religious were less theological than ethical and metaphysical.[120]

She also attributes his pessimism in interviews (particularly in the early 1990s) to fatigue, adding that he experienced a joyful period right before he died.

The Uncanny Coincidence

Kieślowski constantly highlighted what might be dismissed as "mere co-incidence" and pondered whether they are not indices of extratemporal forces at work. Coincidence or Providence? Happenstance or a sign? These questions run through most of his fiction films, but they become most prominent in *The Double Life of Véronique* and the *Three Colors* trilogy.

Dreams, Memory, and Intuition

Memories recounted by Kieślowski's characters often form an interface with the spiritual — a suggestion that they transcend the individual. This theme emerges in conversations, such as Werner's description of his love in *Blind Chance* and Krzysztof's groping speech on death and memory in *Decalogue I*. This approach to dreams, memory, and collective narrative proves compatible with Husserl's phenomenological approach to fantasy and communal perception. That is to say, dreams and memories may or may not have actually happened in any concrete sense, but they carry a strong epistemological weight, and they continually shape our present sense of being. As we reach out, intentionally, for meaning in the world, they are the vocabulary from which we speak. As Tarkovsky once wrote:

---

119. Stok, *Kieślowski on Kieślowski,* 149.

120. Interview with Milos Stehlik, http://www.facets.org/decalogue/holland.html (accessed October 10, 2003).

Time and memory merge into each other; they are like the two sides of a medal. Memory is a spiritual concept. . . . Bereft of memory, a person becomes the prisoner of an illusory experience; falling out of time he is unable to seize his own link with the outside world — in other words he is doomed to madness.[121]

Dreams and intuition are both treated as likely portals to the metaphysical as well. Numerous times Kieślowski's characters confess to odd feelings, strange dreams, and subtle internal leadings in a certain direction. The question remains whether they are psychological anomalies, spiritual premonitions, or messages from beyond.

The Communal

The religious rite of communion is only sparingly portrayed in Kieślowski's films, but the motif finds other manifestations constantly: glasses of tea, milk, and other comforting drinks unite characters, often forming the social context in which true understanding takes place (moments in *Decalogue II* and *Blind Chance* are but two examples among many). Like Tarkovsky, who could not "imagine a film without water,"[122] Kieślowski takes full advantage of the visual aspects of liquid, inherently expressive and suggestive of multiple forms, shapes, layers, and metaphors.

Spillage and Breakage

The broken glasses in *No End* and *Decalogue II* mark the clear rupturing of the communal relationship. Numerous times Kieślowski's characters spill a drink, sometimes breaking the glass, and this counterpoint to the communal is the ideal ruptured. These images carry a heavy metaphorical quality, typically expressing something vital lost (or draining) from a character. Of particular interest is the way Kieślowski films these moments, often in close-up, with emphasis on the formal qualities of the image (sometimes filmed in slow motion to heighten the effect). As the following chapters will make clear, this should not be dismissed as mere stylistics aimed at simply enhancing the semiotic value of the image or merely lending an emotional charge to the scene. In addition to these qualities, Kieślowski

---

121. Andrei Tarkovsky, *Sculpting in Time,* trans. Kitty Hunter-Blair (Austin: University of Texas Press, 1986), 58.

122. Fabrizio Borin, *Il Cinema di Andrej Tarkovsky* (Rome: Jouvence, 1989), 24. Quoted in Angela Della Vacche, *Cinema and Painting* (Austin: University of Texas Press, 1996), 136.

utilizes the phenomenological powers of abstraction to encourage meta-physical contemplation. This contemplation is partly semiotic (metaphors of metaphysical concepts) and partly phenomenological (an intuitive sense of something larger than the immediate denotation of the image).

The Dialectic and Dialogue

Though not a Marxist, Kieślowski did approach questions in a dialectical manner. Rarely did he allow one side of an issue to be simply demonized or another to escape unscathed. An alternative model to the opposing powers of the dialectic is the dialogue, featuring partial truths coming together to contribute to a larger, more complete picture of an issue. It seems that Kieślowski vacillated between these two models, but the constant factor was always there: the unanswered question with many possibilities.

Ambiguity and Duality

Closely related to both the "providence" question and the dialectical approach is Kieślowski's frequent use of ambiguity and duality. By this I mean his propensity for images that would encourage multiple, even opposite interpretations. I mentioned before Kieślowski's story about his mother crying in the rain: were they tears or raindrops? By extension, is the water on Krzysztof's cheek tears of repentance, tears of anger and grief, or drippings from the ice in *Decalogue I*? Is the climax of *Decalogue II* a miracle or happenstance? The answer is often both, though sometimes it cannot be both, and the answer simply eludes us.

Science and Technology

In early Kieślowski, there are many builders, workers, inventors, and so on, and this is consonant with the "progressive" concerns of Poland at the time of the films. In many of the films, technology promises a sort of liberation and enhancement of human life, in the modernist vein (i.e., the "myth of progress"): Filip procures an enabling new camera in *Camera Buff*, Witek's future hinges on the catching of a train (apparently able to whisk him off to a completely different destiny), Paweł and his professor father revel in the powers of their personal computer, and Julie finds one last connection with her dead daughter via a miniature television. The list goes on. Yet, as with most of Kieślowski's themes, there is an insidious shade of gray creeping across the modernist horizon. He acknowledged science's value but questioned whether it had any salvific power. Indeed, there are instances in his films where the impassivity of the technology, starkly filmed, proves menacing (e.g., the gaping camera lens at the end of *Camera Buff,* the computer blinking "I am ready" at the end of *Decalogue I,* and the eavesdropping equipment in *Red*). Other times, technology shows its curiosities and benefits, as with the comforting filmed image of Piotrek's dead mother in *Camera Buff.* The degree to which science and technology aid us is the degree to which we should laud them, yet science will always offer more than it can actually deliver, such as the answers to the deepest questions of human meaning. This Kieślowskian critique (so resonant of Tarkovsky and Zanussi) is also apparent in his own writing. For instance, the original script of *Decalogue I* offers a perfectly "scientific" explanation for the mysterious ice thaw in the film, yet Kieślowski deliberately chose to excise those details from the film, leaving the audience to struggle with the spiritual question Is God responsible? If so, how? If not, who, then, is responsible? For Kieślowski, that question will haunt us, regardless of any scientific facts, and to turn to science is to avoid the issue.

Other gadgets are presented more objectively: the pen in *Personnel* (and *Camera Buff*), the listening devices in *Red,* and the telephone (figuring prominently in almost all his films). Some of these gadgets are talismanic or, at least, a dialogue on the talismanic idea (e.g., the bauble in *Véronique*).

Home and Family

Antek's mother is "not his . . . but married to his father," he says in *Peace.* So many of the characters in the *Decalogue* have either lost a parent or are, in some way, separated from one (or both) of them. Likewise, we might list Lucille and Julie in *Blue,* Véronique and Weronika, and many more. This obviously reflects Kieślowski's loss of his parents as well as his own felt guilt over his daughter, with whom (he felt) he did not spend enough time.[123] On a broader scale, however, the brief history of Poland is a story of a young generation cut off by force from its heritage. Old Poland can be remembered but never fully retrieved. Along these lines Kieślowski constantly employed the theme of home: what defines it, how we search for it, and how it defines us.

---

123. Stok, *Kieślowski on Kieślowski,* 112.

The Iconic

One motif that should not go unnoticed is that of the "iconic" look. This motif, so common in Tarkovsky's films as well, features a character that breaks the wall, so to speak, and stares directly at the camera. The power of these moments is hard to describe (as they happen in nearly every film, but usually only once or twice). They signal a spiritual pause, a caesura for reflection. More importantly, the audience can no longer escape involvement. This is a key point when we consider that Kieślowski was constantly mindful of guilt or indiscretion on the audience's part (as he amply demonstrated in his criticism of the young director Leif Magnusson during the filmmaker's workshop depicted in Erik Lint's film).[124] When he engages the audience directly, he does not do so lightly. Invariably, the metaphysical weight of the scene warrants reflection.

The Liminal Image: A Primer for the Immediate, Abstract, and Transcendent Character of Kieślowski's Style

The themes above might be called "liminal," in that they convey various thresholds to the metaphysical in human experience. They also create a general context of metaphysical possibility throughout his films. This context forms a foundation for the abstract images that complement the themes. Chapter 2 is dedicated to fleshing out how they do this. In short, I call Kieślowski's use of these images "liminal," in part because they reinforce the liminal themes in his work, described above, and partly because they carry liminal properties themselves. That is, they organically illustrate the fault lines between the rational and nonrational, representation and expression, concrete and abstract, universal and particular, physical and metaphysical.

Some may call this approach "transcendental," a term made famous in film scholarship by Paul Schrader (in his evaluation of the films of Yasujiro Ozu, Robert Bresson, and, to a lesser extent, Carl Dreyer). Indeed, some of Schrader's descriptions of the style seem to apply to Kieślowski (at least in the later films): "Transcendental style seeks to maximize the mystery of existence," "[it] chooses intellectual realism over optical realism...."[125]

---

124. Lint, *Krzysztof Kieślowski: A Masterclass for Young Directors* (VHS).
125. Paul Schrader, *Transcendental Style in Film* (New York: Da Capo Press, 1972), 10, 13.

However, Schrader's description of the style, a type of ascetic religious "mode" throughout the form of a film, cannot adequately describe the humanistic compassion and persistent vitality of Kieślowski's films. Perhaps a better term for Kieślowski's style would be *metaphysical dialogue,* as our lives are consistently a struggle between ideals and material reality, form and content, art and science. Indeed, it is the human and the human soul that Kieślowski clearly loved to explore, but his so-called mystical pursuit[126] never quite leaves the earth behind. His look at cinema was existential, yet compassionate and visionary, agnostic but never quite despairing.

The power of Kieślowski's style cannot be reduced to one particular element, but among his stylistic virtues stands his intuitive understanding of the powers of the moving photograph and its heightened power in abstraction. I use this term in a very broad sense, referring to a visual emphasis (at any given cinematic moment) on visual form over visual content and/or semiotic referent. My understanding of Kieślowski's style is one of progression, from the immediacy of the photographic image to its focused power in the abstract, narrative image to its transcendental import via metaphysical themes and contexts. In short, Kieślowski's images are powerful because they are crafted and utilize the powers of abstraction at key metaphysical moments in his films. Not every abstract moment should be seen as a direct index of the metaphysical, but it is not a stretch to say that every abstract shot is at least a point of metaphysical emphasis. Some may be vehicles. I developed this formula, originally, in an attempt to understand Tarkovsky's films, and I believe it holds firm for the Russian's great works. Kieślowski's admiration for Tarkovsky — for his ability to film something that "means something else" — bleeds over into his own cinematic style. The filmmakers can be quite different, to be sure, but in many ways, Kieślowski received the artistic baton from Tarkovsky; the similarities are striking, both thematically and stylistically.

Tarkovsky's cinematic theory, as articulated in *Sculpting in Time*, finds extension in Kieślowski's style. The themes and attitudes that Tarkovsky espouses match many of Kieślowski's sentiments throughout his corpus of interviews: mistrust of structural approaches to cinematic symbolism, belief in the necessity of metaphysical pursuits, revision of "realist" film theories

---

126. Coates, *Lucid Dreams,* 2.

in favor of intentional models, and so on.[127] Although Tarkovsky was far more confident, romantic, and theological in his rhetoric, the two men had the same concerns. As the next chapter will show, they also saw a certain approach to cinematic style to be effective in addressing these concerns.

The next chapter is a summation of my theoretical efforts in this direction. The three-stage process in the style, a genus/species schema, begins with the general aesthetic notion of immediacy, demonstrates how visual abstraction might contribute to the feeling of immediacy (or function as a component of it in some films), and then explores how a metaphysically concerned filmmaker (such as Kieślowski) uses the immediate/abstract strategy as a means of expressing the Transcendent possibility. This process is most demonstrable in the later films of Kieślowski (such as *Three Colors*). This does not limit the study, however, as we see that Kieślowski's entire career is actually a microcosm of the process, from his early days in documentary (and realization of film's immediate powers), to his more extensive exploration of the inner life through abstract techniques, and, finally, to his concentrated efforts in the direction of issues of Transcendence. I believe this paradigm will serve us well.

---

127. Ibid. Within Tarkovsky's *Sculpting in Time* the following themes are present: anti-structuralism (p. 176), metaphysics (p. 168 and throughout the book), and intentional models over naive realism (pp. 184–185).

$$\boxed{2}$$

IMMEDIACY, ABSTRACTION,
AND TRANSCENDENCE

Howhever formidable Kieślowski's screenwriting talents, the elements that make his work truly great are most resistant to verbal description. This chapter precedes the readings of his films precisely because one must have a sense of the enormous weight perceptual experience carries in his work before one begins a standard "textual" analysis.

As mentioned, part of the liminal quality of Kieślowski's style is its efficacy in the zone between the articulable and the ineffable. Much of this liminal style hinges on his careful use of visual abstraction. This chapter explores the nature and functions of abstraction in his fictional narratives as well as its ability to suggest the metaphysical dimension Kieślowski consistently sought.

The main terms of my theoretical model to come — immediacy, abstraction, and transcendence — all have a history in philosophy and/or aesthetics. I will present a short introduction to the terms, followed by some necessary exposition of the model. The second half of the chapter will detail some specific instances of Kieślowski's use of abstraction to illustrate the model presented.

When it comes to cinematic epistemology, there are many nuanced options from which to choose. This is because most film theorists today recognize that perception of the world (let alone the cinema) is a very complicated process that incorporates memory, learning, bodily response, numerous varieties of cognitive response, and raw stimulus, among other factors. The dimension of the perceptive event upon which one focuses often determines the theoretical approach one should take. In my case,

41

the study of the precategorical, nonverbal realm of image perception is best served by a phenomenological model, which approaches experience as a wholistic, bodily, sensuous, and intentional encounter of consciousness with the world. In short, it emphasizes experience over signs. That which is "experience" is also, to some degree, semiotic or coded, but to reduce all experience to coding is to oversimplify the perceptive event and render the term *code* useless, as Dudley Andrew has articulated.[1]

This does not mean that semiotics has no role to play or that I see perception as untainted by subjectivity, but the linguistic bias built into that approach renders it less effective in this particular area. Phenomenology approaches the precategorical epistemological event more directly, even though early phenomenology (like Husserl's) was not correct about all the particulars of that "direct" effect. (It is here that contemporary neuroscience will aid us; a discussion to come.) Cinema is "direct," not because it conveys reality impeccably and impassively, but because its inherent biases and mediations are often similar to our own as we perceive anything. As Andrew has said: "Thus cinema is above all things a representation of visual life itself. It mimics the continual work of seeing by means of its own work."[2]

I conceive of cinema as a microcosmic world, highlighting the process of meaning making. It offers a distilled and concentrated dose of epistemology. As Mikel Dufrenne puts it, art offers up an occasion to examine the intentional moment, where subjectivity meets the objective artwork, where it "induces us to complete the constitutive movement of a truth."[3]

My theory here will build upon the strength of the above parallelism between perceptive process of reality and cinema's simulation of its perception; that is, the harmony between the abstractive process of perception and the abstract image yields a powerful sensory experience with epistemological weight. This study presupposes the phenomenological tenet of intentionality (i.e., that we continually "reach out" for meaning in perception) and its complementary idea in cognitivism (that cinema as phenomenon that is encountered by a negotiating, constructive mind). I don't believe we know enough about the mind yet to be dogmatic on one exclusive theory of the mind, but, in this particular area of inquiry, I do find cognitive theories

---

1. Dudley Andrew, *Concepts in Film Theory* (Oxford: Oxford University Press, 1984), 33–34.

2. Ibid., 35.

3. Mikel Dufrenne, *The Phenomenology of Aesthetic Experience* (Evanston, IL: Northwestern University Press, 1973), 540.

to be more complementary to neuroscientific findings than, say, Lacanian theory.

Whereas most books on Kieślowski have focused on the semiotic realm, here I center on form and style. Semiotics will come into play, of course, as formal, stylistic matters can never be divorced from content issues completely. The narrative, characters, sonic elements, and previous dramatic action all provide an interpretive context through which the image is experienced. However, my intent here is to bring Kieślowski's little-discussed formal powers into relief, so that I might demonstrate the cooperation between them and the semiotic elements toward achieving his expressive goals. In sum, Kieślowski's metaphysically concerned films take more advantage of abstraction's powers than a typical filmic image. Like Tarkovsky, Kieślowski saw the image in a more poetic, less scientific light — a mingling of epistemological strengths. Poetry combines garden-variety semiotics (metaphor, simile, etc.) with formal, structural connections (e.g., alliteration and rhyming) and synaesthetic elements to produce a meaningful experience. Cinema adds the iconic dimension to this, in C. S. Peirce's sense of the term, meaning resemblance,[4] but there is also an epistemological impact that grounds and enables perception of all of these elements and should be considered to be meaning as much as the cognitive overlays that follow. It is this pre-categorical realm I hope to explore.

A Theoretical Mechanism:
Immediacy, Abstraction, and Transcendence

I define *immediacy* as the capacity of cinematic images to directly communicate, exceeding linguistic categories, yielding expressive and emotionally powerful impact. This definition is primarily derived from various ideas on immediacy in art, beginning in eighteenth- and nineteenth-century British aesthetics[5] and generally embraced by thinkers as diverse as Henri Bergson, David W. Prall, and John Dewey.[6] My particular definition has been

4. C. S. Peirce, *The Collected Papers of C. S. Peirce*, vols. 1–6, ed. C. Haretshorne and P. Weiss (Cambridge, MA: Harvard University Press, 1931–1935).

5. For the early, literary origination of this term, see Wallace Jackson, *Immediacy: The Development of a Critical Concept from Addison to Coleridge* (Amsterdam: Rodopi NV, 1973).

6. Discussions of immediacy may be found in Henri Bergson's *Laughter*, trans. Cloudseley Brereton and Fred Rothwell (St. Paul, MN: Green Integer, 1999); David W. Prall's

modified somewhat under the influence of the phenomenological theories of Edmund Husserl and Mikel Dufrenne,[7] as well as George Romanos's insightful essay "On the Immediacy of Art."[8]

I conceptualize abstraction as a visual strategy found in the cinema that deemphasizes the everyday representational approach to image and its referent(s) in favor of formal concerns. I use this term in its broad sense, as found in Malcolm LeGrice's *Abstract Film and Beyond.* That is, the term *abstract* should not be limited to nonrepresentational images, but applied to any image that emphasizes form over "realist" indexicality through a strategy of manipulating time, space, motion, or any constituent elements of the image. LeGrice states that, " . . . in its more general meaning, abstract implies the separation of qualities, aspects or generalizations from particular instances. . . . [S]ome basically 'abstract' tendencies in film are not necessarily non-representational in the photographic sense."[9]

In this study, transcendence is best defined as a cinematic style expressing the immaterial and aiming to provoke metaphysical consideration in the audience. One should not confuse this term with the Transcendent (capital *T*), which is actually the immaterial object of transcendence (lowercase *t*). In the case of Kieślowski, the aim is the expression of metaphysical ideas, and the purpose of this chapter is to show how abstract style suits this aim. These ideas may be conceived as immanent or transcendent (e.g., "love" as a social, psychological, and biological response and/or a marker of a spiritual reality). Kieślowski's liminal images consistently straddle the two realms, typically offering images that suggest both. My use of the word *transcendence* in Kieślowski's case is not to suggest a specific religious idea necessarily, but only to imply the transcendence of what is material (beyond "the things we buy in shops," as Kieślowski himself said).[10] This transmateriality often pushes into the theistic realm, but not necessarily so. Kieślowski's style evokes the Transcendent as part of a search for that very entity. It is a

Aesthetic Analysis (New York: Thomas Y. Crowell, 1936); and John Dewey's *Art as Experience* (New York: Minton, Balch & Company, 1934). George Romanos discusses the individual theories of these thinkers in "On the Immediacy of Art," *Journal of Aesthetics and Art Criticism* 36.1 (1977): 73–80.

    7. Edmund Husserl, *Logical Investigations,* trans. J. N. Findlay (London: Routledge & Keegan Paul, 1970); Dufrenne, *Phenomenology.*

    8. Romanos, "On the Immediacy of Art," 73–80.

    9. Malcolm LeGrice, *Abstract Film and Beyond* (Cambridge, MA: The MIT Press, 1977), 3.

    10. *Kieślowski on Kieślowski,* ed. Danusia Stok (London: Faber and Faber, 1993), 5.

reference, phenomenologically and semiotically, to what might be beyond. Whether there is anything beyond or not is a decision for the viewer, but the style invites him or her down that metaphysical path. There is nothing deterministic here. The viewer of the cinematic image is not forced down this road to transcendence; he or she may stop at any time, rejecting the experience, or the experience may be offset by other personal factors.

These conceptualizations constitute an experiential process that may be visualized as a series of concentric circles:

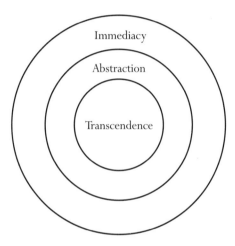

The most suggestive experiences in this mode are necessarily immediate, abstract, and transcendent. However, the model is one of graduated specificity; this does not imply that all immediate experiences are abstract or transcendent or that all abstract experiences are transcendent. Some of Kieślowski's images drive directly to the heart of the diagram, others remain in the second ring, but there is always the sense that they are moving inward toward the transcendent goal. Kieślowski employs multiple abstract strategies, varying in character and effect, but I contend that they all come from the same ground — a rupturing of the everyday tempo-material attitude in favor of an expanded metaphysical view.

Immediacy

Immediacy encompasses cinema's ability to capture qualities of reality that are beyond articulation. The following quote from Susanne Langer articulates the void visual immediacy helps to fill.

> Sometimes our comprehension of a total experience is mediated by a metaphorical symbol because the experience is new, and language has words and phrases only for familiar notions. . . . But the symbolic presentation of subjective reality for contemplation is not only tentatively beyond the words we have; it is impossible in the essential frame of language.[11]

Immediacy may be seen as the operative mode of ineffability, a similar aesthetic concept. Although W. E. Kennick criticizes *ineffability* as a term without any real substance (essentially arguing that words can convey all that the artistic image can), he does admit that "the picture leads us to see certain features and qualities of the landscape [for example] that the prose description *does* not lead us to see." He qualifies, "It is not that there are values and meanings that can be expressed *only* by immediately visible and audible qualities; it is rather that there are values and meanings that are better expressed by immediately visible and audible qualities than by prose descriptions."[12] Kennick's problem with ineffability as a concept lies in its claim to convey some sort of knowledge beyond words. However, Kennick's admission of art's direct efficacy in expressing certain things leaves the door open for a cognitive account of perceptual knowledge that truly does exceed the language we have. Diana Raffman engages Kennick's argument handily, I believe, and maintains that there are many experiences in art that we perceive as knowledge (i.e., some kind of mental representation) but do not have a fine-grained enough cognitive schema through which we can articulate that knowledge. In the end, we are left with an ostensive description, meaning we know an ineffable experience (and take pleasure in it) when we hear it or see it; to convey it to others, we must point to it rather than articulate it.[13] Much of her very helpful article on the topic of musical ineffability is dedicated to parsing out the many different varieties of perceptual knowledge — the one most often labeled "ineffable" being "occurrent sensory-perceptual knowledge."[14]

I pair this concept (and immediacy) with the idea of nonverbal knowledge. Kenneth Dorter's articulation of "nonrational" knowledge is an exemplary study, defending the existence of a nonverbal, nonconceptual

---

11. Susanne Langer, *Problems of Art* (New York: Charles Scribner's Sons, 1957), 23–24.

12. W. E. Kennick, "Art and the Ineffable," *Journal of Philosophy* 58.12 (June 1961): 315.

13. Diana Raffman, "Toward a Cognitive Theory of Musical Ineffability," *Review of Metaphysics* 41.4 (June 1988): 685.

14. Ibid., 701.

epistemology.[15] I am not convinced that the knowledge immediacy imparts is nonrational entirely, but the distinction from the nonverbal is very helpful. In essence, immediacy arises from the way an artwork functions as a sample — a "concrete instance" of a thing — rather than a label (like a word), by virtue of its having "more properties related to its overall symbolic function than does any instance of a label."[16] By virtue of this concreteness, a certain knowledge can be imparted by way of artistic experience:

> It may be that Plato is right in regarding art as cognitively inferior to conceptual knowledge in practical empirical matters, as the third and fourth arguments of *Republic X* claimed. But in terms of the elusive *foundations* of reality, or at least our experience of reality, art furnishes as important a mode of cognition as does philosophy.[17]

It seems to me that this knowledge lies typically in the zone of epistemological "preformulation" (to borrow Dudley Andrew's phrase), a precategorical realm of experience where "sensory data congeals into 'something that matters.'"[18] In this realm of inquiry, phenomenology has much to offer.

In defining where immediate knowledge resides, the phenomenologist forges a compromise between hard idealism and hard epistemological realism — meaning lies not solely in the mind or the world alone, but in their intentional relation.[19] Dufrenne holds a similar view in his discussion of the perception of the artwork.[20]

As for immediate knowledge and the image, the patriarch of phenomenology, Edmund Husserl, conceived of the encounter with "picture-presentations" (including photographs) as phenomenologically similar to the perception of reality in certain respects.[21] We might call his approach "immediate," in that one approaches the photograph and *lives through the perception* in a direct manner, similar to the way in which one encounters the "real" object *in concretum*. Logically, we may extend this to the cinema, and

---

15. Kenneth Dorter, "Conceptual Truth and Aesthetic Truth," *Journal of Aesthetics and Art Criticism* 48.1 (Winter 1990): 37–52.

16. Romanos, "On the Immediacy of Art," 79.

17. Dorter, "Conceptual Truth," 48.

18. Dudley Andrew, "The Neglected Tradition of Phenomenology in Film Theory," in *Movies and Methods II,* ed. Bill Nichols (Berkeley: University of California Press, 1985), 627.

19. Husserl, *Logical Investigations,* 690–692. See also Richard Kearney, *Modern Movements in European Philosophy* (Manchester, England: Manchester University Press, 1994), 15.

20. Such is the essence of his "sympathetic" mode of reflection in aesthetic perception. *Phenomenology,* 392–393.

21. Husserl, *Logical Investigations*, 689.

so we may apply Husserl's primary approach to the analysis of perception: the phenomenological époché. The époché was Husserl's mechanism for filtering out preconceived notions of the world and arriving at a universal essence of perception. This ultimate goal would prove to be doomed, by most accounts, but it is my opinion that Husserl was on to something in his method, and the époché can be carefully and judiciously applied to abstraction.

The époché is Husserl's system of "bracketing,"[22] whereby he seeks to suspend a series of cognitive categories with which we perceive the world, in order that he might isolate "pure" perception in an unadulterated phenomenological state. In the first bracket, we suspend the "natural" or "scientific" attitude, which considers things independent of our existence. In other words, we consider things only in terms of how we perceive them in relation to us, that is, the intentional perspective. As Richard Kearney has noted and Allan Casebier has applied, this includes works of fiction and art, as well as things in concrete reality; all perceived objects are considered equally, as the exploration is of experience, not simply "the world of facts."[23] The époché then continues: the bracketing of objectifying constructs (i.e., "categories" or "presuppositions").[24] The third stage is a stage of free variation, where the imagination or fancy explores the raw percepts.[25] In this stage all possible variants of a percept are pursued.

At this point, Husserl pauses. He summarizes the work so far: "The narrowing of an impure percept which throws out symbolic components yields the pure intuition which is immanent in it." A further reductive step then "throws out everything imagined, and yields the substance of pure perception."[26] In works after *Logical Investigations,* Husserl was to venture beyond

---

22. Edmund Husserl, *Ideas* (New York: Collier Books, 1962), 99.

23. Ibid., 90–92; Kearney, *Modern Movements,* 19; Allan Casebier, *Film and Phenomenology* (Cambridge: Cambridge University Press, 1991), 34. William Earle writes: "Neither phenomenology nor criticism is interested in the *factual* description of anything. Both are indeed interested in grasping the meaning or inner core of the phenomenon, in Husserl's jargon, its *eidos.*" Earle's analysis of Surrealism utilizes Husserl's idea of the époché in analyzing that movement in a fashion similar to its employment here (albeit in a more limited scope); "Phenomenology and the Surrealism of Movies," *Journal of Aesthetics and Art Criticism* 38.3 (Spring 1980): 255–260.

24. Husserl, *Logical Investigations,* 681; Kearney, ibid., 19.

25. Husserl, *Ideas,* 50.

26. Husserl, *Logical Investigations,* 734.

"pure perception," and think about the idea of "essences" of perception as they relate to the "Transcendental Ego" (Husserl's idea of a transcendent, invariable, and universal root of consciousness).[27] My path diverges from Husserl at the "pause" above, as I do not claim any Transcendental Ego or universal essence of perception. Likewise, I am not convinced that "pure perception" is a possibility, as E. H. Gombrich has demonstrated in his critique of "the innocent eye" idea.[28] However, though we cannot wholly escape our presuppositions or preconceptions, we can limit them, and I believe there is great profit in this limitation.

Abstraction

It seems to me that abstraction in the cinema epistemologically functions like the first three stages of Husserl's époché. Abstraction invites us to consider objects in a different way, apart from our everyday approach to the world. We are invited to reckon with form before content. Sometimes we are compelled to see an object apart from its identity (that category-name by which we recognize a thing). In other modes of abstraction, Kieślowski encourages us to rethink the spatiotemporal context of the object. The examples discussed later in this chapter will help to clarify this process.

It so happens that abstraction in the cinema not only mirrors Husserl's model, but it replicates the initial stages of human perception itself, to some degree.[29] Contemporary neuroscientists such as Semir Zeki and Richard Gregory testify that perception is a complicated affair, assembling many elements of an image into a whole through a rationalizing process (a process albeit that is very little understood, even today).[30] In other words, perception is not a matter of our brains seeing a picture. All pictures stop at the retina, where myriad biological sensors break the image down into

27. Husserl, *Ideas,* 51–52.

28. E. H. Gombrich, *Art and Illusion: A Study in the Psychology of Pictorial Representation* (Princeton, NJ: Princeton University Press, 1969), 12.

29. As a general concept, this is not a new idea, with theorists from Hugo Münsterberg to Poland's preeminent film theorist Karol Irzykowski to the postmodern Gilles Deleuze offering some version of it. However, I have not seen much neuroscience applied, as I have attempted to do here.

30. Semir Zeki, *Inner Vision: An Exploration of Art and the Brain* (London: Oxford University Press, 1999); Richard L. Gregory, *Eye and Brain: The Psychology of Seeing,* 5th ed. (Princeton, NJ: Princeton University Press, 1997).

its elements and code those elements into signals. These signals fly to nu-merous parts of the visual cortex, and there does not seem to be one particular place where the signals reassemble.[31] How the percept remains so coherent in our minds is not understood at all, but the initial stages of perception seem to include the isolation of the elements of a scene (color, form, motion, etc.).[32]

The sum benefit of this is that abstraction presents a cinematic image in a primary way closer to the way in which we perceive. This conforms with Zeki's observation that both the brain and abstract art exhibit "a search for constants."[33] This may explain why abstract photographs and cinematic images have historically held such appeal. The phenomenological meaning they carry is beyond words, precisely because it is before words, a streamlining of our epistemological experience, neurobiologically speaking.

The abstract cinematic époché is a setting aside of what Husserl called the natural attitude in an effort to crystallize the fleeting pre-reflective stage of perception. Whereas the audience would have normally reached out intentionally for meaning in the image through perception, imagination, and signification, abstract images throw signification into varying degrees of stasis. One must then deal with the form presented, the image as it is (presentational) and as it might be (possibility).

The possibilities the viewer entertains regarding the identity of the object and/or its time-space context mirror the "free variation" phase of percep-tion in Husserl's époché. After bracketing a percept, one must then imagine the percept in all its possible manifestations, both real and imaginary. Ab-stract images embody the concept of possibility (and potentiality), even as they encourage a Husserlian epistemological response: that of free variation.

At this point, the viewer must utilize more primary categories of under-standing. For example, when one sees a tree, one may, as a matter of mental shorthand, immediately process this image as a part of the group of many thousand trees perceived in one's experience. However, when faced with a

---

31. Zeki, ibid., 65. Zeki suggests multiple brain processes working together, but not necessarily in precise temporal registration.

32. Zeki's survey of the minute levels of perception is remarkable. For example, some cells in the visual cortex will react only to movement from right to left, with color or form having no bearing on the reaction. Other cells respond only to color information. Similar fascinating observations, at the single cell-level, may be found in Margaret Livingstone's *Vision and Art: The Biology of Seeing* (New York: Harry N. Abrams, 2002).

33. Ibid., 7.

tall, slender form, one cannot always be sure the object is a tree; it carries the possibility and visual resonance of one, but it may also be something else, of similar form. Both cognitive and Gestalt schools of psychology see this process of "reasoning" as key to all perception, and it illuminates the union of imagination and perception of the objective real.

It is also exceptionally important that we not reduce these mental concepts to idealist mental representations, as if they were amputated from the body. They are welded to bodily experience — what Maurice Merleau-Ponty called "primordial" experience.[34] Dufrenne also sees a union between body and imagination.[35]

Immediacy and Abstraction as Knowledge: A Move toward Transcendence

At this point, we should consider the epistemological status of the abstract image. In his discussion of nonrational knowledge, Dorter mentions four levels of experience at which art seems to express a certain kind of truth: (1) our emotions, (2) cultural values, (3) sensory experience, and (4) the "elusive significance of our experience."[36] For our purposes, the third point is most important, of which Dorter says, "art reveals something not only about the subjectivity of experience but about the experienced world itself, something that is not accessible to conceptual understanding."[37] He elaborates:

> Since in our normal experience qualities like color, shape, and sound are "absorbed" into the images of perceived things, they are experienced only derivatively — not in themselves but as submerged in the object. . . . Art, however, can make the qualities of color, shape, sound, duration, weight, etc., stand alone as images themselves rather than as mere features of normal physical things. Thus it can give us a framework within which to see these qualities in their own terms. . . . In this way art can *reveal truth about the world* by making conspicuous the primitive qualities of which our experience is composed but which are normally submerged in that experience.[38]

---

34. Maurice Merleau-Ponty, *The Phenomenology of Perception* (n.p.: Humanities Press, 1962). See also the essay "Eye and Mind," in *The Merleau-Ponty Aesthetics Reader,* trans. Michael B. Smith (Evanston, IL: Northwestern University Press, 1993), 124–125.

35. Dufrenne, *Phenomenology,* 345.

36. Dorter, "Conceptual Truth," 37.

37. Ibid., 38.

38. Ibid., 39; emphasis added.

In his discussion of the color white, Husserl describes a similar "surplus of meaning" in the color itself — a meaning that the natural attitude generally overlooks or discards, but abstraction explores.[39] There is some overlap here with what Kristin Thompson has called "excess" in the cinema, residual "structures" that lie outside typical narrative analysis.[40]

The knowledge status of these "primitive qualities" (as Dorter named them) may point to more than just our sensory experience. The fourth of Dorter's points — that art expresses the truth of the significance of our experience — lies at the heart of this quote from Martin Heidegger:

> Genuinely poetic projection is the opening up or disclosure of that into which human being as historical is already cast. This is the earth and, for an historical people, its earth, the self-closing ground on which it rests together with everything that it already is, though still hidden from itself.[41]

Heidegger's concern is with Being, and this Being is present but still hidden. Art, or poetic projection, brings this essence of Being to the foreground but maintains its quality of mystery. Dorter's interpretation of Heidegger is most helpful:

> Art's power of giving sensuous form to significance is also the more fundamental sense in which, for Heidegger, art discloses the hiddenness of "Earth," the Realm within our experience that is not reducible to conceptual clarity. Earth includes not only primitive sensuous qualities but also that which underlies what is as a whole. Because Earth cannot be reduced to conceptual clarity it is accessible only to evocative rather than conceptual thinking, and therefore to imagination rather than reason.[42]

It is precisely this idea of a deep, inexpressible knowledge that immediacy yields and abstraction highlights. Shades of it exist in other aesthetic theories, such as the "sensuous" in Dufrenne's *Phenomenology of Aesthetic Experience.*[43]

In addition to this ontological revelation, an expanded conception of the percept often emerges through Husserl's free variation process (the third

---

39. Husserl, *Logical Investigations,* 775.

40. Kristin Thompson, "The Concept of Cinematic Excess," in *Narrative, Apparatus, Ideology,* ed. Philip Rosen (New York: Columbia University Press, 1984), 130–131. I should note that, for some reason, she seems to resist calling the phenomenon "meaning."

41. Martin Heidegger, "On the Origin of the Work of Art," in *Poetry, Language, Thought,* trans. Alfred Hofstader (New York: Harper and Row, 1971), 75.

42. Dorter, "Conceptual Truth," 40.

43. Dufrenne, op. cit. See Chapter 19 for his discussion of being and art's ability to shed light on aspects of the real.

step of the épochè). Sometimes Kieślowski will reveal the diegetic identity of the percept after its abstract presentation, that is, after predisposing the audience toward a wider frame of reference for the perception. In other words, we may ultimately see what the object "is" in the diegesis, but we have been predisposed to considering it in terms of the many things it could have been. In Kieślowski's images, this expanded view harmonizes with a metaphysical conception of reality, which is, by definition, expansive (beyond the material). This harmony echoes many religious ideas of reality, and so a certain transcendent impulse may be said to be present in the images, particularly as Kieślowski has couched these images in a metaphysical context (i.e., a metaphysical topic or issue present in the narrative).

So far, I have shown how immediacy is a direct, nonlinguistic experience, part of the broad area of nonrational knowledge, and how abstraction functions within this realm. Husserl has given us a phenomenological paradigm for analyzing such intentional, pretheoretical experience. The main functions of abstraction I have mentioned are abstraction as bracket, abstraction as possibility, and abstraction as revelation.

In locating the immediate, abstract experience, we find ourselves primarily in the realm of the visceral. Film theorist Carl Plantinga has outlined a cognitive model of spectator experience and, within this model, the visceral functions as a major source of spectator pleasure.[44] He suggests that the visceral is not simply limited to the knee-jerk, emotional response. The door is open for a visceral experience to link itself to cognitive pleasures and empathy. What distinguishes it from other sources of spectator pleasure is that "a visceral experience is a response to the formal qualities of the

---

44. Carl Plantinga, "Movie Pleasures and the Spectator's Experience: Toward a Cognitive Approach," *Film and Philosophy* 2 (1994), http://www.hanover.edu/philos/film/vol_02/planting.htm (accessed September 10, 2003). On page 1, Plantinga claims five major sources of spectator pleasure: (1) orientation and discovery, (2) visceral experience, (3) empathy and character identification, (4) narrational structuring, and (5) reflexive criticism and appreciation. Plantinga believes these sources are rarely experienced in isolation and are not necessarily exhaustive, but preliminary and suggestive. Indeed, this model helps us locate the immediate, abstract image; whereas the immediate tends to dwell within the nonrational, prelinguistic, and, sometimes, nonrepresentational, the "visceral" experience tends to be where this particular encounter may be found. As this section will show, Kieślowski's setting of a metaphysical context for the abstract image overlaps into Plantinga's "pleasurable" areas of orientation and discovery, empathy and character identification, and narrational structuring.

film and the events it represents, regardless of our allegiance with characters."[45] In our examples here, even the "events it represents" have been neutralized to some degree. So the visceral experience here lies in the realm of immediacy, in that it is an instantaneous, emotional, and pretheoretical response.

In *Logical Investigations,* Husserl speaks of a division between "sensuous concepts" and "categories," refining the "old epistemological contrast between *sensibility* and *understanding.*"[46] However, he qualifies, these two acts are "bound together."[47] Likewise, one can make a parallel with Rudolf Arnheim, who distinguishes between intuition and intellect (intuition being the cognitive ability to grasp the whole; intellect being the ability to grasp particulars and their connections), but acknowledges that the two are inseparable in perception; thus, he entitles his article "The Double-Edged Mind: Intuition and Intellect."[48] Zeki suggests that perception is a matter of systemic synthesis, but also affirms the idea that the sensation and understanding should not be so rigorously distinguished.[49]

In short, perception consists of a complicated process whereby the viewer intends toward meaning in the form of mental categories and sensual concepts. The encounter with the abstract image is not an exception to this rule, but it is distinct from familiar perceptions (which are easily processed both sensually and categorically) in that the forms are different from what is expected, at least in the classic Western narrative tradition. The power of these images should not be underestimated. Arnheim describes the most effective abstract images:

> These passionate [abstract] compositions are not limited to the purely visual celebration of what pleases the eyes. They reach beyond the world of the senses to symbolize the forces that activate life and the physical world with all their overwhelming complexity.[50]

A theological reading of this quote takes us to the liminal plane, the threshold of the transcendent possibility.

---

45. Ibid., 4.

46. Husserl, *Logical Investigations,* 681.

47. Ibid., 793.

48. Rudolf Arnheim, "The Double-Edged Mind: Intuition and Intellect," in *New Essays on the Psychology of Art* (Berkeley: University of California Press, 1986), 13, 29.

49. Zeki, *Inner Vision,* Chapter 8 is dedicated to this issue.

50. Rudolf Arnheim, *To the Rescue of Art* (Berkeley: University of California Press, 1992), 22.

Kieślowski's approach to abstraction is religious in the limited sense that Dudley Andrew has described it:

> Philosophy, Hegel taught, replaced images as Western culture gradually matured. By virtue of its historically countenanced mission, then, Philosophy, at least its main traditions, proudly kneels to no law or power higher than the rules of thought or language. Religion, on the other hand, might be said to begin on its knees, groping toward a power it aims to locate, to corral, and perhaps to begin to comprehend.[51]

Transcendence

The twentieth century held challenges for the idea of the Transcendent. What Paul Coates calls the "postromantic" age,[52] art historian André Malraux named "the twilight of the absolute."[53] Likewise, religious belief has subsided in the academy and the arts. However, the acclaimed sociologist of religion Mircea Eliade maintains that the sacred has not completely disappeared, but rather goes unrecognized:

> The two specific characteristics of modern art, namely the destruction of traditional forms and the fascination for the formless, for the elementary modes of matter, are susceptible to religious interpretation. . . . [N]othing could convince [Constantin] Brancusi that a rock was only a fragment of inert matter; like his Carpathian ancestors, like all Neolithic men, he sensed a presence in the rock, a power, an "intention" that one can only call "sacred."[54]

It is this very "presence" that encourages philosopher George Steiner's "wager on transcendence." In essence, he argues that meaning in human life is an indicator of God's existence, and through meaning from God, all great art flows.[55] As to the nature of meaning, he argues:

> Meaningfulness is not an invariant datum. . . . That is, there can be no end to interpretative disagreement and revision. But where it is seriously engaged in, the process of differing is one which cumulatively circumscribes and clarifies the disputed ground. It is, I have argued, the irreducible autonomy

---

51. Dudley Andrew, "Introduction." In *The Image in Dispute,* ed. Dudley Andrew (Austin: University of Texas Press, 1997), viii.

52. Paul Coates, *Cinema, Religion and the Romantic Legacy* (Aldershot, Hants, England: Ashgate, 2003), 7.

53. André Malraux, *The Twilight of the Absolute,* trans. Stuart Gilbert (New York: Pantheon Books, 1950), 51.

54. Mircea Eliade, "The Sacred and the Modern Artist," in *Art, Creativity, and the Sacred,* ed. Diane Apostolos-Cappadona (New York: Crossroad, 1984), 182.

55. George Steiner, *Real Presences* (Chicago: University of Chicago Press, 1989), 3, 214.

of presence, of "otherness," in art and text which denies either adequate paraphrase or unanimity of finding.[56]

Steiner argues from a postmodern situation, but not a postmodern attitude. He recognizes the ruptures in meaning, but he sees them as simply inadequate to the truth of the world, not to the negation of it.

> Human words and syntax . . . fall derisively, desperately short of the resistant substance, of the existential matter of the world and of our inward lives. Speech can neither articulate the deeper truths of consciousness, nor can it convey the sensory, autonomous evidence of the flower, of the shaft of light, of the birdcall at dawning.[57]

Thus, the poverty of language leaves us with a choice: absence or presence. Steiner chooses presence, as he cannot escape Gottfried Wilhelm Leibniz's pivotal, existential question — the "why" question: "why is there not nothing?"[58] One might argue that Kieślowski thought much the same way. Where words fail us, his art helps to span the linguistic gap to the transcendent meaning.

From a religious point of view, the construct of transcendence found its most eloquent and encyclopedic exponent in Rudolf Otto. His book *The Idea of the Holy* not only defined transcendence philosophically, but also contributed to an understanding of the Holy "Other" in aesthetic terms. The "Other" is not simply that which is not we ourselves, but that which is "wholly" other.[59] The Transcendent is of an entirely different order, and it exhibits itself with a sense of mystery, provoking in the viewer feelings of awe, terror, wonder, and, paradoxically, fascination and attraction.[60]

Otto sees the spiritual life as both rational and nonrational, working together like the "warp and woof" of a fabric.[61] The nonrational part of the spiritual life is a sensation of the "Numinous" — the sense of the ineffable. Again, Kenneth Dorter's conception of a nonrational knowing prescribes a knowledge that arises from the Husserlian encounter in experience. Steiner

---

56. Ibid., 214.
57. Ibid., 111.
58. Ibid., 200.
59. Rudolph Otto, *The Idea of the Holy* (London: Oxford University Press, 1958), 25.
60. Ibid., 26, 31; Steiner, *Real Presences,* 137–139.
61. Otto, ibid., 2–3.

describes this encounter as a moment "when cognition holds its breath,"[62] at "the semantic limit."[63]

But the nonrational knowledge cannot subsist alone. I suggest a parallel between Otto's "warp and woof" of the rational/nonrational in religion and the phenomenological and significative. At this stage in the pursuit of transcendence in film, language, rationality, and narrative return to contextualize and demarcate the transcendent gesture.

Metaphysical Context

As mentioned, metaphysical context refers to any suggestion, narrative, semiotic, or diegetic, of an entity or concept separate from the immanent. The suggestion may be anything from ultimate principles (such as love), moral issues, spiritual issues, and religious symbols, to plot elements regarding spiritual struggle, unexplained forces, or prophet-like characters. The sheer variety of these suggestions prohibits a full catalog here. Typically the metaphysical context expresses a need or desire, on the part of a character, to transcend the immanent in some way.

Apart from the nonrational realm of knowledge that has been the locus of this investigation, some other important coordinate themes have emerged in my survey of Otto and deserve attention here. First, Otto's conception of a Numinous consciousness is one that breaks away from a "profane," everyday conception of reality. Second, Otto's advocation of feeling as primary in the beholding of the Numinous[64] parallels a general phenomenological perspective on feeling as indispensable in the study of the lifeworld.[65] Finally, the encounter with the Numinous may be conceived as something akin to intentional experience; a beholding of something truly real, outside the self, but with the searching, creative mind as a constitutive factor in its apprehension.

Along these lines, some insights from the Jewish philosopher Martin Buber are helpful. Buber's theology is built upon the idea that relation is the highest mode of perception, transforming an "it" or a "you" into

---

62. Steiner, *Real Presences,* 201.

63. Steiner goes so far as to define the essence of art as "the maximalization of semantic incommensurability in respect to the formal means of expression," Ibid., 83.

64. Otto, *The Idea of the Holy,* 8.

65. Dufrenne, *Phenomenology,* 49, 521.

a "Thou."[66] Relation calls for the giving, intentional act — setting aside the quantifying, controlling instinct of the categorical. Husserl's intentional view of perception is given new shape here as the idea emerges that relation holds an ontological weight. In one's encounter with the world, if one pares away the typical, objectifying attitudes of perception, a spiritual kinship can be grasped, made possible because a Transcendent Source exists. As the appendix to *I-Thou* makes clear, Buber's belief is in a personal Transcendent God who 'has intricately woven Himself into the fabric of the immanent, which He has created: "[T]he theophany comes ever *closer,* it comes ever closer to the sphere *between beings* — comes closer to the realm that hides in our midst, in the between."[67]

Buber has given us the experiential locus of transcendence: the between. All the difficulties of conceiving transcendence as the other or the beyond, yet found in the essential, in the immanent, can be summed in the paradoxical between. It is a theological cast to the phenomenological conception of perception as intentional, first given us here by Husserl. Kieślowski's vacillation on the existence of the Transcendent Source does not diminish the fact that his films consistently strained toward the Numinous, born out of a suspicion that it might be there.

Immediacy, Abstraction, and Transcendence: A Liminal Cinema

Having demonstrated that various theological conceptions of the Transcendent are complementary to the immediate and abstract image, it remains for us to synthesize them. Paul Schrader outlines three general approaches to the sacred in the history of art (my summary):

1. The Holy speaks in revelation (e.g., divinely-inspired Scripture).

2. The human expresses the Holy (e.g., iconography).

3. The artist portrays (expresses) the human experiencing transcendence.[68]

Schrader concentrates on his second manner of presentation as "Transcendental Style" in films and attempts to show how three filmmakers from

---

66. Martin Buber, *I-Thou,* trans. Walter Kaufmann (New York: Touchstone, 1970), 57–58.

67. Ibid., 168.

68. Paul Schrader, *Transcendental Style in Film* (New York: Da Capo Press, 1972), 6.

varied cultures utilize it to achieve the expression of the Holy. Yasujiro Ozu, Robert Bresson, and Carl Dreyer all express the Transcendent by means of this cinematic approach that refutes stylized Hollywood realities and hints at a reality beyond. The difficulty with Schrader's theory is that it is so narrow that it limits cinematic expression of the transcendent to a stoic, almost gnostic form. Drawing from Mikhail Bakhtin, Terry Lindvall and colleagues have argued that in the film *Long Walk Home,* transcendence is achieved through abundant means, not sparse means, appealing to the body as a communal entity.[69] Schrader limits the expression of the Transcendent to the expression of "otherness," but this picture ignores some basic theological ideas: the reach of God toward us as well as His presence in his creation. Buber was a Jewish thinker, but the "intimacy" and "immanent intersection" with the Divine is also a theme of the Christian New Testament (see John 1:14: "The Word became Flesh and dwelt among us"). The great paradox of the Divine is that the Transcendent is the Source and Sustenance of the immanent. Divine Transcendence and Immanence cannot be wholly extracted from one another. Many theologies (including the Catholicism of Kieślowski's homeland) are built upon this Transcendent/Immanent paradox, forming a paradigm for understanding expressions of the transcendent in art.

Abstract Form and Color for Transcendent Ends

Consider the following quote:

> How does the straight line feel? It feels, as I suppose it looks, straight — a dull thought drawn out endlessly. It is unstraight lines, or many straight and curved lines together, that are eloquent to the touch. They appear and disappear, are now deep, now shallow, now broken off or lengthened or swelling. They rise and sink beneath my fingers, they are full of sudden starts and pauses, and their variety is inexhaustible and wonderful.[70]

Helen Keller's words shame the rest of us, "whose eyes fail to grasp these qualities of form," art critic Meyer Schapiro chides. Keller's delight comes from the inexhaustibility of the forms, as they suggest to her a boundlessness of something greater — unlimited, fully free. Although her quote makes no direct reference to the Divine, her delight implies not simply an immanent

---

69. Terry Lindvall, Artie Terry, Wally O. Williams, "Spectacular Transcendence," *The Howard Journal of Communications* 7 (1996); 205–220.

70. Meyer Schapiro, *Mondrian: On the Humanity of Abstract Painting* (New York: George Braziller, 1995), 14.

experience, but rather an experience that transcends. Abstract forms have this suggestive power if they are fully seen and appreciated. Perhaps this is why Walt Whitman and Leo Tolstoy, in more direct, theological references, conceived of God as a square shape,[71] or why the Theosophist movement saw Divine qualities in particular colors and shapes.[72] In his seminal work, *Concerning the Spiritual in Art,* Wassily Kandinsky also shows this tendency.[73]

I do not claim anything inherently talismanic about such shapes or colors. Rather, I join Schapiro in saying: "The capacity of these geometric shapes to serve as metaphors of the divine arises from their living, often momentous, qualities for the sensitive eye."[74] However, I have shown that these shapes are not merely metaphors (belonging to the cognitive or rational realm); rather, their "living . . . momentous qualities" emulate and synchronize with human perception, giving them a unique experiential power (in the phenomenological sense) — an aggregate, perceptual inertia. I also maintain that they lend themselves to the enaction of a process, much like Husserl's phenomenological époché, which creates a broader experience than the average cinematic moment.

Clearly, parallels exist between the more mystic abstract painters (like Piet Mondrian and Kandinsky) and ideas presented in this study. Likewise, those attempting to express art's power for immediacy agree that such an experience is beyond words and resonates in a deep manner (similar to Kandinsky's phrase, "sympathy of the soul"[75]). There is not space here to survey all the writings by various artists on this topic, but suffice it to say that artists in this vein sense the spiritual potential of the abstract form.

Abstract images do not simply transcend representation and marshal extraordinary expressive power. They have the ability to transcend space and time figuratively. Space and time transcendence is a quality of the Godhead (Eternal, Omnipresent), and so abstraction has the power to evoke the Transcendent through these shared characteristics. For a full exploration of this possibility, I turn to Mircea Eliade.

---

71. Ibid., 13–14.

72. Maurice Tuchman, "Hidden Meanings in Abstract Art," in *The Spiritual in Art: Abstract Painting 1890–1985,* ed. Maurice Tuchman (New York: Abbeville Press, 1986), 36.

73. Wassily Kandinsky, *Concerning the Spiritual in Art,* trans. M. T. H. Sadler (New York: Dover, 1977).

74. Schapiro, *Mondrian,* 14.

75. Kandinsky, *Spiritual in Art,* 3.

Transcending Time and Space — Mircea Eliade

Few scholars have a more keen observation of the human religious instinct than Mircea Eliade. His book *The Sacred and the Profane* stands as a monumental work on the subject and will help to frame some of the issues related to abstraction, film, and the spiritual. The subtitle of this book is *The Nature of Religion*. Eliade structures his book around the building blocks of reality, space, and time and contrasts the sacred and profane approaches to these elements throughout. He states: "The sacred always manifests itself as a reality of *a wholly different order* from 'natural' realities."[76] The "act of manifestation of the sacred" is entitled "heirophany." Interestingly, the sacred is not constructed in Eliade's assessment of religious life. Rather, to the religious person, "something sacred *shows itself* to us":

> From the most elementary heirophany — *e.g.*, manifestation of the sacred in some ordinary object, a stone or a tree — to the supreme heirophany (which, for a Christian, is the incarnation of God in Jesus Christ) there is no solution of continuity. In each case we are confronted by the same mysterious act — the manifestation of something of a wholly different order, a reality that does not belong to our world, in objects that are an integral part of our natural "profane" world. . . . The sacred tree, the sacred stone are not adored as stone or tree; they are worshipped precisely because they are *heirophanies*, because they show something that is no longer stone or tree but the *sacred*, the *ganz andere*. It is impossible to overemphasize the paradox represented by every heirophany, even the most elementary. By manifesting the sacred, any object becomes *something else*, yet it continues to remain *itself*, for it continues to participate in its surrounding cosmic milieu.[77]

In the religious life the particular and the universal, the temporal and the eternal, the sacred and the profane are all coexistent, inextricable, yet distinct concepts. The challenge for the artist is to create an artwork that brings out the spiritual aspect, which is not readily seen or experienced, as it is beyond words and does not lend itself to simple utility.

Eliade speaks of sacred time and space as manifest in religious man's instinct to reactualize the primordial reality: the moment of Creation. Sacred space is considered the real space, whereas all other space is formless and amorphous; a heirophany gives rise to absolute space.[78] In the end, the search for sacred space is a search for the real:

---

76. Mircea Eliade, *The Sacred and the Profane: The Nature of Religion,* trans. Willard R. Trask (San Diego: Harcourt, 1957), 10.

77. Ibid., 11–12.

78. Ibid., 21.

Religious man's desire to live *in the sacred* is in fact equivalent to his desire to take up his abode in objective reality, not to let himself be paralyzed by the never-ceasing relativity of purely subjective experiences, to live in a real and effective world, and not in an illusion.[79]

As to the construction of sacred spaces, Eliade is quick to point out that such construction is not simply the creation of humans, but "in reality the ritual by which he constructs a sacred space is efficacious in the measure in which it *reproduces the work of the gods.*"[80] For instance, consecrating a territory, according to Eliade, is the equivalent of "cosmicizing it," a reproduction of the act of creation, which created order out of chaos.[81] The space serves as a connection to its spiritual counterpart: "The city of Jerusalem was only an approximate reproduction of the transcendent model; it could be polluted by man, but the model was incorruptible, for it was not involved with time."[82] Thus, the sacralizing of space is reference to an eternal form, from the religious viewpoint.

In summary, the "experience of sacred space makes possible the 'founding of the world': where the sacred manifests itself in space, *the real unveils itself,* the world comes into existence."[83] This is appealing to the religious man because he has an "unquenchable ontological thirst . . . a thirst for *being.*"[84] The appeal of phenomenology here should be clear. Husserl speaks of "spatiotemporal endlessness," that is, an awareness of "the world-whole in its own peculiar form."[85] Similarly, the intentional essence envisions the form in all possible worlds. The concept of inexhaustible space is linked intricately to boundless time, and thus, both are common subjects in religion, as God is seen as the summation of these elements (Divine Omnipresence and Eternality).

Eliade's approach to time in religious life is similar to that of space:

By its very nature sacred time is reversible in the sense that, properly speaking, it is a primordial mythical time made present. Every religious festival,

---

79. Ibid., 28.

80. Ibid., 29.

81. Ibid., 30–31.

82. Ibid., 61.

83. Ibid., 63.

84. Ibid., 64.

85. Edmund Husserl, *Cartesian Meditations,* trans. Dorion Cairns (The Hague: Nijhoff, 1960), 37, 43.

any liturgical time, represents the reaction to a sacred event that took place in a mythical past, "in the beginning. . . . " It is an ontological, Parmenidean time; it always remains equal to itself, it neither changes nor is exhausted.[86]

Eliade describes sacred time with a host of abstract terms: "a succession of eternities," "the time that 'floweth not,' " the "eternal present," and this "sacred and indestructible time."[87]

The reason visual abstraction is so conducive to heirophanous interpretation is that it lends itself to ideas of essence (including a core identity for an object or image as well as its unifying eternal source), creation (i.e., the original building blocks of a thing), and the possibility of redemption (a transformation). Abstraction brackets material reference and often alters one's conception of diegetic space and time.

The following quote from Eliade helps to clarify the interpenetration of spiritual (cosmic) space and time and the natural world (and, by extension, as it might be abstracted in the cinema):

> For religious man, nature is never only "natural"; it is always fraught with a religious value. This is easy to understand, for the cosmos is a divine creation; coming from the hands of the gods, the world is impregnated with sacredness. It is not simply a sacrality *communicated* by the gods, as is the case, for example, with a place or an object consecrated by the divine presence. The gods did more; *they manifested the different modalities of the sacred in the very structure of the world and cosmic phenomena.* . . . This divine work always preserves its quality of transparency, that is, it spontaneously reveals the many aspects of the sacred. The sky directly, "naturally," reveals the infinite distance, the transcendence of the deity. The earth too is transparent; it presents itself as universal mother and nurse. The cosmic rhythms manifest order, harmony, permanence, fecundity. The cosmos as a whole is an organism at once *real, living,* and *sacred*; it simultaneously reveals the modalities of being and of sacrality. Ontophany and heirophany meet.[88]

Kieślowski's cultural touchstone for this idea may have been Thomas Aquinas, the giant among Catholic philosophers. Aquinas approached beauty as a characteristic of God and therefore recognized beauty in the world as flowing from that same Source.[89] Abstract images, should they contain a sort of beauty (which might be defined here as a formal attraction), are pregnant

---

86. Eliade, *The Sacred and the Profane,* 69.

87. Ibid., 88–89.

88. Ibid., 116–117.

89. Thomas Aquinas, *Summa Theologica* I-II, q. 27, a. 1, ad. 3, reprinted in *An Aquinas Reader,* rev. ed., ed. Mary T. Clark (New York: Fordham University Press, 2000), 97.

with a Divine reference — a trace that should be acknowledged as such. Kieślowski's lack of religious commitments only tempers this assertion, transforming it into a question: might God be lurking among the elements? If so, how might He help us? Kieślowski does not approach the order of the world in a dogmatic fashion (as if it were a Divine trace, exactly), but he does continually surprise us by revealing a sort of order hidden among the apparent randomness of existence.

Thus, abstraction in art has the potential to suggest these heirophanous qualities, both in archetype (content, symbols) and experience (form leading to reaction and expression); likewise, the metaphysical context amplifies the elements as a source of divine reflection and insight. Film has a unique power to exhibit motion and is therefore particularly strong in bringing out the processional qualities of abstraction (i.e., abstract images replicating and provoking the experienced religious process). Thus, to reference another filmmaker, to see, in the finale of Godfrey Reggio's *Koyaanisqatsi* an exploding rocket transformed from a catastrophic event into something eerie, primordial, and resonant with spiritual beauty dwelling within flames and destruction, we may be moved to remember and reexperience (even, in Eliade's terms, reactualize) a personal religious, transformative conversion. Does the viewing of such an image, in the right context, become a sort of spiritual ritual for us because of its evocative power of process paired with archetypal religious symbol (having roots in eternal, primordial structures)?

Even outside a religious context, the transformational power of art is clear: evocative aesthetic experience changes "the felt pulse of our daily lives."[90] According to Eliade, the man who has chosen to live in a "desacralized" world will find himself relentlessly pursuing religious forms, even in modern art:

> [W]e are witnessing a desperate effort on the part of the artist to free himself of the "surface" of things and to penetrate into matter in order to lay bare its ultimate structures. To abolish form and volume, to descend into the interior of substance while revealing its secret or larval modalities — these are not, according to the artist, operations undertaken for the purpose of some sort of objective knowledge; they are ventures provoked by his desire to grasp the deepest meaning of his plastic universe.[91]

---

90. Steiner, *Real Presences,* 164.
91. Eliade, "The Sacred and the Modern Artist," 181.

A Summary

Before I plunge into specific examples from Kieślowski's work, a brief summary of the construct I have built is in order: (1) Cinematic perception, as a form of thinking and knowing, can be an experience of immediacy, yielding a resonant, nonverbal knowledge. (2) In contrast, abstraction is the pattern of human visual perception; abstract images and mental abstraction of artistic form can be utilized to provoke immediate encounters with art as well as a grasping after a totalized, expanded view of reality. (3) Such abstract techniques can be utilized in metaphysical contexts in art, evoking and expressing the Transcendent, particularly the theological concepts of divine omnipotence, omnipresence, and omniscience. These three points are seen as a series of concentric circles, narrowing to some very specific sorts of experiences and expressions in art (see diagram earlier in this chapter).

Abstraction lends itself to Transcendent expression because (1) its nature makes it useful for the phenomenological project (abstraction as bracket, possibility, and revelation); (2) perception of abstract images works on a more primary, direct epistemological level in human consciousness, rendering a powerful impact; and (3) its suggestive dynamics paired with its rich mystery suits it to express the theological ideas, which contain both rational and nonrational dimensions.

Just as the theological paradox of Divine Transcendence and Immanence is forever being navigated, the tensions between realism and formalism, so common in cinema since its inception, take on a metaphysical telos in the works of Kieślowski. By creating a metaphysical context and utilizing abstract techniques to offset an everyday attitude in the viewer, Kieślowski harnesses the powers of abstraction and steers them toward transcendence, encouraging us to join his search.

Abstraction: Psycho-aesthetic Investigations

Many, if not all, of the formal techniques to be described in this section have precedence, dating back to the earliest days of the avant-garde cinema through the highly experimental, modernist European cinema of the 1960s and 1970s and the avant-garde cinema of the same time (particularly the structuralist works).[92] The modernists were largely concerned with the

---

92. This modernism is not entirely without spiritual sensitivity, however. Ultimately, modernist techniques (abstraction included) all served Michelangelo Antonioni in his quest

language of cinema and the ideological assumptions that characterized the most popular cinematic vernacular of their day. They searched out new forms of expressiveness, often with an adventurous, innovative, even re- bellious spirit. Other filmmakers had other motivations for their abstract experiments, such as Alfred Hitchcock's creative play with the point of view (POV) conventions for the purposes of suspense.[93]

However, the difference between most of these filmmakers and Kieślow- ski is one of telos. Whereas Kieślowski's cinema has reaped the rewards of the previous era, I do not have the sense that he is defending the honor of the medium, critiquing it, or even concerned with the particulars of its rhetoric. Rather, he uses these techniques as tools in pursuit of a series of important metaphysical questions, and his technique is subservient to this overarching goal.

The images printed in this section are black-and-white still frames. Such is the great limitation of books on film, giving only a glimpse of the power Kieślowski's images contain. Tarkovsky once stated that the great virtue of the cinema was to be able to take "an impression of time,"[94] and books do little justice to this quality either. I can think of no stronger encouragement to the reader to experience these films themselves.

Film Thinking: Abstraction and the Aesthetics of the Moving Image

Much has been written on the modernist movement in painting, but consid- erably less has been written on the role of abstraction in the moving image.[95]

---

for a more complete understanding of the world. He states: "I'm not saying one should slavishly follow the day-to-day routine of life, but I think that through these pauses, through this attempt to adhere to a definite reality — spiritual, internal, and even moral — there springs forth what today is more and more coming to be known as modern cinema, that is, a cinema which is not so much concerned with externals as it is with those forces that move us to act in a certain way and not another." This quote is found in the published version of the *L'Avventura* script (Michelangelo Antonioni, with Elio Bartonlini and Tonino Guerra, *L'Avventura* [New York: Grove Press, 1969], 215).

93. See Branigan's sharp analysis of a scene from *Notorious,* Edward Branigan, "The Point-of-View Shot," in *Movies and Methods,* vol. II, ed. Bill Nichols (Berkeley: University of California Press, 1985), 679.

94. Andrei Tarkovsky, *Sculpting in Time,* trans. Kitty Hunter-Blair (Austin: University of Texas Press, 1986), 62.

95. Maureen Turim's *Abstraction in Avant-Garde Films* (Ann Arbor, MI: UMI Research Press, 1985) and Malcolm LeGrice's *Abstract Film and Beyond* (op. cit.) are among the few

Even in these few cases, there remain to be seen any dedicated studies of abstraction in narrative (i.e., outside the avant-garde) film, although some authors, notably David Bordwell, Kristin Thompson, and Angela Dalle Vacche,[96] have touched upon these issues in a cursory fashion. The goal of this section is not so much theoretical as it is descriptive, in its attempt to establish a point of reference regarding perceptual abstraction and abstract techniques in Kieślowski; it is a working vocabulary for the following chapters, exploring abstract manipulations of time, space, and context of the image.

I do not deny the importance or constitutive power of the diegetic elements such as narrative pattern, characters, and plot (indeed, these elements help comprise the term *metaphysical context*), but the focus here is on the abstract image as it functions phenomenologically. The phenomenological will necessarily intersect with the semiotic in various stages of the discussion, but the primary question, again, is how abstraction functions in perception, and how Kieślowski uses those functions to his advantage in the expression of his themes.

I will also show that abstract images relate to a much more foundational matter: how humans perceive and think. It is Arnheim's position that the human ability to abstract, that is, think primarily in generalities when considering particulars, is not only the thing that makes art possible, but also that which makes *thinking* possible. Indeed, Arnheim maintains that the dichotomy between thinking and perception is categorically false; he testifies: "My earlier work had taught me that artistic activity is a form of reasoning, in which perceiving and thinking are indivisibly intertwined."[97]

Time and Space Manipulation

The following are formal areas within which time and space are manipulated and function as a phenomenological bracket of the viewer's expectations. Some of these areas privilege time over space, or vice versa, but in nearly every case they work with elements of both. Time and space are considered

---

focused examples. Other discussions of abstraction can be found throughout various works dedicated to the cinematic avant-garde, such as *The Avant-Garde Film: A Reader of Theory and Criticism*, ed. P. Adams Sitney (New York: Anthology Film Archives, 1978).

96. See various discussions in David Bordwell and Kristin Thompson's *Film Art* (New York: McGraw-Hill, 1993) and Angela Dalle Vacche's chapter on Tarkovsky's *Andrei Rublev* in *Cinema and Painting* (Austin: University of Texas Press, 1996).

97. Rudolf Arnheim, *Visual Thinking* (Berkeley: University of California Press, 1969), v.

in the broadest senses, including both diegetic and nondiegetic time and space. The three functions of the abstract image discussed in the previous section — bracket, possibility, and revelation — are implicit throughout this discussion.

Consider the following image:

Fig. 1. From the beginning of *The Double Life of Véronique*.

It is lovely but difficult to discern: full of rich blues and violets, slashes of light, and subtle movement (many of the bright spots pulse brighter and darker while the picture is rolling). Kieślowski pushes the audience to encounter the image, bracket preconceptions, and assess it in terms of form — that is, shape, movement, and color — all general categories with which humans think (according to Arnheim, Zeki, and others). Only then, after a few seconds of initial mystery, does the voice-over speak a clue: "That's the star we're waiting for to start Christmas Eve. See it?" Enter the second image:

Fig. 2. From *The Double Life of Véronique*.

Kieślowski, had he been a lesser artist, could have shown the audience the upside down child first, and the clue to the inverted angle of view would have been sufficient. But Kieślowski is interested in more than the represented object. He is concerned with form, and all the wonder, mystery, and connotations that accompany abstract images. Through abstract strategy, a common scene is rendered wholly different from what Husserl would call the everyday or natural attitude. The audience has little choice but to reckon with the formal properties of the image and absorb it for its immediate effect, and consider the abstract image as pure possibility, while drawing upon imaginative faculties in a very primary (nonsymbolic) way. Dorter would call this nonrational knowledge.

Then, in a remarkable move, he reveals the source of our view: a child. The star, the reference to Christmas, and the child all carry connotations of spiritual hope and renewal — a metaphysical context for the image. Abstraction yields to a double revelation: the identity of the image as an inverted cityscape and an expanded sense of time and space through the combination of époché and context.

Of course, this is not a guaranteed result; the audience members may simply be frustrated that they cannot discern the object's identity. A viewer must submit to the process if he or she wishes to experience the benefits of the approach. In line with cognitive psychological tenets, the viewer is free to resist the process. But the metaphysical context is very suggestive, and Kieślowski's invitation down that metaphysical road is very appealing.

Sometimes the identity of the image is clear, but the framing amputates it from its wider diegetic context. The filmmaker may even employ contrast and color effects to heighten this isolation of the object. In these cases, the alienated object takes on an abstract quality. For example, consider the comments of film critic John Simon on Claudia's hand, framed in close-up against Corrado's black hair, at the end of Michelangelo Antonioni's film *L'Avventura:* " . . . white and black, are pitted against each other . . . the whiteness of that hand blessing the black hair is both stunning and meaningful."[98]

As mentioned, Kieślowski is also fond of the hand in close-up. The following still from *Red* is part of a motif stretching back to some of his earliest films. Not only do these hands embody the notions of emotion and praxis, but they also tend to be shown first, without an establishing shot, suggesting a universal notion; for a suspended second, these hands may belong to anyone, and, perhaps, everyone. The lighting, framing, and contemplative pace of the editing all contribute to its abstract quality.

---

98. Antonioni, *L'Avventura,* 267–268.

Fig. 3. The hands of Valentine
and the Judge in *Red*.

The static nature of the frame contributes to the abstract effect; Zeki accounts for this effect as a disengagement of motion-focused brain cells.[99] Arnheim's description is more poetic:

> It is often necessary, first of all, to see the physical changes of the object as deviations from a norm shape, e.g. when various motions of the human hand and its mobile fingers are understood perceptually as variations of the star-shaped organ known to the eyes as the hand.[100]

Like similar shots in Bresson's and Tarkovsky's films, this image yields the effect of timelessness in a paradoxical fashion (the hand being the foremost symbol of human temporal action, rendered cosmic by abstraction); the hand, isolated from its context, gains more and more independence as Kieślowski lingers on it. The formal properties of the hand emerge, and it appears to nearly become something else. The following shot is similar, depicting Julie's escapist haven of the pool in *Blue*. It features her in a fetal position in the water, but Kieślowski's gaze remains on her hair floating in the water, referencing a very similar, timeless abstract shot in Tarkovsky's *Mirror:*

Fig. 4. Julie's floating hair in *Blue*.

---

99. Zeki, *Inner Vision,* ch. 16.
100. Arnheim, *Visual Thinking,* 52–53.

Recall Dorter's words: "Art, however, can make the qualities of color, shape, sound, duration, weight, etc., stand alone as images themselves rather than mere features of normal physical things. Thus it can give us a framework within which to see these qualities on their own terms."[101] These components of the image are, indeed, isolated more than before. At this level, we begin to see the effect of which Russian Formalist Viktor Shklovsky wrote:

> Habitualization devours work, clothes, furniture, one's wife, and the fear of war. . . . And Art exists that one may recover the sensation of life; it exists to make one feel things, to make the stone *stony*. The purpose of art is to impart the sensation of things as they are perceived, not as they are known.[102]

In this abstract isolation, the properties of these components are manifest most directly rather than being "submerged in our experience."[103] That is, in the absence of our everyday or natural attitude, the dynamics of the image more clearly emerge. Arnheim uses the term *dynamics* for perceptual forces, actual or psychologically suggested, present in the work (such as tensions, balance, and imbalance).[104] Though they do not create "isomorphic traces" (i.e., pictures in the brain, as some early Gestaltists believed), there does appear to be a correspondence between them and brain activity, as Semir Zeki and Margaret Livingstone have shown through scientific measurement of brain activity at the single-cell level.[105] Combined with the elementary elements of perception (shape, color, movement, etc.), they give the abstract image a type of primary communicative power.

---

101. Dorter, "Conceptual Truth," 39.

102. Viktor Shklovsky, "Art as Technique," in *Russian Formalist Criticism: Four Essays,* trans. and ed. Lee T. Lemon and Marion J. Reis (Lincoln: University of Nebraska Press, 1965), 11–12.

103. Dorter, "Conceptual Truth," 39.

104. Rudolf Arnheim, *Art and Visual Perception: The New Version* (Berkeley: University of California Press, 1974), ch. 9.

105. Zeki, *Inner Vision,* 61 and throughout; Livingstone, *Vision and Art,* 62 and throughout. Richard L. Gregory (*Eye and Brain,* op. cit., 5) and Robert Solso (*Cognition and the Visual Arts* [Cambridge, MA: MIT Press, 1994], 37–38) both discount the isomorphic theory. Dufrenne references this theory in his article "Perception, Meaning and Convention." He remains cautious of this theoretical postulation, though he does not dismiss it either, calling for more research. He prefers to understand the affinity between subject and object in terms of ontology rather than psychology (*Journal of Aesthetics and Art Criticism,* 42.2 [Winter 1983]: 209–212).

A large part of immediacy is the initial encounter with dynamics. Possibility is created when an abstract form dynamically suggests other objects that share the same dynamic.[106] Revelation occurs when the dynamics in the image reveal something new about the object that was previously submerged.

Likewise, what has emerged from these examples is a process of transformation in the abstract image. Maureen Turim calls this effect in abstract images "metamorphosis."[107] These images portray objects that seem to become something else in their abstract rendering. They do not lose their identity completely, of course (Valentine's hand is still a hand), but the connotations of the image — their indexical qualities (as Peter Wollen might call them)[108] — become multiple. The images suggest a likeness beyond the obvious referent (the hand) and toward like forms (a star). Whereas these connotations are clearly semiotic in nature (i.e., categorical), the initial experience of the forms is an immediate, nonlinguistic perception — a phenomenological "taking-in" of the image that has a dynamic quality quite apart from its identity. Also, the abstract qualities of the image are thrown into relief, to be considered on their own terms.

Another Kieślowskian mode of time-space abstraction is recontextualization. The basic forces behind recontextualization are the same (i.e., it is built upon the interplay of visual dynamics, abstract connotation, and the manipulation of the perceiver's cognitive expectations), but this mode works as a more complicated manifestation of these elements. "If a visual item is extricated from its context it becomes a different object," says Arnheim.[109] Much like the metamorphosis phenomenon described earlier, objects can adopt abstract qualities when they are placed in a context different from their typical environments. This can often draw fresh attention to the form *as* form. In the cinema, this effect can be accomplished in several ways beyond the close-ups discussed earlier: through mise-en-scène (often through the use of reflections), editing patterns, cinematographic effects, and so on. The examples to come will make this concept more clear.

---

106. Arnheim states: "In this more general sense, expression is the capacity of a particular perceptual pattern to exemplify through its dynamics the structure of a type of behavior that could manifest itself anywhere in human experience" (*New Essays on the Psychology of Art,* op. cit., 222).

107. Turim, *Abstraction in Avant-Garde Films,* 25.

108. Peter Wollen, *Signs and Meaning in the Cinema* (Bloomington: Indiana University Press, 1992), 122.

109. Arnheim, *Visual Thinking,* 54.

Sometimes the context is not so much new, but transformed by abstraction. There is a sympathy of movement in Kieślowski's use of the quick, circular pan and the expression of time rendered timeless and space rendered cosmic. The diegetic identity of the subject is not typically lost in these cases, but the diegetic context often is. The world becomes more shape than substance through the movement of the camera, and, in the case of the opening sequence of *Blue* and the "resurrection" scene from *Decalogue II* (both detailed later in this book), through a musico-rhythmic rather than temporal procession. Indeed, the idea of recontextualization through editing opens up the idea of abstract sequences, a linking of images, forming an aggregate abstract effect. In the above cases, it will be shown that the metaphysically concerned Kieślowski combines these effects with repetition as a means to deeper meaning (in a fashion similar to religious ritual, as described by Eliade).

Summary:
Psycho-aesthetics and Abstraction

In discussing the structural categories of perception, Arnheim states:

> The principal reason why these disembodied shapes can be so helpful is that thinking is not concerned with the sheer matter or substratum of things but only with their structure. . . . The perceptual features accessible to thought are purely structural, e.g., the expansiveness of that red, the aggressiveness of that sound, or the centric and compact nature of something round. Thinking treats space and time, which are containers for being, as the structural categories of coexistence and sequence. Both of these categories can be represented in the spatial medium of visual patterns.[110]

Arnheim uses structural language to communicate what are, in effect, the building blocks of our perceptual experience. The qualities of these blocks (i.e., the "expansiveness" of that red) are most likely learned, cognitive associations that are culturally established. In this sense, one might consider them categorical and not phenomenological, but at this primary level, the line between the perceptual and the categorical is hazy at best. Whereas Arnheim leans toward an essentialist position (i.e., that red is inherently expansive), I am more skeptical (e.g., red does not always suggest "expansion"). What does seem inherent to the image, however, is that lines,

---

110. Ibid., 129.

colors, patterns, and forms do work in a phenomenological dynamic relationship, which appears immediately. That is, the audience instantaneously grasps these elements, and their dynamic relationship to each other works a quick, powerful, perceptual effect that is beyond words. Such thinking is, indeed, thinking, but not of the linguistic order. Abstraction is primary in that it is simple, yet dynamic.

As we explore some more of Kieślowski's images, it will be apparent that dynamics, primary elements of the image, and other aspects of abstraction will combine with semiotic categories. This, of course, is an aesthetic strength.

The Liminal Image: Examples from Kieślowski

The power of abstraction has been present since the earliest days of cinema, from Dziga Vertov's energetic forms in *Man with a Movie Camera*, to the evocative, controlled compositions of Alexander Dovzhenko's *Earth*, to the whirling dancers of Maya Deren's *A Study in Choreography for the Camera*. However, there remains another frontier for those willing to entertain metaphysical ideas, and Kieślowski continually takes us to its threshold.

Kieślowski and Tarkovsky: Comparison and Contrast

In Chapter 1, I mentioned some affinities between Tarkovsky and Kieślowski. Indeed, an astonishing number of parallels can be drawn between the two filmmakers in respect to content and form. I will draw out these similarities here as they relate to the abstraction discussion, but it is also important to recognize their differences. To give just a few examples, Kieślowski never used the black-and-white image to any great degree (beyond some early documentaries), and his approach to color was more adventurous than that of Tarkovsky. The overall pace of his films runs faster, though he still edits in a more observant fashion than the typical Hollywood filmmaker. Finally, there is a lighter mood in most of Kieślowski's films, not because they lack honesty, seriousness, or depth, but because he felt free to use humor (an element noticeably absent in nearly every Tarkovsky film, with only a few exceptions).

Like Tarkovsky, Kieślowski found the metaphysical topics to be the most fruitful to explore. The issues of ultimate good, evil, the existence of

the soul, predestination, the existence of God, spiritual search, temptation, and salvation/redemption are consistently present in the work of both
filmmakers, forming the basis for an overall metaphysical context.

However, simple plot themes are not enough to characterize a metaphysical context. To a great degree, the abstract images themselves work in a
reciprocal relationship with the plot and characters to create a metaphysical
aura. Kieślowski excels in this endeavor, imbuing his films with a consistent
sense of wonder and spiritual suggestion. Elements of narrative content,
combined with the form and presentation of the image, create this aura.
It is no accident that Véronique's childhood bauble, which produces an
abstract, inverted perspective, comes to be a key visual motif throughout
The Double Life of Véronique. This motif gains symbolic weight, as the world
literally turns upside down and stretches beyond normal size in Véronique's
experience. Kieślowski is hinting at eternal time and space beyond mere
semiotics, as the cathedral makes its pass through the expanding lens:

Figs. 5–6. From *The Double Life of Véronique.*

These and other shots are examples of the recontextualized, mediated
image, through which mediation the image takes on an abstract quality
through distortion. The use of reflections is quite extensive in Kieślowski's
films and will be covered more fully in the following discussions. In short,
the reflections press two images into relation, distort the "normal" shape
of things, and throw the image into a completely different contextual field.
Images mediated by liquid and glass are most prominent and take full
advantage of abstraction's spiritually suggestive powers. Figures 7 and 8
show Tarkovsky's influence.

Just as Tarkovsky explored and utilized the elements, food, the human
body, and iconic poses for abstract and spiritual effect, so Kieślowski finds
inspiration in these themes in figure 9–12.

Figs. 7–8. Kieślowski utilizes reflection and distortion
in (l to r) *Blue* and *A Short Film about Killing.*

Figs. 9–10. The play of light and dark in the tea of *Decalogue I* and a timeless
moment in still life from *Blue* (in this final image, the light changes from light to dark
in a matter of seconds, strengthening the idea of a fluid, cosmic time).

Figs. 11–12. The "Theophanes" character of the *Decalogue* (l), and the Judge
at the end of *Red* (shedding a solitary tear of redemption).

Coming from Orthodox and Catholic countries, respectively, Tarkovsky and Kieślowski both understood the iconic pose. At the essence of the religious icon lie a transhistorical dimension of presence,[111] the intermediary role it plays between the perceiver and God, and the "inverted perspective" (i.e., a deliberately flat image, intended to exchange Renaissance perspective for a reverse vector, theoretically stretching out of the picture, into the heart of the perceiver).[112] At the heart of this image is a new spiritual dimension that theoretically opens up for the viewer by directly engaging him or her in a visual look. It functions as an arrest of the passive, voyeuristic mode of the spectator.

There are numerous motifs in Kieślowski's works that are not derivative of Tarkovsky, and some of these he used for abstract effect. First, the image of the eye is important in the Kieślowski imagistic lexicon.

Figs. 13–14. This sequence from *Blue* takes place after Julie's car accident, as she heals in a hospital bed.

In this case, abstraction is used to convey Julie's psychological and physiological state as she reemerges into the living world (in the wake of the death of her husband and child). Most of Kieślowski's abstract images can be seen on this very practical, diegetic level. However, his use of metaphysical contexts suggest a wider connotation of the images themselves than their denotational, plot-level referents. It seems that, in these images, Kieślowski is hunting for larger game: a metaphysical seeing and blindness — and Julie's spiritual anguish in the film supports this interpretation. The aggregate effect of abstract images in the preceding sequence supports this interpretation. Here, each shot indeed conveys information, but one is

---

111. Dalle Vacche, *Cinema and Painting*, 144.

112. John Baggley *Doors of Perception: Icons and Their Spiritual Significance* (London and Oxford: Mowbray, 1987), 80–81. Quoted in ibid., 147.

equally struck with the sheer wonder of the forms present; in some cases, in typical Kieślowskian fashion, one cannot immediately identify the image until its identity is revealed later:

Figs. 15–17. Just a few of the many abstract images from *Blue*'s opening sequence. In resonant, abstract close-ups (and very little dialogue) Kieślowski tells the story of a family in a car who, because of a faulty brake line, has an accident.

As stated earlier, this opening scene to the film has a strong musico-rhythmic element that unifies the images. I will give more detail about this rhythm in the discussion of *Blue* (Chapter 5), but suffice it to say, the affinity between music and abstract visuals stretches far back in aesthetics (even further than Kandinsky, who most explicitly made the connection).[113] Music amplifies the abstract nature of Kieślowski's images, particularly in his later films.

As evident in the last images, one of Kieślowski's concerns is with light itself. Light naturally lends itself to abstract patterns, and light has served as a religious symbol in Christianity and Judaism since the beginning ("Let there be light," from the book of Genesis; "Lux Aeterna," from the Mass). In some cases, Kieślowski focuses on the light patterns themselves to evoke a spiritual presence or atmosphere. Many such images appear in *The Double Life of Véronique*; the most obvious is a sequence in which Véronique sees light reflecting around her room. She figures out that it comes from a child with a mirror in the adjacent building. But when the boy leaves, the light remains, suggesting a supernatural presence intertwined with the reflected light all along. Kieślowski's use of the light is certainly metaphorical, but the experience of perceiving the scene endows it with a phenomenological "surplus" of meaning, in Husserl's words.

In *Red,* the Judge interrupts Valentine to remark, "The light is beautiful," at which time the sun seems to rise and set all in the span of a few seconds, suggesting (once again) eternal time. The breathtaking effect can scarcely be conveyed in still images:

113. Kandinsky, *Spiritual in Art,* 20.

Figs. 18–20. From *Red*; "The light is beautiful."

Similarly, overexposure can create an abstract and symbolic moment. In the following sequence, Valentine and the Judge come to a new enlightened understanding of each other as the latter replaces a lightbulb. The cinematographer Piotr Sobociński says he deliberately used a very bright bulb in the lamp, so as to be certain the image would overexpose in the middle of the shot.[114]

Figs. 21–23. Abstraction and overexposure in *Red*.

Space-Time

Just from these few images we can see Kieślowski's films depict a conception of space and time that goes beyond a merely temporal mindset. Many of Kieślowski's films toy with the idea of a wider reality, where cause and effect flow from a cosmic order — where time is timeless, and space is ever expansive and fluid. In this wider reality, the interconnectedness of human beings is one of Kieślowski's greatest themes. At times, his vision of this connectedness is darker and more existential (*Blind Chance, No End*); other times it is an instrument of grace (*The Double Life of Véronique, Red*). In other films the connection is miraculous and predestined (*Véronique*); still others could be explained in more temporal terms like "chance" or "probability" (*Blind Chance*). The interest of Kieślowski, however, is that all these instances hold meaning for us. He makes it his task to probe for these meanings.

---

114. Stephen Pizzello, "Piotr Sobociński, *Red,*" *American Cinematographer* (June 1994): 74.

The wider reality is sometimes conveyed through editing. In a scene from *Decalogue II,* the establishing shot shows a hospital room with a bed containing Dorota's ill husband, whom she has come to visit. She despairs over his seemingly terminal condition and wonders whether it is worthwhile to leave the food she brought for him. In this moment of despair, a solid thirty seconds into the scene, another voice is heard: "Leave it. . . ." The voice seems authoritative, and, because it comes from nowhere, for a moment it seems it might be the voice of God Himself; something akin to what audio theorist Michel Chion calls the *acousmetre,* a haunting, off-screen presence with the power to "see all," "know all," and possessing "omnipotence to act on the situation."[115] In fact, it simply belongs to another sick man who has been on a bed on the other side of the room *throughout the entire scene.* His jarring entrance deliberately breaks the Hollywood convention, suggesting mystery and forcing the audience to be open to revelation. Likewise, it forces the audience to expand its mental assessment of the diegetic space — even to the point of the timeless and cosmic. The editing strategy sets up a dialectic, with the suggestion of transcendence as a possibility pitted against immanent revelation (only a man speaking). The synthesis that emerges is a feeling in the viewer that the transcendent dimension is always lurking amid the immanent.

Later in the same film, we are given an image that broadens as the shot continues, revealing a very different place, perhaps, than the audience expected.

Figs. 24–26. Dorota's visit to the obstetrician becomes a cosmic arena of ethical issues in *Decalogue II.* Dorota's words in the last frame are "I need an abortion."

Like Tarkovsky and Antonioni, Kieślowski often edits against the Hollywood model of parsimony; he will present a place, give it time to be studied, enter his main character, let the character leave, and study the place some more before he moves on to the next location. Such an approach functions similarly to the resonant empty spaces of Tarkovsky; it foregrounds

---

115. Michel Chion, *Audio-Vision: Sound on Screen* (New York: Columbia University Press, 1990), 129–130.

the space as central (and, perhaps, synecdochical of the cosmos), while not reducing its function to the place through which the character moves.

The following sequence from *Red* contains a fascinating case of space expansion, disorientation, mystery, and split identification. This strategy was also a hallmark of Antonioni:

Figs. 27–30. Valentine walks into her own point of view in *Red,* creating an abstract sense of space in the viewer and imbuing the Judge's home with mystery.

Forms and Motion

In his pursuit of mystery, Kieślowski often utilizes the extreme close-up, yielding an abstract image that may be conceived in phenomenological terms (form, dynamics, color, and essential properties), because the identity of the object is often indecipherable (at first). In each case, the image has a dynamic quality that evokes feeling in the audience; as these images arrive in a metaphysical context, the feelings can be seen as immediate and powerful, inviting transcendent interpretation by their very structure. When asked about what he hoped to capture in the close-up, Kieślowski replied: "Perhaps the soul. In any case, a truth which I myself haven't found. Maybe time that flies and can never be caught."[116]

---

116. *Télérama* (September 1993): 93; quoted in Annette Insdorf, *Double Lives, Second Chances* (New York: Hyperion, 1999), 160.

 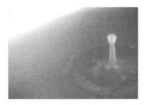 

Figs. 31–33. Abstract close-ups in *Decalogue II* (the resurrection scene).

Figs. 34–36. Abstract close-ups in *Blue*.

Kieślowski discusses figure 36 (from *Blue*) in the film's 2003 DVD release. Whereas he does not articulate the transcendent dimension explicitly, he does talk a great deal about universality and the things that unite people (namely, their most important desires and experiences as humans). He says the sugar cube illustrates Julie's insularity — her obsession with an immediate object as the only thing that matters to her. What is interesting here, then, is the sense of force that the coffee creates. The liquid creeping into the sugar cube appears almost magical: a transcendent penetration into her insular world.

Figures 37–38 portray scarves dragging behind different characters (who are both facing a sense of judgment/doom). In each case, the scarf's contrast and movement on the blank floor creates a haunting moment — as though the long form were struggling to survive amid an all-encompassing background. The editing pattern (i.e., the lack of an establishing shot) and the framing emphasize the formal properties of the scarf to such a degree that the object seems to lose all denotation as a scarf, having been perceptually transformed into a moving black form of mysterious identity. We know the iconic, denotative label for this form ("a scarf"), but abstraction has forced us to consider how many other things it might be.

Of course, these are but a few examples among many. When Ula pours the coffee into the sink at the beginning of *No End*, it is important to note that Kieślowski casts our attention on the liquid in the sink (dark, amorphous). Other directors might choose to focus on her face as the

Figs. 37–38. Scarves from the defending lawyer in *A Short Film about Killing* (l) and Véronique at the cardiologist (r), in *The Double Life of Véronique.*

locus of meaning and emotion, but Kieślowski finds it in form. This pattern repeats time and again, and the aggregate effect is a predisposition on the part of the viewer to perceive in an expansive frame of mind.

Later in *Véronique,* the title character slowly toys with a shoestring while studying her cardiology report.[117] The symbolism is obvious, but beyond this Kieślowski demonstrates a patient attention to form. In what would have been considered empty time by many directors and editors, Kieślowski hangs on the shot longer to absorb the form and allow it to resonate:

Figs. 39–40. The "flatline" from *The Double Life of Véronique.*

As might be expected, the chromatic themes in the *Three Colours* trilogy begged for formalist visual effects, and Kieślowski delivered. His three different cinematographers each utilized filters to complement the color theme of his respective film. In the case of *Red,* the effect went far beyond mere use of the orange Wratten 85 filter. Sobociński and Kieślowski agreed that

---

117. The ominous nature of the cardiology reports becomes particularly eerie when one considers Kieślowski's own fatal heart problems.

massive changes in art direction needed to be effected: red-painted walls, red-painted cars, red clothing, and so on.[118]

This employment of color deserves attention. It serves as a visual thread that holds the film together yet never stands out as an easily discerned, direct metaphor. Here we see how far Kieślowski came from his documentary career. His films are suddenly on the plane of painting — utilizing color as a construct in the film's diegesis, not as an incidental sight. In each case, it is plausible that red would be present in the frame (a stoplight, the Swiss flag, or a billboard), but it is clear from the film as a whole that the look is stylized; the color evokes wider connotations in terms of mood, symbolism, and higher expression. The multivalence of meaning in the colors becomes obvious, as they form an abstract screen upon which we project a variety of emotions. Red is both blood and love, trauma and tenderness. Kieślowski's chromaticism presses the two into relation (i.e., love as sacrifice). It is as though Kieślowski is showing us connections that have always been there, but we have never noticed. There is a unity in the world — a beautiful structure that is noticed when the camera distills it to a celluloid image.

Kieślowski also uses motion to abstract effect. Like Tarkovsky, he sometimes uses slow motion to create a sense of suspended or eternal time, but there are also other techniques. In the only scene where Weronika and Véronique see each other (an eternal moment within the temporal turmoil of an antigovernment protest), Véronique (in a turning bus) spins around Weronika. The result is a blurred, racing background that creates a marvelous abstract effect, suggesting eternal space as well as time (Fig. 41).

Fig. 41. Chronos suspended in *The Double Life of Véronique.*

---

118. Pizzello, "Piotr Sobociński," 68–74.

In other places, such as the following example from *Red,* opposite motions (all moving quickly and abstractly) suggest an eternal space (at a moment of spiritual crisis in the plot).

Fig. 42. Inexhaustible space in *Red.*

Finally, in typical Kieślowskian fashion, the most powerful of images (in the plot and in symbolic power) are often the most visually beautiful, even if this beauty is ironic. In this case, an image from *A Short Film about Love,* the slow motion of the blood rolling into the water lends meaningful weight to the image, suggesting religious symbolism (sacrifice; the wounds of Christ in a Christ figure), and the expressive nature of shape and form simultaneously:

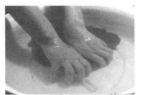

Figs. 43–45. Abstraction and bloodshed in *A Short Film about Love.*

Sometimes motion works as a revelation clarifying an otherwise abstract image. One example is the hospital scene at the beginning of *Blind Chance.* The object in the foreground is not clearly identifiable, but after it moves, we recognize it to be a leg. There is a neurophysiological reason for this: there are some brain cells in the visual system devoted exclusively to motion perception, and so movement in the frame initiates a new set of brain cells in the visualization process.[119] Aesthetically, however, Kieślowski utilizes this process as a dramatic pattern, facilitating a general abstract openness (transcendent suggestion) that is given immanent identity only later. As I

119. Zeki, *Inner Vision,* 143.

describe in the next chapter, the use of the POV in this shot is also disorienting, enhancing the bracket effect, and multiplying the possible owners of the vision (a gesture toward universality). The metaphysical context for this image is that of imminent death: a character's last thought before dying.

It cannot be stressed strongly enough that the abstract image is not the sole cause of the transcendent effect; in every case, the background plot, the concurrent and surrounding dialogue, the music, and the sound design all contribute to the experience. A comprehensive phenomenology of the cinema (and of style in the cinema) must account for all these factors. Although this chapter has focused on the abstract image, Kieślowski has much to offer regarding these other elements, and their expressions of the Transcendent manifest their powers to the fullest. There is not space to survey them all here, but a short discussion on sound is essential.

Audio

Kieślowski's approach to sound follows his liminal aesthetic. There is not adequate space to discuss all the ingenius ways Kieślowski uses sound and music, but Chapters 3 through 5 will examine some of these instances in their context. In general, Kieślowski's primary innovations involve spatiotemporal experimentation and musico-rhythmic influence.

As to the former, the audiotape scene in *The Double Life of Véronique* is a master stroke, marking one of the most creative moments in the Kieślowski/Piesiewicz collaborations. As Véronique wanders around her apartment, attending to mundaneities with a set of remote headphones on (she drinks water, brushes her teeth, etc.), we hear the contents of the mysterious audiotape she received in the mail: equally mundane, though foreign, pedestrian sounds and echoes (what sound like doors, a car, things being dropped, open, and shut, etc.). This creates a bicameral world that is at once marvelous and disconcerting. The effect is difficult to describe, but it serves as an amplification of the central duality theme that has run throughout the film: the idea that two worlds could coexist (in this case, through nonsynchronous aural and visual elements). Indeed, the tape is very like a transmission from another coexistent world, into which Véronique is beckoned, and everything about the production of this scene reinforces that feeling.

Michel Chion's theories on sound give a little more articulation to this experience. In *Audio-Vision: Sound on Screen*, he states that sounds temporalize images along several dimensions (i.e., it gives the image a sense of time). Likewise, sounds naturally tend toward "synchresis" with the image, meaning they weld a cause-effect relation between them regardless of any logical connection; this effect is stronger in some cases than others, but the tendency toward synchresis is always present. In addition, the presence of sounds (their recorded "distance" and timbre) can psychologically appear to be coming from a source within the frame or, at least, the immediate diegetic region off-screen even though they clearly are not (a process Chion calls "spatial magnetization"). In this case, our logical understanding that the sound is clearly not emanating from the frame is synthesized with these effects. The fact that most ambient noises in Véronique's apartment are absent from the frame only bolsters the synthesis. The result is a "vast extension" of space in the experience (the "superfield," according to Chion), to the level of the "phantom audio-vision," a term Chion reserves for the extraordinary sound design of Tarkovsky. I've connected Tarkovsky and Kieślowski throughout this book, and the sonic connection here only strengthens the parallel. Chion's description of Tarkovsky's *Sacrifice* might very well apply to Kieślowski's liminal use of sound:

> [O]ne can hear sounds that already seem to come from the other side, as if they're heard by an immaterial ear, liberated from the hurly-burly of our human world. . . . [I]t calls to another dimension, it has gone elsewhere, disengaged from the present. It can also murmur like the drone of the world, at once close and disquieting.[120]

Kieślowski uses off-screen sound to great effect, particularly in *Red*. Chapter 5 will discuss those instances in their filmic context, but, according to his sound mixer, William Flageollet, Kieślowski often bucks the Hollywood trend (one picture, one sound) and uses sounds that are not in the picture beyond the typical ambient noises.[121] For instance, Valentine's original conversation with her boyfriend is interrupted by a loud, unseen helicopter, forcing her to close the windows. We hear this helicopter a few times throughout the film but never see it until the very end of the film, when we look back and see that it functioned as a harbinger. Eerie silences punctuate the films as well, an important quality that Kieślowski's composer, Zbigniew Preisner, has also noted.[122]

---

120. This final quote comes from pp. 123–124 of Chion's book *Audio-Vision: Sound on Screen* (op. cit.). The other ideas are found on pp. 13, 63–70, 87, and 150.

121. William Flageollet, "Insights into Red," *Red* (DVD, Miramax, 2003).

122. "Zbigniew Preisner," in *Film Music,* ed. Mark Russell and James Young (Boston: Focal Press, 2000), 161–163.

Kieślowski's musico-rhythmic emphasis is discussed in more context in Chapters 4 (*Decalogue II*) and 5 (*Blue*). Chion's observations that both motion pictures and music have rhythm as a trans-sensory core element is most demonstrable in Kieślowski.[123] He often uses music to create an elision of diegetic space and time. The sum result is a sense of spatiotemporal expansion. In addition, Preisner has remarked that Kieślowski always relied on music to express the inner world of his characters.[124] In other cases, such as the opening to *Blue,* the music is absent, but the rhythm of the images and sound effects create a musical sense of the sequence. This has the effect of abstracting the very procession of the sequence itself, that is, distilling the seemingly "random" sounds, sights, and actions of a given world to a common, rhythmic unity, suggesting an underlying metaphysical order to the universe.

Conclusion

In this chapter, I have attempted to present, in a cursory fashion, the liminal vision of a metaphysically concerned director. My study shows only a partial view: still images do no justice to the experience of seeing the images in full motion, on a large screen, and in full color, and there are many more examples threaded throughout Kieślowski's films. He uses other formal strategies that are not articulated here but aim in the same Transcendental direction, all the same. Kieślowski predisposes the audience, through style and subversion of its preconceived patterns of viewing, toward an expanded metaphysical view of the film. The Transcendent possibility resonates in the wonder of both the plot elements (manipulations and expansions of space and time, and themes of mystery, revelation, and predestination) and the dynamics of the images themselves. Kieślowski consistently brackets expository information in a number of ways, revealing that information later. The net effect of this concealment does not appear to be politically motivated, but rather a Transcendent suggestion — a consistent "pointing-to" the human experience of mystery and a suggestion that perhaps more lurks in reality than our semiotic categorizations acknowledge. It should also be evident that Kieślowski continually uses abstraction as a universalizing tool. The bracket is a universalizing strategy — reaching for concepts that

123. Chion, *Audio-Vision,* 136.
124. "Zbigniew Preisner," 168.

unite all human beings, and an attempt to extend the stories, images, and their significance to everyone else.

Kieślowski's work is, first, an "opening up" to his unique comportment, his approach to the world, as David E. Cooper might say.[125] Second, it is a style that often utilizes abstraction, which, by its nature increases the varieties of interpretations a viewer will likely bring to the image. In a metaphysical context, the properties of the abstract image are suited to theological analogy (a kinship between semiotics and phenomenology). Third, it bears a perceptual power of its own, distinct from cognitive predispositions but intertwined with them. The fact that we cannot wholly extract our presuppositions or cognitive associations from these images (à la E. H. Gombrich and the fallacy of the "innocent eye") does not mean we should give up all efforts to locate what is ontologically distinct in these perceptions (à la Rudolf Arnheim), isolated (as much as possible) from our subjective memories, and attempt to understand a dimension of their perceptive power upon us.[126] Indeed, these forces in artworks are often suppressed far beyond what Gombrich himself would likely sanction; that is, they are virtually skipped over in favor of semiotic elements, precisely because words are not adequate to the task of their description. This often leads to a further misstep, I believe, of downgrading these phenomenological aspects of the work from epistemological status as knowledge to "mere" sensation.

This synthesis of transcendent word and image lies in the inner circle of the diagram explained in this chapter's beginning. There is no evidence that Kieślowski ever felt that he concretely found that Transcendent hope, but his films stand as testament to the integrity of his search and his longing.

125. David E. Cooper, "Ineffability," in *A Companion to Aesthetics,* ed. David E. Cooper (Oxford: Blackwell, 1995), 224.

126. The critique of the innocent eye forms the heart of Gombrich's book *Art and Illusion,* op. cit.

Part 2

The Films
(1966–1994)

$\boxed{3}$

EARLY WORKS (1966–1988)

A s discussed, Kieślowski began in documentaries, and this experience exerted considerable influence on his feature filmmaking. What is most clear is that Kieślowski appreciated the immediate powers of the image, even as he debated its efficacy for social change. As early as his film school thesis, "Author, Film, Reality," it is clear that Kieślowski prized "the dramaturgy of reality" and, at the same time, asserted the value of the auteur's personal expression within the documentary form.[1] This is no naive realism, nor is it solipsistic expressionism. He writes: "I'm talking about a film without artistic conventions — instead of a story about reality — a story by reality itself. Instead of an author's commentary, a viewer-director partnership."[2] Even in 1975, as my discussion of *Personnel* bears witness, Kieślowski looked to expand some of his conceptions of documentary to works of fiction. The early films, in general, do not always show the formal tendency toward abstraction that the later works use so effectively, but the path toward that mode of expression emerges here, and this is the ground where the seeds of a more formalistic style are clearly sown. Likewise, the Transcendent is not consistently invoked, but there is still a sense that the issues of ultimate reality — metaphysics — ground the narrative.

Philosophically and politically, Poland languished in a crisis throughout much of Kieślowski's early career, and these films reflect this turbulence. One finds more questions than answers in the films of this period, mani-fest in a dialectical narrative pattern, rather than the elliptical variants on

---

1. *Krzysztof Kieślowski: We Are What We've Absorbed* (Lódź, Poland: Camerimage, 2000), 66.
2. Ibid., 69.

traditional story structure one finds in Kieślowski's later films. A more cynical, pessimistic agnosticism persists as well, rather than the more hopeful, humanistic spirit characteristic of the post-*Decalogue* films.

As mentioned, all close readings will be dedicated primarily to Kieślowski's feature work, with the shorter *Personnel* and *Decalogue* films included as well. Even so, for the sake of unity, concise discussions of his documentaries and shorter films will begin this chapter. Film school projects aside, Kieślowski's professional life began in documentaries in 1968. It was not until 1973 that he experimented with a short fiction film (*Pedestrian Subway*). In 1975 he attempted shorter fictional projects again, and 1976 marked the release of a feature, *The Scar*. He mixed his fictional and documentary work until 1981, when he began to concentrate solely on fictional work (the 1988 documentary short *Seven Days a Week* being the lone exception).

Documentaries and Short Fiction

In style, the documentary does suit itself to abstraction on some levels. Although the documentarian may choose the telephoto lens for different reasons (i.e., to observe from afar), the optics of that lens often create abstract effects through the flattening of perspective and the narrowing of depth of field. The natural reflections of glass windows ("remedied" in many feature films, but championed as authentic in the documentary) create multilayered, abstract images. These elements abound in Kieślowski's documentaries, and there is a sense in the "docudrama" films (like *Pedestrian Subway*) that Kieślowski is steering these techniques toward a more expressive goal.

The Tram (1966, B&W, silent, approx. 5 min.[3]): This short, made at the Łódź Film School, depicts the encounter between a teenage boy (Jerzy Braszka) and girl (Maria Janiec) on a train. After several exchanges of looks between them, he exits the train, only to think twice and chase after it again. His initial run is not revealed to be a run for the tram, at first. We assume he is running out of frustration or internal issues, only

---

3. All running times are approximate and based on my viewing of the films. In some cases (e.g., *First Love*) the version of the film I viewed was significantly different from that listed by Stok, *Kieślowski on Kieślowski,* ed. Danusia Stok (London: Faber and Faber, 1993), 237–264. This suggests that different versions of these films exist.

to see the "revelation" later. In what will become another Kieślowskian trope, he peers at the girl from behind a wall, and the camera gives us his partially obscured POV. Several years later, a scene in *Personnel* will echo this film.

The Office (1966, B&W, 6 min.): Kieślowski's first known documentary shows something of his antipathy for bureaucracy. A close-up on two glasses of tea in this film mark the beginning of a leitmotif running throughout Kieślowski's career. In this case, the image is not so much communal as it is frustrating; employees in the office drink tea while a line of frustrated citizens wait...and wait. The shelves, jammed full of documents and files, make for a remarkable synecdoche of bureaucratic chaos.

Concert of Requests (1967, B&W, 15 min.): This longer short tells the story of a carefree afternoon among youths that soon turns menacing. The film features a young man (looking remarkably like Kieślowski) witnessing a number of incidents between two groups of people: the rowdy, drunken people he is with (but not feeling a part of) and a couple he discovers camping in the woods. The film features many formalist techniques that reappear in his later films with more artistic maturity, control, and teleological thrust. In the end, the couple sacrifices to stay together rather than be separated by the drunken party.

The Photograph (1968, B&W, 32 min.): "An old photograph of two little boys, wearing soldiers' hats and holding rifles. The camera goes in search of these two boys, now grown men, and registers their emotion as they are confronted with the photograph."[4] In Kieślowski's later films (*The Scar, Camera Buff*) he continues to probe the perils of memory, inscribed in the filmic image.

From the City of Łódź (1969, B&W, 17 min.): A documentary portrait of a town full of idiosyncrasies and interesting details: exercise routines at a factory, a community meeting to save the local orchestra from "liquidation," and others. The pedestrian detail, as it reveals what is meaningful to the town's residents, glues the episodes together: old men sitting around, children playing, laundry drying outside a window. These details, pregnant with subtle charm and beauty, will continue to fascinate Kieślowski throughout his career. The shots of the factory machinery

---

4. Ibid., 238.

show his early penchant for the close-up. The final song accompanying the final scene tells of a town that "must be found somewhere, where one can live a peaceful life."

I Was a Soldier (1970, B&W, 16 min.): Blind former soldiers convey to us the only thing they can see anymore: their memories and dreams. This is a touching documentary about the internal world and its importance. All agree, at film's end, that war should end once and for all.

Factory (1970, B&W, 17 min. 30 sec.): A scathing documentary look at the dysfunction of a factory, clumsily limping along, hamstrung by countless bureaucratic entanglements. Honest workers try but simply cannot perform because of circumstances beyond them.

Before the Rally (1971, B&W, 15 min.): Two Polish race car drivers work on their car in preparation for the Monte Carlo race. Their continual stream of troubles stands as an allegory of Polish industrial and economic problems, according to Stok.[5] The film begins with some fascinating abstract visuals on the car assembly line. There are some stunning shots of the white car dashing through the snow, almost dreamlike. The men do not finish the race.

Refrain (1972, B&W, 10 min.): A documentary about a funeral home. Here, at the threshold of life and death, lie endless paperwork, incompetence, and a large profit motive. The close-ups at the beginning of the film (of bureaucratic hands and documents of the deceased) appear distorted and strange (via the wide-angle lens). A pan through a cemetery inspires similar shots of graveyards in later films (e.g., *The Double Life of Véronique*). Throughout the film, a series of pans by a window contrasts the dark, tomblike room of the funeral parlor, where the business of "death care" is carried on, with the living, outside world. The final image of a newborn child rings hollow: a depressingly cyclical affair (perhaps) rather than a joyous new beginning.

Between Wrocław and Zielona Góra (1972, color, 10 min.) and *The Principles of Safety and Hygiene in a Copper Mine* (1972, B&W, 19 min.): Two documentaries, commissioned by the Lubin copper mine. The first film presents the human element: the story of a miner, his aspirations, and economic

---

5. Ibid., 240.

hopes (success is a major subtext in this film). The second is an instructional film, complete with humorous cartoons illustrating the potential dangers of mining work (decapitations, dismemberment, etc.). Both films feature elements uncharacteristic of Kieślowski's work, the most obvious being "elevator" music. It's difficult to know how seriously Kieślowski took these films,[6] but the first does tell a personal story of a worker (a topic close to him). The images of flight (model planes, parachutists, gliders, airplanes, etc.) give something of a transcendent suggestion, though not in particularly strong or focused terms. Similar images gain more strength in *Blue*.

Workers '71: Nothing about Us without Us (1972, B&W, 45 min.): A documentary shot during one of Poland's most strike-filled and politically tumultuous times, "intended to portray the workers' state of mind in 1971."[7] Close-ups of machinery and workers in the factory show a penchant for formalist composition, not unlike Dziga Vertov's close-ups of the same in *Man with a Movie Camera*.

The Mason (1973, color, 17 min.): A documentary account of a bricklayer and his career, riddled with frustrations amid political change in Poland. In the end, he forsakes the success that the Communist Party offered him in bureaucratic positions and returns to laying bricks. He voices a romantic attachment to his trade and the satisfaction of building something that endures.

Pedestrian Subway (1973, B&W, 29 min.): A short drama about a window dresser (Teresa Budzisz-Krzyzanowska) working in a Warsaw pedestrian underpass. Her husband (Andrzej Seweryn), whom she has left, comes looking for her. Their relationship is clearly distant, and the details of that distance are slowly revealed throughout their consistently interrupted, difficult conversation. The complex dynamics of the relationship come to light, strand by strand, problematizing any initial moral judgments of either character. The opening shots are close-ups on postcards, but they are only revealed to be such after a few moments. The entire action of the film carries a curious aura, due to the unusual environment — underground in the belly of Warsaw. Kieślowski counters this secluded,

---

6. Kieślowski showed little enthusiasm for them; see ibid., 54.
7. Ibid., 242.

subterranean feeling with the transparency of the shop's picture window: the stage of the film. The transparency and the voyeuristic dynamic shifts as papers are mounted on the window for privacy, and the couple stares through a small hole at the outside world (a point of view remarkably like Kieślowski's documentary camera and, perhaps, a reflexive comment on such). They watch a crime (like Jacek in *Short Film about Killing*) and a thwarted lover (like Tomek in *A Short Film about Love*) from a safe distance. Abstract impulses can be traced throughout: the detail of the paper floating by on the sidewalk takes on an abstract dimension by virtue of its movement and framing. Likewise, the coffee, thrown at the window and running down the glass in front of the characters' faces, adds an expressive element to the shot. Their attempts to close the distance between them, amid the translucent cocoon they have built, prove insufficient. In the midst of a lovemaking attempt, he looks at his watch. She counters by picking up the phone, steadying it on top of his back as he lies atop her, utterly defeated. She dials a service that gives the time, then dangles the phone at his ear. "Give me a call," she says later as they unhappily part (a backhanded reference to the amorous calls she has received from others that night). Their bitter parting will be partially redeemed through a similar scenario in *Decalogue III,* as two former lovers part in another transportation hub with a bit more understanding between them.

X-Ray (1974, color, 12 min.): A documentary on tuberculosis patients expressing their hopes and fears. This was very personal for Kieślowski, considering his father died after a long battle with TB. The film opens with the close-up on an unknown person's back, a bodiless hand pressing a stethoscope against it. Stark, beautiful shots of a wood at sunrise follow, with a mysterious fog rolling through the scene. The abstract impulse is clearly there in these shots, and they act as a suggestion of eternal space cut against images of people facing death. Many express a felt uselessness after losing their jobs, as well as a determination to defeat their illness. Kieślowski seems to be exorcising some childhood demons here: the stark contrast between the pastoral rehabilitation center and the smog-ridden city is potent visual rhetoric.

First Love (1974, color, 51 min.): This documentary follows a very young couple through an unexpected pregnancy, young marriage, and new birth. She briefly considers abortion (a theme that will return in later films), but that proves to be only the first in a host of decisions ahead of them. They continually face bureaucratic and financial obstacles as they try to plan their new life together. In one instance, a neighbor calls the authorities on them for living unregistered in Jadwiga's grandmother's apartment; it turns out Kieślowski himself secretly sent the policeman in on the couple.[8] At the government wedding, the sterile ceremony culminates in the receipt of their official documents. Each of Jadwiga's parents wishes them lives happier than their own. Her grilling by the school board (over her pregnancy) is vicious, but she bears up admirably. All these weighty, discouraging matters are counterbalanced by the clear love between the couple and their innocent, even naive, approach to the world. By film's end, their view is wiser but still happy. Kieślowski felt that he fell short here, unable to truly access the private world of the couple, but it remains a touching film in many respects. It's clear that the birth of the child influenced his portrayal of the birth in *Camera Buff.*

Curriculum Vitae (a.k.a. *Life Story*) (1975, B&W, 45 min.): A drama of a man accused of disloyalty to the Communist Party and the committee hearings that follow. The film may be called a docudrama, as it is based on the lead actor's similar experiences and features real Poles playing themselves (such as the party review board).[9] The compositions are more stylized, the lighting dramatic, and the camera techniques more formal than usual, but, overall, the looseness of the camera and the consistent use of the telephoto lens are trappings of documentary style. A parade of relentless close-ups marks the interrogation (not unlike the famous close-ups during the interrogations of Joan in Carl Dreyer's *The Passion of Joan of Arc*). The claustrophobic framing is matched only by the suspicious, invasive questions and the sense that the man cannot answer any question in a way that will not be scrutinized. The committee members pick apart his entire, sad life, a bitter narrative that often refers to political events, connecting the story to Polish history. Kieślowski ends the film with a montage of photographs from the man's life after his case is deemed "not straightforward." We never hear the final verdict, but it feels as if punishment has already been meted out.

---

8. Ibid., 64.
9. Ibid., 60.

Hospital (1975, B&W, 20 min.): One might say this film runs contrary to Kieślowski's voiced confidence in Polish doctors, expressed at the end of his life.[10] However, its main protagonists, like those of *The Factory,* are shown to be doing their best amid impossible conditions (overwork, supply shortages, faulty equipment, etc.). The documentary follows these doctors for a thirty-two-hour period. Desperation bleeds through: the film opens with a doctor responding to a report that a patient has jumped from the fourth floor window of the hospital. The physicians discuss this and other tragedies calmly and casually — all in a day's work. The patients are rarely shown, but they are often heard off camera. Their misery is tainted with frustration and suspicion. Compassionate moments peek through occasionally, as when a doctor takes up a collection for a blind and destitute patient. Other moments are starkly gruesome scenes on the operating table — a cold, stark perspective that will return in *A Short Film about Killing.*

Slate (1976, color, 6 min.): While some of these outtakes (from *The Scar*) are "bloopers," others do not appear to be so. The film becomes something of an editing experiment, unified by the musical rhythm of the clapping slate.

Peace (a.k.a. *The Calm*) (1976, color, 72 min.): A fiction film starring Jerzy Stuhr as Antek, a recently released prisoner who desperately wants to return to a "simple" life. He plays a man with similar ambitions in *Camera Buff,* and in both cases, his character finds that no life is simple. The film opens in prison, with the inmates singing Christmas carols over Antek's memories of a girl. He seeks a job, a wife, kids, and a roof over his head — peace. He later adds a television to the list, this after seeing the images of horses mysteriously showing up on a faulty TV set. The horses return periodically, most remarkably on an evening bus trip. This tip of the hat to Andrei Tarkovsky[11] also bears with it connotations of freedom, an elusive ideal that Antek still pursues even after freedom from prison. He marries the girl of his prison dreams (Izabella Olszewska), but soon finds himself caught between a thieving boss (who has been kind to him)

---

10. Annette Insdorf, *Double Lives, Second Chances: The Cinema of Krzysztof Kieślowski* (New York: Hyperion, 1999), 1, 3.

11. Tarkovsky was famous for his use of horses in his films. *Andrei Rublev* is a potent example.

and the workers framed for the crime. Antek attempts to mediate, but this is perceived as betrayal. After leaving the boss's house in anger over an announcement of potential firings, he is viciously beaten by workers. He lies bleeding on the ground, desperately muttering, "Peace, peace, peace." The memory of the running horses ends the film. Abstraction takes a backseat here, though a few shots are stylistically remarkable, namely, the silhouette of Antek lighting a cigarette as an out-of-focus train rushes past in the background. Antek is a cross between *The Scar*'s Bednarz (in his concern for reconciliation between groups) and *Camera Buff*'s Filip (in his desire for a simple life). He also prefigures the third scenario of *Blind Chance,* a man who wishes the simple life apart from any social complications. Such avoidance is impossible, Kieślowski shows us.

From a Night Porter's Point of View (1977, color, 15 min.): A documentary about a factory night porter who cherishes rules and regulations in both his professional and personal worlds. Violent films amuse him and make him happy; films of love hold no interest. Control and power appeal to him, and he speaks glowingly of enforcing the bureaucratic rules among ordinary people. He thinks the young have too much freedom, and has contempt for their dress and behavior. He detests violent people, and supports public hangings where "tens, hundreds of people would see it." In the end, "The rules are more important than the man." The sentimental music runs in sardonic counterpoint to this portrait, which is anything but touching. In the last scene, Kieślowski sarcastically suggests that we must decide "what he is called." In an early formalist move, Kieślowski deliberately chose film stock that would create a "distortion of color" to reflect this "distortion of a human being."[12]

I Don't Know (1977, B&W, 43 min.): A documentary of a factory member, loyal to the Communist Party. His attempt to expose the corruption around him comes to haunt him, as the corruption revealed extends higher up the ladder than he anticipated. Like so many of the other documentaries, it begins with a sequence of close-ups on "machinery," in this case, a tape recorder and film projector. Like a similar opening moment in Ingmar Bergman's *Persona,* there may be a reflexive comment here. In this case, the film is a minimalistic definition — a scene of a man telling his story, intercut only with lonely exterior shots of his

---

12. Stok, *Kieślowski on Kieślowski,* 79.

home as the hour grows very late. These essentials — the human story, the expressive human face, and the concept of home — will all prove important to Kieślowski, and the sentiment "I don't know" echoes his characteristic agnosticism.

Seven Women of Different Ages (1978, B&W, 15 min.): This documentary takes place over seven days in a ballet academy. Each day is dedicated to a different dancer; each one older than the last. The form of the narrative aims at something of a Platonic portrait of "the dancer," even as the title suggests a generalization about "woman" (grace mingled with courage, strength, and persistence). The natural formal properties of ballet shine through brilliantly in the lovely sequence from the Sunday performance and the numerous close-ups on hands and feet. In a fascinating bit of mise-en-scène, Kieślowski will often focus on a background character as soft-focus and abstract dancers move in and out of the foreground. Kieślowski's love of dancers returns in later films (*Personnel, Red*).

Station (1980, B&W, 12 min.): One of Kieślowski's most expressive, and multilayered, documentaries — a portrait of Warsaw's central railway station. The scenes are quotidian and interesting, but the most prominent, recurring image is that of surveillance: a cycloptic camera viewing all from overhead. That same camera returns to the station in *Decalogue III*, but the monitors who are asleep and distracted in that later film show rapt attention here. As the government news anchor reads off the government's propagandistic reports of current economic "progress" and "optimism," the fatigue and disinterest on the faces of most people in the station betray this assessment. People hurry for the platform, complain about the delays, kiss each other goodbye, and simply try to live.

Talking Heads (1980, B&W, 15 min.): Kieślowski asks a considerable number of ordinary Poles some fundamental questions as a portrait of a given histo-cultural moment: When were you born? Who are you? What would you like most? This cross section of Poland's population counts backward, beginning with children born recently and moving toward the older generations. With each interview, the weight of memory gets heavier. Children want everything from "nothing" to a chance "to go to America." One girl would like "the pope to visit Poland." The teenagers and college-age crowd talks in terms of ideals ("I'd like people to realize materialism isn't everything"). The adults are more direct in their appeals ("We all want it...freedom," "For people to live by their principles and never have to fear fear"). Some even directly wish for democracy, though they do not seem hopeful of finding it. A very old Polish revolutionary talks of the Communist Party and his disappointment that not everything he "dreamed of" has been accomplished. Many wish for peace, like the woman born in 1900. The last person interviewed is a one hundred-year-old woman, born in 1880. With a laugh, she says she would simply "like to live longer."

Short Working Day (1981, color, approx. 73 min.): In this drama, a Communist Party secretary attempts to "stay with the ship," as rioting, striking workers echo the Poznań protests of 1956 (shouting "Bread and freedom!") and set fire to the party headquarters. He barely escapes with the help of the police and some party friends. It might be called a docudrama, as it is based on Hanna Krall's journalistic report on a similar incident. Although Kieślowski clearly shows sympathy for the workers, he does not paint them in an altogether attractive light. In the end, the film is a portrait of the times, representing its tensions and seemingly insurmountable difficulties. The camera lens, so ominous at the end of *Camera Buff,* continues its relentless gaze at the party member on television. One can almost hear Kieślowski snickering a few times (e.g., as the secretary speaks into the bullhorn, "Ladies and gentleman," Kieślowski cuts to deaf, empty streets). As the protest tension escalates, abstraction emerges; this is not focused in a transcendent direction, but it does indicate a new internal conflict: that of the secretary's values and conscience. The moral lines become more blurred as the people resort to violence; reflections and the heat of burning fires provide the visual distortions accompanying the violence. The scenes of protest are intercut with scenes of the aftermath: some protesters are jailed; some are inspired to further Solidarity. Kieślowski disliked this film, feeling that he did not adequately explore the character of the protagonist.[13]

Seven Days a Week (1988, color, approx. 18 min.): As Kieślowski's contribution to an anthology of films about European cities, Warsaw is represented by six different people of varying ages, occupations, and interests, each featured on a different day of the week (Monday through

---

13. Ibid., 115–118.

Saturday). Nearly everyone works all the time; some carry two jobs (e.g., the woman who is tour guide and translator by day, paramedic by night). The eldest spends her day fighting the madness that is Polish bureaucratic life: endless lines, regulations, and inconveniences. The youngest does not work as conventionally as the others; he is an artist, a rock musician, and a generally concerned, restless soul. On Sunday, Kieślowski reveals they are all members of the same family, sitting around a communal table. This hopeful portrait of cohabitating generations marked Kieślowski's return to the documentary after eight years of only fiction work. It was also his last venture into the form. The young man of Friday writes a song: "God wanted the *Titanic* to sink, so it sank. And no one thought about the relatives of those who drowned. Now they want to salvage it; what will they find?" Kieślowski's filmmaking career will end with an image of a sunken ship and similar questions.

The Early Features

Personnel (1975)

SYNOPSIS: *Romek (Juliusz Machulski) is a young tailor with the state opera, coming of age. As he rises within the organization, he finds himself at once enchanted with the mysterious beauties of the theatrical arts and conflicted about the treachery, bickering, and politics behind the scenes. In the end, in exchange for financial support from his colleagues, he is asked to denounce one of his only friends. The film leaves him at the signing table, undecided.*

Clearly, the setting for this film is inspired by Kieślowski's own experience during what he describes as a golden time for Polish theater.[14] Kieślowski manages to preserve his early fascination with the art; he once said he was "dazzled" by theater,[15] just like Romek at the raising of the curtain scene. At the same time, this was theater in Poland, and nothing so purely idealistic as art could survive untainted.

In many respects, this film is in the realist vein of Kieślowski's early fictional work. Sumptuous visuals do not abound; lighting is typically more natural and documentary-like in its look (i.e., uncorrected light sources, grainy film, flat lighting, unremarkable shadow patterns, etc.); the Transcendent is not referenced in any direct way; questions of morality are

14. Ibid., xvii.
15. Ibid., 123.

generally tied to political situations; the camerawork is interesting, but more documentary-like, and so on. Yet there are some hints here of the stylistic and thematic interests that would characterize Kieślowski's later work.

Look no further than the opening shot of the film. Kieślowski withholds an establishing shot in favor of a close-up of Romek. The viewer's diegetic placement in the geography of the scene appears to be shifting randomly. Only a few moments later we discover that our dislocation is caused by a series of theatrical mirrors moving in and out of the scene. We see, and know, only the protagonist's face, and that through reflection and distortion. This remarkable little scene stands as an apt metaphor for Romek's own search for identity at this liminal moment in his life. The film traces Romek's first steps from the world of education, full of idealism and promise, to the hard reality of the workplace. The mesmerizing feel of the opening scene places the audience in sympathetic stride with Romek's bewildered internal state.

Kieślowski couples this formalist gesture with the marks of the documentary: handheld camera, natural sound (never a nondiegetic intrusion, musical or otherwise), and liberal use of the telephoto lens (as if the audience were peering in from afar, never intruding on the action). There are, of course, scopophilic aspects to this style (and much has been written on these matters), but the connotations of sexual pleasure and guilt attached to scopophilia do not seem to be active here in any explicit way. It may be more helpful to see this as a documentary shooting style with immediacy as its aim. The audience feels present at an event that the style suggests to be authentic.

Kieślowski's fondness for spontaneous moments also runs in the documentary vein. In fiction, Kieślowski was fond of having his actors and actresses engaged in unposed moments that reflected a certain everyday quality and were not always flattering to the actors. For example, Romek notices the girl on the train as she eats a snack. No music plays, no backlights stream over her gently blowing hair — just a girl eating a snack, whose appearance strikes a chord within him. Although Kieślowski eventually used "stars" in his films as well as more formalist lighting for his actresses (in particular), he continued to pursue these everyday moments, such as when Valentine guzzles a bottle of water in *Red* or Véronique brushes her teeth in *The Double Life of Véronique*. It is also worth noting that Romek's potential romantic encounter is something of a reprise of an idea for one of Kieślowski's first student films, *The Tram* (1966).

Throughout the film, Kieślowski shows a great regard for art but a rather negative view of the artist. In this film, artists receive special entrances, attend parties, behave abominably, and play tennis in the theater workers' much-needed workspace. The height of this conflict between workers' ideals and artistic bourgeois frivolity comes at the moment when the artists' errant tennis ball bounces into the middle of the workers union meeting. Such social criticism must have pleased Kieślowski's Communist censors, yet other aspects would, no doubt, be troubling. It is clear by the end of the film that the world of the workers is far from ideal or ethical.

It is behind the scenes of artistic artifice that Romek's conflict between the ideal and the real comes to a head. In an astonishingly formalistic scene, we follow Romek's supervisor as he walks along a platform. There is a disorienting sense about the scene (reminiscent of the film's opening), the cause of which is revealed at the end of the scene. We hear the supervisor say, "To work here is to soar like a bird," and we assume, at that point, that we are taking Romek's point of view, following the teacher along like a dutiful student. At this point, Kieślowski upends our diegetic comfort by revealing the falseness of our POV as we see Romek walking toward us (on a collision course?). The camera passes the supervisor and ends in an iconic close-up of Romek's face. He stares directly at us, reminiscent of the many visual icons in Tarkovsky's work, and declares that he feels the elevation the supervisor describes, yet his face registers something different. Does he doubt this idealistic statement? Has the collision of the artistic ideal and the real world become disenchanting?

Yet he *is* rising. We discover in the final shot that the platform has been ascending into the flies as the characters, and we, walked upon it. The scene is one of transcendence — a hint of a true experience. The shot at the end reveals a mechanical, scientific explanation for our exhilaration, but we have felt the ascension all the same.

The stylistic use of abstraction should not go unnoticed: the bracketing of an establishing shot in order to create a more expanded sense of space and time. Although Kieślowski's attitude toward transcendent experience is more skeptical here, this very same technique will express the Transcendent possibilities in his later films.

There is a sense in which Kieślowski's films have always been phenomeno-logical in character rather than reporterly. Even in his documentaries, Kieślowski was not so much interested in facts and clear description of an issue, but the feelings and previously hidden experiences of the characters. In the fiction films, we see an emphasis, not on Aristotelian action, but on reaction, internal and psychological. This is particularly evident in *Personnel,* as we are more often looking at the listeners rather than the speakers in any given conversation. This trend is magnified in *No End,* where key narrative events are not shown, but only discussed afterward in their devastating psychological wake.

Romek, like most of Kieślowski's protagonists, indulges in humanizing, tiny transgressions (in this case, smoking in the restroom). This little transgression is linked, via a cigarette, to a later scene. Romek sits and talks with the other tailors, who tell horror tales of the supernatural (one of the only times the supernatural comes up as a topic). As he lights up a cigarette, it explodes in his face: a prank played by another tailor and, perhaps, another critique of the Transcendent. At the very least, Kieślowski seems to be linking Romek's naive idealism with metaphysics.

Romek's disillusion with the ideal becomes clear when he asks his friend, "Is it real?" "What?" his coworker replies. "The Art," he states in reference to the artistic ideal of which his friend had spoken. "Of course it is!" his friend responds. Just a few scenes later, however, this idealist is being muscled out of the theatrical workers union and out of place in the world of workers' politics. The question persists in Romek's mind: can the artistic ideal be maintained in a world of frank political realities?

The theater workers, soaring above the opera in the flies, have conversations about fixing a fireplace and other mundane topics, ignorant of (or disillusioned with) the glories of the aesthetic ideal playing out below them. Romek sees what a gulf lies between people and the Ideal; the central issue is not political, as though the workers had access to the ideal truth and the artists were too arrogant to see it. Even the artists strive, work hard, and beat their bodies in pursuit of the Ideal (a fact most evident in the scene of the ballet rehearsal). The workers, on the other hand, may or may not have a clear vision of the Ideal, but often lack the resources to pursue it.

Kieślowski keeps his film from becoming a despondent picture on the impossibility of art and meaning with a brilliant little scene in which Romek happens upon a practicing violinist. Quite accidentally, Romek hits a set of chimes as he spies on the violinist. His cover blown, Romek exchanges stares with the violinist, who then invites him to continue playing the chimes, culminating in a spontaneous and hopeful duet. A moment of grace emerges where the Ideal reveals itself as possible.

Given eyeglasses, purchased (we assume) by the union, Romek truly does see better, or so he thinks. As he senses his star is rising within the union, he also tastes the artistic ideal once again through his lucky receipt of tickets to the opera he's helped produce. Through his new spectacles, he sits and watches the curtain rise. He senses in that moment, that *immediate* moment, before all the symbols, double meaning, and politics enter in, the feeling of a shudder going through him. That thrill becomes his emotional touchstone to the aesthetic ideal, an immediacy that marks the essence of great art.

However, in typical Kieślowskian fashion, aesthetic ideals are conjoined to ethical ideals when he is asked to testify against his friend regarding a conflict and so hasten his removal from the union. He stares at the pen with which he is to fabricate his testimony, caps it (as if to ethically refuse the task), but fails to leave the signing table. The film leaves him at the table as it moves to the first slate of credits. It returns to the final shot between credits, but nothing has changed; Romek is still caught in the impossible situation, where he must choose between life and ethics, and all he can do is exist, in stasis, at that moment of decision. Kieślowski leaves him in an existential quandary: how can one truly act authentically in a world where values are so difficult to discern?

Throughout this film there is an acknowledgment of art's mysteries, beauties, and transcendent possibilities, from music (abstract sound as immediate communication) to the dancers of the theater (abstract form exuding from immanent bodies). At the same time, Kieślowski suggests that access to those transcendent dimensions is difficult and often fleeting, problematized by social, political, and ethical issues. He offers no remedy here.

The Scar (1976)

SYNOPSIS: *In the town of Olecko, Poland, the city officials successfully lobby the Communist government for a fertilizer factory to be built, against the wishes of many in the community. Stefan Bednarz (Franciszek Pieczka) is brought in to oversee the factory's construction, in part because he has a strong reputation in the profession, but mostly (we learn later) because he lived in Olecko before and is seen as someone who can smooth over the social strife inherent in the project. Bednarz is known as a real humanist, and throughout the film he pursues the project as a great potential benefit for the townspeople, providing jobs and much needed fertilizer for farming. Yet, for all his humanistic virtues, "he forgets that he's mortal." While he struggles to keep all parties happy, he runs into conflict with the politicians, the townspeople, the workers, his old acquaintances, his family, and himself. As he attempts to live ethically in a world of unethical situations, his existential angst becomes more and more prominent. He requests to be relieved of his assignment and is denied. Finally, after a public (and ideological) show of reconciliation and solidarity with his alienated workers, he is dismissed from the project. The film ends with a suggestion that Bednarz will make an attempt to return to his home and his family, including his new granddaughter.*

On multiple occasions, Kieślowski let it be known that he intensely disliked this film. He told Paul Coates that it is "based on a script with a completely false concept," and he went on to deride it in every category, from the directing to the acting to the editing.[16] He suggested to Annette Insdorf that the pretensions of "socio-realism" bothered him:[17] "it all takes place in factories, workshops and at meetings . . . where socio-realists loved to film, because socio-realism didn't consider private life to be all that important."[18] This quote reveals the growing pains Kieślowski experienced as he moved from documentaries to features, and the theoretical frustrations that plagued that change.

Throughout *The Scar,* it appears that Kieślowski is trying to find his new artistic voice. Some visual experiments (such as jump-cut sequences) are not typical of Kieślowski's oeuvre; other motifs and stylistic patterns return in his later films. Although the film is flawed on a number of levels, those who love Kieślowski's work recognize the seeds of genius that will soon come to fruition.[19] Some moments, despite the technical flaws, succeed quite well as moving drama, lending insight into the plight of many ordinary Poles under communism. However, as in *Personnel,* the context for this film is a given political situation, and we see that Kieślowski's ultimate concern is for the universal questions that every man and woman faces. The protagonist, Bednarz, does not really struggle with the authorities politically as much as he struggles with his ability to do good in the world. At the film's end, after his efforts have clearly failed, he asks the journalist (who has been filming him), "In your view, am I good or bad?" The man replies that the answer is "not so simple." Axiological judgments are beyond the journalist, and, perhaps, beyond all of us, Kieślowski suggests. The metaphysical fatigue takes its toll: "The truth doesn't get you very far," say the workers, and

---

16. *Lucid Dreams: The Film of Krzysztof Kieślowski,* ed. Paul Coates (Trowbridge, Wiltshire, England: Flicks Books, 1999), 165.

17. Socio-realism (a.k.a. socialist realism) was an aesthetic designed to exalt the ideals of the Communist state.

18. Insdorf, *Double Lives,* 39.

19. Coates, *Lucid Dreams,* 69, 165.

the journalist says his uncle physically died of "a weak heart," but really died from "loyalty to an ideal." By the end of that conversation, Bednarz does not declare himself good or bad. He defends himself, yet he admits his conscience is not entirely at peace. "You're tired," the journalist says. "We're all tired," Bednarz replies.

The irony that he constantly confronts is that the objects of his efforts are also the impediments to progress: his fellow citizens, his family, and, above all, himself. Of course, the authorities have created a nightmarishly bureaucratic situation, but the sense throughout the film is one of existential struggle — of one individual in a swirling dilemma he cannot possibly control, despite his title of "director." This is, of course, a double for Kieślowski as director, who sees himself failing at his own documentary project (falling short of capturing reality).

This critique is clear near the beginning of the film, as photographs of poverty in the town of Olecko are used to show how people live, a selective (and deceptive) view of reality presented to Communist officials in hopes of attaining the bid for an enormous factory to be built in the town. In the same meeting, townspeople congregate outside the officials' window, purportedly begging for work (but are, in fact, staged for the bidding effort). This show of Olecko's supposed "reality" is carefully controlled and executed, and journalists (remarkably) are deliberately barred from the meeting. The factory effort is farcical, of course, and Polish audiences, no doubt, think of the Katowice Steel Mill project, an equally bloated, wasteful Communist project of the 1970s, famous for draining the local economy.

The sequence depicting Bednarz's initial whirlwind meeting with the authorities can be faulted for its confusing sequence of images; it is not always clear where Bednarz is or where he is going. This might be seen as an analogue to his spiritual struggle, and the sequence is marked by expressionistic imagery and music in contrast with the documentary realism of the main body of the film. When Bednarz is assigned to Olecko, he pauses, as the revelation clearly carries some emotional weight for him. He whisks through the city in a car, yielding a dizzying, abstract view of the street out the car window, while a disconcerting, ethereal soundtrack plays beneath. The combination of image and sound is remarkable, creating something of the transcendent feel described in Chapter 2. The car arrives at its destination (the meeting of the development board, we presume, where Bednarz's assignment is officially given), and the wide exterior shot of the building suddenly snaps to a bluish tint. The following scene shows the silhouette of a man coming into a dark room and screwing in a lightbulb, illuminating his face. The man is Bednarz, and he has come home. The shot is followed by a view of him entering the living room, exhausted, and taking off his tie. He sits down in a chair, his back to the camera, and throws his head wearily back on the headrest. The faceless gesture has something of universal connotation: "We're all tired."

Although these sequences might be judged confusing and a bit awkward, they reveal stylistic trends and motifs that will characterize Kieślowski's later work. The shot from the car is more than just exposition; it is an expression of mood at a decisive moment in the drama. These shots from cars will find repetition in several later films, particularly the very moving car sequence in *Red,* which is also accompanied by music at a decisive dramatic moment. The shift in colors at the government building seems somewhat forced and pretentious, signaling the passage of time while lending a feeling of foreboding to the sequence, yet cinematographer Sławomir Idziak used these colored filters to more controlled effect and richer suggestion in the later films. The lightbulb motif will return at the end of the film, as the conversation between Bednarz and the journalist becomes "enlightened," as well as in *Red,* as Valentine and the Judge come to understand one another.

Other motifs find new life in the later Kieślowski films. Bednarz's daughter's name is Ewa, which may be translated as "Eve" in English. If the biblical Eve is the mother of all humankind, her namesake in Kieślowski's story finds herself considering an abortion. Women facing the same, desperate situation resurface in *Blind Chance, Decalogue II*, and *Decalogue IV.* In a beautiful scene on a hillside, Bednarz and his daughter see a gorgeous display of lights on another hill. "You even lit up the hillside," Ewa says, remarking on the beauty of the moment. In a distinctly Kieślowskian turn, hinging on beauty inherent in the tragic, Bednarz responds, "That's a cemetery, Ewa." After their conversation turns sour (on the abortion subject), Bednarz is forced to look for Ewa amid the abstract candlelight of the cemetery, glowing like spirits in the place of the dead. This same cemetery/candlelight motif, ringing with spiritual connotation, repeats in Kieślowski's *No End.* The paradoxically beautiful, yet deathly, snow-covered fields in *The Scar* will return, to similar effect, in *White.* Likewise, Bednarz's abandonment of his dog and later retrieval of the pup are directly reprised in *Red,* as is the dominating red backdrop to a most distressing conversation between Bednarz and his wife.

On numerous occasions, Kieślowski remarked about the poverty of the photograph and the cinema, by extension, and this film bears that critique. The exploitive, manipulative powers of the image mark the beginning of the film, as the "suits" manipulate the authorities for the factory contract with photographs. Later, the journalist's interview with Bednarz is filled with fits and starts, as the director desperately tries to tell the truth, but only so much of it as will keep him out of trouble. He attempts to retract the statement "It always works on paper, but the reality is very tough," only to have the cameraman tell him, "This isn't a movie. No second takes." Yet Kieślowski also shows how the photograph can provide a human, relational touchstone, as the journalist finds himself (as a child) in one of Bednarz's old pictures, just as Véronique will discover "herself" in a photograph in *The Double Life of Véronique*. Here, Bednarz is a photographer by hobby, and it is clear that he uses these fragments of the past in a therapeutic way.

Throughout this film Kieślowski undermines the pastoral/natural with societal intrusion. The tree-felling sequence, shot in a jarring, jump-cut sequence (a rare use of the technique for Kieślowski), makes a striking impression, if only for its brutal swiftness. We soon learn that the trees took 200 years to grow. Ever mindful of the natural (a long walking sequence shows him sauntering thoughtfully through a park as well as the town), Bednarz notices a deer poised in a yard, immediately after a helicopter survey of the construction site (which clearly shows the habitat of the deer invaded). Within minutes, the men of the housing committee are feeding it cigarettes.

Although Kieślowski may be called a humanist, true to his dialogical form, the very term *humanist* is interrogated in this film. Bednarz, in his attempt to be a humanist, is hit from all sides. He establishes human contact with the town in the beginning, then he is berated in the end (by party officials for allowing the contact and by workers for not giving them enough). The workers' true demonstration at the end of the film sets up a terrible symmetry with the false demonstration in the beginning, and Bednarz, unable to bridge the gap between government and worker any longer, throws himself into the middle of the crowd. This gesture of solidarity may be noble, but he does so only after he is assured the journalists are gone. It also removes him from any position of power where he might enact the social changes he desires.

Even this early on in Kieślowski's features, we see the impulse to move beyond documenting reality (hence the expressionistic moments), and those ventures into the world of feeling are dramatically placed, a pattern that will intensify in its turn to abstraction and metaphysical themes. Consider the remarkable scene from Bednarz's apartment, as he switches his lamp on and off, alternating his view (and ours) between the outside and his own reflection inside: the cosmos and the existential point of "home." It is also instructive that, later in the film, the desperate crowd of workers pushes so hard on the doors of the factory employment office the glass breaks sheltering the exterior/interior division.

The abstract and semiotic come together in great strength in the film's later images. The shot of a lowly worker carrying the flag up the factory smokestack may be called abstract by our chosen definition, in that the size of the worker and the small splash of color the flag provides contrast heavily with the enormity and blandness of the tower itself. This focus on form serves as a cue for extra attention to this image and, perhaps, wider interpretation. The tilt of the camera further emphasizes the great distance to which the worker aspires, a metaphor for the long, lonely struggle of the Solidarity movement. Given the wider metaphysical context Kieślowski has so clearly established, the metaphor is also suggestive beyond the local politics to a more universal struggle for hope amid oppression, and ethical clarity amid vexing contemporary situations.

The final shot of the film begins with Bednarz trying to teach his new grandchild to walk. This hopeful image redeems a few things. We have since learned that Ewa was pregnant with new life as her father chased her through the cemetery and that she has chosen have this child. Bednarz may have a chance to reconnect with his alienated family and truly return home. The shot tracks backward (one of the very few dolly moves in the entire film), and we, the viewers, step away from the private moment to observe from a distance. In this gesture, there is a sense that Bednarz has finally been left alone — a solitary moment Kieślowski himself would increasingly desire near the end of his life. Yet the camera stops on a divided image: a darkened doorway to the outside world on the left; a bright, cozy but small, isolated (if not claustrophobic) picture of Bednarz and grandchild on the right. This stark division between the dark world of politics and all things public and the isolated-yet-comforting home resonates phenomenologically, even as it semiotically functions as a dialogue, summing up the unresolved, yet all-important conversation threaded throughout the film.

The concept of "home" binds the film together, and it is quickly apparent that the term exceeds its geographical connotations. As is his custom,

Kieślowski dialogues on the subject, asking the question where can we be most human between the two necessary poles of progress and rest? Domicility and exploration? Immanence and Transcendence?

Kieślowski's own struggle for home is reflected in Bednarz; Kieślowski often spoke, at the end of his career, of his guilt at not spending enough time with his family due to his filmmaking. He claimed that he only wanted to live in the country, undisturbed with his family, smoke, and chop wood; however, even as he said these words, even after he retired, he continued to write scripts. In this light, Ewa's words to her father prick the conscience: "You left Mom on her own. Is that any way to live?"

The Japanese director Hiroshi Takahashi, in a tribute to Kieślowski, writes: "Once, during an interview, I asked you [Kieślowski] about the last scene in *The Double Life of Véronique* — why did Véronique stop and touch the old tree when she returned home? And you answered with the question: 'Is the notion of a home important in Japan? Because it's very important to us in Poland.' "[20] Just as the deer is driven from its home, Bednarz finds himself wandering, desperately trying to establish a rootedness in Olecko, a former home, poisoned by memory. While touring the bare apartment that will become his residence, his statement "I'm home now" rings ever so hollow. As he fights, nearly literally, to save the home of one Olecko resident, he hopes to reestablish new homes for his workers (complete with newly tiled bathrooms). Consumed with these issues of permanence amid change, he neglects his own home; his daughter Ewa, clearly a disillusioned, wandering soul, cannot settle on a permanent phone number at which her father can call her. Bednarz's wife refuses to return to Olecko, for all the painful memories, and asserts to her husband that her residence is not "her place" (as Bednarz calls it), but "home."

This theme of metaphysical geography between a place to grow and a place of quiet security illuminates a key image in the middle of the film. Photographs of an astronaut and a globe catch Bednarz's attention. At this moment of great spiritual crisis, between a scene of tension with his daughter and the desperate sight of hundreds of unemployed workers, we see a space traveler. This image, the first of many "ascending" figures in Kieślowski, stands for the search for a new home, even as it looks back, god's-eye, on the residence of all humanity. Within the image lies the

---

20. *We Are What We've Absorbed*, op. cit., 6.

film's central tension: the struggles for transcendence and a nostalgia for immanent rest.

Camera Buff (1979)

SYNOPSIS: *Filip Mosz (Jerzy Stuhr) is an ordinary Pole, working in a factory, who declares himself happy with his new apartment, wife (Małgorzata Ząbkowska), and expected baby daughter. This contentedness slowly dissipates as he films with his new 8 mm camera (purchased for the birth of the child). Filip's boss asks him to document a factory party, and the nuances of the film (particularly the moments that reveal a "behind the scenes" subtext to the event) get him noticed by some film critics. So begins his artistic ascension and personal decline. He devotes more time to cinematography, less time to his family. At the height of his artistic career, the political and social repercussions prove too great for him; friends associated with the somewhat controversial film suffer, and his wife leaves him, unable to cope with Filip's continued absence, temptation to infidelity, and obsession with the cinema. In the final scene, having acutely experienced the double-edged power of the cinema for joy and pain, Filip turns the camera around on himself for the first time and begins a retelling of his story.*

This film is about photography, the cinema, reality, the complex dimensions of existence, and moral decision, but it is also about an ordinary man, an amateur, grappling with a larger existential dimension (note the Polish title of the film — *Amator,* meaning "amateur"). Like *The Scar,* I believe the theme of "home" forms an important foundation for this film, as Filip (a rather comical, sheepish, yet inquisitive fellow) experiences the world beyond his own immediate purview via the camera. Filip discovers the irony that often accompanies personal artistic pursuits: one must pull away from the communal to produce truly personal work, which may then be shared communally. In the end, it is one's artistic product that mediates one's social relations — a hollow substitute for the direct contact of a real marriage, friendship, or conversation.

The "modernist" films of the 1960s and 1970s constantly reminded us of the cinema's artificiality, constructed nature, and selective presentation of the world. *Camera Buff* may be seen in this way, yet it seems to me that Kieślowski is using the cinema as a catalyst for a larger discussion of the human condition. Any of us could be Filip: declared a "good" man by his wife in the beginning of the film, enthralled with the power of discovery (inherent in the cinema) and tempted to infidelity with the "outside" — an unsuccessful balancing act between home and the cosmos. The self must be defined in tension between the internal and the external; "home" mirrors a rootedness, and the cosmos reflects a natural instinct toward discovery. In theological terms, the immanent and transcendent perspective must be equally present. A lack of balance can lead to destruction.

Camera Buff stands in a long tradition of films about filmmaking made by auteurs. Just as Guido mirrors Federico Fellini in *8 ½*, Filip reflects the sympathies and struggles of his maker, Kieślowski. In contrast to Fellini, however, the struggle for fame, fortune, and the perils of the artist are not foregrounded here as much as the classic humility that characterized Kieślowski's attitude toward his work; Filip, the amateur, sheepishly declines the title "artist," much as Kieślowski remarked that the term should be reserved for "certain special people and events" who are "worthy of the name," and excludes himself from that category. Like Bergman, he was willing to accept the more humble title of "artisan," for all its rootedness in culture, practice, and everyday life. His work is not simply of his hands, but also something of his heart, a "giving something of oneself."[21]

Also in the "reflexive" tradition, within these films lies a critique of sorts of photography and cinematography: their powers for joy and pain and their weaknesses, deceptions, and mysteries. The celluloid image lies at the liminal point between reality and perception, exhibiting a verisimilitude and a deceptive appearance of neutrality unrivaled by any other art form.

In this particular contemplation of the documentary filmic form, *Camera Buff* itself adapts the documentary style. The camera angle, more often than not, is low and/or handheld. Abstraction is not immediately obvious. Even so, at high spiritual moments (such as the return from Warsaw on the train and the final, distorted reflected image ending the film) abstraction characterizes the metaphysically laden moments.

The film begins with pastoral sounds under the black-and-white titles, eventually yielding to the striking image of a soaring hawk. In a Kieślowskian turn, this image of natural strength and beauty reveals its underbelly, as the bird swoops down and mangles its prey. We are forced to witness the plucking of the chicken at length, and the hideous sound of the hawk's savage work carries over into the next image, a light turning on in a home and Irka awakening from her nightmare in a sweat with the cry "Oh, Jesus!"

---

21. Coates, *Lucid Dreams,* 163. This is the thrust of Bergman's famous passage on the artisans of the Cathedral of Chartres, *Four Screenplays of Ingmar Bergman* (New York: Simon & Schuster, 1960), xxi–xxii.

In a doubly ironic turn, she announces to Filip that it is time to deliver their child. The pain of childbirth mingles with the joy of a new life in the world. In this film, beauty and joy are often inextricably woven with savagery and pain. Just as we, the viewers, first fancied the vicious hawk beautiful, so Filip's fascination with the pigeons outside the window (in his first film) will ultimately prove destructive.

We are given a view of Filip's tender character as he carries his wife to the hospital, flagging down a ride, then, endearingly, running away from the driver because he is drunk. After this narrow escape, in a side alley Irka reveals a premonition: their child will be a girl. These moments of instinct are worthy of interrogation. Are they natural impulses or some sort of revelation (divine or otherwise)? Throughout Kieślowski's films, there is the nagging sense that our existence is peppered with unexplained phenomena — moments of insight that reveal a partial view of something larger, an ultimate reality where time and space may not be as fixed a matter as we believe.

We arrive at the hospital via a shock, the horrifying sound of a scream that we assume, by association, to be Irka. We are informed, to our conflicted feeling of relief and horror, that the voice belongs not to Irka but to a young girl. Her story, we will never know, and, in this moment Kieślowski pricks our conscience while laying out one of the prominent themes for his films to come: what about the other stories — the narratives that cross and run parallel every day, yet remain undiscovered? One man's relief may be another's nightmare.

Lest we become too burdened with the tragedies, the next sequence shows us the humorous side of Filip, a sincere simpleton in the Charlie Chaplin/Buster Keaton vein. Filip, awaiting news of his wife, gets properly drunk. Amid his comical hiccups, we see more ominous images, such as an empty stretcher being carried into the hospital.

A thematic mirror of *The Scar* emerges: a new apartment, a pregnancy, a man simply trying to live in the world. Stanisław sincerely announces that upon seeing the new apartment and the look of Filip's face as Filip weeps for joy through his drunken stupor, he "now sees what happiness is." He offers Filip a symbolic drink of brotherhood ("Bruderschaft!"), and Filip appears delirious with this newfound joy. Indeed, the idea of true friendship and brotherhood between an overseer and a worker in Communist Poland offers great hope. Sadly, Stanisław will ultimately suffer for their friendship.

117

As Filip tries out his new camera on his friends, the shot ends with something of a revelation itself: the pan across the many smiling faces comes to rest on the television. Fancying himself a cameraman at the televised event, a piano performance, Filip asks for the sound of the TV to be turned up as he gazes at the image through his camera. As in *Personnel,* the touchstone for the ideal of artistic beauty is presented through music (a motif that will recur many times in *Véronique* and *Blue*). Filip remarks, astonished, that the pianist did, indeed, play beautifully, but the viewer is left with a hollow sense that this doubly mediated, black-and-white television image seen through an 8 mm camera, is something terribly distanced from the ideal, as incomplete as the shadows in Plato's cave. Filip's love of those shadows and his pursuit of their real objects form the dramatic spine of this film, a necessary tension bringing great exhilaration, joy, and comfort, as well as emptiness, sorrow, and destruction.

As Filip and Irka view their daughter through a glass window, Filip sees a smile on the infant's face and attempts to film it. A close-up casts doubt on his interpretation of the event (she appears to be crying), and the nurse immediately begins to change her diaper. Filip's camera continues to roll until Irka asks him to stop. "Don't film her naked," she says. "Why?" he asks. "Because she's a girl," she replies. This short little scene provides a number of keys to the interpretation of the rest of the film. First, the ambiguity of appearances will continue to be an issue throughout, often in funny scenarios (such as this one), other times in more somber scenes. Second, the ethics of documentation already pose a problem here: is the photograph a value-neutral zone where reality can be captured and discussed later? Irka's comment suggests there are some things that should never be filmed. Filip ponders this question as he sets his camera down. He will wrestle with the proper role of documentary throughout the rest of the film. What is the line between exploitation and endearing documentary (the naked infant girl and, later, a handicapped factory worker)? The other side of the question emerges soon enough: are there some things that *ought* to be filmed (corruption, lies, poor working conditions, etc.)? As the film moves along, Filip discovers that the axiology of the cinema is every bit as complicated as the ethics of existence, and the same issues may be at stake. It is important to note that Filip's inability to handle the ethics of cinematography is coupled with a personal moral collapse. It is not until the end, when his own self and the celluloid merge, that he begins to sort through the existential pairing of the two realms.

Another important misperception occurs soon after as the camera approaches a hearse parked on the sidewalk next to an apartment building. Irka walks into her own POV (a rupturing of the audience's expectation, a technique discussed in Chapter 2), and exclaims, "Somebody died." This moment rings with great irony, as it is the day of a new birth, and the irony doubles once again when Filip tells her that his friend Piotrek drives the car for his work (a point that will prove significant later, when Piotrek's own mother dies).

The misperceptions of the audience reveal themselves in the next scene. Filip wants to restage the entrance of mother and daughter in his apartment, to which Irka replies, "No. That'll be a bad sign." Not only does this scene refer to religious superstition in Polish life (evident several times throughout the film), but it also condemns the equivalency Filip is already drawing between a cinematic rendering of an event and an actual event. If the filmed reality is a poor substitute for the actual (a mere symbol in Irka's world), the reenactment is, in fact, a doubly bad "sign." The reenactment moves a semiotic step beyond documentation, but suggests it in a manner like Jean Baudrillard's simulacra (a copy without an original).

Kieślowski then jars the audience by coupling the words *bad sign* with an apocalyptic scene: men in ghostly gas masks running at the camera. The semiotic impact is extraordinary, precisely because there is no context given. The horrifying image is bracketed away from the narrative. The moment turns comical (and yields a diegetic explanation) as Filip runs in late to join this cold war–era chemical weapons drill. This shot is reprised in *White*, after the fall of communism.

This pattern of misperception and revelation will become less narratively driven and more formally focused as Kieślowski's career moves on. His interest in the ambiguity of the image will intensify. This strategy, as described in Chapter 2, will prove to be fertile ground for the expression of the metaphysical. As Gilberto Perez has noted of Antonioni, this strategy is a modernist impulse:

> Like other modernist works an Antonioni film designedly disorients us, not to promote confusion but in the recognition that our accustomed ways of making sense are no longer reliable, our received assumptions about the world no longer adequate, and in the attempt to find new bearings amid uncertainty, new ways of apprehending and ordering our experience.[22]

22. Gilberto Perez, "The Point of View of a Stranger: An Essay on Antonioni's *Eclipse*," *Hudson Review* (Summer 1991): 235–262.

"Films. They're the most important," Filip's boss says, attributing the line, significantly, to V. I. Lenin. The appearance of reality for the purpose of persuasion (or mystification) will prove to be the crucial issue in Filip's first assignment with the camera. It is worth noting that, after shaking on this Faustian bargain, the next scene shows a hearse barreling down the road, Filip and Poitrek bouncing around in the cab.

Filip is soon told that there are certain things he should not film, such as the board meeting. In his attempt to shoot some pigeons outside the window, he finds that a little manipulation of the documentary scene goes a long way. The pigeons fly away when he bumps them by hand, and they come back when he places bread out for them. The debate over this sort of manipulation, of course, is as old as documentary itself (the making of Robert Flaherty's *Nanook of the North* being a prime example). Later, when asked about the scene, however, Filip says he was just waiting in the corridor and the pigeons simply flew down for Filip to film. So the half-truth breeds lies. As if to say so, a key moment in the middle of Filip's pigeon reenactment is the sight of a frustrated Irka walking away from the building after multiple futile attempts to talk with him. He views her from the window, and music begins to play. This seemingly nondiegetic accompaniment seems odd in that Kieślowski has shied away from such music in this film. An explanation emerges, however, in the next scene.

Irka, in frustration, smashes the hallway mirror with her hand, and Filip, upon learning of this, romances her. He exudes sympathy for her, but he quickly gives up on all efforts to deal with the root of the problem. Instead, after she refuses to answer his questions, he engages in sexual foreplay as he describes the sight of her previously, how she "appeared so small" from the window, and how he'll always remember the scene. This image, which he describes so cinematically, took place in the middle of his filming activities and solidifies the idea that Filip is beginning to see the world, even his wife, as a picture. The music we heard was, presumably, the soundtrack he imagined in his mind (just as he will seek out music for his new film a few scenes later).[23] In his famous essay on technology, Martin Heidegger describes how technology has created this age of the "world picture,"[24]

---

23. The music also returns on Filip's wistful train ride back from the film festival, as he stares out at the countryside, framing the scene with his fingers in directorial fashion.

24. Martin Heidegger, *The Question Concerning Technology and Other Essays,* trans. William Lovitt (New York: Harper and Row, 1977), 115.

which leads to a certain objectivizing mentality, and for all the pictorial beauty Filip discovers through his camera, it soon becomes clear that the film frame has introduced a certain emotional distance between himself and the lifeworld.

Filip's increasingly camera-bound world conflicts with the necessary concreteness of the haptic. Irka's wounded hand acts as a brutal critique of his touch, even as she describes the pain that intercourse after childbirth will cause her. Even so, she consents, but Kieślowski has fully warned us of the bleak future of the haptic realm in Filip's life. As the film progresses and he seeks physical intimacy (both from his wife and his potential mistress), he finds himself unable to attain it. An unbridgeable emotional divide renders the former impossible, while the telephone (a stale, technological medium) proves the nearest intimacy he ever achieves with the latter (beyond an initial touch of the hand). The theme of the haptic recurs throughout. A particularly interesting example occurs when Filip is filming the baby in a babyseat, the seat slips, and Filip commands Irka, "Don't touch her!" He then, on *his* directorial cue, films Irka picking up the child and pronounces the scene "beautiful." Irka's barbed response says it all: "If she'd fall off the balcony, would you continue to film her?" At the end of the film, in his yearning recitation of his own story, Filip emphasizes this lost haptic dimension in his life, describing the sweat of Irka's childbearing and how he carried her almost the whole way to the hospital.

This lack of a haptic anchor to reality is paired with Filip's status as an orphan, a genealogical rootlessness. This may also explain his passion for the camera and his fascination with its revelatory power. Stanisław (a.k.a. Staś) warns Filip about the dangers of a focused passion:

STAŚ: I had a brother-in-law who suddenly at thirty believed in God. . . . He came to a bad end. He became a priest.

FILIP: But you've got your stamps. Everyone's got something.

STAŚ: I've only got stamps. I've nothing else.

This dialogue reflects Kieślowski's own distrust of organized religion while, at the same time, acknowledging humankind's need for meaning. This impulse is channeled through stamp collecting, in Staś's case, a prefiguration of the stamp collector of *Decalogue VIII* and *X*.

Through his film's entry in a film competition, Filip makes the acquaintance of two important figures in his life, Anna (of the Filmmakers Federation) and television producer Andrzej Jurga (playing himself). These new acquaintances catalyze some important developments in Filip's new world. Anna praises Filip's film as "proof of the director's ability to observe," yet refuses to allow him to do anything *but* observe her, a certain impotence born of the camera. As he pursues an affair with her, she entertains his affections but does not permit him to access her (beyond an initial kiss and affectionate touch of the hand); she is called "the Amateur," she reveals, because she has never been able to be attached to anyone or anything (the other meaning of the Polish word *amator,* is "lover"). Her life runs counter to Staś's advice. One must not become obsessed, left only with stamps, yet neither should one be as unfocused as Anna, with multiple lovers but no love. Anna wishes Filip to pursue his filmmaking (despite her privately judging his work as "poor"), and this contrasts with his wife, Irka, who wishes that Filip would not win the film competition and so give up his new hobby.

Jurga, on the other hand, gives Filip a more appropriate channel for his passion via another mode of observation. During his speech on the judges' panel, he chides all the entrants of the competition for observing with a newslike quality — documenting events, not searching out personal meanings. He invites amateurs to flee the news model and pursue intimate stories in the auteurist vein, "films that will be your films . . . about what you think, what you feel about your colleagues . . . who really work hard, so that you have enough to eat." This will prove to be Filip's inspiration — to dig into the nuances of people's lives (consonant with Kieślowski's film school thesis) — as well as his disenchantment (just as Kieślowski grew frustrated with the unattainable ambitions documentary instills).

The director of Filip's plant invites him over to his home for a celebration of the third-place festival award. The director, seizing the role of producer, takes the diploma for himself (so much for Jurga's idealism), and Filip appears powerless to resist (though his contempt is evident, a mark of his new, auteurist instincts and newfound personal confidence). Then, lest we demonize the director too quickly, Kieślowski gives us a remarkable little scene, seemingly extraneous to the plot, where the director gives Filip a tour of his garden. We see that the man also has a human side, filled with a love for his children (the first of which he has tragically lost) and a passion for gardening as memorial to his family. Filip once told Staś, "We all have something" and, clearly, the director's garden is that something — that repository of emotion and personal meaning. Filip's repository is becoming the cinema, but he will soon realize that the medium is unwieldy, so large and far-reaching that it cannot be controlled. The director's tour of the trees (planted in memory of his children) is interrupted by Staś, handing out congratulatory drinks and announcing, "Like buyer, like moviemaker." She is referencing the fact that both are caring fathers, but Kieślowski's implication is wider: Filip must take caution that he not fall prey to the uncaring temptation to power the director represents. Ironically, Filip's next film will be the cause for Staś's dismissal from the factory.

The crisis point with Irka arrives here, on the threshold of Filip's surge into the professional filmmaking world. In the midst of an argument, Irka recalls Filip's description of a film scene in which a woman throws things at a man, the moment when Filip discovered the power of implied action through editing. The action here is anything but implied as she hurls diapers at him, angrily screaming, "Is this how it is like in the cinema?" Enraged, she rubs a dirty diaper in his face, a haptic awakening to the real world. At this point of emotional breakdown, Filip regains his composure and tenderly tries to explain his newfound passion to her:

> FILIP: It started by itself... all this may be more important than peace and quiet... man needs something... I need something more than peace and quiet... and this may be even more important than a home.
>
> IRKA: But what?
>
> FILIP: I don't know what, but it may be more important.

The step is now complete; the door that Bednarz was content to leave closed at the end of *The Scar* now carries Filip into the wider, invigorating, yet more dangerous world. Here, for the first time, the spiritual hunger is laid out in full view. It is not the camera that will satisfy Filip's yearning. Rather, the camera has laid bare that spiritual desire.

The spiritual vacuum, according to Kieślowski, is larger than that which the organized church can remedy. Piotrek's mother's funeral bears all the religious trappings in full view: the priests, the vestments, the casket, the crucifix. All stand quiet, static, and impotent. In the final shot of the scene, a priest stands in the foreground, hands clasped and static, while uniformed officers smoke in the background, sitting on headstones. No one can offer comfort. The critique of religion seals tighter in the next scene, when Piotrek asks Filip to show him the film. Irka, upon hearing that Piotrek wants to view the film, bursts into tears. The paradox emerges: life and death coexist in the camera, an idea I will discuss in more detail in Chaper 5. The hollow life of the cinema is accentuated in the close-up shot of the film, spinning around the projection reel, its circling as endless as the spiritual questions with which Piotrek is plagued. Even so, he finds comfort in this death mask, as he says to Filip: "What you're doing is beautiful. Somebody is dead, but still here."

Filip attends a screening of Zanussi's *Camouflage*. The central theme of *Camouflage* is a man's principles, and whether he should bend them; a principled, traditionally romantic, and idealistic young professor spars with another professor, a Darwinian pragmatist who continually baits him through confrontational rhetoric and challenging ethical situations of his own malicious design. Though not obvious to the viewer unfamiliar with Zanussi's work, the lengthy scene from *Camouflage* shown in this film bears striking parallel to Filip's situation. The two professors (Jakub, the mischievous pragmatist, not unlike his deceiving biblical namesake, and Jarosław, the idealist) discuss their respective votes in an academic paper competition. Jarosław chides Jakub for lacking the principle to vote against a mediocre paper, a clear contrast with Jurga in Filip's film competition. Jakub talks about his own cyncism and challenges Jarosław to specifically critique his pragamatic approach to life — a challenge Jarosław declines. The main tension in the film, later, centers around the overweight rector of the academic institute, an autocrat not unlike Filip's boss. As a mirror of Filip's own life, he must choose: will he be a Jakub, or will he be a Jarosław? Just as Jarosław's animal instincts do eventually emerge (in a fit of rage against Jakub at the end of *Camouflage*), the tensions in Filip's life will, eventually, rupture.

Filip undoubtedly sees patterns of his own existential situation in the film and senses an affinity with Zanussi as he speaks after the screening of the film. Zanussi (playing himself) talks about the quest for the universal mold of a man: the figure that is the true "everyman," desired yet unattainable. He portrays flawed figures and broken situations where the honest man does not receive any more consideration or chances than he does in real life, precisely because that *is* the real situation. When asked if artistic conviction of truth suffices in the creation of a work, Zanussi responds that our "eternal drama" lies in that question and its related problems: the necessity of truth (and its artistic pursuit), and the inability to test whether that truth is correct or not, wise or foolish, just or unjust. Zanussi claims that an artistic strength can be made out of this agnosticism, precisely by using the cinema to "say something more, in a different way . . . more tellingly, more aptly."

The cinema as an existential interrogation, a dialectical arena thriving on its presentation of the questions rather than any answering of them, will prove to be a hard lesson for Filip to learn. Indeed, it provides the basic structure for most of Kieślowski's early films as well. Nevertheless, inspired by this speech, we see Filip venturing into the larger world, ordering copies of the magazines *Film* and *Politics.* The next customer buys razors, a pedestrian object, indicating something of the social drift Filip has undergone. Later, he's seen reading the newspaper *Kultura,* meaning "culture," a Paris-based publication that was one of the few Western European periodicals permitted in the country, functioning similarly to Radio Free Europe. The parallels with Kieślowski's career here are obvious, and, for a moment, we are given the impression that the turbulence in Filip's life may be settling down. He comes home, enjoys a loving, intimate evening with his wife, and begins the shooting of his next film, the story of the crippled worker. Filip's film is something of an idolization of the man: his courage to overcome obstacles and his happiness within his simple life. All that is exalted in the film is something that Filip has lost, though he seems scarcely aware of it.

Filip makes some efforts to integrate Irka into his new world, specifically through his persistent requests that she attend the meetings with Zanussi during the filmmaker's visit to Filip's film club. She blames her absence on the child, whom Filip suggests could be cared for by a family member that day. She does not reply. The absence of the child at this point is most pronounced. Essentially, his films have become his children, and Irka has begun to give up any hope that Filip will interact with little Irenka outside of the camera. This point becomes sharper a few scenes later, after Irka's departure, when Filip's friend Witek says, "She's cute!" of the new 16 mm camera Filip lovingly holds.

On the trip to meet with Warsaw TV, we are given a view from the train rendered abstract by an intervening window. This moment of abstraction is one of the few in the film, and it gleams with Transcendent impulse. Yet this romantic image is quickly shut down by Filip's boss, who accompanies him on the train.

Filip finds himself in the situation where, in order to accept the new assignment from Warsaw TV, he must use the 16 mm camera his boss at the plant provides. This arrangement becomes more complicated when his film reveals a financial impropriety. We might see this as a scandal uncovered, but Kieślowski problematizes this judgment. The money in question, earmarked for improvements to a bank building, is diverted, without authorization, to renovate and build other structures, such as a slaughterhouse and kindergarten. This is not an exposure of corruption but a broken system shown in all its uselessness. Those within the system (however well-meaning) suffer when the truth is revealed.

Filip pursues his filmmaking ambitions in a more spirited, free way when he and Witek dash out on an excursion to another town and make a film about the trip. The director had specifically insisted on coming along, but Filip and his friend duck out on a night bus without him. This highly romantic gesture is not rewarded by Kieślowski; that film is judged indulgent by Jurga later. Perhaps because of this failure, Filip declines the title "artist," when he is offered it by the head of Warsaw TV (a mirror of Kieślowski's own declination of the title). It is also a warning from Kieślowski away from the idealized, romantic view of the artist, who'd champion free vision over a responsibility to the real.

Filip returns home to find Irka moving out. In addition, she makes the jarring declaration that she is five months' pregnant, from the last time they made love. He exclaims that he finally "knows what this is all about," what he is "living for," and cannot understand her departure at this crucial moment. She calmly explains that she seeks peace and quiet, just as Filip did in the beginning. He cannot countenance this, accusing her of not loving him, to which she replies, in a devastating line: "That would be the easiest." As she walks away, Filip cannot help but frame her with his fingers, a dramatic refiguring of his personal life, executed by his alter ego, the filmmaker. This funny, yet tragic moment reveals something of Bergman, who consistently brought up the parasitic nature of art; one thinks of the protagonist in *Through a Glass Darkly,* who is tempted to incorporate his observations of his daughter's mental breakdown into his latest work.

Almost immediately, however, Kieślowski shows how meaningful this parasitic image can be. Another touching moment comes when Filip is teaching Witek some film-editing techniques, using footage of his daughter. Clearly moved by the images, granted access to his daughter only through the cinema, Filip tells Witek: "When editing, you must remember when a person is far off, and then close up he must be facing the same way." The question lingers: is Filip facing the same direction, ultimately, as he was when he was "close" to his loved ones? Clearly not.

Soon, even the professional world starts to crumble for Filip. Upon learning that Staś will be dismissed, Filip cries, in a zealous manner, that he should suffer the consequences of his actions (as his film is the catalyst for Staś's dismissal). The boss assures him that it is not that simple; he will stay on, and others, who are more expendable, will be let go. Kieślowski paints Filip as a zealous crusader for truth, but it is not clear that he is in the right. As Zanussi stated earlier in the film, passion is not enough; we must have a criterion for determining whether the artist is right, and that criteria is nearly impossible to find. Staś's judgment is more direct. He tells Filip not to worry about his firing, but rather to brace himself for further suffering. He implores him:

> You must go on regardless. If you feel you're right, everything else isn't important. You'll never know who you're helping. Who'll take advantage of it. Against whom you're working.... You'll help some, harm others.... Something good was born in you, keep on with it.

This encouragement is not enough for the vexed Filip, who exposes the film of the brickworks and cries, half angrily and half imploringly, for Witek to go after the ruined film he has thrown down the street. Torn apart by the choice, he emits another insecure hiccup, a comic reminder of the old Filip, at this tragic moment. The hiccups, a mark of nervousness and self-doubt, come before his child is born and before the film competition, and return, finally, at the very end, as his doubts return.

The pilgrimage of the amateur has run from naive to personal confidence and understanding. The difficulty, Filip has discovered, lies in the perils of knowledge: a tendency toward bitter cynicism, coupled with a destructive addiction to the experience of discovery. Who can blame Filip for wanting to know more, for reveling in the fact that he's discovered something bigger, more important? Yet at the same time, who can blame his wife for leaving him, raising their child on her own, betrayed by a shadow of the man she married? Most unsettling is the fact that neither discover absolute answers to their problems.

The final scene shows a disheveled Filip in his neglected apartment, unable to remember the day he is living in (in every sense of the phrase), dumping spoiled milk (a death image) down the sink. He loads his camera and points it toward the window, the objective "outside," then turns it around on himself. His distorted, abstract reflection in the lens, warped in spiritual anguish, contrasts with the cold, technological rigidity of the camera. It stares at Filip hollowly, impassively, and hauntingly. In many respects, its apparent neutrality is its most terrifying feature, similar to the computer at the end of *Decalogue I,* blinking "I am ready." The camera is as much an empty hole as it is a reflection — a duality inherent in the cinema itself, both reflecting and impoverished. Kieślowski adds another dimension to this interpretation in *I'm So-So,* stating that Filip has realized, here at the end of things, that he can only portray reality through himself.[25]

We are given here a POV shot unlike any in the entire film: a POV divorced from Filip himself. The cold camera eye is our own, as Filip stares at us, reciting his tale from the beginning (the story we have witnessed). This confessional moment carries a labyrinth of connections — a nexus of different relationships, both diegetic and nondiegetic — between Filip and his narrative, the camera and Filip, Filip and us, our viewership and the camera, and, ultimately, Filip's narrative and our own. The question Filip asks us, implied in the narrative he recites, is, "Where did I go wrong?" This axiological query penetrates us as passive viewers, now called upon to make an existential decision we cannot possibly make, but must face.

Blind Chance (1981)

SYNOPSIS: *This film is about one man and the two other men he might have been, had a few small coincidences been different. The imaginative framework Kieślowski uses (seventeen years before Peter Howitt copied it in his 1998 film* Sliding Doors*), consists of Witek (Bogusław Linda) running to catch a train. In the first scenario (half the film), he catches it. The second scenario portrays him missing it, accidentally smashing into a policeman, and getting arrested for the ensuing disturbance. The third shows him missing the train, but, by chance, meeting his old love on the same train platform. The resultant Witeks, respectively, include a Communist, an underground resistance leader, and an ordinary, professional Pole attempting to avoid controversy and politics altogether. This third scenario is, in fact, the "actual" scenario, in that its conclusion is foreshadowed in the very first scene of the film where Witek screams* "No!," *and a sequence follows, illustrating scenes from his childhood. In the final scene of the film, Witek is revealed to be on an airplane that explodes in midair.*

I mentioned, in my remarks about *Camera Buff,* how a lack of balance can lead to destruction. It seems, in this film, that Kieślowski is showing that such pat phrases are not automatic recipes for success either. In fact, the unwieldy factors of fate and chance loom larger than any self-help directives. The tension between the principled life and the pragmatist viewpoint (articulated in the clip from Zanussi's *Camouflage* and *Camera Buff*) continues

---

25. *Krzysztof Kieślowski: I'm So-So* (dir. Krzysztof Wierzbicki, Home Film Festival, 1995).

as a theme here but under a much darker existential cloud. One reading of the film may be the futility of principles and a Camus-like indictment of the man who avoids an existential choice. Yet Kieślowski's own take on the film is that of an essential man (maintaining that Witek is essentially the same person) engaging the same principles in each scenario (despite his widely varying political allegiances, or lack of them). In this light, one may read the film as a more humanist project, asserting the holistic and essential nature of the person and pushing the metaphysical search for universals forward, albeit with a pessimistic air.

The narrative structure is somewhat unique, a three-stranded exploration of possibility. The visuals also tend to be more adventurous, in line with the strategic use of bracketing already discussed. Also in harmony with this Husserlian concept, there are certain expository elements that remain ambiguous at first (characters, motivations, relationships between characters, etc.). That is not to say that, at this early stage in his career, Kieślowski explicitly intended a transcendental suggestion, but it does show that he was often willing to sacrifice narrative clarity in favor of other factors.

This film stands as one of Kieślowski's most philosophically complex efforts: the by-product of disillusion and great upheaval in his homeland. A turbulence in his own personal convictions appears to be present as well, as evidenced by the films of this period. Synchronous with this philosophical transition, there is a stylistic move in this film that, from the very outset, contrasts strongly with the realist, documentary aesthetic of *Camera Buff.* This is a transitional work in every sense, in its new formal emphases and expanded concern beyond local political issues.

This film and *No End* (1984) are the darkest of Kieślowski's oeuvre, and it is no coincidence that they both deal heavily with ghostlike reflections on memory as a means of assessing a tragic and turbulent present. Identity, whether it be that of a person or an entire nation, is the first foundation imperiled in a time of great transition, and the efficacy of history (and, by extension, memory) remains the only hope for healing or comfort. The great paradox is that during times of transition, present existential circumstance calls that very efficacy into question: you do not know as a nation or an individual who you will be on the other side of the unstable present. To my mind, *Blind Chance* speaks to the crisis of identity as strongly as any other theme, offering up suggestions of human essence and running it, dialectically, against powers greater than the individual.

Considering the realistic mode of Kieślowski's previous films, the beginning of this one is audacious. A man, whom we will quickly identify as Witek, sits in close-up before the camera. His blank expression is difficult to discern, though it quickly moves to something like anger (or is it fear? or both?), and the man screams, "No!" as the camera dollies into his mouth. As tragic music sweeps in, joining the ongoing screams, the titles come up in the midst of this black hole that was the vestige of a man. There is no denying the power of this camera move and its suggestive function: Kieślowski will take us on an interior journey, and the view may be very, very dark. Kieślowski, quite literally, marked this film as his shift from the outside world of documentaries to the inner world.[26]

So, from the very first frame, Kieślowski has delineated his new stylistic territory. This moment of diegetic crisis demands a formal means of expression; the next sequence is as formal as anything Kieślowski will do, and it lays out some of the territory he will retraverse in later films. We are presented first with a strange, canted frame with an object blocking it.

Fig. 46. From the opening of
Blind Chance.

As discussed in Chapter 2, this is the sort of ambiguous image that will continue to fascinate Kieślowski, the powers of which he uses to great effect later. Faced with the difficulty of the image, we must reckon with it in more formal terms, bracketing our attitude of expectation and yielding to the dynamic forces at work. The music cues us to its tragic connotation, and, as the obstructing object falls, the camera rights itself: the object was indeed a bloodied leg, and we guess we are in a hospital, as a body is hurriedly dragged past us, leaving an abstract stripe of crimson along the floor. As a doctor approaches, we appear to have taken the POV of an injured person in the hall, and the leg belongs to us. This alienation from

---

26. Stok, *Kieślowski on Kieślowski,* 113.

our body matches the experience of semiconsciousness, and Kieślowski has masterfully structured the viewing experience to accentuate that alienated feeling. So the abstract powers are twofold here through strategies of epistemological and ontological ambiguity. The cue for the latter, the POV, is that of the eyeline, made manifest when the image rights itself (a suggestion of a moving head).

It does not seem that the leg could be ours, however, if we are the man in the first shot (who is, we will shortly discover, Witek, the protagonist). The leg appears feminine, and the shredded tatters of clothing on it appear to be something like panty hose. All the same, this ambiguity and disorientation persist in the next frame with the close-up of a young boy; the camera tilts to reveal the image to be that of a mirror — a reflection of "ourselves." The camera continues to "our" hand writing mathematical problems in a notebook, which seems *not* to be our hand due to its perpendicular angle. No sooner have we surmised that our identity is not that of the boy, but that of the detached observer, when the father of the boy looks up, directly at the camera, and speaks to "us" about how our "mother" once wrote her 8s in a similar way.

This tumultuous identity shifting only persists as we are next presented with a highly stylized wide shot (Fig. 47). A large, empty hill leads to the top of the frame, where a lone car (in silhouette) stands next to a barren tree. This opening shot is, in many ways, the complement to a similar scene in the beginning of *Blue* (Fig. 48). Both hold the same pictorial elements (earth, sky, car, and tree), and both appear at important, establishing moments near the beginnings of their respective films. The difference, a tracing of Kieślowski's evolving concerns, is that the predominant factor here is earth, a hillside that the characters entering the shot must traverse and ascend.

Figs. 47–48. Wide shots from *Blind Chance* and *Blue,* respectively.

The picture in *Blue* emphasizes sky (or overemphasizes it, compositionally speaking), suggesting the metaphysical beyond and its immensity (and the tragic, unanswered question of the problem of evil).

The style of the composition in *Blind Chance* suggests our position as passive observer, only to be ruptured as one of the two figures ascending the hill runs back at the call of an off-screen voice (our own?). The boy comes to rest and converses with the character at the far right of the frame, an ambiguous position complemented by ambiguous eyelines: not quite off-screen, not quite POV. This child (Daniel) will return as a man later in the film, as will many of the other characters we see in this sequence. The reappearance of characters, as their paths coincidentally cross, becomes a defining theme in Kieślowski's later works.

The series of hands in close-up continues. A child's hand (our own?) prowls along a window, peeking in on one of those typical Kieślowskian meetings of the bureaucracy, where the lives of named workers rise and fall by committee. The boy at the window catches his father's attention, and it is important to note that the father is considerably younger than two shots ago. It demonstrates the chronological collapse of memory. He is thinking of his father, recently deceased, while also thinking of his childhood.

A girl, set up against the sky, looks down on the camera while she walks; an arm extends (again, our own?), taking her hand and helping her down to camera level. As she happily descends, our POV becomes objective; the arm belongs to a young Witek, who kisses this young girl (who will appear again). Cut against a shot of a corpse being sliced open, the audience is not only assaulted with the Freudian connection between sex and death, but we must wonder if we have returned to the blood-stained halls of the hospital in shot number 2. We realize we are wrong as the camera follows a woman in a white coat (clearly a medical student), then stops on Witek's face as he watches her. Their ensuing conversation reveals that the woman knew the cadaver as her elementary school teacher (whom, significantly, she loathed) and that Witek used to be this woman's lover. Like the first woman, she will reappear. What will also reappear is this strong connection Kieślowski makes between fate and moral action; the circumstance of the teacher's death has refigured the woman's feelings toward her. The issue of guilt is clearly present (she regrets her hatred of the woman now that she faces her corpse). In a strange bit of Kieślowskian synchrony, Peter Keough (of the *Boston Phoenix*) reports that as Kieślowski was filming this autopsy scene, his mother was undergoing one, having been killed that day in a tragic car accident.[27]

A conversation with Witek's father follows in which he demonstrates his heartlessness (confessing his annoyance at his son's good grades), while also laying out a theme of the film: he suggests that rebellion against the establishment is a virtue he prizes. A hollow, snowy television flickers in the background, a useless technology of communication, an image of alienation (complemented by the working but equally ineffective televisions in *Decalogue I* and *Blue*). Witek is revealed in this same shot to be a young man, and he meets his father's nurse, only to find his father making love to her in the next shot. A matched action cut links the father's sexual touching with that of Witek initiating sex with the medical student. He halts their passionate moment to make a phone call to his father ("Why do you keep phoning and not saying anything?" she asks). During this call, however, he announces himself, only to hear his father declare he is going to the hospital and that Witek is "under no obligation." "To do what?" Witek desperately implores. "To do anything," is the haunting reply. This polysemous phrase will prove key to the film in that every scenario will exhibit a different interpretation of it. Insdorf insightfully remarks that this phrase ironically spurs Witek to action.[28] The next shot shows Witek at the train yards, mourning his dead father in the darkness, mistaken for a drunk by a passing policeman ("Are you pissing or throwing up?"). The next scene shows Witek talking with a doctor friend, discussing how his father's deathbed thoughts made him rethink his chosen career as a doctor. He then rushes to catch the train that will define his existence.

With each dash for the train, certain elements persist. The image of the coin is most interesting, an image of fortune that will reprise in later Kieślowski films, most notably *White* and *Red*. The finder of the coin purchases beer with it, and Witek's trajectory with this man makes a difference in his ability to catch the train.

It is important to note that, apart from some musical cues, there is a seamless slippage from the opening flashbacks into the flow of the diegetic "present." Despite the fact that the entire film can be seen as a variety of flashbacks, the foundational story of the film really begins with the death of

---

27. Peter Keough, "*Red* Giant: Is Krzysztof Kieślowski the greatest living director?" *Boston Phoenix,* January 20, 1995, 6.

28. Insdorf, *Double Lives,* 59.

the father and Witek's subsequent race to catch the train. The conflation of time and space, ambiguity of identity, and general dislocation of the film's opening seven minutes function as an expression of psychological trauma: a man rethinks his life, memory being a sort of bifurcation of time[29] or a set of haunting ghosts screaming, "What if all had been different?"[30] In light of Kieślowski's career, however, it can also be seen as a move toward metaphysical questioning that will eventually lead to explorations of transcendence in other films. Even here, the ambiguity of identity recalls a sort of *geist*-like presence — a swirling consciousness that will become more personified in Kieślowski's next film, *No End,* and more pervasive stylistically in the films after *The Decalogue.*

This film is a microcosm of Kieślowski's stylistic transition. The surreality of the opening sequence yields to a certain documentary quality (very like *Camera Buff*) for most of the film's remainder. However, at critical diegetic moments, the film is spiked with stylized compositions: the handheld camera often gives way to a tripod shot, the angle of view typically moves lower, away from eye level, and the frame sometimes becomes carefully composed (and often divided) between foreground and background elements (with one or the other in abstract shallow focus). In the most general sense, one may call these shots abstract, but accuracy demands that we see these as steps toward abstraction — an exploration of the formal possibilities of the film for metaphysical suggestion. In this film, metaphysics does not necessarily synchronize with these images, but the images do appear at crucial narrative moments that often carry spiritual import.

Scenario 1. Here Witek catches the train and so initiates a series of events that will lead to his membership in the Communist Party. Yet it is important to realize that Witek transcends the political brand. He is shown to be a man of compassion, offering to help a prisoner escape, who, like Camus's "Guest," chooses not to do so. Werner remarks that "some people don't escape. They don't want to," a telling insight from this anti-Communist leader who had suffered in prison, accused of spying against the government.

29. A hallmark feature of Gilles Deleuze's *Cinema 2: The Time-Image* (Minneapolis: University of Minnesota Press, 1989), 98. Although I do not read Kieślowski's film as a Deleuzean interrogation of the filmic form, his approach to time and memory does show a slippage between actual and virtual times that lends itself to Deleuzean interpretation (as Emma Wilson has shown).

30. Slavoj Žižek, *The Fright of Real Tears: Krzysztof Kieślowski between Theory and Post-Theory* (London: British Film Institute, 2001), 79–80.

Witek is given the choice to lead a particular type of life in each scenario, and he perceives the choices as his own, but the overarching sense is that his path is a product of causes and effects quite beyond his control, hinging on moments never perceived as liminal. Yet Kieślowski once remarked that the point of the film is that Witek remains fundamentally the same person, carrying essentially the same values (regardless of which political direction from which he chooses to approach them), offering a measure of agency to the characters beyond historical determinism. The dialectical structure that characterizes so much of Kieślowski's work emerges here as well, in the tension between chance, human agency, social effect, and destiny.

We see Kieślowski interrogating these factors through the characters Witek encounters. We are given the strong impression that Adam (Zbigniew Zapasiewicz) and Werner (Tadeusz Łomnicki), political antipodes, are products of chance and in other circumstances could very well have held different political views. As a foreboding cigarette smolders in the background, Czuszka (Bogusława Pawelec) reveals she has had three abortions in her life (one of them, at least, a harrowing experience), and one perceives that ethical choices have shaped her life as much as any twist of fate beyond her control. Olga, having made a choice to hate her teacher as a child, finds the scales of justice tipped against her as she becomes witness to the excavation of the old woman's body.

The reflection of Kieślowski's burgeoning political disillusionment is most clearly seen in the character of Werner, however. Our first introduction to him shows a drunk man, one who has suffered and lost a great deal. Werner is a man who cannot run after trains anymore, as the rest of his life appears set before him. Werner breaks the milk bottle on the floor, reminiscent of the spilled milk in *Decalogue V,* an image of vital resources wasted. Later, he says, "If we haven't done things right, maybe your generation will. You, for instance. . . . " In contrast to Werner is Adam, the Communist pragmatist who will exert his influence on Witek in this phase of the film. He lectures his listeners on his journey for an ideal. He compares the political ideal (that "the world can be ordered in a more just or better way") to both a hopeful beacon and a drug, whose initial effect is exhilarating, only to turn sour later. In the end, Werner confesses that the beacon is considerably less dim for him (consonant with the depression among activists in this era), but without this hope and bitterness, life is a sorry thing. In sum, Kieślowski and Werner both testify to the frustration and agony of ideals unrealized yet necessary. Despite Kieślowski's lack of political zeal in this film, the government still chose to ban it for Polish audiences. Apparently the film struck a little too close to the bone, employing all sorts of current events in its plot (the "Flying University," political protests, strikes, etc.).

The scene of Witek emulating Werner shaving in his bathroom postulates a clear connection between the two: will Witek follow in Werner's footsteps? Or will he follow Adam, the Communist pragmatist, played by Zbigniew Zapasiewicz, who played a similarly Machiavellian character in Zanussi's *Camouflage*. He will return to Kieślowski's screen as the State Police Inspector in *Decalogue VI*.

At the very time when Werner meets his first love in the park, Witek meets Czuszka, his own first love. These sorts of coincidences will become foundational for Kieślowski's later films. They showcase the very moments we see as meaningful, and often center on love or death or suffering. The significance of these moments hinges on their appearance of purpose. Are they random occurrences or teleological efforts from beyond? Kieślowski does not attempt to solve this problem, but our human investment in these moments fascinates him.

At the end of the institution scene, where Witek is the party member chosen to mediate a political protest, Witek shouts, "Besides, they're in the right!" to his superior over the phone. His effort to be an ethical party member is running into obstruction at every turn. After his release, Adam refigures this moment of weakness as a great pragmatic strategy for overcoming the situation. Witek dispels this notion, affirming that the rebels truly were in the right. "Never concede a case unless there's a percentage in it," Adam advises. "I was trying to be fair," he responds, but Adam indicates that fairness is not something easily distributed in a public capacity (recalling the speech of the director near the end of *Camera Buff*). At this point he meets Krystyna, Werner's love, stolen by his former cellmate, Adam (of whom Werner has remarked, in a loaded statement, he "doesn't see well and refuses to get glasses").

A discussion of Werner ensues, during which Adam remarks that, had Werner been released earlier, they'd be in each other's shoes. This aleatoric teleology does not sit well with Witek, who affirms the importance of personal character in determining one's existential position. Adam twists the discussion skillfully, affirming that personal ideals do, in fact, persist, even when political movements have their inevitable periods of error. He affirms the Communist Party's ideals, despite its errors (which include his and Werner's imprisonment), just as people "went to the stake, still believing in

God" during the Inquisition. He argues that Werner's leg problems (from a prison beating) kept him from doing leg exercises, implying that his entire political future would have been changed in light of the benefits of regular activity. In Adam's view, personal suffering and existential situation precede any sort of essence.

Witek's unstable position within the party spills over into his relationship with Czuszka, which continues despite the bitterness of their last encounter (a searing rebuke for his party membership in the form of a cigarette burn). The road Witek sees before him, the role he is increasingly taking on for himself, is that of a redeemer: of his own childhood, his own lost ambitions, his party, and Czuszka herself. His ability to redeem, however, will quickly be called into question — swallowed up by political pressure and circumstance.

At this moment of spiritual crisis, Witek's glass spills on the ground when he gets drunk. The abstract nature of the close-up signals the moment's significance dramatically and sets the metaphysical atmosphere for the revelations to come in the scene. This image of emptying also stands as a metaphor for the confessional release of his inner world to Czuszka: his defenses down, he tells Czuszka everything; how his father was arrested in Poznań on June 26, 1956, and how that very night his mother gave birth to Witek and his twin. "I was born first. That's why I'm alive," he asserts in a vein similar to that of Adam's determinism (we assume his brother was born weaker and died). The death of the twin and Witek's claim of a "second sight" (a memory of his birth, "like an image printed behind my eyelids") prefigure the themes in *The Double Life of Véronique*. Witek's claim of extraordinary vision gains dramatic power as the sound of a siren anticipates the next shot, a curious return to the initial abstract scene in the hospital, leg in the foreground, a dragged body striping blood on the tiled floor. Birth and death are linked by supernatural vision and conveyed as deeply embedded intuition.

This is a vexing moment, diegetically, as it seems this scene should belong to the final scenario of the film, when Witek dies. As with many Kieślowskian metaphors, several interpretations of this sequence are plausible and not exclusive, but aggregate. They all combine to form a multidimensional zone of meaning. The first possibility is that Witek is given a premonition of his potential end, as he will be scheduled on a doomed flight to Paris.

The second interpretation is broader than the first: Witek was born on the night of the Poznań massacre (see Chapter 1). This event was the beginning of the crisis defining modern Poland, and so, Witek represents modern Poland metaphorically. A memory of his birth is a memory of the death of that night, and Kieślowski uses the hospital image to draw out this historical symmetry. In the next scenario Witek will strengthen this metaphorical suggestion by reciting his lineage, each of his forebears having fought in a defining military conflict in Polish history.

A third, complementary possibility is that Witek is given a sort of intuition of his other self, much as Véronique perceives her other self, Weronika, at the moment of her passing and has always felt "watched" throughout her life. These doubles in Kieślowski's films are portrayed as ontologically real connections between people, but Kieślowski traces the essence of these connections to the metaphysical realm. This is the same realm where "possibility" may lie, as only a divine mind would possess what theologians call "middle knowledge," apprehension of all possible worlds as well as the actual. From a temporal perspective our limited minds are always haunted by possibility. It is true that, nonreligious, postmodern fictions (e.g., Jorge Luis Borges' *Garden of Forking Paths*) root these possibilities in immanent ground, running like innumerable tributaries from the founts of subjectivity, polysemy, and virtuality. Likewise, one might be tempted to conceive this film as the converse of Luis Buñuel's *That Obscure Object of Desire,* where two actresses play one woman. Deleuze describes this strategy as a welcome departure from Buñuel's previous "naturalist cosmology" into a "plurality of simultaneous worlds."[31] However, Kieślowski's project seems wholly modern and fully "naturalist," lamenting the loss of a grand narrative (rather than reveling in its *jouissance*) and searching for the unifying ideal between these disparate outcomes. In the end, the unifying factor is existential; Witek has chosen to be a decent man in each scenario.

In Chapter 1, I discussed Kieślowski's fascination with technology as well as everyday pedestrian items. His curiosity about the power inherent in these tools and his interest in how things work are expanded to their larger thematic correlates in the scene of Werner's return from abroad. Werner is transfixed by a multipurpose calculator he brought back with him. He speaks with Witek across a table filled with consumer goods, including a portable television, American cigarettes, a bottle of wine, and a Slinky. The next scene, a demonstration of the Slinky, is a seed of things to come: a contemporary object, usually mundane, is given an unusual

---

31. Deleuze, *Cinema 2,* 103.

amount of camera attention with an emphasis on form. In this particular instance, the metaphor becomes obvious: as the grounded Slinky shifts its weight back and forth incessantly until it stabilizes, Witek remarks, "It's like it died." One cannot shift back and forth between political poles, opposing convictions, or even personal allegiances, without hitting some sort of deathly stasis. It is worth mentioning that this scenario, the "Communist" scenario, features a man disillusioned both with the Communists (who arrested his girlfriend) and with the opposition (who kindled false hopes for him). This scenario receives far more time than the others, and so perhaps, Kieślowski fancied it to be most resonant with contemporary Poles during this dark period of Polish history.

The heavy symbolism continues in the form of the globe Witek carries away after fighting with Adam and screaming at Werner ("You taught me to believe in something! Screw . . . your committedness!"). At the airport, globe still in hand, Witek meets the man he redeemed from his prison in the drug treatment center, and who, in the third scenario, will ironically perish with Witek in the exploding plane. It is not clear whether or not they actually board the doomed plane in this first scenario, as it ends shortly. Just as they are about to board, they receive word that the strikes and sit-ins are beginning, and this social unrest drives Witek to a frenzied anger (fueled by his personal anguish over Czuszka's arrest). He reels back and smashes the globe on the floor. We learn later that the year is 1977, the beginning of a period that will witness the rise of Solidarity and the establishment of martial law in 1981 (the year this film was intended to be released).

The symbol is rather obvious and forced, but it is worth pointing out that the theme of "home" continues even here. At the airport, asked if he's "trafficking in globes," Witek responds: "I've just moved out. I've nowhere to put it," as he struggles with the globe and his suitcase. Witek is an orphan, and much of his "run for the train" has been about his own identity. He not only feels the weight of the world in his struggle for principle, but his own private world is something he must carry with him. This image of rootlessness is only enhanced by the time-space shift to the second scenario, a seamless link via the return of Wojciech Kilar's urgent musical theme.

Scenario 2. As Witek begins to smash the globe, the image shifts to slow motion, and the theme music rushes in dramatically. The sequence cuts to Witek re-running his route through the train station. Witek's collision with the lucky beer drinker accounts, perhaps, for his missing the train this time, but also exemplifies a surprising desperation and rebellion in this run that did not appear in the first, as if his second self were acting subconsciously upon the anger generated at the end of the first scenario. His collision with the policeman seems to border on rage. Witek's decision to rebel against authority is born in this very collision, it seems, as we watch his anger over his father's death elide into an anger against the world.

Scenario 2 is a separate telling of the story, but it is impossible to assess it in isolation. Witek's desperation here should be analyzed apart from all the frustrations revealed in Scenario 1 (as, diegetically, they have not yet happened), yet this is not the nature of the drama, and, as the opening sequence and the flash forward to the final plane crash demonstrate, Kieślowski has an interest in cosmicizing time and space. That is to say that Kieślowski is rolling potentiality and actuality into one metaphysically laden fictional life. This is not quite the theologically certain cosmicization Eliade describes in his religious sociology, but it emerges from the same ground. There is a sense that fate is a universal affair — a metaphysical shifting of the scales that necessarily effects everyone in the temporal system. Witek's three runs for the train flow out of Kieślowski's phenomenological impulses — a testing of all the existential possibilities in Witek's life to locate something of an essence, as in Husserl's imaginative phase.

At Witek's trial, the authorities are literally faceless, and Witek's image appears quite small against the enormous hands grasping the Polish emblem in the foreground. His rage intensifies in his sentencing ("Up yours," he mutters to the judge, beyond her hearing). In the next scene, Witek's community service takes on a caustic political tone; we see him planting flowers within the same Polish emblem — an attempt to beautify the government symbol that sprawls across the native Polish land. Buried deep under this example of historical cosmetology lies a time capsule, a little box of buried history (symbolic of all of Poland's history, a chronology of culture trampled underfoot, inaccessible).

This second scenario is, in many ways, the most interesting philosophically, in that Witek truly wrestles with his foundational principles. In this scenario we see him not only angry, but spiritually searching. His first meeting with the priest yields the idea that the missing of the train was providential (not randomly "lucky," as in the first scenario). Witek confesses that he often thinks such happenings are by chance, but his pilgrimage in this scenario shows him examining the opposite possibility. Kieślowski often remarked forcefully that he did not make religious films, but he acknowledged that this scenario was, indeed, the most forthright religious portrayal in his career.[32] It is also remarkable that this scenario does not place him on the downed plane. We must not draw too strong a causal connection here (surely Kieślowski would resist it), but the suggestion lingers that God may in fact "be" for Witek here, and may be protecting him more than he knows.

Foreshadowing the roadside boy in *Blue,* Witek finds a necklace and cross pendant in the destroyed home of the woman from the Free Trade Union. The cross is not simply a symbol of the woman's faith, but an index of her true cross to bear in this world. She tells Witek that doctors gave her three years to live twelve years earlier. Her unexpected survival has forced her to "make a present of life" and "not fear anything." She is alone, like Witek, literally in "the shadow of death" figured in Psalm 23. She softly preaches to Witek:

> Don't look so sad. He can come to you if you do what He expects of you. He can come to you if you help others. Or you could try asking Him to come yourself. He'll understand.

A cut to one of the government enforcers outside, looking in the windows, reveals how invaded this woman's life is, a bitterly ironic image cut against her next statement to Witek:

> Do you know what Mother Teresa of Calcutta said when she was asked what you could give a person half an hour before death? The belief that you are not completely alone. For a moment I was alone. Then you appeared and I no longer am. I'm glad you came.

Witek's childhood friend, Daniel (Jacek Barkowski), echoes Kieślowski's own feelings of the world outside Poland; his father has become "acclimatized" to Denmark, but he has not ("I keep thinking I'm somewhere far away"). As if speaking out of a national consciousness, the trouble with memory is clearly revealed in this conversation. Witek recalls the scene shown in the beginning of the film: his friend Daniel ascending the embankment to a waiting car. Despite the concreteness of our perception, Daniel adamantly insists there was no such car. Much like Hitchcock toyed with the "authority" of the image by feeding the audience false flashbacks in *Stage Fright,* we must now question the veracity of *everything* we have seen, a radical subjectivization of the film and critique of the entire film and media enterprise. These sorts of rifts cause critics like Emma Wilson to justifiably

---

32. Interview with Coates, *Lucid Dreams,* 168.

seek after postmodern conceptions of time and narrative (in Wilson's case, that of Deleuze). Indeed, it seems this inconsistency could be seen as a subversion of the whole classical narrative, just as the entire film has been an unorthodox exploration of narrative possibility. This difference of memory calls to mind the conversation with Adam in which Witek desperately questions whether we can be sure we are not making terrible mistakes at this current moment, mistakes rooted in a misperception (or misuse) of a lost history. What access have we to history except through memory and interpretation of someone else's memory?

Kieślowski often chooses to deemotionalize the camera; for example, when Daniel is crying in his sleep and Wera helplessly watches him, Kieślowski refuses to give us a full frontal view of Daniel, in blatant disregard for the first rule of Hollywood cinematography (i.e., heighten emotion by shooting both of the subject's eyes). In this case, much as Bednarz (in *The Scar)* and Werner (in his first conversation with Witek) have their backs to us, we are given a quarter view of Witek's face — just enough to register his shock and disturbed expression, but never enough to invest ourselves in a deep emotional way, steeped in empathy and sentimentality. In fact, the only truly full frontal view we've been given of Witek is that of his death, seen as the first frame of the film, before any possibility of true empathy. Kieślowski's directing lesson at the Amsterdam Summer University shows him specifically avoiding the personal, emotional moment, a violation he called "indiscreet."[33]

However, Kieślowski does engage the full-frontal view in the next sequence, where Witek himself in iconic pose gazes at a hologram of Christ's crucifixion, creating a doubly iconic sequence. Witek shifts his perspective to reveal the effect of Christ's eyes closing in death. This scene initiates a crucial series of scenes in which Witek approaches Stefan, the priest, about becoming a Catholic "to know why I'm alive." The use of abstraction in the prayer scene is the most clear example yet of Kieślowski's stylistic trajectory for films to come. We see Witek in a church and an out-of-focus orange object in the foreground. A candle, perhaps? But it doesn't flicker, so perhaps it is something else — something orange, vibrant, hopeful, and, perhaps, transcendent, in contrast to the muted colors and grays

---

33. *Krzysztof Kieślowski: A Masterclass for Young Directors* (VHS, dir. Erik Lint, Editions à Voir, 1995).

that pervade the film. Witek makes one request, outside of which he will never ask for anything else: "Dear God . . . Be here."

The next few scenes exhibit a dance of fortune, between life and death, with the question of fate lingering overall. Witek goes to work in a print shop, the first link in the underground publication chain that ends with Czuszka's distribution efforts. Czuszka is very near, yet so far from Witek's mind, and they never intersect in this scenario. Perhaps, had the printing efforts continued, he would have met her again; we cannot know. In another twist of fate, the moment after being asked by the authorities to spy on French youth when he travels to a Paris Catholic Youth convention (a proposal he refuses), Witek saves an old woman by pulling her back from speeding traffic.

This life-affirming gesture is, in turn, cut against Witek's conversation with Wera (Marzena Trybała), where she tells of the "nothingness" she experiences when visiting her dead mother's grave. She remarks that she now has her own grave for the first time, and this creates an ironic sense of "home," as she "was from nowhere" before. For her, a place to die is a marker of rootedness, much as the Polish people of this time had watched their home deform and twist into something unrecognizable. Like the drunk man in *Decalogue III*, they cannot find their home, but they know where they will die.

Likewise, Wera's family echoes this loss of national history and identity. She knows nothing of her grandparents (her mother never talked about them, and Wera "never got round to asking"). By contrast, though he had "never thought about it," Witek realizes his heritage: his great-grandfather fought in the 1863 uprising, his grandfather with Piłsudski at the Vistula in 1920, his father served with Kutrzeba in 1939, and later protested at Poznań in 1956. Witek does not remark here about the coincidence of his birth that year, perhaps a signal that his demons have been partially exorcised. "You have them all at hand," Wera remarks, and the statement holds the force of revelation for him; while orphaned, Witek still has a history and culture to root him, even if resistance to oppression is the only thing that unites his forebears.

Witek's intimacy with Wera is quite unlike that with the other women in his life; the conversation flows easily, and their histories are a matter of mutual giving, unlike the necessary interrogations he and Czuszka undergo. He alludes to Olga, who becomes his wife in Scenario 3, but that union is never realized here. However, she does function as a catalyst of the conscience, her incident of guilt at the medical school having provoked his own thinking about the things he won't talk about with anyone: fear, his father, and God. Finally, he suggests there is something he doesn't know *how* to talk about with her, having "a little to do with you, and maybe with me too." This secret (which will never be revealed) is epitomized in the time capsule he discovered while digging earlier, which he hopes to show her, but brings up empty. The message about the past, the future, and the way things actually turned out has vanished — vaporized in the air of potentiality — a suggestion that even history might be changed by human action and decision.

We discover Witek will survive this scenario, as he has been denied his passport and will not go to France on a foreign plane, the likes of which Wera's husband services (an ominous fact, in retrospect). At the mention of her husband, in clear reaction, their relationship turns sexual. In another ironic turn, Wera notices the cross around his neck during their lovemaking (presumably the one found at the old woman's house). After a discussion in which Witek affirms his belief in God (albeit it rings somewhat hollow and institutional), Kieślowski gives us a tableau of the couple, Witek kneeling before her, head in her lap, nearly a pietà.

We are given the impression that Witek has skirted the edge of the Transcendental ground, having found faith and a remarkable connection with Wera. Kieślowski problematizes this, of course, steeping the Transcendental in an illicit affair. This is, after all, the liminal ground. Kieślowski's characters are never saints, and they often glimpse grace in the most immanent, worldly situations.

After this, the scenario becomes a tangle of misunderstandings and missed connections. Witek is suspected of treason to the Underground for not having been at the shop when it was raided. He seeks out Wera, asking directions from a man on the street who appears to be Werner (and whom he does not appear to know in this scenario, having missed his opportunity to meet the man on the initial train). His search ends up fruitless, as they both pursue each other in opposite places. They miss each other just as the strikes begin, a synchronicity not quite clear (a cause-effect relationship?), but ringing with significance all the same. Witek finds his aunt listening to reports of the uprising on Radio Free Europe, and the musical theme returns to carry us into Scenario 3.

Scenario 3. If Witek was the redeemer in Scenario 1, and the seeking crusader in Scenario 2, he attempts to be the honest peacemaker in Scenario 3.

As he runs for the train, little varies from the other scenarios: the woman still yells at him, the man finds the coin and buys the beer, Witek runs into him (though not in a violent fashion, as in Scenario 2), and the delay is enough to make him miss the train. This missed opportunity opens another possibility: Olga (Monika Goździk) has been waiting at the platform for him to see him off. She indicates that she was at his father's funeral and waited for him afterwards, to no avail. Her pursuit is successful here, and of all the sexual situations depicted in the film, this is the first scene that depicts the lovemaking without reference to politics, belief, or history. There is a sense of sensual abandonment here away from troubling ethical, political, or existential issues.

"You said you'd lost your vocation," the dean of the medical school says after Witek begs for readmission to the school. "It seems to have come back." Witek's decision to return to normalcy — to the familiar — to interpret his father's dying words as merely a relinquishing of obligation to the dying man (not to the world, himself, or anyone else), will shape this scenario. Olga becomes pregnant, they get married, and Witek graduates. He is rewarded with a teaching position as well as a hospital position ("I'm getting too lucky," he exclaims, more prophetically than he could ever know). We are given another frontal/iconic look at Witek as he gazes at his wife's naked form, framed by the bathroom door, a beautiful whiteness in contrast with the darkness of the apartment. His religion is love, family life, and a peaceful domicile. He will settle down into a comfortable routine in his own home, just the sort of life Filip found ruptured in *Camera Buff*. A charitable man, he makes house calls, accentuating the importance of home, and resists the efforts of his elderly patient's family to move her to a nursing institution.

Outside the house, he witnesses a pair of jugglers and remains transfixed by the give-and-take image, even as the first Witek remarked on the Slinky shifting back and forth in Scenario 1. Why do they juggle? The woman replies: "No particular reason. According to them, they hold the world juggling record." The camera shows as much fascination as Witek, focusing on the abstract patterns of the balls in the air and the blur of hands as they work to maintain them. There is a sense that these men are biding time, trying to make something beautiful and creative amid the dead time, the stasis, for no particular reason except to exist beautifully. This is, indeed, Witek's enterprise, and his resistance to both the Communist Party and the opposition is his own juggling act, in every sense of the phrase. He doesn't want to join the party, but he clearly states his disbelief in God. When asked why he doesn't want to join the party, he replies: "I just don't." Witek is compassionate, a family man, and entirely without conviction, lest it destroy him.

Those activists seeking his support encourage him: "It's no crime to be afraid." The theme of fear pervades the entire film, and this statement seems to shake him. He attempts to juggle some apples in his kitchen, only to drop them. Left with one in his hand, he takes an Adamic bite, a marker of his temptation to remain disengaged from the political turmoil around him. This is the only scenario in which Witek does not hear of the strikes throughout the country; he has turned a deaf ear to the protests, and he's rewarded with eternal silence in the end.

His trip to Libya for the dean of the medical school is postponed one day for his wife's birthday. The fateful irony here lies in the fact that this change of plans puts him on a doomed plane. The wedding of birth and death events has been a hallmark throughout the film, and this irony is amplified here. More interesting is Olga's suggestion that she watched her husband sleep once but then refuses to state what she saw. There has been only one instance in this film so far that might be called a dream, and that is Witek's drunken vision of a blood-stained hospital floor in Scenario 2. Did Olga witness a death dream in Witek that he does not remember (or has repressed)?

Of course, the real reason she wishes him to stay is that she is pregnant with his second child, a girl. This bit of pathos before the end is not really a sentimental wringing out of the audience; on first viewing, we're not at all sure what will happen to Witek and may have forgotten Witek's scream of "No!" in the beginning. Even so, it is enough to make the audience uneasy, a feeling that only grows worse upon the "coincidence" of seeing the priest and his group of Catholic workers from Scenario 2 and a party comrade from the group in Scenario 1 at the airport. The plane explodes at the end of Scenario 3, bringing us back to the beginning of the film, and the defiant "No!"

Kieślowski makes his own frustrations with ethical action manifest in this film, set on the eve of martial law. The three Witeks attempt to remain "honest," as their father wished for them. Each tries a different path toward that honesty. In the end, all paths are problematized, and the final scenario, ending in tragic, unexpected death, rings the most nihilistic. It is our fate to die, and this is why Kieślowski said this scenario meant the most to him of the three.[34] Kieślowski maintains the ethical ideal as essential, while constantly showing us the great difficulty of maintaining it, particularly under oppressive circumstances. Kieślowski's view here is pessimistic, as the chasm between the immanent and transcendent appears unbridgeable; at the end of his next film, a character will read a poem that speaks a prayer for mercy and grace in this impossible time.

No End (1984)

SYNOPSIS: *This film begins with a family in the aftermath of the death of Antek, the father. Antek (Jerzy Radziwiłowicz) was a lawyer known for defending striking workers and other members of the Solidarity movement. He died of a heart attack and abides, in ghostly form, throughout the film as his family struggles to survive in his absence and his clients struggle with their legal predicaments amid the turbulence of 1980s Poland. Antek's wife, Ula (a.k.a. Urszula, played by Grażyna Szapołowska), tries desperately to pull the broken pieces of her life together and reconstitute her husband's affairs. Via Joanna, the wife of an imprisoned worker (Darek, played by Artur Barciś), who Antek was defending, she meets a small network of people aligned with Solidarity. Ula's suffering runs parallel with the sufferings of this network. Joanna engages Antek's former mentor to defend her husband, a man named Labrador (Aleksander Bardini), with some sympathy for the Solidarity movement, but looking for a compromise maneuver from Darek to secure his release. Though Darek refuses initially, eventually he and his fellow inmates call off their hunger strike, and he is released on a suspended sentence. It is a hollow victory for him. Ula's personal grief slowly swallows her throughout the film as she reaches out in different ways to deaden the pain (anonymous sex, hypnotherapy, etc.). In the end, she commits suicide, and the final image of the film shows her walking down a path with her husband.*

No End stands as an important film in Kieślowski's career for many reasons. It is his first collaboration with Krzysztof Piesiewicz, his first film with composer Zbigniew Preisner, the most formally oriented of his films to date, the final feature before the watershed series *The Decalogue* (and international renown), and one of the most criticized films of his career (from the Left, arguing the film lacked political commitment, from the Right, arguing the film criticized the government, and from the Catholic Church, which decried Urszula's suicide as immoral).

These imperative formal experiments formed stylistic zones that would soon bear his most distinctive marks. Kieślowski's construction of more

---

34. Interview in Stok, *Kieślowski on Kieślowski*, 113.

dense and complicated mise-en-scène, use of abstraction, foray into the spiritual world, and innovative use of sound and music set *No End* apart from all of his previous films.

Many of these innovations will recur in *Blue,* often in improved fashion: typical Kieślowskian visuals (close-ups on hands, for instance), the prominence of the color blue, striking abstract compositions, a car accident, grief, intimations of suicide, and prominent use of music. Kieślowski's childhood burden of shock, dislocation, and grief finds partial redemption in his later ability to express these themes in his films. As my preface noted and Kubrick's quote suggested, Kieślowski renders visually and experientially the moments in life where words fail us. In *No End,* this often manifests itself through a narrative strategy of reaction rather than action. For instance, we see Joanna's surge of emotion at the door and only find out later she has been told the hunger strike has begun (imperiling her husband's life). Kieślowski's frequent denial of such establishing information forces the audience to respond immediately and emotionally before more rational thought sets in.

No End begins with a high, overhead shot of a cemetery. The angle is deliberately flat and striking, reducing the three-dimensional caskets and monuments to two-dimensional squares and rectangles with convoluted, maze-like paths running between them — the paths of the dead that, we shall see, also run among the living. Candles flicker, the only sign of movement or warmth in the cold scene. All is dark (or blue), except for these memorial lights. The scene darkens, vaporizing the caskets and all traces of the temporal, leaving only the suggestive candles struggling to survive amid the vacancy of any other form.

We see a hand, amputated by the frame from any body, slowly stretching and expanding, shrinking and contracting.

Fig. 49. From the beginning of *No End.*

Our intent view of it isolates the hand as a form, the deadly twin of Monica Vitta's hand at the end of Antonioni's *L'Avventura*. The form itself moves in a slow, persistent way, similar to the plant in *Decalogue II,* rising slowly to life after being picked and crushed. Once again, Kieślowski has denied us an establishing shot. The anonymous hand touches a young boy sleeping, and the camera pans across the room, revealing a backpack (with the word *Joy* on it), toys, a piano, and other joyful things (in eerie counterpoint to the funeral dirge on the soundtrack). The camera focuses on an abstract, single black line dangling in the foreground: a telephone cable, we presume, transmitting the ominous message, "This call is monitored. The time is 7:20 A.M."

Antek, the presumed owner of the hand, is seen only by reflection in the glass of a cabinet, just as his final appearance in the film will be equally mediated. It is a transitional image, as Antek makes his way to our world, his former home. He is a figure of memory, yet he demonstrates to us a certain will of his own. Ula rests on her bed, and the camera cranes high, soaring over her and Antek's head as he sits on the bed's edge. It drops in front of his face as he stares directly at us, iconically. "I've died," he announces flatly. It is difficult to explain how profoundly stunning this paradoxical moment is. The oxymoronic quality of the living image speaking is but one level; his unyielding eye staring directly at us shatters the objectivity we have been granted thus far in the film, exposing our scopophilia in the most disconcerting fashion. Perhaps most disturbing, Antek implies that *we* are part of the deathly vision by our participation. We see what he sees (an omniscience denied the other characters on screen).

There is also an important semiotic component here, in that Kieślowski very deliberately chose Jerzy Radziwiłowicz for the role of Antek. Radziwiłowicz was a face known around Poland for his roles in Wajda's films, and his characters often carried the weight of national aspiration in many respects. Kieślowski chose him precisely because he would be seen as "morally pure" and "evidently honest."[35] His deadness may be seen as an inability for the people of Poland to do good during this bitter time (i.e., after the crushing blow of martial law). "People with such clear consciences didn't stand a chance anymore," Kieślowski said, and *No End* is a film about the dark mood of that desperate time.

---

35. Ibid., 134.

As Antek speaks, the film cuts away, strangely, to different still lifes around the room: a sugar bowl with spilled sugar on the table (a parallel to a shot of a sugar cube in *Blue*); a basketball under the table, coming to rest at the end of some slight movement. These cutaways function, in a formal way, like a formal interpretation of the mood behind his statements. This imagistic pattern is something like the transcendental style of Ozu that Paul Schrader describes in his classic book on the subject. In his description of Ozu's *Tokyo Story,* Schrader remarks on the consistent return to a vase intercut with a daughter's conversation with her father (who eventually falls asleep) on the most momentous night of her life: the night before her wedding. As she bursts into tears, Ozu continually shows the vase by means of a cutaway:

> The decisive action — the miracle of the tears — has little meaning in itself but serves to prove the strength of the form. The transcendental style, like the vase, is a form which expresses something deeper than itself, the inner unity of all things.[36]

This is one of the more explicit examples of the transcendental style, a mode of filmmaking that Kieślowski will rarely imitate exactly, but the metaphysical goal of which is common to Kieślowski's own style. The "still life" is an apt title for these shots, because they appear both dead and alive, exemplifying once again the paradox that resides in all forms of photography. The basketball coming to rest also functions narratively, visually articulating Antek's own death ("... and that was it," he says) and foreshadowing Urszula's final temporal breath at the end of the film.

The prominence of hands in the film, initiated by Antek's stretching fingers, recalls the end of Ingmar Bergman's devastating film *The Silence*, where the dying message of Ester reads "face" and "hand." Hands, by their formal virtues, express a great deal: the one and the many, power and lack of power (when still, as the hand protruding from the wrecked car later demonstrates). Hands extend certain directions — toward us and away. They grip and hold dear (as the two hands clasping each other in the opening of *Decalogue VIII* aptly shows), and they destroy (as Dorota pulls apart the plant in *Decalogue II* and Julie drags her bleeding knuckles along the brick wall in *Blue*). Antek, in recalling his funeral, describes his young son in terms of his expressive hands, a telling, rich, and human moment demonstrative of Kieślowski's marvelous attention to the expressive details

---

36. Paul Schrader, *Transcendental Style in Film* (New York: Da Capo Press, 1972), 51.

of human existence: "His hands were frozen, but he was ashamed to put them in his pockets."

A phone ringing interrupts Antek's soliloquy, a temporal intrusion in the spiritual realm (a call from Tomek, a friend of Antek's, who wakes Ula up here and will later, quite literally, attempt to enter her bed in Antek's stead). Kieślowski's fascination with technology may be summed up in his use of the telephone, a consistent feature in many of his films. Beyond the fascination with the gadget's power, the telephone embodies synchronous intimacy and distance, the voice without a body, the word without the vision/image, and the symbols (words) without their immediate context in the lifeworld. By way of these characteristics, the telephone often functions in crucial spaces of human relationships: the desperate reach for a lost daughter in *The Scar*, the illicit dream of an affair in *Camera Buff*, the last words of father and son in *Blind Chance*. There are many more examples in later films. At the same time, the telephone is very much like the voice from beyond that Ula seeks throughout the film, though it always proves disappointing; at one point, when asked who she is calling, she replies that she has forgotten. The most ominous example of this symbol is the cutting of the telephone line at the end of the film. No more temporal intrusions, no more half-embodied communication for Ula. Her cutting of the phone line is both a denial of human contact and an affirmation of the full communication experience (with her husband).

After the phone call, Ula gets up, moves to the window, and waters a flowerpot (a gesture of routine, as well as a symbol of new life). By equal force of habit, Ula makes coffee for two. As discussed in Chapter 1, Kieślowski consistently uses beverages as both a communal symbol and a formal tool. This marks an ingenious and devastating twist on the theme, signaling the absence of communion. The liquid's phenomenological powers of suggestion heighten here as Ula pours it down the drain. Kieślowski chooses to focus on the form, not her face, as the locus of emotion and meaning. At the same time, this moment expresses the symbolic weight that everything carries for the grieving, a documentation of the amount of semiotic investment made in the temporal, even (or, perhaps, especially) the most mundane things. They are markers, this investment of meaning in the deceased, the way they shaped our everyday lives.

As if to counter the symbol of absence, Antek's reach for the newspaper signals his pedestrian presence. Antek's temporal intersections are rife with coincidences that suggest something close to causality. For instance, we see Kieślowski's metaphysical wink when Labrador's watch breaks (a literal stopping of time) as Antek walks by. The many interactions between Antek and the temporal world suggest not two realms that occasionally converge, but rather one realm, laid out in concentric circles, the wider realm being truly metaphysical.

As the funeral theme plays, we see Jacek running off to school, the English word *Joy* ironically emblazoned on his backpack. Ula watches him, deflated by grief, unaware of her husband sitting beside her. A black dog approaches them and licks Antek's hand. Like the dog at the end of Tarkovsky's *Stalker,* the canine's connection to the spiritual realm is unmistakable, functioning as a sort of docile Cerberus, pointing the way to (rather than guarding) the entrance to the afterlife. The dog will bridge the gap between the dead and living and regularly show up throughout the rest of the film. Jacek is the only one, besides Antek himself, who touches the dog (hugging him later). The poem Labrador recites later aligns all earnest, human souls with the wandering dog, even as his own name alludes to the canine (at least in English).

Labrador posits some of the key questions in this film, and the following statement anchors a major subplot: "I'm quite aware of the times. But what do we do with them?" This persistent query yields a counterpart question, running parallel throughout the film: What will time (or fate) do with us? The synchrony motif that pervades Kieślowski's films articulates this question: a large clock in the foreground overshadows the scene where Labrador hears he will be forced to resign from his position. This happens precisely at the time he must decide whether or not to take Darek's case, an offer he initially refused but will now accept. To Darek's family, this must appear as divine provision, but Kieślowski rarely makes the metaphysical world any easier than the temporal; the question mark that appears mysteriously next to Labrador's name on the lawyer roll suggests that Antek may be working against fate.

Ula makes her way through Antek's belongings, and Kieślowski's focus on these items, many of them very curious, raises their status to repositories of meaning. The investment of the grieving, as discussed earlier, is made manifest in these items. This semiotic archeology project proves transformational for Ula. She later acknowledges that her relationship with Antek, which she would not have characterized as "close" before, reveals itself to be more dear than she thought.

Then we see the photographs of Ula from a time in her life before Antek, when she posed nude for money. After sending for them, Antek had cut out her face from every image instead of discarding the lot. He resealed them in the package in which they had arrived. Ula destroys them and breaks down in tears for the first time — a confluence of grief, shame, and agonizing questions ("Why did he cut out the faces?" she asks). Up to this point, her expression has been a bit too sentimental, happy even, but now the floodgates have been torn open, even as the lone dog sits watchfully under the street lamp outside.

It is not clear why Antek kept the images or why he modified them, but the complexity of the action rings true with the complexity of the emotional scenario. Obviously, Antek attempted to disassociate the commodity of the photos and his wife's face. It is important to note that he did not look for the photos; some "well-wisher" sent them. Perhaps he cut out the face to keep them in the past — to preserve her self. At the same time, he cannot discard her image completely, for that would be tantamount to hiding in a fantasy. The modified photo is a compromise with reality.

Ula's car dies unexpectedly, and the frame focuses on the vertical line of the wiper, nearly bisecting the frame. We see that same wiper, from the reverse angle, as the car miraculously jumps to life. As the providential interval keeps Ula from the car accident ahead of her, the mystery of the moment is accentuated by Kieślowski's emphasis on form. The mystery of the crash is also heightened by the abstract pool of oil and the series of hand shots (on Ula's stomach, on her car bumper, smearing grease on her face, and the disembodied hand through the broken car window).

One facet of grief, to which Kieślowski was particularly sensitive, is the horror of unreliable memory. Ula's memory of Antek is perilously open to revision, and her conversation with Marta, Antek's former lover, about him becomes something close to a battle over Antek's identity. Marta claims he wanted to be a judge in 1967. Ula flatly answers that he always wanted to be an attorney, and that is what he was. At home, she angrily scours through photographs until she finds one from the time in dispute. Grief rides on symbols; photographs become evidence (i.e., signs) of some sort of reality that no longer persists; people are reduced to the sum of their representations within people's subjective recollections. It is this grand semiotic equation that makes grief so difficult, and that is precisely why Kieślowski, the cartographer of meaning, focuses on it.

Ula's sexual episode with the stranger also flows from grief and takes place as a double reaction: in resistance to Tomek's overture (intimacy with a known person is too much at this point) and out of memory of Antek (the stranger's hands resemble Antek's). Afterwards, amid the emotional and spiritual poverty of the impromptu, anonymous sex, Ula's confession rushes out of her. She first makes certain he doesn't speak a word of Polish, then launches into a monologue about her love for her husband (who has, unbeknownst to her, been looking on in spiritual form). Ula's profession as a translator comes into play here, in that her action is the converse of her productive occupation (i.e., establishing meaning between people through communication). In this case, communication is negated, leaving only expression, and meaning is localized to Ula herself. The tie between psychological need for expression and the semiotic impulse is most vivid, as the scene demonstrates the impossibility of her circumstance, the need to communicate, and the lack of true receivers. Perhaps she speaks to a non-Pole in Polish for the same reason Antek cut away the faces in the photographs: it stands as an attempt to distance the carnal event from the person in order to preserve some sense of the ideal.

Memory, for all its malleability, also functions as a lens in which some things become clearer. Ula confesses to the American (in a language he cannot understand) that she realizes, in retrospect, that she was happy with Antek, though she scarcely realized it when he was alive. Again we recall the semiotic tensions and similar themes at the end of Bergman's *Silence* (the foreign tongue, hands, and face), when Ula tells the man that he has hands like Antek's. He cries, "If only you would say it in English!" She then touches his face with her finger and states, "You wouldn't understand." Words simply fail her. Her compassion extends to him, as she realizes she has used him as a screen upon which she can project her emotions for Antek.

Hands and faces figure prominently in the scene when Ula turns to hypnotherapy as a means of forgetting. The ringing sound of Antek circling the glass with his finger intrudes upon Ula's hypnosis, waking her. This sound, increasingly louder as the scene goes on, might also be seen as a siren's song, calling her to death. Her playful communication with him works through emulated hand signals, which themselves move through different semiotic forms, ending with an extended middle finger (obscene gesture) and a disapproving wag of the single finger from Antek (the playful punch line to the joke). If Marta went to this hypnotist to forget, Ula finds her memory intensified to the point of spiritual access. The session ends with Ula's hand, spiderlike, and mysteriously abstract on the floor. By contrast, the hypnotist's hand gets caught in a mousetrap (perhaps a jab at his quackery from Kieślowski).

Ula's hand, her communicative link with Antek in the previous scene, reaches for intimacy with Antek as she masturbates, calling his name. As in *Camera Buff,* Kieślowski interrupts this adult affair with the needs of a child. Jacek confesses to his mother that he saw his parents having sex once. She tells him they were making love, an important admission, far from the faceless pornography of her earlier days and the wordless liaison with the American. She then makes a startling statement, that Jacek, through his embrace of her, is her lover now. One could have a Freudian heyday with this scene and miss the main point. Kieślowski has always seen sex as, in its essence, more a matter of spiritual need and desire than biological function. A monumental task stands before Ula in her relationship with Jacek, a task for which she is ill-suited and will ultimately fail. She must redirect and transform her affections and their dedicated energies to her son. Kieślowski's meditation on love and its complicated transmutability is also the subject (and abiding tension) of *Decalogue IV.*

Meanwhile, in the other plotline, Darek's lawyers are a bit like the biblical Job's friends, offering lots of advice with little understanding. Labrador wishes Darek to be free, whatever honor need be sacrificed. The younger lawyer zealously urges Darek to push on, for the sake of political revolution. Darek's conversation with the younger lawyer stands as one of the more important in this plotline. In it, he traces the lawyer's zealous rhetoric to hate, an attitude Darek cannot abide. This lawyer offers no better answers than his older counterpart with the same name: two sides of the same coin. Darek holds his ground, and later wakes up in his cell to a supposed noise. As he dismisses the noise and reclines again, the camera subtly shifts to reveal Antek beside him.

In her conversation with Tomek, Ula announces, quite sincerely, that she literally saw Antek in the psychotherapy session, and "could have asked him. . . . " To what? To stay, quite clearly, just as Antek himself testified to us in the beginning of the film, that he could have chosen to refuse death as he hovered above his body in cardiac arrest. He chose to leave, because it felt better, and Ula understands now that Antek will not choose to return. Her anguish is made palpable by her slow twisting and tearing of her stocking, an abstract image pregnant with a certain undefinable emotional power (discussed in Chapter 1).

At this point, the film runs the risk of careening off into a Hollywood-style sentimentalism about the afterlife. However, to the Pole of this time it would be clear (as it should be to us) that the character of Antek doubles for the optimism of the entire youth movement and the pessimism surrounding its survival. The movement exists better, for the time being, at least, on the ideal, metaphysical plain. It is too messy in the temporal realm, where impossible choices are posed amid impossible circumstances. Kieślowski leaves little hope the movement will return, and, describing the mood of the times, wonders if things might be more bearable on the other side of death.

Ula dashes through an apartment building. She encounters a man trapped in an elevator, pounding on the window, begging for help. Her rush through the building, ignorant of those who need her, indicates her solipsistic descent, morally inexcusable, but humanly understandable. She desperately heads for the stairs. The shot changes to a POV frantically dashing up the staircase, only to catch Ula herself running up the next flight (an agitated and deliberate breaking of the continuity code and expansion of the time-space structure). The sequence continues, an extended tracing of Ula's desperate ascension, exhausting and endless. We note the old woman on the stairs, whom Ula pushes by thoughtlessly, and might see this as a prelude to the predicament for all three protagonists in the *Colors Trilogy* to come. She is akin to grieving Julie in *Blue,* who cannot escape her own problematized line of vision to see the elderly woman in need of help at the recycling bin.

She finally arrives at the door of the hypnotherapist and begs to repeat the treatment as a means of seeing Antek again. As they talk, the therapist traces his finger on a glass, emitting the tone she heard from Antek throwing the entire previous scenario into question (was she in a hypnotic state, imagining Antek, and the sound from the therapist?). "I'm not in communication with the Beyond," he flatly asserts. Ula takes the glass from his hand.

The next scene depicts Ula at home, glass in hand; it is a different glass, but the theme is obvious. She holds a delicate trace of him, and it's slipping from her grasp. We are privy to its slow, painful descent, articulating the dramatic pressure of the scene.

Jacek innocently pounds out the funeral theme on the piano. The tune is "Mury" (translated as "Walls"), a perennial hymn of Solidarity that will play throughout the memorial scene to come, just as the candles in Ula's window function as a silent protest for Solidarity (a custom of the time, taking place on the thirteenth of each month).[37] Ula drops the glass, a shattering that repeats in other films, most notably *Decalogue II.* As in that film, the breaking vessel is simultaneous with the emotional cracking in the character. The scene following Ula's breakdown in the bathroom is that of the cemetery. The beauty of this scene mingles with a foreboding sense of doom. As Jacek, not yet politically jaded, stares at student protesters and a memorial plaque honoring an Underground Resistance solider known as Zawisza,[38] Ula stares at the camera, iconic, lighting matches one by one. "I love you," she utters, then repeats the words again and again. The shots often veer toward abstraction, a kind of dark transcendence. Ula's fingers burn as the matches burn down, an eerie recall of the crazy man in *Blind Chance* who lights his hand on fire, and a foreshadowing of the flare of Dorota's matchbox in *Decalogue II.*

Ula cannot see herself a part of the political equation again. She desperately upbraids Jacek for his interest in the resistance movement. In the scene to follow, the image of Jacek reflected in the car's rearview mirror is enough to illustrate their distance. They communicate via the reflection in the mirror, and Ula is giving her son over to his grandmother, the woman who raised her husband to be the revolutionary he was. "How far is it?" the grandmother asks Ula, regarding her supposed trip. "Not very," she ominously utters, as the camera tracks back and away, dramatically heightening the sense of departure. Ula does not see herself leaving her home as much as *going* home, or redefining it, a reestablishment that is only possible through a complete renunciation of the temporal.

Jacek insists on a proper goodbye, but not Ula. One would expect the opposite to be true, as goodbye is reserved for longer absences, and Ula's "so long" would be more appropriate for a short parting. However, it is clear that Ula's conception of time and space has cosmicized; she does not see time as short and long in the same way, as she intends to join her husband in a timeless space. This is no justification for her selfish act, of course, but it does articulate a transcendent theme in Kieślowski, the cosmic dimension.

---

37. Tadeusz Lubelski, "From *Personnel* to *No End*," in Coates, *Lucid Dreams,* 72.

38. *Zawisza* means "dependable." The plaque connects the new political resistance to the old. My thanks to Stephen Krauss for this translation.

I cannot confirm it, but it does seem that Kieślowski himself provides us with a cameo in the courtroom scene. Appropriately, he appears to play a judge. In one sense, as the "author" of his films (a title he accepted), he arbitrates and rules on what is portrayed in the film. In another sense, his role of judge echoes Antek's interest in a fictional judge, the "penitent judge" of Camus. That man, Jean-Baptiste Clamence of *The Fall*, confesses his complicity in the evils of the world and sees no easy way to hold legitimate moral judgment over others. Not only does this reference seem appropriate for Kieślowski, who constantly shows us the difficulty of moral action, but it also foreshadows another conflicted judge to come, Auguste of *Red*.

Having lost his honor, Darek sits through his sentencing, a guilty verdict with a suspended sentence. The verdict is the picture of compromise, and all that Darek hoped to avoid, ironically. On the one hand, he is free. On the other, he loses the force of principle that self-sacrifice earned him. He no longer holds the ideal.

Sensing Darek's dissatisfaction, Labrador recites a Polish poem that reflects many dimensions of the film, tying him (through his name) and Antek (through the black dog) to its themes:

> And I don't even know how I happened to change from a wolf into a mangy dog. Maybe my muzzle lost the dark wind's touch. My yellow eye no longer scowled at the sky? A flicker of fear, not a boisterous flame, stormed upon my back? Maybe no one needed to put this collar on me. And I myself crawled over to beg, fawning and dog-like? Lord, who loves even those who grovel, and can kindle pride in a worm's pale blood, help open the throat of one mutely shouting and tell me I walk free, even though I am weeping.

As Labrador says "dark wind's touch," the camera reveals Antek, sitting in the back of the court. For the first time, Darek seems to notice his presence, a clarity of vision that has come through a sort of grace, an acceptance of mercy (or is it judgment?) amid human helplessness. By virtue of the eyeline and the cutting pattern, we make this inference, but it cannot be proven, of course, leaving us with an ambiguity that Kieślowski considered valuable.

The final sequence is horrifying, precisely because it is so calm. No music. No outbursts of emotion. Ula quietly readies herself; she brings in an empty milk bottle (the perennial Kieślowskian death image), cuts the telephone wire (a terrifying response to the phone call initiating the film), and brushes her teeth. At this watershed spiritual moment, Kieślowski's images become more formal, more deliberately composed, and less documentary-like. As Ula changes into a black shirt, a rack focus reveals her hand one more time, knuckles clenched in counterpoint to her otherwise calm demeanor.

Fig. 50. From *No End.*

She covers her mouth with tape, a terrifying image for the synesthetic response it elicits in the audience, but also symbolic of her eternal silence to come. As the translator, she has been quieted. She has gagged herself to increase the efficiency of the gas, and so she may not cry out. Silence prevails when words have failed us. The only sound is the eerie seeping of the gas. The camera dollies slowly into the mouth of the stove, just as it drove into the dark pit of Witek's mouth in *Blind Chance,* and with similar mortal suggestion.

The funeral theme returns only as her head bows, in death, and, one might argue, in prayer. For the second time, Antek looks directly at us, an icon to match her iconic look in the graveyard scene. The camera reveals Ula next. Her head collapses, slowly and deliberately on his shoulder (an otherworldly, ballet-like gesture). The camera then moves to their reflection off a glassy surface. As they move away to a wooded scene, the glass appears to be that of a door with beveled panes. Just as Kieślowski ended *The Scar* with a door, prominent in the image, the door closes the film here with a more transcendent suggestion (the threshold of the afterlife). The abstract quality of the image is unmistakably transcendent, and the posture of the couple (walking side by side, deliberately, never touching) is also of that mode. The asceticism with which they behave lends the film to metaphorical interpretation. Which interpretation is largely up to us. I believe Kieślowski is suggesting that something lies beyond this life, but he refuses to romanticize what he does not yet understand.

As mentioned, the film did not please the critics, the government, or the church officials, but Kieślowski maintained that the public appreciated the film very much, often telling him that he told the truth about the time period, and, as Lubelski puts it, captured "the mood of the time."[39] Antek is, in part, the haunting ghost of Solidarity, of a young nation's lost hope. The mood was dark indeed — a political depression from which Kieślowski would never fully recover.

The Watershed: The *Decalogue* Films

Throughout this chapter I've consistently tried to point out how Kieślowski's style was beginning to move in the direction of abstraction. I trust that Chapter 2 made clear that this stylistic shift is not merely a matter of changing aesthetic fancy, but a very deliberate engagement with a particular mode of communication, grounded in the phenomenological and focused on the metaphysical. The *Decalogue* films, the subject of the next chapter, show a shift toward universal themes and issues and away from the imma-nent ground of Polish politics. Many of the films will also show aggressive formalist experiment in a transcendent direction.

---

39. Stok, *Kieślowski on Kieślowski,* 134, as well as Tadeusz Lubelski in Coates, *Lucid Dreams,* 73.

4

THE DECALOGUE
(Ten film series, 1988)

These ten films, released in 1988, function as a watershed moment in Kieślowski's career. Many demonstrate the formal emphasis that will fully characterize his work after 1988. Some films hearken back to the more subdued, documentary-influenced style of his early features. Kieślowski set out to use ten different cinematographers for the ten films (in the end, he had to settle for nine, utilizing Piotr Sobociński twice, in *III* and *IX*). The experiment would prove very rewarding: each of the cinematographers he would use for his later films worked with him on the *Decalogue.*

In an interview with Danusia Stok, Kieślowski tells the story of a passing conversation with Krzysztof Piesiewicz outside in the cold, pouring rain. "Someone should make a film about the Ten Commandments. . . . You should do it," Piesiewicz suggested. Kieślowski didn't think much of the idea at first; then, walking around Warsaw, Kieślowski was overwhelmed by the impression that he was "watching people who didn't know why they were living."[1] At that point, he began to think Piesiewicz might be right.

Regardless of one's theological commitments, the commandments demarcate ten universal arenas of moral choice. These are the loci of our most important decisions as humans, and Kieślowski shows how rich and complicated these arenas are. No theological dogma is trumpeted here, but it is not a stretch to say that Kieślowski shows respect for the Judeo-Christian tradition, even if only by acknowledging that the commandments continue to haunt us. Respect is not equal to adherence, however. Several

---

1. *Kieślowski on Kieślowski,* ed. Danusia Stok (London: Faber and Faber, 1993), 143.

times Kieślowski seems to be indicating how difficult the commandments are to keep, or even understand, amid the complexities of contemporary life. All of the episodes might be seen as stories in Plato's cave. Occasionally, the characters get to turn and see the ideal, even if only in the periphery. Most of the time, however, they encounter shadows of the truth, lots of lies, and the mundane sounds of their surroundings.

In the current literature on Kieślowski, there is a surprising amount of debate on the numbering of the episodes and their thematic alignment with the biblical Decalogue. Those finding the relationship awkward are typically working from the Protestant numbering of the commandments, not the Roman Catholic,[2] and it seems very clear to me that Kieślowski is using the Catholic system. Some assert that no direct parallel can be drawn between any of the episodes and any one commandment, but rather that all the episodes touch on themes of several.[3] Kieślowski did deliberately avoid titling the films to broaden their application, recognizing the inherent connections and overlap between the commands themselves. The biblical Decalogue itself is bookended by ultimacies. On the front end, God shall be the only thing worthy of worship, and breaking any of the commandments, in a broad sense, is worshipping something else (one's self, at the very least). On the other end, the root of covetousness is discontentedness, and each of the commandments flows from some form of discontent. So, whenever a commandment is broken, one always breaks at least two, often three. This

---

2. Catholics typically combine the assertions "You shall have no other gods before me" and "You shall not make unto yourselves an idol" into one commandment (Commandment 1), whereas Protestants count them as two (Commandments 1 and 2). Thus, the Catholic numbering is always one commandment ahead of the Protestant commandments in numbering, until the end, where the Catholics split the assertions "You shall not covet your neighbor's house" and "You shall not covet your neighbor's wife" into two commandments (9 and 10) whereas the Protestants treat them both as Commandment 10. Joseph N. Kickasola, an Old Testament scholar, explains that the Bible totals but does not enumerate the commandments of the Decalogue (Exodus 34:28). He demonstrates that Protestants (other than Lutherans and Anglicans, who follow the Roman Catholic enumeration) follow the ancient Jewish tradition of Philo (a Jew of Alexandria, d. 50 AD) and Josephus (a Jew of Jerusalem, d. 100 AD). The Eastern Orthodox Church also perpetuates this enumeration, refusing the conflation of polytheism and idolatry (the Sanctities of God and of Worship) and affirming the union of the kinds of covetousness (the Sanctity of Contentment).

3. Monika Maurer is just one of several popular critics taking this position. See *Krzysztof Kieślowski* (Harpenden, Herts, Great Britain: Pocket Essentials, 2000), 40.

aside, I believe the themes of the individual episodes are quite clearly related to foundational concepts inherent in their sequentially parallel commands.

Kieślowski bookends his series in a rather deliberate fashion as well. The first film, by far the darkest, initiates the series as "the curse of the law."[4] Just as Paul cited the redemption of Christ as the fulfillment of the law, and salvation from its curse,[5] so Kieślowski ends his series with a comedy and image of reconciliation: a lighthearted story of grace between two brothers (a Jerzy and Artur to remedy Jacob and Esau).

The following chart of the Ten Commandments (see page 164) I borrow from my father, an Old Testament and ancient language scholar. Joseph N. Kickasola articulates the object of each commandment, that ideal which the commandment was instituted to preserve. Kieślowski does not necessarily pursue each of these ideals directly, so I have added the themes that Kieślowski derived from each ideal in a third column.

Theophanes

As a thread of continuity between the scripts, Kieślowski and Piesiewicz designed a character originally intended to be present in every scene (but appearing fleetingly in episode *VII* and not at all in *X*[6]). Annette Insdorf calls him "The Angel," partly inspired by his affinity with Wim Wenders' characters.[7] I opt for a more formal theological term: Theophanes. In part, this a nod to Tarkovsky's *Andrei Rublev*, which features a character of the same name, moving in spiritlike fashion and appearing to know much more than most mortals are ever given. Etymologically, Theophanes means "Appearances of God," and this term has been used for various enigmatic characters in the Bible who seem to mark divine presence of some kind.[8] I do not

---

4. Galatians 3:10.

5. Galatians 3:13.

6. Kieślowski experienced technical difficulties including him in *Decalogue VII*, and chose not to show him amid the dark-humor atmosphere of *X*, a decision he later regretted (in Stok, *Kieślowski on Kieślowski,* 158).

7. Annette Indsorf, *Double Lives, Second Chances: The Cinema of Krzysztof Kieślowski* (New York: Hyperion, 1999), 73.

8. In Christian theology, a theophany is a sign or wonder of the appearance and presence of God, a manifestation of Him, but not His direct revelation, "for no one can see God and live" (Exodus 33:20). This is never his unveiled glory, but his veiled theophanic glory, as in speaking to Moses "face to face as a friend" (Exodus 33:11). Some other biblical

Commandment (Roman Catholic Enumeration)	Ideal	Kieślowskian Theme
1. I am the Lord thy God ... thou shalt not have other gods before me. Thou shalt not make unto thee any graven image ... Thou shalt not bow down thyself to them, nor serve them.	The sanctity of God and worship	Idolization of science
2. Thou shalt not take the name of the Lord thy God in vain.	The sanctity of speech	Names as fundamental to identity and moral choice; the importance of one's word in human life
3. Remember the Sabbath day, to keep it holy.	The sanctity of time	Time designations (holidays, day/night, etc.) as repositories of meaning
4. Honor thy father and thy mother.	The sanctity of authority	Familial and social relationships as regulators of identity
5. Thou shalt not kill.	The sanctity of life	Murder and punishment
6. Thou shalt not commit adultery.	The sanctity of love	The nature and relation of love and passion
7. Thou shalt not steal.	The sanctity of dominion	Possession as human need and temptation
8. Thou shalt not bear false witness against thy neighbor.	The sanctity of truth	The difficulties of truth amid desperate evil
9. Thou shalt not covet thy neighbor's wife.	The sanctity of contentment	Sex, jealousy, and faithfulness
10. Thou shalt not covet thy neighbor's goods.	The sanctity of contentment[9]	Greed and relationships

theophanies include the "three men" who appear to Abraham (Genesis 18:10, 14), the "angel of the Lord" appearing to Manoah (Judges 13:18, 32), the flaming bush before Moses (Exodus 3:4), and the angel with whom Jacob wrestles (Genesis 32:30). These incidents are not to be confused with appearances of ordinary angels, as these specific texts allude to some variety of beholding of the divine, whereas other passages merely describe angels as messengers *for* the divine.

9. Repeated, in the Protestant conception of the commands.

mean to overdeify the character or invest him with too much significance, but he does appear to be a reference point for the biblical themes embodied in the films. Likewise, he bears traits of God: his secret knowledge (one perceives that he knows something by his iconic stare), his omnipresence in the lives of these neighbors who barely interact with each other, his apparent affection for certain characters (*VI*), and the consternation of conscience and judgment he exudes (*IV* and *V*). One might say he is the *Dei oculi,* the "seeing" dimension of God's connection with the world, a manifestation of the idea found in the Old Testament, 2 Chronicles 16:9: "For the eyes of the Lord move to and fro throughout the earth that He may strongly support those whose hearts are completely His."

Theophanes may not be the only dimension of the Creator-creature interface, but he serves as a strong reminder of God's relentless, searching gaze. Indeed, throughout the *Decalogue* there are numerous instances where God's eye may be inferred (e.g., the vaulted angles above the cars in *III* and the wide shots of the countryside during the murder in *V*). Theophanes completes the divine omnipresent field of view, complementing the Transcendent angle with an immanent perspective.

Often his look is indecipherable, like Mozhukhin in Kuleshov's famous experiment, and we invest him with meaning in the same way.[10] I call him Theophanes, not because he is God, but because he references Him like an icon, materially bearing His presence and eternal gaze in the broken, desolate community, and reminding us that the commandments have always been perceived (by the faithful) to have a living, transcendent dimension. Although Kieślowski and Piesiewicz simply call him "the young man" in the script, the actor playing him (Artur Barciś) apparently thought of him as Christ. According to Christopher Garbowski, Kieślowski told Barciś to play him "as if you were five centimeters off the

---

10. For those not familiar with the experiment, the famous Russian actor Ivan Mozhukhin was filmed giving a neutral expression. Lev Kuleshov edited this image against a bowl of soup, a dead woman in a coffin, and a girl playing with a toy bear. Audiences often read the expression on the actor's face as three different, subtle reactions to the scenes, reflecting hunger, sorrow, and joy, when, in fact, the expression never changed. This account may be found in most film history texts; Robert Sklar's *Film: An International History of the Medium* (New York: Prentice-Hall, 1993), 151, and David Bordwell and Kristin Thompson's *Film History: An Introduction,* 2nd ed. (Boston: McGraw-Hill, 2003), 132, are but two examples.

ground."[11] Kieślowski said of him "He's not very pleased with us," and in the screenplay wrote: "It is the same man who sat around the fire in the first story, who stood in the hospital corridor in the second story, and who will continue to appear, forever."[12] He is the eternal witness.

The apartment complex functions as the battle-scarred immanent ground. Within this context of community, a strained cohabitation that Kieślowski will probe for true human connections, the themes of home and family persist in every episode. A child is lost in *I*, gained in *II*. A family is tested and threatened in *III*, while the very definition of family is questioned in *IV*. *V* demonstrates the devastation of losing a family member, whereas *VI* demonstrates the effects of not having a family. *VII* involves the intrafamilial struggle over a child, and *VIII* involves a young girl in need of parental protection. *IX* exhibits the delicacy of bond between spouses, and *X* exhibits the delicacy, and necessity, of bonds between siblings. The home is where we receive our first sense of identity and learn how to relate to others. In this fragile, personal arena Kieślowski confronts us with the heaviest issues in human experience.

Decalogue I

SYNOPSIS: *Krzysztof (Henryk Baranowski), a scientist with full faith in the scientific method and no theistic beliefs, loves his boy, Paweł (Wojciech Klata), and much of the film is dedicated to their activities together (conversations, chess games, machines they've constructed, solving math problems with a computer, etc.). Through various events, such as the death of a neighborhood dog, Paweł's thoughts turn to mortality. His father gives biological explanations. His aunt provides a more theological and truly metaphysical perspective. Paweł's desire to try his new ice skates is subject to the thickness of the ice, which Krzysztof deems safe after consulting the scientific method (running some calculations on his computer and testing the ice himself with a stick). Even so, the ice breaks and Paweł drowns, causing Krzysztof to angrily run to the*

---

11. Christopher Garbowski, *Krzysztof Kieślowski's Decalogue Series: The Problem of the Protagonists and Their Self-Transcendence* (Boulder, CO: Eastern European Monographs, 1996), 18. He is translating from a Polish interview with Barciś ("Grasz to, co masz w sobie. Z [. . .] rozmawia Tadeusz Sobolewski," *Kino* 24.2 [1990]: 9).

12. Found in the script for *IV*, scene 23. Krzysztof Kieślowski and Krzysztof Piesiewicz, *Decalogue: The Ten Commandments*, trans. Phil Cavendish and Susannah Bluh (London: Faber and Faber, 1991), 111.

nearby church and overturn the altar. Wax from the ruptured candles splashes on the face of the Madonna icon, simulating tears.

It seems deliberate that the first adult character of the series, a skeptic in faith matters, bears Kieślowski's name. It is also worth noting that Krzysztof is quite literally a "Christ"-ian name, referencing the tension of belief and doubt in Kieślowski's own life.

The film begins on a lake, which actually resembles something closer to a swamp amid the dead of winter. The camera lingers on the dark surface, half-frozen, flowing abstractly on the right side of the frame, dully reflective on the left. This image, which might have come right from a Tarkovsky film, begins the series in a stylistically distinct mode. Though this film rarely utilizes a pure form of abstraction, the patient camera and editing isolate objects in unusual ways, pulling them from the ordinary flow of time and embuing them with phenomenological impact and metaphorical suggestion.

The lake will become something of a character in the drama to unfold. It forms a proverbial chasm between the church and the people of the apartment building. Children play on its surface and die beneath it. Theophanes sits upon its banks, warming himself next to a fire. The flames are at once hopeful, a warm glow amid the bitter cold, and unbearably frightening in view of the tragic ice melt at the end of the film.

We see the man's back, and, indeed, he is turned away from us throughout much of the film, as though in judgment or abandonment, or both. Then, Theophanes stares at us, as an icon. The heat, rising from his fire in the foreground, blurs his definitive shape a bit, rendering him not quite solid; in addition to the abstract virtues of the moment, the symbolic connotations of the fire (he sees us through judgment, and weeps) must not be lost. His face is paired with a crying woman (equally unknown to us) staring at a TV monitor. On the television, the image of happy children running slows and finally stops in freeze frame on the face of a boy, plucked from the time-flow of life and ossified on the screen. The woman's tears are matched by those of Theophanes, framed in the next shot; his back may be turned, but he is not emotionally removed. The aunt weeps for Paweł. Theophanes seems to weep for much more. His tears may reference the whole human condition.

A low, abstract shot of a building facade follows, dominated by stacked, cross-shaped balconies, textured in cold, gray cement against an ominous sky. In an unexpected flurry of life, birds scatter in the foreground. One of those birds lands on little Paweł's windowsill, and we have been carried, via flight, across the temporal rift. We have arrived at the beginning of the story. The seamless flow of these shots shows a maturity of style in the chronology of Kieślowski's films. As mentioned, there is a transcendent reach here, not simply in the metaphysical context, but in the formal elision of time-space boundaries. This sequence might be called a metaphysical chain. Theophanes, with his iconic appearance, cuts with Paweł's aunt (Maja Komorowska), whose embrace (she tells Paweł later) incarnates the love and presence of God. Paweł's frozen face on the television provides an eerie counterpart to the iconic pose of Theophanes, and the man's tears follow the image, implying a relation between them. Mediated by technology, the television image is liminal, carrying the powerful emotional weight of memory (just as Peter wept over his mother's posthumous image in *Camera Buff*), but lacks the necessary ontological weight of existence. The image is rich, but falls short of real presence.

The father, Krzysztof, is a professor. He has a theory that a computer can someday be built to such specificity that it carries "aesthetic preference," a liminal characteristic, hovering on the threshold of humanness. His lecture is most instructive, beginning with a semiotic discussion of the concept "Judas" and the intricacies of connotation inherent in it (a lecture reminiscent of the linguistic discussion in Zanussi's *Camouflage*). Through this educational trope, Kieślowski has not only plunged us into his most prominent theme (a discussion of meaning in human life), but he has also suggested that a Judas-like betrayal will occur. Indeed, multiple betrayals exist in this rich, potent film: technology that destroys rather than serves, a father who fails to protect sufficiently, and, in Krzysztof's mind, a God who gives and then takes away. In each case, the betrayal is complex: a mingling of good intentions, inability, and mystery. Even in the case of God, where agency is most traceable, Kieślowski suggests that God is not so heartless as He appears (e.g., the tears of Theophanes and the Madonna), but we are still left without answers. Even Job, the biblical paradigm of suffering, received no answers, only divine presence.[13]

Krzysztof's prophecy regarding technology comes mysteriously true, at least in some respects. He calls the computer "colleague," and it responds to Krzysztof's voice. Krzysztof asks his colleague what it "wants" ("I am ready..." is its ominous reply), then chides himself as "silly" for asking a

---

13. See Job, particularly chapters 38 through 42.

volitional question of the machine. It is instructive that the machine refuses to turn off at Krzysztof's command — refuses to "die" — and a frustrated Krzysztof manually shuts it down.

This is the first suggestion that the computer has a will (reminiscent of Kubrick's *2001*), and it apparently turns itself on as well. This uncanny self-generation resonates as an everyday mystery, a commonplace unexplained event with suggestions of a transcendent reality lurking behind the material world. The computer falls short in the face of the most important questions.[14] Technology cannot convey the divine love that Aunt Irena conveys in her physical contact with Paweł. All the gadgets, with which Kieślowski was so fascinated and which generate such happiness between Krzysztof and Paweł, ring very hollow at the film's end, failing in the liminal space. Even the computer's memory, which is often mentioned throughout the film, is shown to be a cold, factual memory lacking the nuances of meaning in human recollection. The green glow of the computer becomes ominous after Paweł's death, rising like a specter on Krzysztof's face — an angel of death declaring, "I am ready." Ready for what? For more scientific "progress"?

It seems that the computer is a combination of symbols. At once it functions as a critique of technological materialism and judgment on the sin of idolizing the myth of progress. At the same time, the computer is a locus of divine presence and judgment, a call to the conscience, and a harbinger of disaster ("What if it really wanted something?" Paweł asks, a question Krzysztof dismisses as silly, to his own detriment). It is important to note that the original script of this episode clearly explains the scientific reason the ice breaks; a power plant unexpectedly released warm water into the lake overnight.[15] It is more important to note that Kieślowski chose to excise this from the final film, implying that the event is not the result of a scientific factor overlooked by the computer, but an utter failure on its part.

The scientific paradigm is critiqued elsewhere in the film for its lack of nuance in the metaphysical arenas of human life. For instance, Paweł's encounter with a pretty girl and a dead dog (yet another stark pairing of

14. Indeed, Kieślowski often shows a blank computer screen in the face of these important questions, just as Douglas Sirk used a dead, hollowly reflective TV set as a poor substitute for meaningful human relationships in *All That Heaven Allows*.

15. Kieślowski and Piesiewicz, *Decalogue*, 24. The indictment of the computer's limited ability to handle metaphysics is also much more pointed in the excised portions of scene 26, where the computer cannot recognize the terms "sense" and "hope" (pp. 26–28).

life and death images in Kieślowski) provokes a very emotional reaction in his young, searching mind. He vents his emotions and explores his questions with his father through a conversation that stands among the most metaphysically and spiritually direct Kieślowski has ever filmed. It is in this remarkable conversation, a metaphysical context if there ever was one, that we see one of the first examples of Kieślowski's abstraction in full bloom.

As Krzysztof answers Paweł's question ("What is death?") in cold, physical terms ("The heart stops pumping blood . . . it doesn't reach the brain, movement ceases, everything stops . . . "), Paweł is not satisfied. "What's left?" he asks, to which the father answers achievement and memory. Indeed, Paweł himself knows the value of memory. His relationship with his mother is entirely dependent upon it, in a certain respect; we never see her, he continually asks for her, she rarely calls ("Do you think Mother will telephone before Christmas?"). "The memory's important . . . " Krzysztof continues. "The memory that someone moved in a certain way, or that they were kind, you remember their face, their smile, that a tooth was missing." Paweł makes note that he has forgotten the soul, and Krzysztof at first denies it ("Some people find it easier believing that," he remarks, echoing Karl Marx), then confesses he doesn't know. At this crucial point, Kieślowski cuts to an inordinately long close-up of cream being poured into coffee. He lingers on this transcendental image, an abstract meditation, rich in both phenomenological impact and connotation. The image here richly demonstrates the formal dynamic system described in Chapter 2, as the swirling light and dark forms exude an aura of the transcendent dimension. On a symbolic level, the milk is sour, just as the father's explanations are impoverished in light of the eternal questions.

Milk, a life-giving substance in many contexts, deathly sour in this scene, thematically bridges the narrative to the next, in which Paweł's school is undergoing an experiment on the nourishing properties of milk in children. A documentary crew is covering the event and provides the footage of the children running, which we view in the beginning and ending of the film.

In sharp contradistinction to Krzysztof, his sister Irena offers spiritual answers to Paweł's questions. In the end, she finds herself weeping with everyone else, of course, but there is a strong sense that she is better equipped emotionally and spiritually for the tragedy. "One is alive, and it's a present . . . a gift," she tells Paweł, echoing Witek's persecuted Catholic friend in *Blind Chance.* Her photographs, which she proudly displays for Paweł, prompt him to ask her if he understands the meaning of life. (Who?

we ask.) The camera then reveals the pictures of the pope, an editing gesture carrying the force of revelation. "I think so," she says. Irena represents the hope Poland placed in its favorite son, articulated explicitly by the young girl in *Talking Heads* longing for a papal visit. At the time of this film, Solidarity was still underground but gaining strength again. In 1989, the year after *Decalogue*'s release, everything would change.

Irena explains to Paweł that his father was raised in a Catholic family but fell prey to the idea that everything could be measured. Even so, she says, his scientific paradigm "does not rule out God." When asked who God is, she hugs Paweł, announcing that He may be found in their embrace. She does not answer the question, but points to where he may be found (i.e., within a feeling, an intuition). This is theology in the vein of Kierkegaard and other Christian existentialists. It is important to note, however, that Kieślowski cuts this touching, theologically affirming scene with a shot of Theophanes, back turned to us, tending his fire by the frozen lake. This hollow, foreboding image presents us with the other side of God — his judgment and wrath. Though he seems to weep for them, he is far from Irena and Paweł and never touches them, let alone embraces them.

Having been presented with these two paradigms, it is important to note that Paweł finds himself in a chess game in the next scene. The original script calls for a chess master and presumes a man in the position, but Kieślowski cast a young woman. She appears to be a teenager, a child genius, who circles the room playing multiple games, one move at a time. Paweł and Krzysztof challenge her, strategizing over each move. She moves with an extraordinary, decisive authority, almost God-like in her power. She has won six games already, but after Paweł claims to have figured out the girl's "system," he castles. The strategy prevails, and they win the game.

The chess match calls to mind Bergman's *Seventh Seal,* where a character buys an extension on his life by playing chess with death. The connection to death may be made here, but there is the suggestion that we, as mortals, do not have full control of the game. Paweł, on the other hand, may have secret knowledge that helps him win. Garbowski has suggested that perhaps Paweł has a special intuition of God, symbolized by his winning the match, and so God took the boy to be with Him.[16] Another likely interpretation is that God's "system" in the ultimate chess game is beyond understanding.

---

16. Garbowski, *Krzysztof Kieślowski's Decalogue Series,* 17.

Apart from the obvious thematic overtones in the scene (choices, strategy, and the place of reason, etc.), I cannot say enough about the brilliance of this little scene. It stands as a gem in Kieślowski's oeuvre, simply for its pacing. The tension generated by the actors and the rhythm of the edits (measuring the walk of the genius, round and round the table) is perfectly controlled, building anticipation, particularly in Paweł, and culminating in a marvelous burst of happiness from the little boy after victory. Wojciech Klata's performance as Paweł is astonishing throughout the film, and when his character kisses his father on the cheek, we see the sheer delight of their relationship epitomized.

I have discussed the importance of Krzysztof's lecture to his students, but it is equally important to notice Paweł's actions throughout. He views his father through gaps in some equipment that frame and reframe different aspects of the man. As his father speaks of semiotics (communication, meaning, and language), Paweł, rather than listening, explores him phenomenologically (through sight, bracketing, and intentionality). This sequence carries an abstract, depersonalized, and objective quality that is difficult to articulate. Krzysztof speaks of T. S. Eliot's belief that poetry is what is untranslatable (or incommunicable) then challenges Eliot with the aesthetic potential of the computer. At the same time, however, Paweł is engaged in this very human, nonverbal, personally meaningful process of visual abstraction that transcends any computer's brute analytic mode. Paweł's natural curiosity, which dissects a familiar image (his father) in order to see it anew, shows the computer's cold, impersonal aesthetic to be pale by comparison.

It is also important that Krzysztof speaks of the intimacy of one's mother tongue and the computer's ability to emulate that relationship. The political reference is blunted and oblique here, suggesting a universalization of language over national experience (expounded here on the verge of another revolution in Poland). While the sequence resonates with these political suggestions, it also beautifully illustrates Paweł's nonpolitical, precocious, and curious mind in contrast with this rhetoric.

The experiment with the frozen milk bottle is interesting in light of the modernist paradigm; Krzysztof fully expects the bottle to thaw, but Paweł eagerly wants to see what will happen. There is this childish sense of possibility in Paweł's world, and the scientific explanation of milk freezing is greeted by him as every bit the miracle as the thawing of the ice will prove to be in the end. Krzysztof's testing of the frozen lake on his evening off reinforces the security of his own scientific judgment. The ice has been subject to two calculations: the computer's assessment, based on temperature, and his own, physical testing with a walking stick. On this walk, as he assures himself, he comes across two unnerving scenes: Theophanes, their eyes meeting through the roaring flames of his fire in the foreground, and a nighttime gathering of silent men and women in front of the church (a wake, perhaps? A political gathering? Whatever it is, the occasion is solemn, and the people stand holding hands).

And so, the harbingers continue to mount. As Krzysztof works at his desk, an abstract, black cloud of ink grows in the middle of his papers, devouring all his scientific work bit by bit. We don't know why his ink bottle suddenly starts leaking, but the ink stains everything and looks like blood in the sink as Krzysztof washes his hands. Judgment has come.

Beginning with a little girl asking for Paweł at the door, Krzysztof begins to piece together the tragedy that has befallen his son. He calls the boy on their walkie-talkies (a last grasp for a technological connection). He calms himself at the stairway, logically deciding to take the elevator instead, where he faces an aged man on the ascent (an image of age, death, and time). He learns from Paweł's friend that the boy had a dream the night before. We don't know what dream, but the suggestion is one of premonition.

Night literally overtakes the day. After a long, excruciating sequence by the lake, the boy's body is pulled from the depths. All around kneel, but Krzysztof refuses. He returns to his empty apartment, and, quite visibly, a green spectral glow slowly rises on the side of his anguished face. The computer has awoken, quite on its own. "I am ready," it announces. "Perhaps it wants something," Paweł had once said.

At the church, the cross is both a looming, mouthlike, empty hole (in the building's facade) and a doorway into the sacred space. Krzysztof turns the altar over, and the wax spills, but several seconds after the disturbance the tearlike spots continue to appear, suggesting something more than temporal cause and effect. Perhaps the Madonna does cry, symmetrical with the tears of Theophanes: a film beginning and ending in divine grief. Such would be the Catholic perspective; a Protestant might reflect Coates's interpretation: she could not protect the child because "perhaps she is mere mortal."[17] Garbowski suggests the tears are not for Paweł, who now has "all the answers

17. Paul Coates, "Kieślowski and the Antipolitics of Color: A Reading of *The Three Colors Trilogy*," *Cinema Journal* 41.2 (Winter 2002): 45.

173

to his innocent questions," but rather for Krzysztof, "the one who is most in pain."[18] Another theological interpretation might reach even broader; the divine grief extends to all His Creation affected by the Fall. God's tears bear all the characters in mind, all the suffering souls in *The Decalogue,* and perhaps ourselves as well. We may ask Him, along with Krzysztof, "Why haven't you done anything about this?" The image is silent, but visibly effusive.

The holy water is frozen. Krzysztof pulls the chunk of ice from the vessel and touches it, baptismally, to his forehead. This gesture bears a double power: a claim for Paweł's baptism and Krzysztof's shell-shocked reach back for his own.

The final image of the film is a return to the television set, upon which Paweł's form was also frozen, plucked (via abstraction) from the temporal flow. Here, after death, we see it echo his frozen death. It moves again, slowly, abstractly, until the boy's face blurs out of focus and leaves the temporal frame, forever.

Decalogue II

SYNOPSIS: *Dorota (Krystyna Janda) finds herself in an ethical tangle, the complexity of which slowly reveals itself throughout the film. She seeks out her neighbor, an old doctor (Aleksander Bardini), currently treating her cancer-plagued husband, Andrzej (Olgierd Łukaszewicz). She begs him to make a declaration on Andrzej's fate, which he adamantly refuses to do. She eventually reveals that she is carrying another man's child, unbeknownst to Andrzej, and this may be her last chance to bear a child. If Andrzej lives, she will abort; if not, she will keep the baby. The doctor is unwilling to make a judgment, and his own personal losses during World War II clearly haunt him in this matter. He gives Andrzej little hope for survival, and his condition appears to be desperately bleak. Dorota breaks off the relationship with her lover, but continues to press the doctor for a decision. He suddenly asserts that Andrzej will die. Miraculously, Andrzej recovers and happily announces to the doctor that he and Dorota are having a child. The doctor clearly understands the complexities behind this announcement, but remarks that he understands what it means to have a child.*

There is a certain deadness that permeates the entire *Decalogue,* and the opening of this film is no different. Kieślowski's construction of the dramatic tension is most remarkable in these first few minutes, and, because there

18. Garbowski, *Krzysztof Kieślowski's Decalogue Series,* 92.

is little dialogue, descriptive summary is necessary to bring out what is happening stylistically.

A clandestine approach to exposition is not unique to Kieślowski, of course, but the ambiguity of character and future revelations typify his aesthetic, a sort of abstraction. Some, like Hitchcock, hide details for the purpose of generating suspense; others, like Martin Scorsese, for generating dramatic tension. Both ends are served here, of course, but I believe Kieślowski's work carries the additional virtue of making us think about these images in broader, more universal, and cosmic ways. Kieślowski is always generating a metalevel of meaning through experience with the image, and I do not believe the nature of the metalevel is simply reflexive (i.e., comments on the film itself), but rather signals a reach toward the Transcendent possibility. This film demonstrates this reach more succinctly than any film in Kieślowski's oeuvre.

In a hopeful image of renewal, the groundskeeper clears away dead brush, but the day is still terribly gray (like the lighting for the rest of the film), and he comes across a dead animal (the second in as many episodes). This death image is axiologically turned, however: the rabbit was clearly food for someone, at a time when people needed food in Poland. There lingers the abiding feeling that, after the crushing crackdown on Solidarity, life has grown terribly stale in Poland. Very small glimmers of hope exist; the doctor, for instance, listens to Radio Free Europe as he attempts to revive his dying cactus and feeds his bird. The lack of running hot water indicates government neglect, as do the signs of decay in the doctor's hospital workplace (peeling paint, leaking ceilings, etc.). Even so, the doctor calmly boils his water for his bath, with no visible sign of complaint, like unto the noble, persistent doctors in *Hospital.* He appears tired, and that fatigue culminates in the bathroom, where he nearly faints. The nature of this spell is never explained, and one gets the impression he may be suffering from more than physical fatigue. Once again Kieślowski gives us a close-up on a hand, grasping for more than physical support. The disassociated, abstract feeling the shot yields empowers it with metaphorical force, and the clear view of the man's wristwatch only heightens its effect; the doctor represents old, hardened Poland, weary with fatigue, afraid to hope. (One cannot help but think of Bardini's previous role as Labrador in *No End,* another old man surrounded by clocks.) We will discover much later the personal nature of the doctor's burdens, but for now, we only know that he suffers, and Kieślowski seems to be asking whether that is not enough for our sympathies.

The doctor's continuing (somewhat reluctant) conversation with his housekeeper, Barbara, will slowly reveal the source of this spiritual stasis. In bits and pieces, he remembers his lost family, including a charming detail about his father's lost tooth, synchronous with the teething of his infant child. These sorts of unique stories (the stories that are left out of many Hollywood films) permeate Kieślowski's films, striking us as both unusual and wholly believable. They are the curious memories of the lost — mundane, immanent things that reveal their deep symbolic value for us all (sentiments echoed in both *Blind Chance* and *Decalogue I*).

We first see Dorota with her back toward us. We have no initial clue that she will be a main character any more than the groundskeeper in the beginning of the film. Her cigarette, a palpable index of her internal distress, falls to the ground. Kieślowski fixates upon her foot grinding it into the floor. This proverbial cigarette will gain prominence in a later scene when Dorota, almost masochistically, drops the ashes in her hand (echoing the fiery hand in *Blind Chance*) and puts the cigarette out in a box of matches (a blazing climax that Kieślowski captures in slow motion and extreme close-up).

The tug and pull of the unspoken build in intensity, climaxing with the doctor catching her at his door. Words are then spoken, and the bitterness between these strangers bleeds out; they have clearly not spoken much before, but the doctor remembers that she ran over his dog two years before. This acidic connection between the two characters is jarring, reeking of the pessimism regarding humanity that abounds in Kieślowski's previous two films. This film, however, will attempt to find a way out through suffering. Although Dorota never comes to love the old man, it becomes very clear that a compassion for her situation grows in him, synchronous with his own recollection of personal loss.

Dorota directs her bitterness at the doctor's God-like quality, as he is the only one in Dorota's purview with any power in the situation. When Kieślowski references God, it is often through immanental means: a human character as liminal ground. Just as Irena encouraged Paweł to find God's love in her embrace, Dorota projects God's apparent callousness onto the doctor. He is terribly resistant to any further personal investment in life, whether his memories of past loved ones, his own life, or the lives of his patients (he remarks that he cannot remember his patient's names).

Stylistically, the seeds of abstraction sown in earlier films grow rapidly here, culminating in the astonishing resurrection sequence (where the transcendental aim of the style is most pronounced). The modes of abstraction described in Chapter 2 all appear here, from slow motion to close-ups to the withholding of expository information (discussed previously) to, most prominently, the long meditation and the denial of an establishing shot. Although some of these scenes were discussed in Chapter 2, a discussion of a few of these examples will profit us here.

Dorota's hand often destroys things. She crumples a letter (from her lover?). She's constantly crushing cigarettes, and she slowly tips a glass off the table (Kieślowski treats us to a dramatic, close-up, slow-motion rendering of its destruction). These gestures are often shot in the abstract mode, carrying resonance of both the temporal destruction permeating her life and the encroachment of evil into her metaphysical sphere. The most pointed example exists in Dorota's mangling of the plant, a counterpoint to Barbara's efforts to revitalize the doctor's dying cactus. Coolly and deliberately we see Dorota pull one leaf after another from the stem, working her way down, and finally crumpling the empty stem. Long after she leaves the frame, rather than cutting away, Kieślowski lingers on the plant, watching its warped stem gradually rise, refusing to die.

To simply describe this image in a literary fashion and interpret it symbolically is to limit its power. Clearly, there is a life-death image here, and the plant's attempted return to its original shape strikes us, on a semiotic level, as a defiance of death (foreshadowing Andrzej's resurrection to come). There is nothing quite like seeing it unfold, however, and Kieślowski's patient, close-up camera pushes us into that experiential realm. It is not a picture of anguish (in the semiotic sense) but nearly an *instance* of anguish, which is, itself, rarely a verbal matter. This is yet another liminal space, between sign and experience, and bridging the gap is living, abstract form, extracted from the lifeflow by the camera.

Whereas many Hollywood directors emphasize clarity of plot, dialogue, and characterization, Kieślowski often sacrifices those elements for the sake of pace and resonance. On the other hand, he preserves other long moments of experience (that appear quite incidental to the plot and yield no imperative information for story comprehension). Kieślowski also seemed amenable to certain forms of the jump-cut, particularly the conjoining of two shots of a single character in two different diegetic times. One would be hard-pressed to argue that this functions in the same way abstraction does, that is, as an expression of cosmic time and space, but it does illustrate Kieślowski's dismissive attitude toward classic narrative cutting and the preservation of consistent time-space relations. Kieślowski's approach to diegetic time and space is much more internal, fluid, and, ultimately, metaphysical and cosmic than many directors.

As I detailed in Chapter 2, the frequent denial of the establishing shot forces the audience to reconsider the narrowness of its diegetic space. Kieślowski gives us several strong examples of this in this film, including the scene where the despairing Dorota first comes to visit Andrzej, and a mysterious, God-like, off-screen voice encourages her to leave the jar of berries she has brought ("He might eat it later," the now-revealed roommate says). In a later surprising scene, a terrified Dorota sees a sheeted corpse being wheeled from her husband's room, only to find Andrzej there and his roommate gone. The other key example of this "dislocational" strategy exists in the scene in the gynecological office, as described in detail in Chapter 2. The rhetoric of such a sequence amounts to an emphasis on the internal (i.e., beginning the scene with a close-up of Dorota's face) and a revelation of the surroundings as complementary to that internal expression (in this case, the revelation that she is in a doctor's office, considering an abortion). As discussed in Chapter 2, the strategy also forces the audience to reconceive its view of the space — to expand it and receive the suggestion of wider, more cosmic times and spaces (consonant with the eternal issues involved). For Kieślowski, the world is always wider, and time is far more fluid than the temporal constraints permit. It is precisely the time-space dimension of human meaning that he attempts to trace, not in a delineating fashion (as if meaning had boundaries), but as a metaphysical explorer.

The metaphysical context of the abstract strategy is clear. Dorota's confession to the doctor is followed by numerous, probing questions. She asks him if he can understand the possibility of loving two persons at once, an anticipation of the doppelgänger theme to come in later Kieślowski films. Dorota talks through her dilemma in personal, emotional terms. The doctor responds to her in probability statistics and figures, then brackets those predictions with his own experience of the "outliers," the medically inexplicable cases, like an older, wiser Krzysztof of *Decalogue I*. Her remark, "One shouldn't wish for everything . . . that's pride," brings us back to the axiological root of these films: the Ten Commandments. Multiple sins are represented here, but Dorota's comment leads us to the principle that the tenth commandment, covetousness (a by-product of pride, springing from the sense one deserves what one does not have), permeates all the commandments. This statement leads to a more theologically direct question: "Do you believe in God?" The doctor's response that his "private God" is only big enough for himself points to his constant confrontation with the problem of evil and his inability to extend God beyond himself. It is clear that he cannot extend Him to his own family, whose tragic death continues to sear his soul. Dorota needs a bigger God than that, however.

Her internal tension reaches a peak as she nears the time of her rendezvous with her lover. She speaks to his erstwhile emissary, a man who we think is her lover but turns out to be simply conveying instructions, much as a spy would in international espionage. The clandestine, politically resonant nature of this situation would ring loud and clear to Polish viewers, and clearly Dorota's response is equally suspicious. Her coffee goes cold, just as Krzysztof's milk went sour in *Decalogue I*. That which is good, the sacramental drink between two communing friends, is spoiled here. It is synecdochal of the condition of the world — the fallen world, the good creation gone rotten, in need of redemption.

The time surrounding Dorota's critical turn also marks the entrance of Theophanes, working as a hospital orderly. As the doctor confirms, via microscope, "progression," in Andrzej's case, Theophanes looks on with interest. There is a terrible ambiguity here that Kieślowski may have intended. Coates and Insdorf both suggest that the word (which is *progress* in the script, but seems to be *progression* in the film[19]), refers to Andrzej's *treatment,* and therefore stands as a sign he might be recovering. In this case, the doctor clearly lies to Dorota about death being imminent, in order to save the child. Monika Maurer agrees, suggesting the slides tip him off to the idea that "recovery is already under way."[20] I see nothing in the script or the filmed version to indicate that this interpretation is absolute. It could very likely be that *the cancer* is showing progression, as they are clearly looking at slide samples of the tumors, taken over a series of weeks. There is nothing in the doctor's reaction, or that of the assistant, to suggest anything encouraging. The reluctance of the assistant to say what he thinks ("But you always taught us . . . ") could very well be in response to the doctor's previous decree that physicians not make predictions at all.

A great deal hinges on how this tiny scene is to be interpreted. If my alternative is to be believed, the film depicts a bitter doctor, reluctant to

---

19. My thanks to Stefan Krauss for help with this translation.

20. Insdorf, *Double Lives,* 80, Paul Coates, *Lucid Dreams: The Films of Krzysztof Kieślowski* (Trowbridge, Wiltshire, England: Flicks Books, 1999), 99, posit this as a likely interpretation. Maurer's position is more dogmatic, *Krzysztof Kieślowski,* 44.

make a judgment, forced to do so through the pressure of his own personal, moral universe. After the decision is made, a miracle occurs. If the first interpretation holds, we may still have a miracle (and the presence of Theophanes in the scene confirms this), but it may be a more "modern miracle," providence laced with science. It would also problematize the ethics of the doctor. This complicated situation is revisited in *VIII*, as Zofia addresses the situation in her ethics class. The important thing, she says, is that the child survives. Perhaps that is the focus, and Kieślowski's narrative ambiguities simply bring that fact into stark relief. In any case, the ethics are most gray, the situation most desperate, and the spiritual tension most palpable.

I do not see this film as an anti-abortion treatise on Kieślowski's part (a political commitment Kieślowski would be hesitant to embrace, I imagine). However, it is very clear to me that the focus in this film is on life and death, and Kieślowski portrays the abortion issue as a life or death decision (or, at the very least, the termination of a potential life). The symmetry between the situation of Dorota and the doctor is undeniable: the doctor lost a spouse and his children, Dorota stands to lose both as well. The last lines of the film ("Do you know what it means to have a child?" — "I do.") reinforce the place of the child in this life-death arena. For Kieślowski, the name of someone, his or her identity, is a core issue, and the commandment to not take the Lord's name in vain is rooted in a grand principle: respect the identity of another. This child will be raised under a false name, perhaps, but *III* will show us that ambiguous identity can be redeemed, and familial love has the power to transcend the specter of dubious paternity. The return of Andrzej and a pregnant Dorota in *V* creates a contrast between their decision for life (however difficult) and a gruesome, impending death in that film.

In the next scene, Dorota's cigarette smoulders in the ashtray, and she finally breaks things off with her lover. She announces her intention to have the abortion and end the relationship. His "I love you" never reaches her ears, lost over the close-up that Kieślowski gives us of Dorota's hand, limply holding the telephone before she hangs it up.

The next scene prefigures the hopeful turn this story will take. The doctor's cactus still appears weak, but it perseveres in its new pot. The close-up of the coffee reveals that it is hot, and its communal significance returns in the doctor's final conversation with Barbara, where he completes the horrifying story of his family's final hour. The sadness of this scene is only assuaged by the fact that the doctor is finally talking about and, perhaps, dealing with the loss of his family. We had seen him reinstate his family's picture in a previous scene (turning it back into view).

The scene cuts with the horrifying possibility that Andrzej lies on that stretcher coming out of his room, only to reveal a weak but awkwardly sitting Andrzej in the room after Dorota anxiously enters. She brings herself to speak to him for the first time in the film, parallel with the doctor's verbal breakthrough in the previous scene. Significantly, Theophanes looks on, first in abstract soft focus, then in a full close-up. His thoughtful reaction *follows* her words to him ("I love you very much") and her touching of Andrzej's face (also a new step for her). God sees this new development. The abstract close-ups of water droplets, falling around the room, bolster the transcendent surge in the scene even as they amplify the tortured, anguished time of sickness. The drops bring to mind a host of connotations, resembling the drips from an IV, to the slow leakage of blood. Andrzej is fighting, it is clear, but it appears he is losing.

Dorota fears the same, as her conversation with the doctor reveals in the next scene. When faced with the inevitable prospect of the abortion, the doctor finally commits himself to a verdict: "He's dying." She makes him swear to it, which he does, following with the unqualified pronouncement, "He hasn't a chance." He urges her not to follow through with the procedure, perhaps out of concern for the child, like the child lost to the bomb in the war, lost to the hole that stood in place of his home that dreadful night.

In typical Kieślowskian style, it is only now, nearly fifty minutes into the film, that we discover Dorota herself is a musician, proof that Kieślowski sought to emphasize the universal issues over the particulars. In a marvelously hopeful turn, the doctor ends his final conversation with Dorota by remarking that he'd like to come hear her play in the symphony. She does not comprehend the relevance of this statement and walks out, but the doctor clearly considered it before he said it. Music has often been called the international language, emotion made palpable and capable of transcending numerous social, cultural, and personal boundaries. It is his reach, beyond his own crisis, to another suffering human being. It is also the prelude to what is, in my estimation, one of Kieślowski's greatest sequences.

It is difficult to adequately describe this sequence. Such labels as "poetic" and "lyrical" address the aesthetic character and ineffable reach of the artifact, but they lack the explanatory power for analysis. I addressed this lack at length in Chapter 2, and can only reiterate that I believe Kieślowski is functioning on a unique epistemological level here. Just as I would characterize music as meaningful beyond any typical semiotic categories (largely built on insufficient linguistic models), this sequence demonstrates immediacy through abstraction amid a metaphysically charged context. The result is a powerful Transcendent expression — a mystical utterance through image and sound. The similarity with music is further reinforced by its prominence in the scene, both in the diegesis (through the shots of Dorota playing violin) and the moving score on the soundtrack (a different piece of music entirely, masterfully written and executed by Zbigniew Preisner). The marriage between the musical and imagistic powers for immediacy here is both astonishing and unusual.

The sequence begins with a shot of Dorota staring out her apartment window, less shaky than she was as she peered from the hall window in the beginning of the film. She does not smoke, and her expression seems to indicate a beseeching, prayerful posture. Her gaze is directed upward, and she remains unmoving, immobile in the iconic, cosmic time. The camera begins a slow, deliberate descent. For what seems to be an eternity, we see the cold, abstract texture of the building's concrete facade, a surface we first viewed intently in the crosslike formations of the balconies at the beginning of *Decalogue I.* One floor. Two floors. Three levels down, we come upon the face of the doctor, bathed in an infernal red glow, staring iconically right at the camera. The theological parallels emerge in this phrase from the ancient Apostle's Creed, speaking of Christ, who "suffered under Pontius Pilate, was crucified, dead, and buried; he descended into hell." The next phrase will be represented as well: "The third day he rose again from the dead; he ascended into heaven, and sitteth on the right hand of God the Father Almighty; from thence he shall come to judge the quick and the dead."

The camera swiftly pans right and makes a seamless passage through cosmic space to the hospital room, where Andrzej lies still. The music suddenly shifts mode as his eyes miraculously open (an echo of the opening eyes of Christ in the hologram Witek beholds in *Blind Chance*). The camera seamlessly moves again, spiritlike, to a close-up of the glass on the table. Dorota's berries, which she brought him and left at the behest of the roommate, sit in the bottom of the glass, staining the water red. A single bee desperately fights for a way out of the liquid that threatens to engulf it. We wonder if it will survive the arduous struggle, as Kieślowski never wavers in his long, watchful shot. In an astonishing, life-affirming gesture, the bee emerges from the syrup to crawl along the glass rim, under Andrzej's watchful gaze. The scene cuts to Dorota playing with the symphony, and her face suddenly registers a change, an intuition that something has shifted in the cosmos. The very slightest beginnings of a smile emerge, as though she were looking at the next image: an empty doorway, like the entrance to a tomb, into which walks Lazarus himself.

This resurrection stands in the Transcendent mode of other films.[21] Among the differing themes in the Transcendental style, the miraculous turn is among the most difficult to effectively execute without lapsing into a fairy tale–like ethos. In my judgment, Kieślowski succeeds admirably here. This film also follows what has been known to Christian mystics as "the dark night of the soul." It is the mode of the Passion, completed by the resurrection, a sacramental mode in film, traced beautifully by Peter Fraser in *Images of the Passion*.[22]

Other Kieślowskian themes reappear and find redemption here. For example, the pictures of the mountains that decorate Dorota and Andrzej's apartment echo the home versus exploration theme in *The Scar* and other early films. This theme fully expands here, however, to the temporal versus extratemporal discussion. In *No End* Antek struggles at his liminal death-life moment, with the choice to stay on earth or move on to the next world, where it is easier (opting for the latter). In this film, Andrzej confesses to the doctor that he felt as if someone were convincing him not to return but, unlike Antek, resists that choice.

The child we never see (counterpoint to Dorota's equally hidden lover) carries an enormous burden in this film, and the meaning with which Kieślowski invests it is not simple or dogmatic. On the one hand, it is clear the abortion would be terminating something wondrous: "Such a beauty?" the gynecologist asks, and Dorota later tells her former lover, "This call is going to cost you a fortune," a foreboding statement carrying meaning well beyond monetary significance. Yet, at the same time, the situation is something of a catch-22, and Dorota's choice to abort the child may be, in her mind, something of a faith statement that her husband will recover, against all odds. It is this faith that she demands, but cannot extract, from the doctor, and she then seems to think the force of existential action is

---

21. Some prominent examples are Carl Dreyer's *Ordet* and Pedro Almodóvar's *Talk to Her*.

22. Peter Fraser, *Images of the Passion* (Westport, CT: Praeger, 1998).

needed. However desperate this "faith step" may appear, she does not go through with the abortion, perhaps as part of a plan to raise the child on her own. After Andrzej's resurrection, all are saved (Dorota, the child, Andrzej), but, of course, the lie persists.

Kieślowski seems to be elucidating the epistemological dynamic surrounding a name, implying that the *choice* to love a child as one's own carries more importance than the status of one's biological lineage. The final, devastating lines of the film reveal this:

ANDRZEJ: Do you know what it means to have a child?

DOCTOR: (somber pause) I do.

There are, of course, many levels to this conversation, and the genius of the script is the aggregate dramatic weight of all these components. Several children, and their significance, are contained in that statement. The unborn child will persist as a hopeful image in Kieślowski's later films as well, most vividly at the climax of *Blue*. In the end, reflecting on the commandment, we wonder what name this child will truly bear — to whom it will belong.

Decalogue III

SYNOPSIS: *Janusz (Daniel Olbrychski) plans on a quiet Christmas Eve with his family, but Ewa (Maria Pakulnis) interrupts his plans. She claims she cannot find her lover, Edward, and desperately implores Janusz, an ex-lover, to help her find him. Through a series of manipulations (most of which Janusz is aware but with which he plays along), she engineers Janusz's presence with her the entire evening. They struggle all night in their search for a lover that will never, indeed, can never be found (a fabricated story). They plow through the difficult terrain of their relationship — infidelity, deceit, regret, and many unhealed wounds. In the end, Ewa reveals that she was near suicide earlier that night, and her successful machinations with Janusz have stayed her hand. As the Christmas Day sun rises, they part, having resisted an affair, avoided death, and finally settled their past.*

Piotr Sobociński's cinematography begins the film in abstract fashion, and his penchant for color splashes, obvious lens flares, and distorted reflections persists throughout.[23] Here, we begin with impressionistic dabs of blue

---

23. Sobociński became a key cinematographer for Kieślowski. The only cinematographer to shoot two *Decalogue* episodes (this and *IX*), he was also Kieślowski's final cinematographer, for *Red*.

and white light, overlapping and shimmering. As the visual cue suggests, this is no ordinary scene, and this night is far from typical. Kieślowski's exploration of the third commandment will focus on the sanctity of time, the eternal space the sacred day delineates, and the mortal struggles found there. Running in ironic counterpoint to this visual evocation is the sound of a raspy, wandering voice singing a Christmas carol in a drunken stupor. We may aspire to the eternal, on this night above all, but we live here on the broken earth, an existential tightrope upon which Kieślowski forces us to walk throughout the film. Garbowski observes that the musical theme for this episode is the Polish Christmas carol "Bóg sie rodzi," translated "God is being born."[24] Kieślowski's ironic use of Christmas carols extends back to *Peace* and also recurs in the nursing home scene of this film. The lens rolls the city into focus, viewed from above (the first of many potential God's-eye shots in this film). The drunken caroler staggers past, dragging a Christmas tree behind him. This poor drunk may be the object of humor here, but, in typical fashion, Kieślowski forces us to consider his plight from a more human perspective later in the film.

Janusz, dressed as Santa, rings his own apartment intercom and converses playfully with his child through it. Lest we slip too comfortably into the holiday mode, he is greeted by a neighbor, a man who leaves the apartment building quite alone. "Merry Christmas," Janusz says. "I'm sorry, I didn't recognize you," Krzysztof (from *Decalogue I*) replies. Krzysztof, sans Paweł, gazes into the family scene unfolding in Janusz's window. It will not be a blessed night for everyone.

Once again, Kieślowski denies us full disclosure of his characters in the beginning. We are not always sure to what or whom characters may refer, and it is incumbent upon us to put the pieces together later. This mode of discovery and investigation sometimes proves taxing for the first-time viewer. However, this curious positioning places us in a subservient role: subservient to God (if He exists), fate, existence, the future, and so on. In short, we are agnostic about so many things yet still forced to view patterns of the past (a suggestion that all is not merely chance). This narrative strategy is, yet again, a form of abstraction, a posture that demands the suspension of normal expectations and a willingness to receive the images to come.

---

24. Garbowski, *Krzysztof Kieślowski Decalogue Series,* 82.

An example of this is Janusz's wife's comment, "Do you think we'll be able to go?" Janusz's response ("We can try") reveals nothing about the object of their conversation, and it is not until the next scene that we discover the referent: a midnight Mass at the church. Our introduction to the church is equally hidden: a wide, high angle of the church with several foreground pillars blocking our view. The metaphor of the partial view lacks precision but is nonetheless present: is God partially hidden (and this his point of view, so to speak)? Is this our view, similar to Ewa's (outside the church doors), as we struggle to look upon the Holy? It is here, looking through the gates of the church (a liminal space), that Janusz and Ewa begin their troubled odyssey.

Our introduction to Ewa is not unsympathetic, and it is very important to keep in mind that, upon first viewing, it is not at all clear she has concocted her story (though we suspect that she is lying, we also have reason to be suspicious of Janusz's account). We teeter between truth and lie throughout this film, just as Kieślowski forces us to balance a mixture of empathy and contempt for these desperate souls. She must never be a monster (any more than any of the characters in the *Decalogue*).[25]

Ewa watches as a boy runs outside in the cold to view the Christmas tree and an adult rushes after the child. Ewa's face reflects certain loneliness — a loss — and our sympathies heighten as she goes to visit her aunt (her only family?) that evening. Her aunt, seated by herself in a room at the retirement home, cannot make sense of the time and falls asleep in the middle of sentences (a loss of communicative ability). In this respect, the old woman parallels Julie's mother in *Blue,* another brutal reminder of what the loss of memory means (a loss of history and teleology — the bitter opposite of cosmic time). To add to the tragedy, Garbowski points out that most Poles would recognize that Christmas Eve is Ewa's name day in Catholic tradition.[26] Here her name is barely remembered. Ewa gives her aunt a Christmas present: leather gloves, upon which Kieślowski chooses to

---

25. Even Jacek, the killer in *V,* is shown to be human. Kieślowski never rationalizes an immoral or morally questionable action, but, in the same turn, attempts to show us our own capacity to commit the same act, through a careful portrayal of the agent's human dimension (i.e., the qualities we associate with empathy, desire to be loved, love of family, past wounds, etc.). The same principle holds true in his films after the *Decalogue* (consider the Judge in *Red,* for instance).

26. Garbowski, *Krzysztof Kieślowski's Decalogue Series,* 82.

dolly in and linger his camera. Kieślowski's hand motif takes on another manifestation here: the gloves are limp, helpless, empty hands.

The shot of Ewa leaving the retirement home is a rather complicated sequence. In short, where several shots would normally be edited together to depict a narrative event, the director has chosen to preserve the continuity of the event in one shot (through careful camera and actor movement). In this case, Ewa leaves the room where her aunt sits sleeping (gloves on her lap). The camera, as if taking on its own identity, makes a move toward the window, carrying the viewer with it. As we approach it, we see the prominent reflection of a lamp on the glass, and, in the same window frame (within the camera's frame), we see Ewa enter her car and drive away. In addition to the obvious preservation of time in this shot, the authenticity of which so enchanted Bazín, the shot poses a juxtaposition not unlike the home/exploration dichotomy so prominent in Kieślowski's early work. In this case, however, home is a cozy, but ultimately dead space, and Ewa's drive away is far more significant than mere perfunctory action. We learn later that she is driving toward her death, with only one twisted hope of salvation.

A carefully composed, high-angle shot reveals Ewa's car entering a traffic island. A foreground pillar (a government building, perhaps?) bisects the frame, isolating Ewa's car (on one end of the island) from a hopeful, glowing Christmas tree on the other. This is followed by another dense image: a voyeuristic look through the blinds into Janusz's apartment as he opens a bottle of champagne. A camera move reveals Ewa in the foreground, and a close-up (to follow) reveals Janusz's deliberate decision to unplug his telephone for the evening. This wordless sequence, complete with themes of technology, intimacy (or lack thereof, generating suspicion and mistrust), and the necessity of communication will reprise in the opening sequence of *Red*. As Janusz and his family toast the occasion, and his mother-in-law reminisces about the pleasantness of "the old times," the darker side of the past arrives at the door, interrupting the peace of the moment with a buzz on the intercom.

In a bewildering transfer of glances, we view Janusz's rush outside (allegedly to track down his "stolen" car) from inside the apartment (a position only revealed by the reflections of the outside light on the foreground glass, as the camera pans). A subsequent shot reveals Janusz's wife in close-up, observing. As he disappears from frame, the comic drunk from the opening of the film returns, dragging the Christmas tree, crying, "Where is my home?" The parallel with Janusz here is obvious.

Janusz's wife observes his consequent meeting with Ewa and hides her knowledge. She suggests that "perhaps it's not worth it" to search for the taxi. Janusz's pretext for leaving the house ("it's our living") is equally significant; their way of life is, indeed, at stake, though the taxi has hardly anything to do with the situation.

His rendezvous with Ewa in the taxi takes place in close-up, bathed in a red Christmas light that almost looks infernal. Indeed, Christmas Eve forms liminal time, both temporal and cosmic. The red of the Christmas lights also bounces between semiotic poles: the cheer of the holiday and the color of hell. Ewa starts their odyssey with a lie, denying that she attended midnight Mass. Janusz, accustomed to Ewa's habit of deceit, presents the truth and quickly deflects it: "I saw you there . . . let's not talk about it." The holiday Mass functions as the first touchstone of truth and the site of its abrogation.

Their experience at the first hospital provokes a return to the triangle, where Janusz's snow-white taxi blends in with the surroundings and Ewa's red vehicle stands out in contrast. Though it is hardly clear, upon first viewing, what situation generated all the present tension, Kieślowski approaches this as a narrative bracket, forcing us to think of the many situations that might have given rise to such tension, theoretically increasing the likelihood that we will find ourselves in sympathy with one of these possible scenarios. We must constantly suspend judgment (in every sense) throughout this series, from our semiotic inclinations toward the image to our moral assessment of characters. As I explained in Chapter 1, Kieślowski never considered himself a moral relativist, but he did, however, view the broken world with great sympathy.

As in his other films, Kieślowski's view of "caring" institutions, such as hospitals and social centers is rather bleak. An orderly sleeps at his desk in this hospital; Janusz offers to turn off the light for him. The man callously describes a nameless, legless corpse, despite the fact that it may be Ewa's "husband." The second hospital carries this corpse, the face of which is half-destroyed. Ewa's reaction is stony at first, then a violent recoil. Horror? we wonder, as she buries her face in Janusz's jacket. Again, she surprises us: the corpse is not her lover, but she seizes on the image as a visual aid, to articulate to Janusz how much she hates the men in her life ("I wish it was him . . . or you. How often I've pictured your faces crushed by truck wheels . . . "). This unsparing portrayal of the depth of Ewa's hatred wrenches us from our compassion for her.

Whereas death is a perennial Kieślowskian theme, it is important to note that he only rarely and judiciously used gory, violent images. Thus, an image of stark horror in his films merits great consideration. Typically, the scenes of blood and/or gore are faces and hands, reminiscent of the wounds of Christ. The bloodied, abused face here will return in *V* as the contemptible cabbie cries out, "O Jesus," even as his visage resembles the battered Savior. This visage stares almost directly at us, even as the eyes of Christ stared back at Witek in *Blind Chance*. It is here, in the horror — where the world is revealed to be most broken — that Kieślowski reveals the depths of Ewa's hatred and expands it to something of a universal statement ("I wonder who this one hurt and who is going to rejoice," she says). The divine paradox, according to Christian tradition, is that this is where salvation may also be found: amid the wreckage. In Ewa and Janusz's case, there is a sense that such hatred must be articulated, even if it is not entirely genuine (an overstatement in service of bitter expression, perhaps). It must be articulated, because the dialectic toward honesty and healing pivots on these outbursts.

The scene where they race away from the police is significant in that it clearly could have been avoided. The police only take notice of the car after Janusz's calculated decision to gun the engine and flee from the area in a most conspicuous fashion. The chase, marked by some interesting abstract visuals, such as the rush of streetlights over their faces, and the combination of the front windshield view and rearview mirror (a shot reprised in *Red*, also shot by Sobociński), turns into a flight from much more than the police. It is, perhaps, a flight from the past — from the web of deceit the characters have woven — but it very quickly evolves into an existential test, a tempting of death (to which they both agree). After the police pull them over and let them go because "it's Christmas" (a fact we've nearly forgotten), an abstract shot follows: an overpowering red frame, revealed to be the car's taillight bursting away from our view as the shot progresses. Janusz rushes the car directly at a train conducted by none other than Theophanes, who, again, exhibits a subdued, knowing look rather than shock or horror. He is available, as an angel of death or life. The choice remains with the couple.

Janusz turns away at the last second and asks Ewa if she's had enough. Indeed, she has not, she replies, and the full scope of her misery begins to unfold. Within her apartment, her machinations become even more explicit. She wanders around installing props that are supposed to indicate a male presence there, one clearly lacking for some time. She fakes a casualty report on her lover over the phone, and a rack focus from the telephone to the Christmas tree outside articulates the yearning, spiritual void from which Ewa's actions flow. The close-up of the telephone (a reprise of many in Kieślowski's films) functions as an image of metaphysical reach. Here, it is an instrument of deceit. A great loneliness, far greater than any individual circumstance, resonates throughout the shot.

This film is a mini-pilgrimage, the darker side of Bunyan, as if "Faithful" was betrayed once and now must be coerced into the journey. As they sit down for tea, that perennial image of community and honesty, Janusz and Ewa begin to talk straightforwardly for the first time. They discuss the night of their parting years before, when Edward, apparently in response to a phone call, walked in on them making love. That day she chose Edward over Janusz, but her meeting him tonight and the gesture of her hand are clear indications she would like Janusz back. Although the moment is tender and a welcome respite from the bitter tension pervading the film to this point, it has a bitter edge. To come back to her now requires that he betray his family. Perhaps this is why Kieślowski avoids the close-up on their hands joining together across the table, a romantic flourish that would be worthy of a Hollywood weepie, but would diminish the veridical value of this modern parable. Kieślowski and Piesiewicz go further, as the tender conversation turns acid once again, Ewa insinuating that she is the real victim in the situation, Janusz having made a happy life for himself. However, our initial impression of Janusz's current family life is that it leaves something to be desired.

"It's Christmas Eve . . . sorry I lied to you," she says, acknowledging that the holy day requires a regard for truth. She immediately follows this with a lie, which Janusz has confirmed to be so: "I am with him [Edward] in the usual way." After they split a stick of gum that looks remarkably like a communion wafer, their false ritual is interrupted by the door buzzer (reminiscent of Edward's interruption of their lovemaking years before). This time, it is children caroling (quite badly) in costume. Apart from the comic relief, the scene becomes something close to a romantic/familial fantasy for Ewa, who cuddles up to Janusz as the visitors sing. It is a lie, of course, like everything else, but Ewa consistently shows us how easy and convenient it is for us to deceive even ourselves. Commandment 3 is "Remember the Sabbath day, to keep it holy." Ewa and Janusz continually forget the sacrality of the holiday, fighting against it at times. Ironically, "remembering" (memory) is their downfall. How are we to remember *and* keep a day holy? Is not memory tinged with the unholy, the broken, the sinful, the wasted?

The scene in the alcoholic center addresses Poland's bitter past. The drunk who comically opened our "silent night, holy night" is naked, abused, hosed down brutally, and still miserably cries, "Where is my home?" The nation's struggle for identity, the product of numerous wars and occupation, rings through the drunk man's pitiable sobbing.

The orderly represents one of the few "monsters" in Kieślowski's films; he is evil unqualified and even looks like a Nazi doctor (Mengele?). He keeps cards on all his admissions and clearly pays attention to ethnicity (particularly the Jews, we note). As he cruelly hoses the caged men down with freezing water ("See how they jump?" he sadistically giggles), Janusz steps in with force, wrenching the hose out of the man's hand. They leave, but the resonance of the scene is unmistakable: this wandering, indecisive journey Janusz and Ewa have taken, replete with lies, half-truths, and manipulations, is as much about identity in the face of moral decision — for themselves, their nation, and the human race — as it is anything else. "It's senseless," Janusz says. "I'm going back . . . I'm going *home.*" Which home? Is there a home left? Ewa's hand on his thigh attempts to coax him back to her. Her hand on the steering wheel forces the issue, and the car, off the road. The collision with the Christmas tree (a collision that has been happening symbolically all evening) bathes the entire car in a hellish light. They have reached the lowest circle, where her willingness to die has been proven (the incident with the train and the dull razor on her hand being harbingers), and her desperate loneliness laid most bare. She begs to be taken to the train station, a point of departure (perhaps eternal). Only later will we understand this is a desperate act of survival.

A lone Christmas tree stands in the middle of the empty, deserted station. The guard is asleep, but the security camera moves on its own, watching in an eerie, distanced fashion so similar to the stale utterances of Krzysztof's computer in *Decalogue I*. The boisterous steadicam shot interrupting this silence is a young security guard on a skateboard. She must move around lest she fall asleep. This emerges as an image of new Poland, particularly when contrasted with the rigid, attentive surveillance of Kieślowski's documentary *Station.*

The clock (turning from 7:02 to 7:03) initiates Ewa's first full disclosure of the evening. Edward has lived in Kraków for years with his new family.

She found it hard to be alone on "a night like this. . . . People shut themselves in and draw the curtains." She thought "everything would be fine" if she could keep him with her until seven that morning, and she would kill herself if she couldn't (the dramatic close-up of her hand on the pill is the first real evidence that suicide was in the plan). Then, in a remarkable turn, she sees the boy who was running from his "parent" earlier that evening; it turns out the mood of the scene was ambiguous, and, in retrospect, desperate. The boy was escaping from a hospital on Christmas Eve. Where he was trying to go we can only guess, but he is caught at the very same station at the very same moment that Ewa has survived the evening. We can never really escape, and we must do our best with what we are given.

We return to the God's-eye view of the traffic triangle where Janusz and Ewa say goodbye. They flash their car lights at one another, a tender, affectionate gesture that highlights the need to communicate with something beyond words. They then go their separate ways. Janusz returns to his wife (Joanna Szczepkowska), who, of course, has guessed the events of the evening (at least in general). "You'll be going out again in the evenings?" she asks, implying (for the first time) that the noble Janusz's "honorable" behavior in his relationship with Ewa was, in fact, rooted in an adulterous context. He is not the saint we made him out to be, but a human being, who has perhaps now finally learned the value of contentment.

"Weeping may endure for a night, but joy cometh in the morning,"[27] the psalm says, and salvation comes, but it is a remarkably existential salvation — a duration of time, a getting through. Ewa has survived until this Christmas, but will she survive to the next? Perhaps, like Sisyphus, she will muster the strength to roll the rock again, but there is no real assurance. For Janusz, the answer lies in a return to family, a stability that does not bear the excitement of his affair with Ewa, but the persistence of a previously unappreciated and abiding love. If, as Vincent Amiel has noted,[28] the beginning of the film bears resemblance to Eric Rohmer's *My Night at Maude's,* the final scene of the film resonates like another Rohmer film, *Chloe in the Afternoon,* where the protagonist returns to his wife after a time of adulterous fantasy. As Janusz affirms, in the film's final line, he is staying home.

---

27. Psalm 30:5.

28. Vincent Amiel, *Krzysztof Kieślowski* (Paris: Jean-Michel Place, 1997), 84.

Decalogue IV

SYNOPSIS: *Michał (Janusz Gajos) and Anna (Adrianna Biedrzyńska) attempt to reorder their relationship after she discovers that he might not be her biological father. Anna's mother, who died when she was five days old, wrote Anna a letter, which may carry the truth of the matter. Anna informs Michał she has read it and that he is not her father. She says she now understands why she has always had trouble with guilt when intimate with other men: she loves him in more than a familial way. Eventually, after conversation, Michał confesses to similar feelings toward Anna as well as jealousy over her other relationships, a conflicting emotion that has hindered his ability to parent her. After a moment of great sexual tension, Michał reassures her that a relationship beyond what they had as father and daughter is impossible. The next morning, relieved to find Michał has not abandoned her over the incident, Anna runs to him (whom she calls "Dad" once again), and confesses that she never actually read the letter, but made up her own version of what it might say. The two of them embrace and agree to burn the unopened letter. A remaining scorched fragment suggests their fears about Anna's paternity may be well founded, but any certainty on the matter has been destroyed forever.*

The preface to the film, as the opening credits appear, consists of two shots: one close-up of a woman, mostly in shadow, staring out a window, and one close-up of a man smoking, staring out another window. Both are pensive and wear searching expressions. Both are partially lit, visually suggesting parts of themselves undisclosed.

The commandment behind the film is "Honor your father and your mother. . . . " Very clearly, the definition of "father" and "mother" and the role of intentionality in the definition of human relationships are key themes in this film. Like the other episodes, this story features the commandment, not as a didactic point or lesson, but as ground for the articulation of modern ethical complexities. Also, it is worth mentioning this is the only command in the biblical Decalogue with a promise attached ("that you may live long in the land the Lord your God is giving you . . . "). There are also traces of this concept as Kieślowski skillfully weaves the two themes — family and country — together through questions of Polish national identity. Though this is not a political film and is demonstrably less so than his previous films, there is an abiding sense throughout that the story may be about more than these two, conflicted but loving people. We always are to love one another, but identity shapes how one is to love. The crisis that vexes Anna's relationship with her father bears resemblance to Kieślowski's relationship to his country, and the paralysis ensuing from a lack of identity mirrors the difficulty Poles suffer when looking back on their country's subjugated, fractured past.

The story begins on Easter Monday, the day after Easter, which has been traditionally regarded by Christians as a time of great levity and euphoric joy, celebrating the resurrection. Traditional activities on this day include jokes, pranks, and the eating of lamb. The Easter water from the previous day is often augmented with perfume and then used to bless the food and possessions of the celebrants. In some countries, on Easter Monday morning, men wake their wives with a spray of the perfumed Easter water as they whisper, "May you never wither." On Easter Tuesday, the favor would be returned, often by the bucketful.

So it is not merely amusing that Anna soaks her father with water. It is the first suggestion given that Anna may see her father in more than a familial light. Just as Kieślowski problematized the Christmas holiday in *Decalogue III,* so he throws the general ethos of Easter into question. Anna and Michał's relationship will mirror the Easter mode: a death and resurrection.

What must be kept in mind here, as with so many Kieślowski films, is a lack of establishment in the narrative. We have seen, over and over, how he hides an establishing shot from the viewer to create an arena of visual ambiguity. The same ambiguity operates here on the narrative level. We simply do not know who these people are or the precise nature of their relationship. The opening scenes show intimate activities (sleeping, bathing, dressing), but the characters' relationship remains ambiguous (spouses? lovers? father-daughter?). It is not until nearly four minutes into the film that she calls him "Dad," and the tension is resolved.

The use of this narrative strategy is obvious (a foreshadowing of future ambiguities), but the impact on the audience should not be underestimated. Couple this with the cinematography (the work of Krzysztof Pakulski), which consistently utilizes deep mise-en-scène to place the two characters within the same frame. They cannot escape this relationship, however undefined.

Michał's eavesdropping on Anna's phone call with her boyfriend is the benevolent, fatherly flip side of the Judge's clandestine audio surveillance in *Red.* Or is it so innocent? In addition to the theme of communication technology that runs through most of Kieślowski's films (often in the form of telephones), the darker side of such technology is also revealed: an invasion of privacy, whether it be out of paternal concern, jealousy, or curiosity.

We see Anna in a doctor's office, and we have no idea why she is there. Her previous conversation with her boyfriend prompts the idea that she might, in fact, be pregnant (particularly in light of the pregnancy theme in *II*). It is only later that we discover she is at the optometrist. The bracketed mode of the narrative primes us for the rather obvious metaphor of sight, an odd blatancy, generally uncharacteristic of the authors. All the same, the metaphor provides more than just a narrative layer. It ushers in another Kieślowskian theme, coincidence/fate, as Anna confesses that her vision blurred as her father flew away just after she spells "F-A-T-H-E-R" during the eye exam. The connotations are obvious: Anna cannot see her father's identity clearly, and her glasses in the next scene signify that she sees him clearly for the first time. The sight metaphor continues as Anna considers her mother's letter, and we receive the abstract visual experience of seeing the letter come into focus.

As Anna walks through the woods toward the lake, the camera takes some initiative similar to the sort of authorial volition common in the films of Michelangelo Antonioni; what begins as a submissive following of the subject through a common pan becomes, at the very least, a subversion of the typical code, and, at most, a wild, searching, exploratory act on the part of an "other."[29] The movement of a camera away from a subject is not remarkable on its own, but to begin a shot in a manner that typically suggests a documentary approach (a submission to the subject) and to rupture it, midshot, with an anticipatory attitude, is to force the audience to rethink the sum total of characters in the scene, that is, to wonder, whether this shot might be the POV of another character. Indeed, it is this scene where Theophanes appears. Although he comes from a different direction (across the lake), his knowing look at Anna as she ponders the letter in her hands suggests the omniscience with which we have begun to associate him. The "other" may very well be the "Wholly Other" of which Rudolph Otto has written: the numinous, the divine. Kieślowski solidifies this connection by finishing the pan on a recently vanquished campfire similar to the flames

---

29. Much has been written about this third "person" (or "presence") in film theory. Examples range from the referenced study of reflexivity in Antonioni (K. Johnson, "The Point of View of the Wandering Camera," *Cinema Journal* 32.2 [1993]: 49–56), to a famous Lacanian application in Daniel Dayan, "The Tudor-Code of Classical Cinema," in *Film Theory and Criticism,* 4th ed., ed. Gerald Mast, Marshall Cohen, and Leo Braudy (New York: Oxford University Press, 1992), 179–191.

with which we began *Decalogue I,* — flames through which Theophanes first looked at us knowingly.

Theophanes' emergence here stands among the most dramatic in the series. Across the water, a speck on the horizon, the boatman comes, evoking the mythological tale of Charon ferrying souls across the Styx to Hades. The gulls swarm like vultures in the foreground as he approaches the shore, where Anna sits pondering her biological identity. She faces a choice: to read or not. Theophanes' ambiguous yet intense look gives her pause. A second look, over her shoulder, reveals a strange view of Theophanes from behind, his body engulfed in the enormous white form of the canoe he carries. In the previous frontal view, the canoe's sharp point seemed particularly phallic and threatening (and appropriately so, as this film, more than most from Kieślowski, suits itself to a psychoanalytic reading). From behind, it resembles an enormous white costume with a pointed hat, not unlike that of the pope. This duality embodies the warring forces in Anna's situation, and the sight of Theophanes has clearly impacted her. Kieślowski's attention to detail, particularly the expressivity of the human hand, reaches full height as she returns the letter to its envelope.

Anna's scene in the acting class further illustrates her difficulties with intimacy. As she struggles to concentrate on the amorous scene, she finally achieves authenticity when her professor (an older, father figure of a man) steps in. This moment seems to be decisive for Anna, signally to her the efficacy of her father's affections and the need to define her relationship with him. We soon see her contemplate the letter again, back at home. In the basement, as she rummages through her mother's personal effects she comes across a photo of her mother with three other people: a woman and two men (neither of whom is Michał). The lighting in the scene suggests lit candles, but Kieślowski brackets this certainty from us. The orange glow creates something of a mystical ambience, and it occurs to Anna (and us) that she may be looking upon her father's image for the first time.

In the next scene, the enormous globe light returns as Anna traces her own handwriting in comparison to that of her mother's. Her father's friend tells her she is her mother's double (another Kieślowskian theme), and her similar handwriting seems to confirm this observation. The scene exudes a marvelous human quality, an endearing, nonverbal expression of quotidian musing. Later we learn Anna's motives are not entirely wistful: she is forging a weapon.

It is worth noting that, in many of the scenes of Anna's room, American paraphernalia is prominent. An American flag hangs on the wall, as does an enormous American cigarette advertisement, sporting a photo of an aggressive explorer (a sportsman in a kayak, not unlike Theophanes in the earlier scene). The tensions in *The Scar,* between old Poland and new Poland, emerge once more (communism would fall shortly after the films were finished). There is a sense that the identity conflict in this film might be extended to Poland itself, searching for its true heritage and attempting to find some stability.

Anna meets her father at the airport wearing new eyeglasses and a new vision of her relationship with him. Little does he (or we) know, the test has begun. Her acting abilities are formidable, we later realize, as she delivers her recitation of the forged letter with great command. It is important to note that we have no hard proof the letter is forged, and Kieślowski has placed us in Michał's position epistemologically. We only know what we see, and that vision is constantly battling with our hunch that more is happening. Likewise, Kieślowski and Piesiewicz continue to reveal new motives in this little mystery, particularly when Anna and Michał finally have a straight talk about the matter. But there is little talk here. He slaps her. She leaves.

Anna and Michał meet again in the apartment complex elevator. The doctor from *II* walks in, another reminder that all these characters live together in the same building and of Kieślowski's interest in the hidden stories of those who are buried in anonymity, social distance, and unfamiliarity. The doctor also functions as a reference to all of *II,* reminding us of the common themes between the episodes: a question of paternity, identity, and the possibility of abortion (which will be revealed in full in the conversations to come). His presence lends something of a strange, reassuring air to this episode — that even here miracles may be possible.

Based on Michał's violent reaction at the airport, Anna assumes that he knows he is not her father. While she hastens to her boyfriend Jarek's house, pursuing her escapist intention to marry him, Michał stews at home. The shot of Michał slamming the door, the glass breaking, and revealing him in the door frame, is one of the more powerful shots in the film. It speaks to the idea that he can no longer hide from the paternity issue.

Their discussion after meeting in the elevator bears an ingenious mixture of brute honesty, gamesmanship, and dramatic machination. Anna's confession that she has desired Michał sexually is not reciprocated at first, but her insistence on the truth drags a similar confession out of Michał. His desire to be her father — to not admit jealousy — has established such denials as the modus operandi, but this will not do anymore. He eventually reveals that he has always subconsciously wished for her to find the letter, just as he has continually laid the groundwork for something "irreversible" to happen with her past boyfriend Marek. Anna turns the tables on his revelation, revealing that she was formerly pregnant by Marek, but could not raise the child with Michał because of her inner conflict about their relationship (she has doubted her paternity since she was a teenager, she reveals). The news of her abortion deeply upsets Michał — the irreversible act has turned out to be different than that what he had imagined.

Anna attributes her failure to achieve intimacy and constancy with boyfriends to her fragmented feelings toward Michał. Her statement, "I am constantly searching for someone," echoes numerous other personal searches in Kieślowski's films (*The Double Life of Véronique* and *Red* are but two examples). All of these searches — for doubles, lovers, friends, and parents — are shadows of *the* search in the Kieślowskian oeuvre for the ultimate answer — the metaphysical key.

Kieślowski's handling of this conversation is remarkable in the manner in which he allows the mise-en-scène and resonant detail of the image to express the emotional subtext of the scene. After learning of the abortion, Michał moves to a table in the foreground, where two glasses sit, like a couple in a relationship, even as he moves away from Anna to headless anonymity.

Fig. 51. The two glasses in *Decalogue IV*.

He delicately pushes one of the glasses along, and we anticipate it being shattered (remembering Dorota's episode with the glass in *Decalogue II*). In this case, however, Michał sweeps up the two glasses in his hand, saving them for a toast later in the film. He resists the impulsive action in other scenes as well. As Anna cries on her bed, her bare side is exposed. Now knowing the sexual charge she received as a girl when he would touch her skin under her pajama top (an innocent tactile moment then), he is tempted to redefine their relationship in a single gesture. Instead, he carefully pulls her shirt down.

But why does he do so? For her sake, or his? She asks him this directly, and it is the sort of question at the heart of all moral action. There is a suggestion that human action can never be completely free of selfishness and self-protection.

After Anna removes her shirt and forthrightly attempts to seduce him ("I am grown up now, and I am not your daughter"), Michał makes his decision. He covers her with a sweatshirt and confesses to her that he wanted her to read the letter because he'd hoped for "the impossible." What, exactly, is the impossible here? That she *is* his daughter? That she *is not* his daughter, and may, therefore, be his lover? It seems clear that the latter is correct. He has found that they cannot so quickly change their relationship, and it is incumbent upon him to make a choice to define it. He does so lovingly. They may still love each other as father and daughter. This becomes clear as Anna begins singing the children's song, and Michał joins in.

She awakens in the next scene dressed in her childlike bedclothes. She desperately searches for him, weeping, and finds evidence he has only left on a temporary errand.[30] She shouts after him, out the window (for all to hear), calling him "father." He had left to get milk, as any father would for his child. She runs after him and confesses the entire deceitful plan. In midconfession, Theophanes passes, carrying his boat, no longer the feared boatman on the river Styx. Anna and Michał burn the letter.

Anna needs to know, beyond all doubt, that Michał will be her father whatever the biological circumstance; in essence, it is the relationship that is fundamental and must never be undermined. Kieślowski and Piesiewicz seem to be highlighting the importance of our choice in our relationship roles. In whatever ways biology, society, or circumstance define us, ultimately we also have volition in determining the contours of meaning in our relations with others.

The final image of the film transforms the Winston cigarette poster on Anna's wall to a wild image of exploration — a new, undiscovered frontier

---

30. In the screenplay, he does make plans to leave, dissuaded only by Anna's confession. Kieślowski's choice to veer from the script heightens the nobility of Michał's character.

to be pursued. Yet it is hemmed in by the walls of a child's room — a home. The presence of the teddy bear confirms its domicility (a foreshadowing of *Decalogue VII*). The graceful pan glides over the moonlike lamp (with its further connotations of exploration as in *The Scar*), and finally comes to rest on the mysterious photo of Anna's mother and her friends. The actual truth of the matter still exists, but only in mute fashion, in the trace of the photographic image. The image references a historic event that cannot be escaped, but it is the words of the letter that give it authority, and those are destroyed.

Decalogue V and *A Short Film about Killing*

Kieślowski took *V* and *VI* and made them into features entitled *A Short Film about Killing* and *A Short Film about Love*. I believe one should resist the temptation to interpret the shorter films in light of the longer ones. We should not presume that extra material for the longer films was merely cut for efficiency or television censorship standards in the shorter versions; his pattern throughout his career was to allow multiple manifestations of his film to exist (note, for example, the different endings of *A Short Film about Love* and *VI* as well as the many proposed endings for *The Double Life of Véronique*). Such an attitude might be expected from the maker of *Blind Chance,* in which completely different outcomes of a film hinge on one, seemingly trivial event. The only sensible thing is to consider each film on its own, as a complete work, exhibited as such.

Decalogue V

SYNOPSIS: *Three characters are introduced. Piotr (Krzysztof Globisz), an aspiring attorney, passes his final exam. The cabbie Waldemar (Jan Tesarz) takes pleasure in cruel pranks on strangers and leering up women's skirts. The tense and enigmatic youth Jacek (Mirosław Baka) wanders around town ignoring suffering and sometimes causing it. The only evidence of tenderness in him arises when he considers a picture of a young girl at her first communion (which he submits to a photo shop to be enlarged). To decide which character is more contemptible, Waldemar or Jacek, is a tough choice indeed, up until Jacek decides to kill Waldemar, without apparent motive. After failing to strangle him, he viciously beats him to death. Jacek's capture is not explained. We are immediately presented with the guilty verdict at his trial, Piotr's defense of the young man having failed. Several arduous scenes follow, detailing Piotr's conversations with prison staff and Jacek himself. Jacek reveals that the picture was of his twelve-year-old sister, who was accidentally run over by a tractor. The vehicle was driven by Jacek's friend, with whom he'd been drinking before the incident. Jacek's execution is every bit as long, detailed, and starkly visualized as his murder of Waldemar. The film ends with Piotr sitting in his car in a field, desperately screaming, "I abhor it!"*

Many small details present in *A Short Film about Killing,* but excised in *V,* create a more coherent, thickly layered narrative. On the other hand, the cold, factual, starkness of *V* seems appropriate for this episode in the series. The prohibition against murder is a central commandment (numerically) and appropriately so. It demonstrates "the wages of sin" at their most intense level. In the *Decalogue* version of this story, we are given less chance to sympathize with either Jacek or Waldemar; Kieślowski treats them with equal distance. What we must see, despite our contempt for their cruelty, is the starkness of their deaths — the acts themselves.

Piotr's thoughts on capital punishment open and close this film. In the beginning we hear a voice-over, a directed soliloquy from Piotr on the law. This little essay on legal theory makes its way very quickly to the subject of capital punishment, remarking on its alleged inadequacy for prevention of crime and suggesting the real motive may be revenge. On the other hand, it is a mistake to simply view this film as a political tract on a given penal issue. The central concern of the film remains that of the entire *Decalogue* series: the deep ground from which evil emerges. Kieślowski and Piesiewicz do not attempt to posit an answer to this age-old question, but they ask it as blatantly and unflinchingly as any filmmaker in history.

"The law should not imitate nature . . . it should improve nature," Piotr's monologue begins. But what is nature? Jacek's confession at the end, as he talks about his mother and sister, suggests that each of us might be a hair's breadth away from senseless killing. Piotr's attempt to separate Jacek from his act is swiftly rejected by the murderer:

JACEK: They're all against me.

PIOTR: Against what you've done.

JACEK: It's the same thing.

The question, of course, is the degree to which our actions define us. The answer to that question leads to another, darker question: the extent of evil within us. According to his translators, Phil Cavendish and Susannah Bluh,

Piesiewicz once said that his motivation to write *Decalogue* flowed from his own "attempt to return to elementary values destroyed by communism."[31] One senses throughout the films that the lack of a standard has hindered the ability to think about these questions, let alone answer them. Piotr himself alludes to this problem later in the film as he laments the loss of common values whereby meaningful action can be measured. Piotr's monologue runs over an image of his own face doubling himself in a mirror, an image of reflexivity and introspection.

For this episode of the series, Kieślowski returned to one of his most trusted cinematographers, Sławomir Idziak. The story of their collaboration on this film is most fascinating, because it demonstrates the degree to which Idziak played a role in shaping the look of the film. He ordered over 600 custom-made, green filters for the "crueller, duller, emptier" look of the film.[32] Eidsvik cites a Polish interview wherein Idziak suggests the filters should evoke the thought of urine.[33]

The sickly green filter also renders other colors ill; the sky is a mucky yellow, human faces are often a purplish gray, almost ashen. Apart from the skewing of color, another effect of the filter is the amplification of contrast, plunging the world into stark divisions between inky blackness and points and slashes of light. Even the light of day appears impotent in the face of this darkness. One of the earliest shots in the film shows a reflection — a somewhat blurred, abstract portrait of the colossal, prisonlike facade of the now-familiar apartment complex — a suggestion that Polish society may not be so different from the lonely halls of the penal institution seen later.[34] The reflection moves again as Waldemar emerges. Within seconds, someone is throwing dirty, wet rags at him from the balcony, a sign of the contempt the residents have for him. The falling rag is also part of a motif of things falling from heaven. In the beginning of *II*, the groundskeeper finds a hare, supposedly fallen from a balcony (and the doctor remarks that he would be lucky if it belonged to him). In this case, filth rains down.

31. Kieślowski and Piesiewicz, *Decalogue,* i.

32. Stok, *Kieślowski on Kieślowski,* 161.

33. Charles Eidsvik, "*Decalogues V* and *VI* and the Two *Short Films,*" in Coates, *Lucid Dreams,* 85. The original interview is found in Arkadiusz Jaeckel, "Kameraleute: Handwerker oder Mitautoren?" *Kameramann* (January 1995): 48–52.

34. The observation that these buildings are prisonlike comes from a former student of mine, Blake Royal.

Everything about this city is dirty, dirtier than usual. As Waldemar washes his cab, Kieślowski's camera places us inside, giving us the paradoxical feeling we are trapped (rather than cleansed) by the abstract flow of water. A trinket dangles from the rearview mirror — an eerily grinning, demonic face. This ghoulish visage remains unchanged throughout the film, embodying the cynicism and cruelty of the characters and ultimately mocking their demise.

The image of the glass of tea, reminiscent of *Decalogue I,* returns here to similar effect as Piotr discusses his exam with his examiners. The swirling, abstract liquid acts as a conduit for the expression of the ineffable while synchronously functioning as a communal symbol (as in so many other Kieślowski films). Here, the communion rings ironically hollow, but the metaphysical suggestion remains potent. Indeed, weighty issues, of infinite and ultimate value, permeate the discussion. Piotr's experience here is somewhat communal; the examiners ultimately like his answers and pass him, but the seeds of his alienation from the legal system are also first revealed here. The inversion of this communal image occurs at the end of the film when the unfiltered (and thus potent) cigarette is shared between the guilty and his executioner before Jacek's death.

At the film's beginning, we know nothing of Jacek's family; it is only at the end that the details are revealed, and we learn that Jacek's pull toward the photo of the young girl is both personal and moral (the girl is his beloved late sister, and the image appears to be of her first communion). His affection for young girls runs throughout the film's first half and represents one of the few traces of unjaded, human feeling within him. Alternately, the ambiguity of Kieślowski and Piesiewicz's presentation of this feeling might easily be interpreted as a perverted fascination, initially. He carries around this picture and wants it enlarged (it is not clear why at first). He is both fascinated and repelled by the girl posing for a portrait on the street (note the alternate version of this scene in *A Short Film about Killing*). In the midst of a display of internal torment, manifest in his writhing exercises with the rope under the cafe table, he breaks away for an interaction with some young girls outside the window, hurling food at them (a playful moment with a sadistic, misogynistic edge). After a moment of shared laughter, they leave the scene, unease registering on their faces. Something close to bitterness registers on his, a suggestion of the popular aphorism that it's a thin line between love and hate.

203

A remarkable indicator of Jacek's cold-heartedness is exhibited in the scene at the overpass. We see here another testament to Kieślowski's mastery at maximizing the efficiency and potency of the cinema's expressive power. In this wordless scene, Jacek loiters on a highway overpass. He keeps peering under his arm at the taxi stand behind him (later revealed as murderous premeditation). He notices a fist-sized stone next to him and begins to toy with it. Just as so many characters in Kieślowski's films toy with objects — tapping, pushing, nudging them along with delicate fingers — Jacek flirts with the universe and its laws. The creeping hand, matched with the rolling, shaking rock, exhibits a testing of fate, as though the rock might move itself and Jacek not be held responsible (he might say, "I bumped it; it rolled on its own over the ledge"). Like so many of Kieślowski's scenes, it parallels Zeno's paradox: if the rock is nudged only half the distance to the edge, it will never actually reach the limit, because one can *always* halve the distance. This theoretical flirtation with the physical laws of the universe amounts, in Kieślowski's characters, to a probing of cause-effect relations, with divine intervention tested in between. Despite the calculated trajectory, Zeno's wall is hit eventually, and Jacek's rock plunges to the traffic below, causing an accident that sounds terribly destructive, perhaps even deadly. Jacek casually extracts himself from the chaotic scene and moves on toward his own personal destruction.

Several references to other parts of the *Decalogue* exist in this film, despite the fact that not one scene takes place within the apartment building. Dorota and her now-healthy husband (*II*) try to catch a ride with Waldemar, who blatantly drives off to spite them. The old car that Paweł mentions in *I* gets prominent screentime in *A Short Film about Killing.* Finally, Theophanes makes two appearances in the extended film and one in this episode. Here, he appears as a worker on the highway, carries a proverbial measuring stick, and catches Jacek's warning eye as he moves past him in Waldemar's cab (on his way to murder). Backlit by the sun, Theophanes' face remains in foreboding shadow here. In the extended film, he also appears as a worker in the prison carrying a ladder (a tool for escape?).

At one point, Jacek asks a curious question: can you tell from a photograph whether someone is dead or alive? This odd, seemingly random question reflects the general disorder of Jacek's internal world, but it also cries out for an answer. The actual answer, remarkably, is no, and it is this embalming property of the photographic image that so captivated the film theorist André Bazín and comforted poor Piotrek after the loss of his mother (in *Camera Buff*). We learn later that Jacek tore the picture from his mother's hands as he ran away from home after his sister's death. He wants the photo enlarged (a simulacra of growth for a dead child) and, in the end, wants it delivered back to his mother. This pathetic but touching reach for redemption proves to be one of the last things Jacek says before he is executed.

But every sympathetic moment is overwhelmed by random anger and cruelty toward strangers. Jacek deliberately scares away an old woman's pigeons. He pushes a man into a latrine. He drops the rock on a busy highway. In the same callous manner, Waldemar leaves Dorota and her husband, sexually harasses Beata (the vegetable market worker), and cruelly honks to scare a passing man and his dogs. This point/counterpoint of cruelties leaves the viewer with the impression that the two men (who have not met) are actually engaged in a game of bitter one-upmanship. Their solidarity in contempt is a poisonous kinship, and one wonders whether Waldemar might have just as likely killed Jacek as the other way around.

As Jacek eats his cream cake in the cafe, it is a messy affair, reflective of his lack of parenting. As he goes to leave and commit his crime, he drinks from someone else's dirty soda bottle and steals a butter knife from the dirty dish bin. The close-up Kieślowski gives us of this dull instrument is remarkable in its visceral effect; it is difficult to shake the eerie feeling evoked by the image of Jacek wiping the globs of butter from the knife. There is a visceral sense that something is terribly wrong, and the suggestion of murder is unmistakable. Kieślowski could well have chosen a plain knife and quickly dispatched the shot, but the lingering camera lends phenomenological weight to the meaning of the scene. In the same manner, Kieślowski lingers on the cup into which Jacek rudely spits — a twisted, negative still life.

In the fatal cab ride, Jacek is given two moments of pause: one when he sees Theophanes, the other when the cabbie stops for a group of passing, waving schoolchildren. Even so, it is not enough to dissuade him ultimately, and the children's music after the killing haunts him to the point that he rips the radio out of the cab in anger. The radio floats in a pool of water surrounded by a wilderness of strange, earthy forms. Kieślowski's camera lingers on this image once again, simultaneously abstract and symbolic. The radio stands as a medium of conversation, a technology of connectedness, tragically discarded. The formal effect is transcendent, but in a negative, demonic direction, as Will Rockett describes in other films.[35]

Other moments of cinematographic insight illuminate the prelude to the killing and its execution. As Jacek pulls the rope taught, preparing to strike, reflected light flashes over his hands with a blinding effect. The killing itself is nearly unbearable, for all its strange (but believable) detail. The majority of the scene has no music under it, just the natural sound of a man being killed in all its unnatural ambience. Close-ups of the man's feet, writhing in agony, exude a morbid curiosity as a shoe, then a sock are scraped off by a desperate foot. This naked foot takes prominent foreground space in the shot where Jacek moves the half-dead man into the passenger seat. This undignified fleshy index of life nigh lost cross-cuts with spinning wheels in an associational edit; his feet get him nowhere, and his flight is pointless. The end has come.

But the end does not come quickly, or easily. As the man dies in agony, various shots of the surrounding environment, hauntingly beautiful and seemingly indifferent to the man's plight, engender intense anxiety and frustration. One might ask God for intervention here. Near the middle of the scene, Jacek pulls the man's battered face up, and the corpse-to-be stares back at him. "Oh Jesus," Jacek mutters, and the image is, indeed, an evocation of the crucifixion. Though this is no savior, and redemption is nowhere to be found, the crushing weight of evil is clearly seen in the battered visage. At this point, Preisner amplifies the significance of the moment with a minor chord on the soundtrack.

Every pathetic attempt Waldemar makes to escape (e.g., the blaring of the horn) magnifies Jacek's brutality. Part way through, we see Waldemar begin to weep, sensing the end. The final attempt, an appeal to reason and compassion ("money . . . my wife . . . please") brings the final horrifying blow.

Jacek's behavior after the killing is odd, to say the least, but after that display, we might question what normal is for this young man. He throws the taxi sign away, something akin to denying the man's vanquished past (but given a more practical interpretation in the extended film — that of stealing the car for himself). He eats Waldemar's sandwich and amuses himself, temporarily, with the demonic trinket on the mirror and the radio.

---

35. Will H. Rockett, *Devouring Whirlwind: Terror and Transcendence in the Cinema of Cruelty* (New York: Greenwood Press, 1988), xiv–xv.

His callous smile and pleasure at these stolen bits of happiness are ruptured by the song playing in the car, which sounds much like a children's song. The lyrics sing of a strong lion and the need for someone strong to love. This provokes Jacek's anger and destruction of the radio.

After Jacek's trial, the emotional impetus of the film shifts to Piotr. He cries out Jacek's name as the boy is led away to the prison van; we learn later that Jacek cried at this moment, touched by the simple fact his name was called by anyone. Piotr drags himself to the judge's chamber, his scarf in tow. In Kieślowskian fashion, the scarf is shown first, abstract against the floor and resonant with the heaviness of the moment (a shot discussed in Chapter 2 and reprised in *The Double Life of Véronique*). His conversation with the judge reveals his presence in the cafe at the precise moment Jacek sat there contemplating murder. This is bitter synchrony for Piotr, who asks himself if he should have done something, whether he bears some responsibility.

The rest of the film, the process of Jacek's final thirty minutes, rings every bit as cold, precise, and dispassionate as the view of his crime. Significant time is dedicated to long walks of characters in the lonely halls of the prison. The executioner (Zbigniew Zapasiewicz) puts in his normal day's work. Whereas Piotr was accused of being too sensitive for his profession, no such charge could be laid against this man, who calmly oils the crank on the noose. His maintenance work in the execution chamber is an astonishingly cold bit of documentary, bearing the marks of Kieślowski's earlier, unrelenting views of people going about their ordinary routines. As Piotr walks to his final conversation with Jacek, he is caught by another bitter synchrony: the prosecutor wishes him congratulations on his newborn son. Once again, life and death mingle in the frame, and we are not given the option to avoid one or the other.

Jacek's conversation with Piotr reveals several things about Jacek, most of which I have already discussed. What is most remarkable, however, is the fact that Jacek mentions the family grave no less than four times. His obsession with this grave intensifies to the point that he insists that Piotr tell his mother that she should give the plot up for him. At first we think he wishes to be buried next to his father, but it is finally revealed that his sister, Mary, is also buried there. They loved each other, and we are given the impression that her tragic death marked the last relationship of mutual affection Jacek ever had. He suggests that "everything might be different" had she not died.

The rest of the film consists of deathly stillness, punctuated aggressively with moments of manic activity. During the sober reading of the sentence, Jacek is forced to give his parents' names (choking with emotion at the recitation of his mother's name). After the last rites, he vomits. An ironic line of characters watch as silent witnesses (carefully ranged behind the prosecutor): a physician, Piotr the lawyer, and the priest. All these professions, dedicated to healing, justice, and restoration, seem oddly out of place, yet they all have a function here, ironically. After his final cigarette, Jacek falls apart, scrambling to the floor, thrashing and flailing wildly. The guards hustle him to his feet and to the noose, screaming at each other ("Higher! Higher! Move him up higher!"). The orderly cranking the noose is wild with something akin to madness as they move him into position. Everyone's back is turned, and a sudden, brief caesura follows; before it seems proper, Jacek's pedestal drops. The death is eerily simple and quick. There is no emotional buildup to the final moment, no dramatic flourish at the climax. Rather, Kieślowski dedramatizes the killing with minimalist austerity, throwing us into fits of panic, never allowing us to settle into a steady, emotional pattern. We cannot sympathize, empathize, or dramatize this easily. It is not to be assimilated. Rather, we are left to grapple with its reality in the empty chasms of time, the slots normally earmarked for dramatic catharsis.

The final shot of the film shows an abstract reflection — a symbol with metaphysical irony — something like a star shining across a gorgeous field at twilight. The camera pans right to reveal Piotr agonizing in his car. "I abhor it!" he screams.

A Short Film about Killing

While both films revolve around the universal topic of killing, the extended film is less focused upon the capital punishment issue. The first evidence of this is the opening of the film, which replaces Piotr's soliloquy (about the nature of law and punishment) with a montage of sickly green images, many abstract. The first images exude an intense, dirty, watery, decayed feel. A series of deathly images follow, usually presented in half of the film frame; inky blackness (overlaid with titles) fills the other half. A dead rat lies in a puddle. Children run away from a cat they have just hung from a railing. All is nausea, amplified by the foreboding music.

There are few essential plot differences between this film and *Decalogue V*, but several elements and characters are richly expanded. Jacek's character is rounded out as more allusions to his sister arise earlier in the film, and his emotions are given more screen time through extended close-ups. For instance, his indifference is amplified here through a scene where Jacek coldly ignores the beating of a man by two others.

The narrative differs overtly in the scene with the artist. In this film, Jacek inquires about the price of the portrait and has a discussion with the artist about talent. The conversation is revealing, showing Jacek's insecurity (he says he has no talent) and bringing out an odd element that will return later: Jacek's ability to plant trees, which connects him to his dead sister, who also loved trees. She was headed for the woods when she was tragically killed, and they chose her memorial plot because of the greenery around it.

Another remarkable expansion is Jacek's relationship with Beata, the vegetable market worker who is harassed by Waldemar in *V.* There is a possible motivation for murder here, as Waldemar offers a ride to Beata in both films, and Jacek returns to Beata in Waldemar's car after the murder, attempting to impress her. Jacek speaks of the car in terms of its possibilities: the places they could go together and the escape it offers them. It empowers him, and he has effectively usurped Waldemar's role. In fact, Jacek discusses these possibilities in a tone that is not unlike the elation Piotr describes after his exams, a rare moment when anything seems possible. In Piotr's case, it is a marking of achievement. In Jacek's case, it is a product of delusion. Beata's somber expression, iconic, "Where did you get this car?" is immediately followed by the courtroom scene, suggesting that Jacek's delusion of freedom and romance with Beata has proved his undoing.

The story takes precedence over the abstract themes of the commandments. For instance, the long soliloquy that began *V* is nowhere to be found, and the final shot of the film reveals Piotr weeping, but never crying out (didactically), "I abhor it!" Kieślowski makes a deliberate decision to steer this film away from an overt political association with the anti–death penalty cause.

Piotr's character is also rounded out. It is more clear that the question he answers in his oral exam is "Why do you want to be a lawyer?" He sees his occupation as a way of meeting and understanding people — a wonderfully naive view. Piesiewicz's concern over a loss of values is given more screen time here and is more clearly articulated. We witness Piotr's glee at passing the bar exam; he meets his wife in a joyous, circling motion in the town square (similar to Tomek's joyous circle in the next *Decalogue* installment, the background swirling into an abstract blur). We see the two of them at the cafe at the very time Jacek is there deciding to commit murder. (In *V*, this coincidence is mentioned but not emphasized.) Their conversation there bears all the Kieślowskian marks: irony, synchrony, and metaphysical questions. The counterpoint between this discussion and Jacek's actions is remarkable. Piotr seems to sense that all his optimism — the feeling that everything is open and anything is possible — is fragile, almost destined to be shattered. Indeed, as he confesses this suddenly ominous feeling, Jacek is about to kill. Piotr's face is iconic, knowing.

Waldemar also receives a fuller treatment. We discover that he hates cats ("They are treacherous, like people") and that he plays the lottery. He is deemed to be lucky in this category, but he confesses that he wants more. Unbeknownst to him, the day will be far from lucky.

The murder of Waldemar is more gruesome and disturbing in this longer film. Several gory and/or disturbing shots make their way into this cut, including an unnerving view of Waldemar's frothing mouth pressed up against the car window and a shot of his dentures flying out upon the ground after being clubbed on the head. The shots are bloodier, more disturbing and more extended, and the sounds of Waldemar's last, desperate minutes are more clearly heard.

Likewise, Jacek's execution is more detailed, including the spattering of dark liquid in the pan below Jacek's hanging corpse. Blood or feces, we do not know, but the effect is the same: it is abstract, eerie, and undignified all at once. This is not gratuitous violence, nor is it in the least bit titillating. Rather, the details all reflect the dishonor of the moment, the horrifying messiness of killing, and the casual way in which it is culturally processed. What is remarkable is the way this film brings to light details that are often left out of horror movies or other films. Piesiewicz once remarked to Annette Insdorf that Kieślowski's approach to the violence in this film emulated police photographs.[36] There is no thrill factor here, just emptiness. This emptiness resounds through the final shot of Piotr, who says nothing, but weeps.

---

36. The Harold Lloyd Master Seminar, the American Film Institute, September 25, 2000. Annette Insdorf interviewing Krzysztof Piesiewicz. My thanks to Annette Insdorf for the transcript of this interview.

Decalogue VI and *A Short Film about Love*

As in the previous episode, the extended version of *VI,* called *A Short Film about Love,* rounds out the characters a bit more and features more of the abstract style discussed in Chapter 2. Unlike *A Short Film about Killing,* however, this extended film significantly alters the end of the story, a suggestion of the lead actress, Grażyna Szapołowska. Both the short and the long versions focus on the ideal behind the commandment against adultery, the sanctity of love. Both films hinge on the essence of this ideal, and the difficulties it posits, in both its definition and its implementation. The different endings represent pessimistic and hopeful possible outcomes to the given scenario.

Kieślowski picks two unlikely protagonists in this drama: an awkward young man who spies on a female artist with a sexually loose reputation. Both of these characters are broken, complex, and fully human, in some ways contemptible, in other ways pitiable, and in still other ways admirable. The film is "about love," the title says, but the commandment is about that which demeans the ideal. Kieślowski's films, both versions, show characters trying to glimpse that ideal from their own position, mired in personal struggles. The short film is more about distance than intimacy and the poverty of modern optics to span the gap between two worlds. In the longer version, the scopic apparatus becomes an occasion for self-reflection and a possible redemptive agent.

The theme of these films, the relation of sex and the ideal of love, will return in force in episode *IX.* It is all the more appropriate, then, that Roman, the protagonist of the later film, appears here. As he incidentally crosses paths with Tomek, Kieślowski leaves us to wonder how their stories might be different had they struck up a friendship and learned from each other. Both are searching for an ideal that transcends mere sex (Tomek by emotional need, Roman by sexual dysfunction).

The different endings of the short and long films solidify the idea that they should be seen on individual terms, not as extensions of or retractions from each other. Just as the ambiguities of character and narrative served to give *V* more clinical austerity than *A Short Film about Killing,* certain curiosities emerge from the parsity of *VI.* To give an example: in *VI,* it is not clear at all, until the middle of the film, that the woman living with Tomek is not his mother, but his landlady. This ambiguity adds a rich dimension to our initial understanding of her character, while it sharpens the irony of

Tomek's orphan status (revealed later in the film). For all its virtues, the longer version of the story reveals her identity right up front.

Decalogue VI

SYNOPSIS: *Eighteen-year-old Tomek (Olaf Lubaszenko) works at the post office, and in his off time he spies on his neighbor, Magda (Szapołowska), an artist who lives across the apartment complex from him. Magda's reputation is that of a sexually loose woman, and Tomek first began spying on her after learning this. It is clear he has become obsessed, when he manipulates her existence in multiple ways (taking a second job as her milkman, calling in false gas leak reports to scare off her lover,[37] stealing her mail from old boyfriends, etc.). After his machinations result in Magda's being falsely accused of attempted embezzlement, he confesses his activities to her. She accepts his invitation for a date, and it is clear that she finds Tomek's sincerity amusing. He proclaims his love for her and, remarkably, distances his definition of love from sex. Magda declares that love does not exist and takes him back to her apartment to teach him something of sex. This occasion ends without consummation because she humiliates Tomek for his embarrassingly premature ejaculation, and he dashes out of the apartment, humiliated and disillusioned about love. She attempts to contact him again but fails because he has attempted suicide. As she waits for his recovery, her affection for him grows. She finally sees him again after his recovery, but her hopes of a relationship are dashed as he announces, "I'm no longer spying on you."*

Magda's character exudes sensuality. She is often scantily clad as she walks around her apartment (alone as well as with male company). She paints, she touches (even dabbling in the milk she has spilled), she eats, and often does all three at the same time. She revels in the sensual, and her conversation reveals a disillusion with anything beyond it (to the point of despair, we discover).

By contrast, Tomek is bound by the gaze, rarely experiencing much that is sensory beyond the scopic, never partaking of the full sensory feast in which Magda indulges; his drinks of water from the dirty bathtub faucet are impoverished versions of Magda's glasses of milk. He longs for this fuller experience, and his bursts of self-inflicted harm articulate this desperation. After foiling Magda's tryst with her lover, he punches the wall in a flash of manic passion, eerily smiling despite the pain. On another occasion, Magda

---

37. It's worth noting that Kieślowski and Piesiewicz originally conceived of the *Decalogue* series ending in an apocalyptic fashion, with the apartment complex utterly destroyed by a gas explosion.

informs a present lover of Tomek's peeping. The man calls Tomek out for a fight, and Tomek obeys with a strange sense of resignation and accepts the punch to the face almost as a type of penance (a theme in this film). The film's apotheosis follows this misguided search for full sensation to its terminal point, a cutting of the wrist. The amorphous cloud of blood, billowing eerily through the water of the basin, is another bitter complement to Madga's spilled, white puddle of milk. The abstract forms exude both a power and resonance that extend toward the transcendent: desperate, spiritual yearning made palpable.

The cinematography of Witold Adamek exhibits a penchant for abstraction, but not always in the intense fashion of Idziak's relentless close-ups. The close-up of spilled milk displays a formal beauty that is difficult to articulate; the pure whiteness of it acts as a contrast to all the drab surroundings of Magda's apartment and functions as a hopeful visual in ironic counterpoint to the negative connotations of "spilled milk." Even after Magda sobs during this intensely dramatic moment, she interacts with the form by dabbling her finger in it, a nonverbal moment akin to finger painting.

As with so many of Kieślowski's characters, neither Magda nor Tomek can be easily demonized or exalted. The anchor of "home" that consoles Bednarz in *The Scar* is not an option for the orphan Tomek, who lives with his friend's mother, in his friend's room. There is a strong sense that Tomek cannot find his own sight, his own home, or his own identity. He is constantly straining beyond his immediate borders to find something that will define his individual essence. In paradoxical fashion, this petty criminal possesses the fullest understanding of love of all the characters in the film, but he has only a concept of how the ideal *should* be. Magda's cynicism toward the ideal functions as the culmination of a thousand disappointments, driving him to despair.

The peeping tom routine has, over time, ironically revealed its poverty to him. He knows she is not simply the village slut, as his friend has stereotyped her, and the pleasures of looking have changed significantly (he used to masturbate as he watched her, but now, quite sincerely, insists that his looking has taken on a more platonic attachment). He has observed moments of great loneliness (her ongoing game of solitaire) and deep emotional pain. Given his consistent desire to control her and interfere with her life, we cannot say he has attained the metaphysical ideal of mutually sacrificial love. Yet, ironically, he does know her better than anyone else as a result of his spying. We get the sense that those who actually interact with her (i.e., her lovers) do not know her at all. In this respect, his view is God-like, seeing behind Magda's social facade. The difficulty will arise in the attempted divine union of this transcendent view with an immanent presence; the closer Tomek gets to her physically and geographically (apart from the scopic), the more complicated the attainment of the metaphysical ideal proves to be.

Tomek's scopophilia inevitably brings to mind *Rear Window* and all that has been written about that seminal film. Robert Stam and Roberta Pearson have applied Jean-Louis Baudry's Apparatus theory and Christian Metz's thoughts on the scopic regime to Hitchcock's film.[38] Given the same psychoanalytic presuppositions, those ideas apply here as well: the desire for control and possession of the object via the gaze, the necessity of voyeuristic distance, and the fear of the returned look all seem to operate. But this is no ordinary film on voyeurism, and the psychosexual pathology of Jeffries (in Hitchcock's film) does not exactly repeat in the character of Tomek.

Garbowski calls this film "voyeurism redeemed,"[39] precisely because the sexual aspect of the gaze has proven unsatisfying, and Tomek has truly fallen for the object of his look. Of course, one cannot eliminate the sexual dimension entirely, and a psychoanalytic critic like Christian Metz might argue that Tomek's despair after his embarrassing climax in Magda's apartment is directly related to the loss of "retention."[40] However sexual influence continues to operate — and it does — it seems clear from Tomek's forsaking of gratification, his tender, sympathetic observation of her sadness, his words about nigh-platonic love, and his generally idealistic approach to Magda that he hopes to transcend the scopic and integrate the sexual with a truly mutual ideal. His despair may be related to the threat of Magda's sexual power over him, but it more likely flows from her cold, calculated deconstruction of his ideal and his inability to restore it. His laughably premature orgasm highlights his current inability to approach mutual love, and Magda cruelly demeans the entire ideal on this occasion: "That's all there is of love. Clean yourself up in the bathroom; there's a towel," she seethes.

---

38. Robert Stam and Roberta Pearson, "Hitchcock's *Rear Window:* Reflexivity and the Critique of Voyeurism," in *A Hitchcock Reader,* ed. Marshall Deutelbaum and Leland Poague (Ames: Iowa State University Press, 1986), 193–206.

39. Garbowski, *Krzysztof Kieślowski's Decalogue Series,* 28.

40. A sexual suspension of orgasm, foundational to the scopic regime, that Christian Metz articulates in *The Imaginary Signifier: Psychoanalysis and the Cinema* (Bloomington: Indiana University Press, 1982), 60.

Throughout this film, there is an abiding sense that Kieślowski is playing with the familiar clichés (scopic ménage à trois suggested by the landlady's spying on Tomek and Magda), films (like *Rear Window*), and Freudian theory. Amid this intertextual playfulness — a pageant of references — emerges an emphasis on the need to transcend the merely sexual. The story begins with smiling filmic references and humorous situations arising from a competition between two flawed characters. Then the tone shifts from a slightly off-color romantic comedy to something closer to tragedy.

Abstraction assists this dramatic shift through its expansive, suggestive powers. The partial view of the telescope may be impoverished (compared to the authenticity of Magda's presence), but the view can also function as a bracket, creating revelatory formal moments. Our first views of Magda in her apartment are far from standard: one shot shows her next to a decorative half-sphere attached to her window, which both multiplies and distorts her image. This image refers to all views of Magda in this film, as the woman is replicated, distorted, and stereotyped. Tomek's scopophilic addiction distorts his view of her but simultaneously expands it.

Another abstract view of Magda reveals a more explicit metaphysical idea. Magda's body is blocked by the building's facade, the window framing (within the cinematic frame) her eerily amputated hands and arms holding a gravity toy. The theme of abstracted, amputated hands has been thoroughly established in nearly all of Kieślowski's films to this point, and the results of this technique remain just as potent here. Her delicate, graceful fingers seem to float in an eternal, limitless space.

Supplementing this extended, metaphysical resonance is the pendulum with which her hands play, a predecessor of the toy with which Antoine will play in *Blue* (and bearing the same metaphysical heaviness). Suspended by a string, it bears connotations both of otherworldly force (in its independent motion) and of divine order (in its eventual adherence to the physical law of gravity). It functions like the ancient divining rod, a quasi-mystical tool purportedly used in the Middle Ages to find water or metal under ground. This metaphor becomes more obvious in the middle of the film, when Magda holds it over Tomek's outstretched hand, attempting to discern what is truly beneath the surface of his persona.

The paradox of the partial yet expanded view persists in the soundtrack to the film. Magda's actions, her lovemaking, her emotional breakdown, and so on, are all seen clearly, but the sound is that of Tomek's limited perspective (the stillness of the evening). At the same time, the perception of Magda is partial (limited only to the two-dimensional visual, further compressed by the optics of the telephoto lens). Yet this amputation of the visual and the sonic creates a marvelous bracket — a feeling of the action happening in something like a timeless space, ripped from its temporal roots. Without the everyday sounds of Magda's apartment, she appears to glide from place to place, an ethereal beauty. This otherworldly aura runs in marvelous counterpoint to her earthy activities with the men in her apartment. Kieślowski embodies in this character our temporal struggle between heaven and earth, a dialectic that forms the foundation of the entire *Decalogue* series.

For all Tomek's efforts to control Magda's life (with some success), it is also clear that Magda's life controls and defines his own. He sets his alarm clock by her schedule and takes on occupations based on their proximity to her. That control becomes most disturbing once his relationship exceeds the safety of the virtual realm. Once he is rendered helpless by the physical thrill he has desired, the cleft between his ideal and Magda's world is complete. The despair at this moment is coupled with his sense of childhood abandonment, and the combined emotional force is too much for him to bear. There is some suggestion that guilt may also play a role here, as just before this incident Magda taunted Tomek about masturbation and lust. ("You know it's a sin?" she says cynically. "Yes," he answers, quite sincerely.) However, it's important, in my judgment, not to write off Tomek's experience as simply a guilt-ridden complex; there's a strong sense throughout that Tomek believes Magda's worldview to be impoverished, to fall short of what love is and can be. His decision not to treat her as merely an object of lust (as least not overtly) is an affirmation of an ideal of which Magda knows nothing, and which he desperately needs to exist. His previous conversation with her outside her doorway confirms this.

Framed by a beautiful red-and-white window, the two characters talk. Their backs are toward us, much like Jacek and his executioners in *V*. They do not look at one another initially. It is a reverse icon: they stare stoically ahead, but not at us. We are left only with their silhouettes and the abstract blocks of the window. When Tomek says, "I love you," they turn toward one another, and their faces emerge with the force of revelation. He declares, in keeping with his discovered ideal, that he wants nothing from her: not a kiss, not a trip away with her, not sex. In this light, her sexual pursuit of him later demonstrates her utter lack of understanding, both of the ideal and of Tomek himself. His desperation flows from the realization that he will never be known, and, therefore, never truly loved.

After the conversation outside her apartment, Tomek's joy can barely be contained. She has agreed to his boyish proposal for a date, and he dashes outside, milk cart in tow. As discussed in Chapter 2, he makes an enthusiastic circle on the sidewalk, the camera following him throughout in a dizzying pan. The speed of the pan renders the whole world a blur, an abstract evocation of pure joy. The shot reaches toward the Transcendent, beyond chronological time, and rejoices at the glimpse of the ideal and the possibility of its realization. The shot is not merely a boy's excitement at a first love, but a supernatural view of pure, Transcendent possibility. "Innocence" is a naive term in our day and age, but in the context of the *Decalogue*, it marks the teleological end of all the commandments.

Theophanes' appearance in this scene supports this interpretation. He witnesses Tomek's joy and immediately pulls the audience back to the Source of the commandment. Though his face still remains ambiguous, something approaching a smile appears. That smile fades when he observes Tomek, dashing away from Magda's apartment after his humiliation.

As they approach the end of their first date, Magda proposes they play a fate game; if they catch the bus, they go back to her place. If not, that is the end of the evening. The bus leaves, then stops for them, and so the suggestion is made that they are ordained to be together. This suggestion becomes stronger to Magda after Tomek dashes out of her apartment. While thinking over Tomek's ideas on love, she finds the bus tickets in his abandoned jacket and is reminded of the fatefulness of the evening.

After Tomek's flight from her apartment, Magda does not know how to communicate with him. All she can hope for is that he will continue spying on her (an ironic twist). She desperately makes a sign saying she is sorry and wishes him to call. Later, she receives a silent phone call she assumes is from Tomek. She confesses to him her change of heart — that he was right (about love, we assume) — and receives no reply. She hangs up, and the phone rings again. The second call makes the first more mysterious: the caller says he did not call previously. The question remains: who did call? The suggestion that God may be placing a call of conscience is a motif that reappears in Woody Allen's *Crimes and Misdemeanors* (1989).

As she awaits Tomek's recovery from his suicide attempt, Magda's solitaire games evoke not only loneliness but also the role of chance in the narrative. When she goes to the post office to inquire about Tomek,

Kieślowski himself appears in cameo (back toward us). The visit reveals nothing, so she waits for the postal worker. As she does, she stands by a window, the apartment building looming in half the frame and an abstract dot on the window. A close-up on her hands reveals her agitation as she toys with her belt (the sort of gestural shot at which Kieślowski excels). The converse of this close-up is the subsequent expressive long shot of Magda sinking to the floor after hearing of Tomek's suicide attempt.

Magda's final tragic conversation with Tomek tells us he no longer peeps at her, and she wishes he would. The peeping had evolved into the beginning of a meaningful relationship, a spark of communication, and a missed opportunity. During his hospitalization, she'd taken to searching for him with her opera glasses, a realization that the scopic might possibly flow out of genuine love and concern rather than mere possession or gratification. It is a crucial discovery, found too late.

A Short Film about Love

SYNOPSIS: *The longer film shares essentially the same plotline with VI, but adds more detail. A major exception comes at the end of the film, after Tomek has attempted suicide. He returns home, and while he is sleeping, Magda comes to visit him. Rather than turning her away, the landlady talks with her about him, although she is still defensive of the boy and suspicious of Magda. Magda looks through Tomek's telescope and "sees" herself crying (from an earlier scene), with an additional projected vision of Tomek coming in to comfort her. The film ends on her thoughtful expression, a suggestion that a relationship between her and Tomek may yet materialize.*

As with the previous extended film, this extension of *VI* proves easier to follow for the average viewer. Kieślowski presents the plot points in more detail and gives more roundness to the characters. Likewise, other themes become more solid. For example, Tomek is shown studying languages with a language tape, raising a passing detail in *VI* to a genuine theme in this film. In light of Tomek's background, this hobby functions synecdochically for a broader desire for human communication. Magda laughs when he mentions he is studying Bulgarian, but he then reveals that he had friends in the orphanage who spoke it. This moment reveals both Tomek's desire to reach out in communication and his lack of a home and a mother tongue.

Other examples abound: the landlady watches the Miss Polonia pageant on television (strengthening the theme of visuality as a contemporary measure of beauty), and in the scene where Magda eats, Tomek also eats as he watches her (strengthening the idea that he desires her rich sensory life).

We learn more about Tomek. His pathological resort to danger and pain becomes a stronger theme when he plays a game with scissors, poking them between his fingers on a table with increasing rapidity (ending with a cut). This is yet another tempting of fate, of course, as if the likelihood of divine existence ran in direct proportion to the time of the game. A discussion with the landlady reveals that Tomek has cried only once in his life, when his parents left him. We are not given more information, but this passing detail gives more intensity to Tomek's emotional issues.

Kieślowski makes an interesting, demystifying change to the scene with the mysterious phone call. The caller Magda rings again, referring to "Mary Magdalene," and reveals the previous call to be a failed call attempt due to a broken phone line. She had been talking to nothing at all. This heightens the pathos of the scene but diminishes the metaphysical possibilities. It could be that here, outside the *Decalogue* context, Kieślowski wanted to explore the story in a more standard mode. It ends up, after all, as a love story.

The difference between Magda's and Tomek's views of the relationship is highlighted through Tomek's gift of a snow globe. The simplicity and toylike nature of the gift reflects Tomek's boyish innocence. The object within the globe is a home, a rootedness that Tomek has never had and Magda, perhaps, longs for. This ideal, romantic symbol seems to be Kieślowski's tip of the hat to Orson Welles, whose *Citizen Kane* features the same metaphor. Kieślowski claimed to have seen *Citizen Kane* "a hundred times."[41] Žižek connects another toy sphere, that of Weronika in *The Double Life of Véronique,* with the same film.[42]

The end of the film moves in obvious slow motion, an unusual technique for Kieślowski. It is a sentimental denouement, but not entirely so. Kieślowski leaves the ending of the film open. A relationship may or may not materialize, but we know that Magda has received something of a revelation, and Tomek's suicide attempt has been transformed from tragedy into a possible redeeming catalyst in her life (refiguring Tomek's bleeding wrists as Christological). Perhaps Annette Insdorf has best understood the nature of this revelation: "The film ends with Magda closing her eyes, unable to continue as either voyeur or object."[43]

---

41. Stok, *Kieślowski on Kieślowski,* 34.

42. Slavoj Žižek, *The Fright of Real Tears: Krzysztof Kieślowski between Theory and Post-Theory* (London: BFI Publishing, 2001), 51.

43. Insdorf, *Double Lives,* 99.

Decalogue VII

SYNOPSIS: *Six-year-old Ania (Katarzyna Piwowarczyk) has nightmares. Her sister, twenty-two-year-old Majka (Maja Barełkowska), does not know how to calm the child as she cries in her sleep. Their mother, Ewa (Anna Polony), clearly despises Majka for this. Stefan (Władysław Kowalski), the father, works in his woodshop, removed from the situation. Clearly, there is great tension between Majka and Ewa and affection between Majka and her father. Likewise, it is clear that Majka is emotionally distraught. While Ewa and Ania attend a children's show, Majka successfully executes a plot to kidnap Ania. She steals the girl away to another town, where she reveals a long-hidden truth: Ewa is not her real mother, and it is Majka herself who has been robbed of her own daughter all these years. She takes Ania to meet her father, a former schoolteacher turned reclusive teddy-bear maker and aspiring screenwriter. Wojtek (Bogusław Linda) dashes any of Ania's hopes of forming a family with him, and the backstory of the situation is finally revealed: Ewa is a headmistress at a school where Wojtek once taught and Majka attended. Then sixteen years old, Majka fell in love with her teacher, and Wojtek apparently reciprocated. After her pregnancy was discovered, Ewa engineered a cover-up, forcing Wojtek's compliance through threats of legal action against him. Ewa has always wanted another child but could not have one, and so Ania stands in as her own daughter. She had convinced Majka the arrangement was best so she could finish her education. At this point, Majka's desperate plan to break out of this web of lies includes taking Ania away to Canada. Wojtek attempts to reason with her, suggesting Ania would be better off in a stable home (i.e., Ewa and Stefan). Majka escapes Wojtek and flees to the train station, child in tow. Just as the train arrives, they are discovered by Ewa and Stefan. Ania runs to her "mother," and Majka, despairing, jumps on the leaving train. Her hollow gaze never leaves the child as the train pulls away. Little Ania runs down the platform after the train, shocked and bewildered.*

Kieślowski and Piesiewicz chose a familiar theme: a child with her patronage in question; *II* has laid the groundwork for this theme, and *IV* articulated its implications. Now *VII* will play out this problem with a different emphasis, not identity as much as possession, in keeping with the command not to steal. Whereas Kieślowski's earlier films struggled with the notion of home versus exploration in the midst of a nation's desperate search for its own lineage, the very notion of home is deconstructed, in a sense, in the *Decalogue*. Although Kieślowski's work (and attitude) bears little resemblance to the cynicism and smirking nihilism of contemporary deconstructionism, it certainly remains true that Kieślowski interrogates concepts and ideals, often with a nostalgia for more idealistic times and a sense of tragedy at their loss.

The strategy of bracketing of which Kieślowski has shown himself a master falters some here, denying the audience enough identification with the diegetic world and rendering the story rather stale and unfeeling. All the same, multiple viewings of the film are rewarding, as knowledge of Majka's predicament garners sympathy for her. Multiple viewings also allow one to put aside the deficiencies that hampered the initial viewing, and the richness of the theme and pattern in the narrative emerge.

In my judgment, this film may be the most difficult of the series, in both its harsh realism and its troubled presentation. As to the former, no character immediately elicits our sympathies. It is not until nearly two-thirds of the way through the film that one can really begin to pity Majka, as her cruelty toward her mother seems boundless. Ewa, on the other hand, elicits pity for the first third of the film, but she soon proves that she can be as cold and calculating as her daughter. Stefan remains a lovable man, but he is clearly impotent in nearly every way; not only does he fail to provide his wife with another child (whether this is his fault or hers is not clear), but he is also reluctant to intervene in this worrisome situation, works obliviously in his woodshop while Ania screams through her nightmares, and caves in to all his wife's demands, however unreasonable and cruel. Wojtek comes closest to our sympathies, as it seems he would genuinely like to do the right thing in the situation, but we are reminded that he too has fled his responsibilities (even if forced into silence by Ewa), and the entire situation arose from his sexual relationship with a young student.

As to the second factor, the presentation of this film is indeed troubled, from the script to the editing. Several things strike me as unlikely and forced. One example is Wojtek's new occupation as a teddy-bear maker. This carries some poetic resonance (a cathartic occupation in light of the loss of his daughter), but it seems overly obscure and inconsistent with his character. As to the editing, Ewa Smal's work in the nine other *Decalogue* films is so exemplary, I wonder what happened in the filming of this episode that so marred the final product. It is worth noting that this episode does not feature Theophanes (except for a fleeting glimpse) because Kieślowski claims he "didn't film him right."[44] It is possible that the fatigue of the gargantuan project was settling in on the crew, and they were simply not

---

44. Stok, *Kieślowski on Kieślowski,* 158.

able to produce enough working material for effective editing, even the cinematography, though often beautiful, sometimes makes diegetic night look like daytime. The chronology of the events (designed as, roughly, a twenty-four to thirty-hour period) becomes confusing at times because of these problems.

However, the film begins with extraordinary power: a person screams, terrified. Who, what, or why, we are not told. The cold facade of the apartment complex, our cosmic theater for this series, receives another inspection over the cries. Multiple pans create a searching feeling in the audience, giving the impression that any of the hundreds of windows in the building could reveal this desperate person. The crosslike concrete design exudes, once again, the feeling of suffering, coldness, death, and imprisonment. The cry is universal, troubling, and without explanation, let alone remedy. The scene cuts to Majka, a failed student, not only expelled, but also bitterly and defiantly confessing to the destruction of a library book.

Once again, hands are important. The first hand we see, rather abstractly, is that of a child: at first we see only rope, in a lattice pattern. As the camera pans, a child's hand comes into view, clutching desperately at the rope. It then becomes obvious this is a crib, but only after we have assumed a larger interpretive posture (i.e., we were open to the many things it could be) clear of the phenomenological bracket.

Wojtek says to Majka, "With you it's either-or, no half measure." If there has been a single theme throughout the series, it has been the complexity and difficulty of moral decisions. Majka's black-or-white attitude is not a clarity of moral vision, but its obfuscation. Her dichotomous vision also tilts her toward biological determinism in Ania's case: Majka is the biological mother, and therefore all will be well when they are together. The truth, of course, is that Ania is as socially conditioned as any other human being, and she misses the "mother" who raised her. Though she is affectionate toward Majka, she will not call her "mother" despite Majka's repeated, desperate requests. Likewise, Majka lacks any real power to comfort the girl. The child's nightmares persist in this scenario.

The nightmares remain mysterious for all involved; Majka reports that Ania has never divulged the content of the dreams. They remain the mystery, like the self-powering computer in *I* or the empty phone call in *VI*. They carry transcendent resonance, for all their mystery; one need only to look at the biblical story of Joseph to grasp the significance of dreams in religious narrative,[45] and this is but one story among many. Typically, dreams serve a prophetic function, and Wojtek suggests that this case is no different ("She's afraid of things to come," he says).

Ewa's compromise suggestion in this standoff with Majka rings terribly hollow, as if Ania were a piece of property (hence the commandment). She suggests that they trade her presence on appointed days, like a custody arrangement in a divorce ("Ania will be mine and yours. When I die, she'll be all yours"). These arrangements are commonplace in divorce proceedings, but the possessive language rings hollow here, because no one appears to be thinking about the child's best interests. Majka's counterproposal suits herself (insisting that Ewa give written permission for the child to go to Canada, or Ewa will never see her again). She gives Ewa to the count of five to agree. She rushes through the count and immediately hangs up, just as Ewa says yes; a missed connection, much like the unheard "I love you" from Dorota's lover in *II*.

Wojtek urges Majka to give the child up, fearing that she will ruin little Ania with all this instability. Stefan urges Ewa to do the same, and for similar reasons (we suspect). The bitter scenario (two neurotic, dysfunctional women and two reclusive, impotent men) reaches no satisfactory conclusion here. No lives are changed or transformed. No revelations emerge, except in Majka's case, as she recognizes, finally, that dichotomous vision cannot stand amid the complexities of the moral universe. If Wojtek's advice is correct — that the child needs a stable home — we have come to doubt the stability of that home and Ewa's maternal abilities. Ania's face, the final image of the film, suggests that she may very well live with the emptiness of Anna in *IV*, who can never be sure of her real lineage.

It seems noteworthy that the woman minding the train station is reading Gustave Flaubert's *Madame Bovary*, a story about a woman with similarly unrealistic, even woeful ideals of love and happiness. The tragedy shared between Flaubert's Emma and Kieślowski's Majka seems obvious enough, and there is a sense that both characters lack a certain resolve in the world — a heartiness that accepts the brokenness of things and endeavors to stay put and work patiently for solutions. Majka is not quite the hopeless romantic idealist that Emma is, but their shared inability to face reality makes them kin.

---

45. Genesis chapters 37–50.

In the end, like Ewa in *Decalogue III*, Majka has kept Ania for an evening, in hopes that everything would change by daylight. But it is not to be. Majka begs Ania to kiss her and say she loves her, and Ania complies, but Majka longs for the day when Ania will call her mother and kiss her voluntarily. When Ewa and Stefan arrive at the train station, Ania shouts, "Mummy," and runs to the woman she has always known by that name. Majka's predicament is beyond remedy, she decides, and she dashes for the train, which has tragically (fatefully?) arrived at that very moment. As she quickly boards, a crippled Theophanes disembarks in the background — a train of broken, marred, damaged people, shuttled away.[46] Such are the trains of Kieślowski's own experience: decisive moments of transport. Majka stares emptily out the train window, a self-imposed prison of visibility. Ania runs after the train, then stops in complete incomprehension.

Decalogue VIII

SYNOPSIS: *Zofia (Maria Kościałkowska) teaches ethics at the university. Elżbieta (Teresa Marczewska) is a scholar from New York who has translated Zofia's works into English. Elżbieta returns to Warsaw and receives permission to visit one of Zofia's classes. During this class, several ethical discussions arise, including one (the story from II) during which Zofia remarks that the saving of a child's life is of paramount ethical concern. This provokes a "hypothetical" scenario from Elżbieta: a six-year-old Jewish girl is being hidden from the Nazis in Warsaw, 1943. She is forced to move to another safehouse, that of a Catholic family who have agreed to house the child if she carries a certificate of christening. The couple facilitating this christening suddenly stop the transfer, remarking that they could not bear false witness by artificially naming this child a Christian. The child is turned out of the couple's house, right at curfew time, into almost certain death. So ends Elżbieta's story. A few students engage the ethical discussion (suggesting the action was not truly Catholic, perhaps there were other motivations for the decision, etc.), but the story distresses Zofia. Later, it is revealed that the story is Elżbieta's childhood memory, and Zofia is the one who turned her out on the street that night. Elżbieta is clearly angry and searching for peace about her lifelong sense of abandonment. Zofia has obviously been tormented by her decision for nearly forty years. Zofia takes Elżbieta back to the very location of the story, a group of houses on Noakowski Street. The younger woman hides, effectively abandoning and*

---

46. It is difficult to recognize Theophanes because the camera never gets close enough, but the script calls for him (Kieślowski and Piesiewicz, *Decalogue*, 188, 212).

scaring the older woman. She reappears in Zofia's car. They proceed to Zofia's house for dinner, where they talk out the situation some more. Elżbieta comes to terms with her situation and the difficult decision Zofia faced. The secret behind the abandonment was that Zofia was a member of the Underground, and the new family destined to be Elżbieta's protectors were named as Gestapo collaborators, threatening the destruction of the entire Underground movement, not to mention Elżbieta herself. The two women reconcile, discuss ethics, God, and hope, and, later, Elżbieta is seeing praying. The next day Zofia takes Elżbieta to see the man who might have been her protector, now a Warsaw tailor falsely accused of collaboration with the Gestapo (Tadeusz Łomnicki). He refuses to talk to Elżbieta about the war, much less her story, despite her repeated attempts. The film ends with Zofia and Elżbieta, clearly affectionate and reconciled, and the thoughtful face of the tailor looking on.

This remarkable film stands as the most philosophically direct of the ten films and, in my opinion, ranks among the greatest. Kieślowski and Piesiewicz wrote a strong script, and the actors convey a clear sense of the characters' inner worlds. Andrzej Jaroszewicz's cinematography, while not an explicitly abstract style, still carries a good deal of ingenuity and emotional impact. His framings of human hands — touching, reaching, pulling away — fulfill Kieślowski's career-long vision for wordless expression of universal human emotion.

The opening shot of the film shows a remarkable joining of hands, adult and child, in close-up as the characters walk through the Warsaw streets. The child's fingers move playfully in the larger, adult hands, suggesting innocence and trust. The sequence ends with the young girl looking back at the camera behind her. This remarkable little flashback sequence (a reenactment of Elżbieta's story) initiates the film and sets its tone. The girl's look is difficult to describe: fear mixed with questioning, perhaps. Similarly, the film itself dances between raw emotions and logical questions (a mode of rationality) and focuses on the places in human life where the two intersect.

A truly beautiful image follows this somber sequence: that of a flower in the wild. This postcardlike vision may strike us as foreign after the long winter shadowing the *Decalogue* so far. Even the prisonlike apartment complex appears transformed on these balmy spring days. An image of a woman exercising follows. We observe her throughout her routine, her run through the park, to a close-up on her hand grasping a handrail. This hand matches the doctor's hand grasping the tub in *Decalogue II,* and to similar effect: Zofia (the runner) attempts to exercise some more, but finally stops, her face resting on her hands in a contemplative, even disturbed manner.

The next few scenes follow Zofia, documentary-like, through her daily routine: she is a disciplined woman, loves beauty and pursues it, and lives an orderly life (we watch her bustle around her organized, neat apartment). She rights a crooked painting on her wall, a pastoral scene. This ideal landscape wrenches itself crooked again almost immediately, as though by some Schopenhauerian evil will. The ideal will constantly be skewed in this film, and there is a strong sense that the crooked will be at constant odds with Zofia's attempts to order her life. This explains why Kieślowski brings out details like her car's failure to start until the second try. There is an abiding sense that brokenness permeates Zofia's world despite its beauty and her efforts to heal it.

While Elżbieta tells her story in the classroom, two curious things occur. First, as she reaches the climax of the story, a drunken and disoriented student staggers in, interrupting her. This bit of comic relief is anything but comic; we recall the drunk in *III* and pause in our mockery since he is a signifier of the brokenness and the callousness of the world. After some agitation on Zofia's part (fueled by her clear recognizance of Elżbieta's story), Elżbieta continues. As she discusses the supposedly Catholic reasoning that led to her abandonment, the camera reveals a thoughtful Theophanes in the classroom. He turns and looks at us or Zofia. The ambiguity doubles the power of his gaze.

As she spins her tragic tale, with some difficulty, Elżbieta toys with a gold cross and its chain, hanging around her neck. Zofia's parting words to the class are to think about the woman's perspective in the scenario; we assume she speaks of the *Decalogue II* story here, but the referent might be expanded to the present story. We must consider the tragedy of Elżbieta's abandonment from the woman's point of view, even if that means both women. Zofia's predicament does have motivations outside of those listed in the class. Elżbieta writes off fear as an insufficient justification for the action, but it is clear (later) that fear was but one component of the entire complicated ethical equation Zofia faced in 1943, including danger for herself and the entire nation.

Zofia, somewhat deviously, takes Elżbieta to Noakowski Street, the site of her abandonment. A shrine/memorial is there (a remembrance of the past), but the place is gloomy. Elżbieta attempts to turn the tables on Zofia, in one sense, hiding from her and abandoning her even as she was abandoned in 1943. Yet, as with all of Kieślowski's complex characters, the motivations are mixed. Brute revenge is mingled with deep need; Elżbieta wants to be sought after, an attention she feels she needs and deserves but is yet to be realized. Kieślowski amplifies this idea (extending the original script of the scene) in the next sequence: Zofia searches, even desperately. She discovers that five families are squatting in her old home, and at least one person appears to be a prostitute. The old world is not only gone, but also thoroughly broken. The five families do not like each other much, yet cohabitate. This home is utterly lost and filled with a confused, disillusioned generation.

Numerous times throughout the film, cinematographer Andrzej Jarosze-wicz signals a character's emotional realizations with changes in lighting, a pattern that will continue with later Kieślowski films and cinematographers.[47] As Zofia and Elżbieta sit in the car, the headlights of a passing car wash over Zofia, who comes to terms with the fear that she had lost Elżbieta once again. Kieślowski matches Zofia's sudden emotional clarity with intense disillusionment in Elżbieta; she comments on the inefficacy for research and learning to bring about true justice. She asks Zofia if she knows why some are rescued and some are not. In a hollow, defeated tone, Zofia responds that she does not. Elżbieta maintains that it is not fair. Garbowski notes Kieślowski's affinity for Dostoevsky throughout his work, and it seems as if this conversation could be taken from *The Brothers Karamazov*.[48]

Entropy is the nature of nature, and only a few, like Elżbieta, escape its grasp. In Zofia's apartment, even Elżbieta cannot permanently right the crooked picture. As she looks over a book in Zofia's apartment, the table lamp flashes on and off, a struggle for enlightenment.

Amid these eternal questions, the two women share the Kieślowskian communion, a cup of tea. Zofia tells her story — her rationale for abandoning the girl — and the emptiness she has experienced ever since, wondering and worrying about Elżbieta for nearly forty years. She affectionately lays her hands on the woman's shoulders. Eventually, Elżbieta grabs the older woman's hand, another close-up to redeem the initial image of the film.

---

47. The most obvious examples include the passing blue lights in *Blue* (Sławomir Idziak, cinematographer) and the replacement of the lightbulb during Valentine and the Judge's discussion in *Red* (Piotr Sobociński, cinematographer).

48. Garbowski, *Krzysztof Kieślowski's Decalogue Series,* 23, and throughout his book. Kieślowski himself expresses great reverence for Dostoevsky's ability "to capture what lies within us," and lists him as a strong inspiration for his films (Stok, *Kieślowski on Kieślowski,* 34, 194).

In the course of their conversation, Zofia reveals her moral theory: that goodness lies in all of us. Situations release good or evil, and that particular situation did not release the good in her, she says. We assume that evil also lies within us. The question of culpability and responsibility, of course, is most prominent here: if situations release these latent tendencies, at what level are we capable (and therefore, responsible) for controlling their release? Elżbieta does not ask this question, but a related one: who evaluates the goodness or evil of our actions? Zofia's answer alludes to a God within us, though she does not always call Him "God," she confesses. She argues for God based on axiological grounds (similar to the discussion Zanussi has with the film club in *Camera Buff*). The basic thrust of the argument is that ethical evaluation is impossible without an Ultimate Evaluator, and a world without ethics is chaotic, empty, hopeless, and, Zofia says, lonely. Loneliness is something with which she is familiar, having lost her husband and been deserted by her son (a story to which she alludes but does not fully tell).

The ethical quandary of 1943 is clearer to Zofia now: no cause is worth the life of a child. Innocence must be protected at all costs, apparently. Kieślowski's films do tend to present children as innocent (if *I* and *VII* are any indication). By contrast, however, one might point to the vicious children running from the dead cat in *A Short Film about Killing,* not to mention the youthful, but vicious, Jacek himself. All the same, the clear suggestion from Kieślowski and Piesiewicz is that something in children is worth preserving. Through more oblique suggestion, Kieślowski's tender, grandfatherly eye will fall upon children again in *The Double Life of Véronique,* and a conscientious youth will prove to be the courier of hope for Julie in *Blue.*

The beauty of Zofia and Elżbieta's discussion lies in its seamless weave of personal narrative and philosophical speculation. The conversation is wholly natural, flowing from characters who are truly concerned with the answers to these questions because they have import in their existential dilemmas. Ethics matter to Zofia, because without them one ends up without an anti-dote for loneliness, a problem with which she has been vexed. Loneliness, for Zofia, is not merely a personal problem flowing from personal issues, but a core, universal matter of philosophical importance.

As if to drive home this point, an interruption of the discussion takes place. The neighbor arrives to show Zofia his newly purchased stamps. Not only does this man love his stamps as others love their children or grandchildren (we will meet his children in *X*), but they are ironically prewar

German stamps, parading the glory of the German war machine. That an image of such destruction, doom, and ethical turmoil could be turned into something beautiful, endearing, and life-giving remains the hopeful tenet of the film. Reconciliation and redemption are both possible, even in the face of genocide, impossible ethical choices, and doubts about God's existence.

The apotheosis of the story may well be Zofia's request that Elżbieta stay the night, a redemption of her turning out the child in 1943. She confesses that she does not get many visitors, and, we have learned that her own child has little contact with her anymore, compounding the number of children she has lost in a lifetime. Elżbieta agrees. We have seen throughout the *Decalogue* a motif wherein one character uses an evening to define the nature of their relationship with another: *Decalogue III* explicitly and *Decalogue VII* implicitly. In contrast to those manipulative and deluded machinations, the night here will secure a relationship because of the solid philosophical and theological ground that has been laid. That night, kneeling in Zofia's absent son's room, Elżbieta prays. We get the strong impression it is the first prayer she has been able to manage in a very long time. With Zofia, we peep through the door on the intimate moment. It is the redemption of Tomek's peeping in *VI,* even as Zofia's friendship with Elżbieta becomes the redemption of Tomek's landlady's loneliness.

The next morning, Zofia goes out for her morning run. While in the park, she encounters a contortionist practicing his strange craft. He is at once grotesque and fascinating, even beautiful at times for all his skill. He remarks that his abilities are simply a matter of exercise, but he doubts that an older woman, such as Zofia, can learn to bend as much as he can. In contrast to the disillusioned picture of the young generation back at Zofia's old apartment on Noakowski Street, this young man stands as metaphor for a more malleable, adaptable generation, able to adjust to the broken past. Zofia laughs as she attempts a similar contortion, accepts defeat, and leaves the scene happy. This humorous little scene stands as a picture of the twisted, the mangled, and all that has been askew in her life, utterly redeemed into something fascinating, entertaining, and, ultimately, joyous. The picture on her apartment wall may always hang crooked, but the scene is still pastoral, and the crooked vantage point may reveal hidden elements that carry their own strange beauty. The contortionist is, on one level, hideous. On another level, he symbolizes pure possibility, even redemption of the twisted circumstance. Such is grace emerging out of bitterness.

Zofia returns with her daily flowers to a thoughtful Elżbieta, who has also purchased flowers. Their gifts are clearly not wasted effort, but doubled kindness. Zofia merges the two clusters of flowers into a gorgeous whole. Yet, lest we are coaxed into sentimentality, Kieślowski and Piesiewicz end the film with an example of how difficult this reconciliation can be. We are not taken to another sinner or betrayer (as Zofia was originally portrayed by Elżbieta), but to a potential savior, now utterly disillusioned. The road to visit the tailor includes a long, dark tunnel, featured prominently and unsparingly in a wordless shot, an image of long, dark time, with only the glimmer of hope at the end.

The tailor himself, Tadeusz Łomnicki, who played Werner in *Blind Chance*, returns in a very different role here. Werner survived "ethical hell" (Zofia's term) by jading himself and treating life pragmatically. The tailor is simply broken by the war and his inability to effect good. He was nearly executed by the Underground, under Zofia's instruction, but the mistake was caught in time. Zofia had apologized (it was all she could say), but that was clearly insufficient for this broken, disillusioned man. He refuses to discuss the war with Elżbieta, even after she thanks him for his generosity toward her. He is hell-bent on making her a dress, continually returning her to that topic. Kieślowski once said that evil came about by not knowing how or not being able to bring about good.[49] Having failed at this in the war, the tailor concentrates on the little bit of good he can manage (dressmaking) and fears to venture beyond the safety of that arena.

Ultimately having failed in this contact, Elżbieta returns to the street. There, Zofia comforts her, smiling, affectionately touching her arm. She asks Elżbieta if she prayed the night before, and, after a pause, Elżbieta affirms it. Their friendly conversation, hopeful and full of tenderness, is framed by the tailor's window. Kieślowski ends the film on the tailor's intense, thoughtful expression witnessing the scene of reconciliation. Zofia and Elżbieta have discovered that the inability to bring about good is sometimes matched by the power of grace to fill the void. Though he has not been a central character, the tailor embodies the thematic core of the film: deep, abiding pain brought on by false witness against him and the slight hope of reconciliation, as we see a new glimmer flickering in his eye.

---

49. Stok, *Kieślowski on Kieślowski,* 135.

Decalogue IX

SYNOPSIS: *Roman (Piotr Machalica), a successful surgeon with a philandering past (he admits), has discovered he is now impotent. He encourages his wife, Hanna (also known as Hanka, played by Ewa Błaszczyk) to take a lover. She asserts that love is more than sex and desires to remain faithful. However, Hanna already has a lover in the young student Mariusz (Jan Jankowski). Roman discovers evidence of the affair and grows jealous. He soon becomes obsessed with spying on his wife, driving to confirm what he already knows. Hanna can only continue the affair so long and breaks it off while, unbeknownst to her, Roman eavesdrops in the closet. She discovers him, and the two of them fight, then reconcile. They proceed along the lines of adopting a child, but Mariusz continues to pursue Hanna. Having found evidence of this, Roman interprets this to mean Hanna was not sincere and will continue the affair on a weekend ski trip. Roman writes a suicide note, then drives his bicycle off the edge of a broken highway overpass. Simultaneously, Hanna darts home, furious that Mariusz has followed her to the ski resort, and intuitively concerned about Roman. She finds the suicide note and despairs. The phone rings, and it is Roman, calling from the hospital, where he is being treated. He has learned of her dash home to Warsaw and reassures her.*

As mentioned, the Catholic rendering of the ninth commandment is a split of the Protestant account: covetousness as two distinct categories (wife and goods). The ninth commandment, therefore, follows after the subject of adultery, though not in the same way that VI pursued the topic. Covetousness is linked with the desire for possession, and here this translates into jealousy. Kieślowski gives us two characters, equally culpable in the sin of adultery: Roman confesses up front that he has had many lovers, and the suggestion is made that he has been unfaithful to Hanka. Upon learning of his dysfunction, Hanka's words are comforting and noble, but it appears that she very quickly moves to an affair, or, perhaps, has been in the affair for some time. Roman suggests that she might have been in one already, which she denies, but she lies several times throughout the film. The relationship with Mariusz, while juvenile in many ways, is clearly advanced in his mind. In short, we are presented with two characters who love each other, but only in broken ways. Roman is impotent, like Karol in *White,* and like the couple in that later film, Roman and Hanka must navigate some very difficult terrain before they truly realize the depth of their love for each other.

It may very well be that *White* is a more full realization of Kieślowski and Piesiewicz's vision for this short film. Like *Decalogue VII,* this film suffers from a certain bluntness of character and general awkwardness of plot, while *White* presents fuller characters. Similarities of theme exist: jealousy, impotence, desperation, and bawdy jokes (e.g., the obvious shot of the funnel and gas tank in *IX* compared with the phallic bottle and recycling bin in *White*).

Sobociński returns to the camera here. Immediately one notices the change in style: the deep mise-en-scène, the abundance of reflections, rack foci, and a general penchant for abstraction. Here, at the end of this series and into his later features, we see Kieślowski choosing cinematographers that work in an abstract style (Idziak for *The Double Life of Véronique* and *Blue,* and Sobociński for *Red*). The comedies (i.e., *X* and *White*) will prove to be less abstract, though not wholly so. It is my contention that Kieślowski chose to amplify the metaphysical themes that concerned him in his early work, and so the abstract style suits the expression of these themes.

The film begins with Hanka asleep, then sitting up in fear, as if from a bad dream. The camera, agitated, pans to the left to reveal her reflection in a mirror and the noticeably absent place on the bed beside her. This sequence suggests parallels with *No End* that continue throughout the film. Urszula feels premonitions throughout the earlier film and awakes to find her husband gone, not simply from her bed, but from the earth entirely. Those premonitions continue throughout the film, including a sense of her husband's spiritual presence, just has Hanka senses Roman's state of mind (despite his absence) throughout *Decalogue IX.* Such premonitions give credence to her suggestion that love is more than sex, more than biology; the spiritual nature of this sixth sense is amplified through the iconic looks she gives the camera on several occasions. The bond is spiritual, and both Kieślowski and Piesiewicz suggest throughout the rest of their films that any meaningful connection between human beings shares the same nature. The themes of suicide, jealousy, and desperation also persist throughout both *No End* and *Decalogue IX.* They also exist in *White,* where suicide is averted, jealousy becomes the source of a maniacal chain of manipulation (ultimately redeemed), and desperation settles into a strange contentment.

After seeing Roman receive the news he is impotent, we return to a worried Hanka in her apartment. The moving shot hinges on the telephone, a key motif throughout this film that will repeat numerous times. Next to the phone is a glass object of some kind, and we view her partially through it, with some abstract distortion. The power of this shot is threefold: a moving shot (carrying a revealing power as it moves), abstraction (with all its suggestive qualities articulated in Chapter 2), and the hinging element of the telephone, a Kieślowskian emphasis on both technology and human communication, referenced in Chapter 1.

The car accident Roman suffers is a direct extension of his internal agitation, and Theophanes' leisurely pass on his bicycle confirms the metaphysical significance of the moment. This introduces the personification of the glove compartment, which pops open its yawning mouth at more than one uncanny moment (and once stubbornly refuses to open for Roman, as if it has a mind of its own). Like the mysterious happenings in *No End,* the computer in *I,* and the curiously crooked picture in *VIII,* this chance event carries the weight of metaphysical significance, leading Roman to evidence of Hanka's lover, and, later, a nigh-spiritual reminder of his jealousy. These uncanny moments are not always easy to interpret theologically, but Kieślowski's agnosticism seems to highlight that difficulty. To him, the spiritual life was a mysterious, vexing possibility, for all its seeming intersections with temporal life.

The moment of high crisis for Roman and Hanka, which will generate the entire spiritual struggle to come, is articulated through a sequence of images, nearly all of them abstract or, at least, stylistically formal. Roman's return to the apartment complex is obscured by rain on the window. Hanka's sight of Roman is a reflected image. Their ascent to their apartment is shown in an alternating patterning of light and darkness, with the spots of light alternately illuminating each of them as well. This flashing pattern of light suggests something like throbbing pain, and dark deeds exposed. The same pattern reappears after the scene of Hanka and Mariusz's illicit lovemaking; Hanka sits overwhelmed in her car, while the camera reveals a flashing headlight, pulsing to the sound of the car alarm.

Hanka's insistent denial of the medical opinion leads us to believe a miracle (of the sort portrayed in *Decalogue II*) may occur to heal Roman's condition. Rather, another sort of miracle occurs as Hanka leaves her lover and Roman learns to trust her. It may be considered miraculous that Roman survives his suicide attempt; it remains a possibility that Theophanes himself rescues the seriously injured Roman, as we know he witnessed the accident. In either case (be it miracle or no), intervention is thematic.

Another point of grace for Roman is a young girl with a beautiful voice and a critical heart condition. Ola (Jolanta Piętek-Górecka)stands as a clear prototype for the character of Weronika in *The Double Life of Véronique,* as she also sings the music of Van Budenmayer, Zbigniew Preisner's fictional pseudonym. She functions in two primary ways: a sexually alluring, bitter reminder of Roman's loss of prowess and a spiritually wise counterweight to the youthful immaturity of Mariusz. This duality is skillfully expressed in a close-up of Ola's moving hands conducting the music of Van Budenmayer and the subsequent tilt down to her knees, revealed by a suggestively short robe. She is unquestionably beautiful, the sort of woman Roman might have slept with in his decorated sexual past. Yet it is this same Ola who inspires him with music and the general beauty of the world, who urges him to think about the reasons for his pursuit of his career, and to think harder about having children and a more stable family life. In the screenplay, Ola dies in surgery,[50] having decided to pursue singing, according to her mother's wishes. Not only does this solidify her connection with Weronika in *The Double Life of Véronique,* but her passing becomes something of a watershed event for Roman as he attempts suicide shortly after. It is not clear why Kieślowski cut this scene from the film, but Ola's power in Roman's life remains all the same.

But before any experience of grace, Roman is simply a tortured man, so much so that he constructs a device whereby he may listen in on his wife's phone calls. The theme of surveillance will persist in *Red,* and, like that film and the peeping of Tomek in *VI,* expresses a desire for divine omniscience — to know the truth about another person through unlimited observational power. This desire for power, indeed, this covetousness, forms the central concern of the *Decalogue;* it is no secret that the serpent's archetypal temptation to Adam and Eve was "Ye shall be as gods."[51]

Mariusz studies physics, and the physical laws of the universe guarantee him a dominant position in the competition for Hanka's profession: young men are typically virile; older men may become impotent. Yet the struggle between physics and metaphysics is, indeed, a fair match in Kieślowski's world. Hanka's need for sex will pass, but love for Roman will ultimately remain.

However, without the establishing dialogue or any visual clues, we might think that Hanka is leaving on a trip. In fact, it is later revealed, she works for the airline KLM. By initially hiding that establishing fact from us, some

---

50. Kieślowski and Piesiewicz, *Decalogue,* 271. She mentions her need for the surgery on 247.

51. Genesis 3:4.

dramatic tension is generated: we sense that Hanka is always on the verge of flying away, darting out of the situation, when she is simply going to work.

As Hanka makes her final decision, to break things off with Mariusz, she is forced to turn down the television. As with so many other instances in Kieślowski's films, the program makes some commentary on the scene, in this case the cartoon flood disaster prefiguring the events to come. Roman's voyeurism during this meeting between Hanka and Mariusz might have proved somewhat satisfying for him, had he not been caught. He curls in shame beneath her gaze, just as Tomek jumped back in fear from his telescope when his "object" suddenly demonstrated a will to power through her own gaze. This has a humbling effect on Roman, and the two reconcile, confessing their sins to one another. It appears we have reached something of a resolution in our family drama, but nothing is ever that simple with Kieślowski.

After putting Hanka on the train for a ski trip to Zakopane, Roman observes Ania from *VII* playing with a doll, reinforcing idealistic notions of children and family in Roman's mind. (Having seen *VII*, we know life and family are rarely that easy.) An empty phone call follows, like that in *VI*. A suggestion from beyond, perhaps? An echo of the mysterious glovebox? Perhaps the call speaks the unspeakable truth, but, for Roman, it proves to be a catalyst for anxiety. In short order, Roman contradicts his own words to Hanka ("I trust you") at the train station: the first suggestion that Mariusz is also going skiing sends him into a frenzy. Confirmation that Mariusz is also going to Zakopane literally sends him over the edge.

The telephone, which has played a central role in this film, becomes a tragic missed connection as Hanka attempts to contact Roman from Zakopane, suspecting something is wrong. Set on suicide, he ignores the call. These missed connections become strong themes in Kieślowski's later films, and the telephone looms very large in the frame throughout this episode.

As Roman churns his bicycle toward his own doom, the music takes some prominence. Most natural sounds fade away as Roman's trip takes on the appearance of a spiritual glide to the end. The lack of natural sound promotes an abstract, dreamlike ambience, just as the lines on the pavement become a staggered, abstract pulse of life. His body glides, slow motion and birdlike over the edge, but not beyond Theophanes' gaze. A second shot of Hanka's iconic look synchronizes the spiritual elements in the sequence. Theophanes is revealed by a rack focus, beyond a leisurely spinning wheel (abstract, spiky lines in the foreground, rotating this way and that). This cuts to a virtuosic overhead shot not unlike the climactic overhead in the nuclear holocaust scene of Tarkovsky's *The Sacrifice*, revealing Roman's sprawled body, then suddenly revealing a foreground, in this case the end of the road from which he fell (abstract white line dangling off the edge).

Roman's POV in the next scene lingers between the anchored gaze of the temporal and the drifting view of the spiritual. The canted angle rolls upright as it pans, only to cant to the other side. Roman is assured that Hanka is home. When we see her, all we see is the beautiful sprawl of hair in the foreground (an abstract view of women that Tarkovsky also loved, prominent in films like *The Mirror*).

"God, you're there," she says. "I am," he replies. The double meaning of this interchange should not go unnoticed: just as Theophanes arrived in time, God is there. In *VIII*, Zofia told us He is in all of us. Roman's reply, "I am," affirms his own survival, while echoing God's own ontological assertions throughout the Old Testament and the biblical Decalogue itself. For all tragedies in these films suggesting God's absence (*I, V, VI, VII*), this stands as another story of grace, where a character should not necessarily have lived, but survives all the same.

Decalogue X

SYNOPSIS: *The stamp collector from* Decalogue VIII, *a man named Czesław Janicki, has died. His two grown sons, Jerzy (Jerzy Stuhr) and Artur (Zbigniew Zamachowski), survive him and must handle his estate. They've been estranged from their father for years, so the discovery of his world-class stamp collection holds some shock for them: it is worth millions. The brothers have not kept in touch much in recent years, with Jerzy starting his own family and Artur singing in the hard rock band City Death. Both assert that they are not attached to material things the way their father was, but they would like to sell the collection and use it for some dreams they have always had. As the movie progresses, their individual attachments to the collection and its inherent wealth intensify. The men begin to get somewhat paranoid about the security of their late father's apartment (beyond the old man's substantial, original precautions). In the process of assessing the collection's precise value, they are swindled out of a stamp series (the Zeppelin series mentioned in* VIII), *and their attempts to remedy that situation bring them into contact with the underworld. One particular shop owner, a key figure in the swindle, makes a most audacious proposition: Jerzy will donate one of his kidneys to him (for the sake of his young daughter, in need of a transplant) along with a smaller stamp from the collection that holds particular sentimental value for a contact of his. In return, the contact will give the men the pink/rose-colored Austrian Mercury stamp, a very, very valuable stamp that will complete the priceless Austrian Mercury series their father had so long sought to finish. After much comedy and drama, Jerzy agrees. While Jerzy is in surgery, a thief steals the entire collection. The brothers turn bitterly against each other, suspecting one another. At the same time, they both develop an interest in collecting stamps, an activity for which they derided their father in the past. In the end, they confess their false suspicions to one another and realize they have both purchased the same stamps. They laugh, reconciled.*

In the introduction to this chapter, I stated that covetousness acts as a collective command as it deals with the problem of discontentedness (a "heart" issue, in theological terms, that generates many, if not all sins). It is significant that Jerzy, at the end of this film (and the *Decalogue* series), makes a simple confession: "I've done a terrible thing." This is one of the few truly forthright confessions of wrongdoing in the entire series, and it amounts to no serious consequence, except that Jerzy recognizes even *pecadillos* can rupture relationships, and relationships may be all that truly matter in this life. This message is something of a humanistic gospel. The *intentional* relation, what Martin Buber calls the "I-Thou" relation, rises to the fore here as the crux of all morality.[52] Implicit within this is the relation to God, which several characters have asserted is within us (the aunt in *I* and Zofia in *VIII,* at the very least).

In a clever turn, Kieślowski and Piesiewicz begin this film with the very antithesis of Buber's I-Thou relation. Artur leaps onto the stage in front of hundreds of screaming City Death fans, a significant name in light of the principle that sin and the law (that delineates sin) bring death in Christian theology.[53] Artur sings/screams through the song, articulating the double edge of the law, encouraging the individual listeners to break all the commandments, item by item, because everything belongs to them (a type of metaphysical materialism). It is a godless, selfishly pragmatic brand of existentialism: to boldly and independently make your way in the world because you are the only one who can make your life meaningful amid the darkness and hopelessness. It will also prove to be the great temptation of possession that will vex the protagonists throughout the film.

---

52. Martin Buber, *I And Thou,* trans. Walter Kaufmann (New York: Touchstone, 1970).

53. Coates makes specific mention of this point, articulated by the apostle Paul in Galatians 3:13 and Romans chapter 7 (*Lucid Dreams,* 105).

Artur is a lovable character, and we perceive that the brashness of his lyrics may be more an act for the stage than a personal credo. However, it is also clear that he is a classic case of the neglected child, wandering from place to place and job to job, shiftless, a bit reckless, and morally loose. His indiscretion with a nurse during Jerzy's operation is both humorous and didactic: while Jerzy is recklessly giving up a kidney and Artur is sexually romping with the nurse, they are both being robbed. The words of Christ become most poignant here:

> Lay not up for yourselves treasures upon earth, where moth and rust doth corrupt, and where thieves break through and steal: But lay up for yourselves treasures in heaven, where neither moth nor rust doth corrupt, and where thieves do not break through nor steal: For where your treasure is, there will your heart be also.[54]

Cut directly against Artur's decadent song is a gentle, gliding tracking shot through an apartment. The camera crosses the still figure in the bed and finishes upon the dead, floating fish in the brackish aquarium. Sin and death are clearly paired (in agreement with Paul's assertion in Romans 6:23), but lest we become too serious, the graveyard scene provides some levity. The eulogy, provided by the head of the Philatelic Association, talks about the noble passion for which the old man sacrificed his family, professional life, and, perhaps, emotions. This laughable tribute turns slightly tragic as we see the family members old Czesław neglected. Jerzy and Artur stand opposite the somber mourners; they shift uneasily throughout the ceremony, and the gravediggers smoke and socialize casually behind them.

Zofia's statement, in *VIII,* that Czesław treated his stamp collection like his children, carried an endearing quality back then. Now it emerges as the man's tragic flaw, having supplanted his own children as a material surrogate. A consistent theme throughout the *Decalogue* is that we rarely know the full story of any given person. The genius of the *Decalogue* scripts lies in our original sympathy for Czesław and our evaluative turn in the final episode. In *VIII,* it was natural to project Zofia's situation upon the old man; we might have assumed he loved this stamp collection because he had nothing else. This apartment building is full of lonely, discontented, restless people, and such is the human condition. Kieślowski and Piesiewicz's universal vision (the Warsaw apartment complex as universal microcosm) has been so consistently present, there is a sense that both our evaluations of Czesław

---

54. Matthew 6:19–21.

are correct: each character stands for someone like him or her in the world, regardless of the accuracy of our judgments at any given time. Kieślowski and Piesiewicz force us to suspend judgment of people and more fully account for the complexity of the human condition.

As they look over the collection, Artur wonders about the root of the human desire for material possessions — the urge to have things. This is, of course, an allusion to the tenth commandment, but it is most important to note that Kieślowski has not focused on the prohibitive voice of the commandment as much as on the root of the sin problem. The episodes in this series never function as a "thou shalt not" proclamation, but rather as an investigation why one would desire to break the command in the first place. Throughout the *Decalogue,* Kieślowski casts a tender, compassionate eye on our sinful tendencies, recognizing that we are all capable of these acts (even killing). At the same time, he does not excuse them or avoid their consequences, even here, where the tragic loss of Jerzy's kidney is intended to be funny. Jerzy says of his father, "I never understood the old man." In short time he will, and so will we.

Amid their father's possessions, they find clippings about Artur and his notorious band. This humanizing element, a suggestion that the old man thought about and cared for his son on some level, prevents us from completely demonizing him. At the same time, lest we deify the two sons, it is revealed that Jerzy has neglected his own son's toothache to spend time with Artur.

The head of the Philatelic Association urges the young men to put aside their personal bitterness and see their father's collection as the sum total of a life. The inherent question, of course, is to what degree should we measure a person's life by material things? Such thinking promotes all sorts of excuses for blatant materialistic pursuits, such as the men's drive for the Austrian Mercury stamp to complete their father's work (and make them rich), or the human gesture of donating a kidney for a sick girl (and to gain a very valuable asset). On many levels, the good that we do is always tainted by some degree of self-interest. On the other hand, the collection Czesław amassed in his lifetime is meaningful to many people, and it is an astonishing example of dedicated work. The focus, for the head of the Philatelic Association, is clearly not the monetary value of the collection, but the symbolism of the collection — the amount of work and dedication for which it stands. Kieślowski and Piesiewicz shy away from any obvious ideological commitments here, refusing to turn this film into a materialist or antimaterialist tract. Rather, they probe the complexities of moral life, attempting to decipher the mysteries of the moral ideal and the multivalence of any particular existential situation. In this light, the figures and symbols in Czesław's philatelic journal prove a hermeneutic challenge similar to the task of interpreting the Scriptures.

As Jerzy and Artur stand outside the apartment assessing the security of the apartment, a most interesting conversation ensues. I should point out that the sequence begins with a now-familiar shot of outstretched hands, in this case reaching upward. The shot reveals them to be Artur's, gesturing toward a balcony, but the abstract presentation of the shot suggests something more universal: a transcendent reach, perhaps. "We're here, and somehow nothing else matters," he says. His speech here echoes, in part, the speech Piotr gives in *A Short Film about Killing* regarding the fleeting glimpse of possibility that one experiences at life's liminal moments. Life is spiked with moments of liberation, glimpses of heaven, and release from suffering. In the brothers' case, greed will overtake this epiphany.

The growing obsession between the two men regarding their recent wealth becomes most acute. Jerzy has spoken about how he likes a comfortable level of living, but very soon he literally draws blood over the Zeppelin series. In Zofia's terms (*VIII*), the stamps are not releasing the good in them.

A word about the operation: the manner in which Kieślowski presents the operation is a sequence of close-ups. Because of the lack of establishing shots, there is the suggestion that every shot is part of the same operation, and so the shot of the blowtorch is most jarring when it appears. In fact, there are three operations going on, all covetous at their base: Jerzy's operation (a self-sacrifice, not for life or any other noble purposes, but for greed), Artur's anonymous sexual romp (for gratification), and the thief's obvious covetousness of the stamp collection.

As the thief looks over the collection with a magnifying glass, the image warps and distorts, an abstract presentation of Will Rockett's "downward transcendence" idea, perhaps. In fact, the stamp resonates far beyond its primary diegetic and narrative function; it is close to a form of currency (a symbol of materialism), a marker of history (and its fleeting nature), and progenitor to the filmic image as an image. In the spirit of Emma Wilson's reflexive approach to Kieślowski's abstraction, there may be some reflexive issues at play here. One gets the impression throughout this film that the stamps — the old man's passion — are a bit like Kieślowski's films. He suffered guilt over the time they consumed, pulling him from his family. He acknowledges their poverty in contrast with the most important things in life, yet testifies to their beckoning allure.

The reconciliation between the two brothers marks a beautiful end to the series, in part because of the ingenious thematic resolution it brings to the commandments themselves. The two men have coveted, desired, been selfish, possessive, and suspicious of others. Yet in the end, they share their new material interests, combining the stamps to make a series. The final shot, that of the two brothers laughing, foreheads touching over their joined stamp collection, can be seen as the beginning of an answer to the many questions the ten episodes have raised: giving oneself away to a loved one marks the beginnings of morality and its teleology. The final, uncanny "chance" occurrence precipitates the miracle of reconciliation.

As the image fades and the credits roll, Artur's song returns, as the script says "telling people to sin."[55] This wry, sarcastic smile from Kieślowski keeps us from tying up the story in a neat little bow. Sin, selfishness, and brokenness will undoubtedly persist, but, perhaps, with Kieślowski's help, we will be more thoughtful about how — and why — we live within it.

Conclusion

The virtues of the *Decalogue* are multiple, but two of these qualities best serve the telos of this study: (1) the more universal, less political, scope of the narrative and (2) the stylistic move toward abstraction in many of the episodes, often at key metaphysical moments. These two trends will continue to grow in Kieślowski's later work to the point that they characterize his unique later style. Likewise, a prominent thematic concern emerges here that will persist throughout the rest of Kieślowski's career: the possibility of grace. Kieślowski's keen eye for the negative ironies of life — the coincidences that perpetuate the problem of evil — will persist. Paired with these instances, however, will be moments of intervention: uncanny coincidences that work in the favor of his characters. Kieślowski never fully commits to the term *divine grace,* but he does not hesitate to plunge headlong into the metaphysical terrain. The *Decalogue* points in this direction, beginning in high austerity and judgment and ending with self-effacing comedy and reconciliation, Theophanes' watchful presence lingering throughout.

---

55. Kieślowski and Piesiewicz, *Decalogue,* 302.

$$\boxed{5}$$

THE LATER FEATURES (1991–1994)
The Double Life of Véronique and *The Three Colors Trilogy*

T his final chapter discusses the films that epitomize Kieślowski's metaphysically aimed formalism. Much of the discussion in Chapter 2 center on these last four films, so this chapter will not discuss form in the same detail, even though, to my mind, form is a fundamental emphasis in Kieślowski's later aesthetic. Here, the emphasis will be on the culmination of Kieślowski's career-long thematic concerns. For a full picture, this chapter should be read in concert with Chapter 2, as Kieślowski's constant goal is to transcend beyond words and, ultimately, beyond image.

The synergy between the abstract image and the metaphysical themes becomes most pronounced in *The Double Life of Véronique*. In *Blue*, the formal impulse persists, but the connection between the style and metaphysical expression is more subtle and controlled. In *White*, the formalist aesthetic exists in subdued form, and the reasons for this tempering revolve around generic considerations (i.e., the demands of a satiric comedy, rather than a contemplative drama). Finally, *Red* demonstrates an extraordinary balance of Kieślowski's approach to form, the image, and metaphysical issues. It also ends his remarkable filmmaking career.

The Double Life of Véronique

SYNOPSIS: *An expansion of the character Ola, in* Decalogue IX, *Weronika (Irène Jacob), a young girl in Poland, is a naturally gifted singer. As an opportunity unfolds for her to perform in a major concert, she begins to suffer chest pains, but only after she has caught a glimpse of a tourist who looks exactly like her. She confesses to her father that she has always sensed the presence of someone else connected to her, but*

242

she scarcely understands that intuition. In the midst of her debut concert, she suffers a heart attack and dies. At that moment, the very tourist Weronika saw feels grief, though she cannot understand why. She lives in Paris. Like Weronika (though unbeknownst to her), Véronique (also Irène Jacob) survives her mother, sings professionally, has trouble securing stable relationships with men, carries the same spiritual restlessness, and is plagued by the abiding sense that she "is in two places at once." Véronique's attempt to understand her shift in mood leads her to follow intuitive, internal direction. She quits voice lessons, though she does not understand why. Later, a cardiology report reveals problems, and Véronique understands that she has avoided a possibly mortal stress. While sorting out her feelings, she begins receiving mysterious signs that someone is interested in her: mysterious objects ("clues") in the mail and a cassette tape with the ambient sounds of a train station on it. Each of the signs intermingles with traces of the supernatural: unexplained sights — visions and dreams. The clues lead her to Alexandre (Philippe Volter), a puppeteer and children's book author who noticed Véronique at the elementary school where she teaches. Initially, Véronique is heartbroken to learn that his baiting of her is part of a character study experiment for his new book. Later, Alexandre finds her and apologizes, declaring his love for her. She feels that he may be the other soul to whom she has always felt connected. While getting to know her, Alexandre discovers a photograph Véronique took on a trip to Poland: it reveals Weronika, her double. This confuses and torments her, but she persists in her relationship with Alexandre anyway. He constructs a new children's story based on Véronique and Weronika's symmetrical lives. In emotional desperation, she runs home to her father, tightly embracing him, the camera revealing a double image of the pair.

Emma Wilson begins her reading of Kieślowski's later films with *The Double Life of Véronique*.[1] She sees the radical, adventurous, formal strategies evident in this film as a negotiation of imaging, exploring the impossibility of realism, the perils of representations, and the inherent collusion of multiple subjectivities (including that of the audience and the camera itself). It is probable that Kieślowski considered these reflexive issues, but I see this film as a struggle toward an end: that of metaphysical articulation. This film is full of abstraction, more so than any film before or after. After the *Decalogue*, it stands as Kieślowski's great formal experiment. The film is also saturated in spirituality, metaphysical suggestions, and superstition, so much so that we might say it lacks any specific theological focus. At times, the formal explorations seem almost ostentatious. All the same, it lays the

---

1. Emma Wilson, *Memory and Survival: The French Cinema of Krzysztof Kieślowski* (Oxford: Legenda, 2000).

foundation for a mature, transcendentally aimed style in *Blue* and *Red*. It also continues the metaphysical trajectory Kieślowski had long pursued, and this is why he adamantly denied that the film betrayed anything he had done before.[2]

This film is about longing — deep, internal longing — and the attempt to follow one's intuition, which is part of the reason it is so difficult to write about. In grasping for words, one is left somewhere between Jonathan Romney's assessment ("luminous, numinous, ominous") and that of Wilson ("a film which simply does not make sense").[3] Kieślowski himself struggled with his mode of expression in this film, and its aim of visualizing "feelings" and "sensibility."[4] He lived in the material world, but he dreamed and thought far beyond it.

In discussing *Véronique,* we are left with descriptions of general impressions such as the feeling throughout this film that little understood, herculean forces are shifting and moving through our midst. So much of the essence of the film hinges on the experience of watching it, not simply on an understanding of its story, characters, and use of metaphor. This type of abstract, nonverbal "rhetoric" can be very persuasive, as Kieślowski found out:

> At a meeting just outside Paris, a fifteen-year-old girl came up to me and said that she'd been to see *Véronique.* She'd gone once, twice, three times and only wanted to say one thing really — that she realized that there is such a thing as a soul. She hadn't known before, but now she knew that the soul does exist. There's something very beautiful in that. It was worth sacrificing all that money, energy, time, patience, torturing yourself, killing yourself, taking thousands of decisions, so that one young girl in Paris should realize that there is such a thing as a soul. It's worth it.[5]

There is a sense throughout *Véronique* that a radical break with the documentary has finally arrived, and this stylistic shift is complemented by a change in scope. *Véronique* stands as Kieślowski's first feature film after the fall of communism in Poland. Kieślowski has mentioned in numerous places how he and Piesiewicz were becoming disenchanted with politics, even at

---

2. Interview with Stok, *Kieślowski on Kieślowski,* ed. Danusia Stok (London: Faber and Faber, 1993), 193–194.

3. Jonathan Romney, "La Double Vie de Véronique," *Sight and Sound* (March 1992): 43. Wilson, *Memory and Survival,* 10.

4. Stok, *Kieślowski on Kieślowski,* 188.

5. Ibid., 210–211.

the very apex of the revolutionary changes in the country.[6] Kieślowski's thoughts and style, for some time, had been straining toward the universal issues, both sociologically and philosophically, and beyond local politics or national concerns. A few political images in *Véronique* mark this departure: the removal of an old Communist statue while children run happily in the streets, and the chaos that erupts when Weronika sees her double. In this latter instance, Weronika is, significantly, oblivious to the political demonstration around her in light of the present, transcendent concern. Indeed, Kieślowski seems to be using politics to serve the old myth of the doppelgänger, rather than the other way around. The myth declares that one may have a double in the world, and seeing one's double portends death.

Véronique was also Kieślowski's first international production, partly financed in France and set in France and Poland. The significance of this sudden link between Poland and Western Europe has not been lost on critics and theorists,[7] and there is some cause to interpret the films in a wider, European political context. However, I believe the universal interpretation remains stronger. It is not that European politics (and Poland's place in them) have no bearing, but that they seem to function as Kieślowski's immediate frame of reference for issues beyond them (a launching pad for universal philosophical reflection, if you will).

In Chapter 2, I discussed the remarkable opening of this film, which stands, in many ways, as an archetypal Kieślowskian moment. The phenomenological bracket functions through the child's inverted perspective, while Weronika's mother hints at the metaphysical context surrounding the image (and, indeed, the entire film): the Christmas Star. According to the New Testament, the Magi found the Christ child by following a bright star in the East, and Christian tradition commemorates that journey through symbolic use of stars at Christmas. The stars and inverted perspective continue as themes in Weronika's toy ball, through which she sometimes views the world. Near the end, we discover that Véronique carries the same toy.

---

6. See "The Ten Commandments of Krzysztof Kieślowski" (BBC, prod. Adam Low, 1990). Both men talk about the depoliticization of their stories, as manifest in the *Decalogue* films. These films were shot before the fall of communism and shown on Polish television just after.

7. See Janina Falkowska, "The Double Life of Véronique and Three Colours: An Escape from Politics?" in *Lucid Dreams: The Films of Krzysztof Kieślowski,* ed. Paul Coates (Trowbridge, Wiltshire, England: Flicks Books, 1999).

The Magi story initiates the film in a mythic mode and serves as a metaphor that generates the theme for the rest of the film: spiritual search. The child Véronique's enormous eye (amplified through the magnifying glass) enforces this theme immediately. Like so many characters in Kieślowski's film, the adult Weronika and Véronique both feel that their existence lacks something. A spiritual vacuum lies at the center of their existence, and they seek out a means of filling it. The characters all seek out love, acceptance, and identity, but the film suggests that all these manifestations of desire are drawn from the same spiritual well. Desire, in Kieślowski, is a deeply rich concept not limited to the sexual. Indeed, even when the sexual is involved, as it is several times in this film, it is revealed to be insufficient for ultimate fulfillment.

The two images opening the film exhibit two primary modes of searching: an inverted perspective (a new angle) and the microscopic perspective (a detailed, enlarged view). Loosely interpreted, these approaches parallel the mysticoreligious approach and the scientific method. The film portrays both approaches as helpful but ultimately insufficient by themselves. Both opening images show children perceiving through these modes with the interpretive, didactic aid of their mothers (both of whom die young). At the end of the film, Véronique returns to the site of this first investigation; the tree she touches functions as an index of home, as does the leaf she first investigated by magnifying glass. By film's end, her father is the closest substitute for her mother she has. His love for her remains a constant; salvation is not be found here, but it remains a respite from the nagging eternal questions. Perhaps love is the beginning of the answer to those questions. For Kieślowski, sociocultural entropy is the norm, but human love remains the abiding miracle.

The credit sequence features a hazy, abstract view of actions to come accompanied by a delightful choral song. This foreshadowing is not a typical convention on Kieślowski's part and may be read as an indicator of predestination or fate; these events are metaphysically prescient long before they play out. The sequence ends with Weronika's extraordinary suspended note. This elision of the future and the diegetic present, combined with the miraculous duration of this final pitch (testing the limits of disbelief), encourages us to adopt a cosmic view of time wherein any moment may be spiritually suspended and examined. The moment is like an aural freeze frame with ontological vitality. The ambiguity of the tears and/or rain on Weronika's cheek not only continues Kieślowski's motif, but it marks a certain liminality of her position between her transcendent experience of music and the natural world.

By this time, the viewer has gathered that the cinematography in this film is the most adventurous since Kieślowski's *Short Film about Killing*. As might be expected, Sławomir Idziak stands behind the camera on both films. On *The Double Life of Véronique* he uses a golden filter,[8] which gives the whole film a feeling of "amniotic well-being," according to Romney (this in contrast to the *Decalogue*'s "analytical realism"). Romney says of *Véronique* that the film is "cerebral as well as sensual, and using the stylistic devices characteristic of a Resnais."[9]

Weronika approaches her boyfriend, Antek, with passion, but that energy dissipates as the story goes on. While making love, she shows embarrassment at an old finger injury, which would have been disastrous had it not happened just after her successful piano exams. This near miss provokes thoughts of providence. At the end of their lovemaking, she smiles at her photo on his bedroom wall, ethereal light and dancing shadows animating it. The suggestion is one of presence, transcendence, and the odd feeling of estrangement one can receive while looking into the mirror. In Weronika's case, this "other" image who is also herself takes on flesh and blood, though she does not yet fully realize it.

As her health deteriorates, her singing opportunities increase. As her sense of not being alone in the world increases, her relationship with Antek proves increasingly unsatisfying. This is not for his lack of interest, but rather a result of a great psychological disturbance, as though he were a shallow answer to a deep question of desire. As she runs home from his apartment, she stumbles into a puddle, a foreshadowing of their faltering relationship and a literal misstep to recur in Véronique's flight from Alexandre to her father later.

The sketch on her bedroom wall depicts a Polish town with a prominent church steeple. Weronika surprises us by sitting up into this same cinematic frame, having awoken from a disturbing dream or premonition. The next shot shows a similar sketch through the microscopic, yet abstractly distorted lens of her father's spectacles, not unlike the magnified view through

---

8. Stok, *Kieślowski on Kieślowski*, 186.

9. Romney, "La Double Vie de Véronique," 43. He refers to the French filmmaker Alain Resnais, maker of numerous stylistically progressive films such as *Hiroshima, Mon Amour*, and *Last Year at Marienbad*.

Véronique's childhood look in the film's opening. This same scene will be echoed on the bus and briefly abstracted by a defect in the window, an amplification of the mysticality of this eternal space. After an iconic look upward and directly at the camera (as if sensing Véronique's eye or God's look upon her), she turns the cosmic gaze to the more common buildings of the town, which invert themselves in her toy ball, surrounded by floating stars.[10] All space — not just the traditionally sacred — is cosmicized as Kieślowski encourages us to bracket the ordinary, pragmatic way of seeing. The toy ball resembles a proverbial crystal ball, a tool of divination (not unlike the divining pendulum in *Decalogue VI* and *A Short Film about Love*).

Weronika's discussion with her father, taking place immediately before this bus trip, provides critical metaphysical context for this scene. Weronika confesses to the intuition of another presence intended for her in the world and her parallel awareness of an internal void ("What do I really want, Papa?"). When she speaks the words "I have a strange feeling" (to be concluded with the words "I am not alone"), Weronika's shadowy profile dominates the frame, fleetingly illuminated by dancing, animated flashes of light reflected from the outside, much like her photographic portrait seen in the previous scene.

The next scene reveals playing cards, an image of chance or fate. We hear an older woman's voice speaking for some time before her face is revealed; she is Weronika's sickly aunt. Their discussion reveals an ominous fact about Weronika's family: numerous people, including her mother, died suddenly while in perfectly good health.

A visit to her musician friend in Warsaw yields the opportunity for a vocal audition in a prestigious competition. Her happiness at the news causes her to bounce the toy ball to the ceiling, raining the old plaster dust down upon her face. She basks in the feeling of the flakes on her skin and the joy of the moment. Embued with potent formal and synaesthetic suggestion, emotional tableaux such as this mark Kieślowski's work from here on.

In Chapter 2, I discussed Véronique and Weronika's encounter in detail. It is truly a masterful bit of filmmaking and a clear demonstration of Kieślowski's use of abstraction. It is worth noting that the scene ends quite

---

10. See still images of this ball in Chapter 2. Weronika's look at the camera is not resolved by her subsequent POV, contrary to the expository practice of traditional film language. Such is the nature of the "iconic" look, keeping the object of her gaze in mystery.

concretely (a return to the temporal from the abstract), with Weronika staring after the tour bus with a line of faceless policemen lined up behind her. This shot is not only a return to temporal time, but also a reminder of a historic time (circa 1990) and the accompanying societal stress in Poland.

In the next scene, the audition, Weronika's passionate singing culminates in the breaking of the cord on her music folder. We watch in close-up as she winds the string around her finger, and we naturally feel the increasing tension of the string as it nears and reaches the breaking point. At this point, we do not know why Weronika has done this, but it is rational to assume that she has become carried away in the passion of her singing. Only later do we realize this is the beginning of her bodily failure. The important thing in this moment, however, is the poetry of dynamics at work here (as Arnheim might put it): the tense cord creates a sensory memory for the viewer that will match other experiences in the film, and the wavy-then-taut shape of the cord will "rhyme" (in Insdorf's words) with the shoelace Véronique is given later. The dynamics inherent in this simple visual form (a shape-shifting line) function not only on the phenomenological level, but also on the metaphorical level: Véronique's emulation of the cardiogram with the shoelace, ominously pulled taught at the end, seals the connection.[11]

This is the beginning of the end for Weronika according to the dop-pelgänger legend. After the audition, as she staggers home, Weronika finally collapses on a sidewalk bench. The appearance of a passing flasher is an odd, carnivalesque element here, similar to the oddity of the midget lawyer hired to finalize her aunt's will. As we have seen in Kieślowski's other films, it is not uncommon for him to intermingle the mundane, pedestrian, and even the unusual with the highly tragic, and not without humor. Such a gesture exists here, to Weronika's amusement. It is important to note that she is in obvious distress when the dark man appears, and he makes no move to help her. Rather, he symbolizes something of the illicit, daring sexual enterprise that Weronika relished describing to her aunt a few scenes earlier and its ultimate poverty. He also functions as a threatening specter — a dark figure of death. In addition to her collapse on the bench, the sight of the old woman outside her window functions as yet another reminder of mortality. The elderly in need of assistance persists in all of Kieślowski's films to follow, as Kieślowski himself pondered his own mortality. It also may be seen as a penitential gesture on Kieślowski's part; he described how,

---

11. See image sequence in Chapter 2.

as a young man, he and his friends used to privately make fun of an elderly woman in their town.[12]

After this incident, Weronika continues her preparations for the big concert, rubbing her eye with a ring, carefully pushing the eyelashes down. The geometrical pattern of circles becomes prominent here (the ring and the eye). In this vein, we also remember the circle of the magnifying glass and Véronique's magnified eye, a circle within a circle, something close to a vortex. One must speculate as to the exact meaning of the forms, but these scenes do highlight Kieślowski's tendency to drift to visual form at moments of high metaphysical importance. This quirky habit with the ring unites Weronika and Véronique (the latter apparently has the same habit), but the time and detail given to these images suggests a connotation beyond mere narrative connection. Kieślowski shifts from conventional metaphor to transcendental speech, the imagistic, phenomenological language of the ineffable, the nonverbal poetry of form. Véronique's breath on the mirror obscures the image in a suggestive, impressionistic, abstract cloud, then she quickly looks away, as if startled by something. What? We can only guess, but the suggestion made by the next shot is menacing: a very slow fade-in from black.

The concert text is old Italian — Dante, to be specific.[13] Clearly the gallows march has begun. From an editing perspective, the sequence of Weronika's collapse breaks the standard: we see her fall in a medium close-up, followed by a shot of the conductor, whose eyes clearly follow Weronika down, and *then* the shot emulates her fall, purportedly as a POV shot. This delay could be written off to cameraman error, but the mystery is why Kieślowski did not correct the problem in postproduction (a shorter edit would clearly have solved the problem). I maintain that the cosmic element plays into this decision — a stretching of the time just enough to suggest an alternate chronological scheme, and, perhaps, even to suggest the presence of Véronique in the scene as a falling, tandem spirit. The following shot, an aggressive, inverted overhead sweep of the audience, further suggests a spiritual transport, and the next scene, that of Weronika's POV through a translucent coffin, further solidifies the idea that Véronique participates in this death; in fact, the spiritual movements appear to be shadows of Weronika's spirit. Or, perhaps, we are witnessing the alternate chronology

---

12. Stok, *Kieślowski on Kieślowski,* 49–51.
13. Ibid., 179.

of the eternal, a time into which Weronika fully enters, and we encounter in the liminal image.

The quasi-temporality of the death scene elides into a passionate sex scene between Véronique and an unknown man. Abstraction is in full play here, from distortions of the lens to innovative lighting: Véronique unexpectedly clicks on the light near them. The question, of course, is why she clicks on this light. Kieślowski and Piesiewicz do not give a literal explanation, but perhaps it is in reaction to the great darkness that has just consumed Weronika, buried under the earth. Her lover remarks that it has been since graduation that they have seen each other (an indicator that Véronique's sexual life is just as unrooted and inconstant as Weronika's was), and Véronique grows sad, as if "grieving," she says.

Cut to a profile shot in shadow, a visual match to that accompanying Weronika's previous line, "I feel strange." Véronique's face disappears into blackness (a tunnel, as she drives) and reemerges, then shifts back to darkness. The significance of this very short scene must not be missed; it establishes that Véronique has traveled somewhere (her voice teacher's apartment, we learn), but such establishing links of dramatic action were never important to Kieślowski, as we have noted in discussions of past films. Rather, the scene remains for its metaphorical qualities and transcendent resonance, a pulsing movement between life and death. Véronique scarcely understands the experience herself, but she immediately knows by intuition what to do (an internal premonition she has always had, she claims). She quits voice lessons to the consternation of her teacher. Only later will she understand why her intuition was correct.

The marionette show is lovingly filmed and beautifully executed. The story is an ancient one dressed up in new circumstances: life, death, and rebirth. Véronique later describes the protagonist as having broken her leg as opposed to dying, and the matter is up for debate, but this connects the falls of Weronika and Véronique more solidly with the show; Véronique's fall is to come, as she runs from Alexandre.

After the show, she teaches schoolchildren about a newly discovered composer, whom we surmise to be Preisner's fictional alter ego, Van Budenmayer. After the class, she feels faint and ducks behind a tree for some respite. The next scene shows a very distressed Véronique emerging from the cardiology center. The camera follows her curious pace, then focuses on her dragging scarf. The wavy fabric becomes an abstract line, pulsing against the backdrop of the white floor, and the stop-start motion of its dragging bears a dynamic similarity to the cord Weronika snapped from her music binder.[14]

A few scenes later, the shot of Véronique on her pillow is barely identifiable as such; rather, we see patches of light in varying intensities broken up throughout a dark field and concentrated in various places closer to the bottom right of the frame. It might be an abstract painting of a darker shade. Not until she moves do we understand it is a close-up of Véronique sleeping, hazily illuminated in patches by incidental light through the curtains on her window. This abstract beginning will initiate a critical scene and a chain of abstract imagery that will bolster the primary theme of the film: the idea of intuitive, nonverbal communication. The anonymous phone call, at once disconcerting and intriguing, becomes the first in a series of nonverbal encounters between Véronique and her admirer. The language used in these encounters is later called "psychological" by Alexandre. In fact, they are associational clues with a heavy dynamic resonance; the power with which the music ruptures the intimate silence of the evening is every bit as important as the connections the piece signifies (i.e., the very piece Véronique has been teaching her class and, unbeknownst to the caller, Alexandre, the piece Weronika was singing when she died on stage).

This is the type of scene postmodern critics might interpret as a recognizance of the interstitial image and a critique of the medium. I believe it is much more likely that the scene visualizes a buried intuition, not quite clear or concrete enough to be called a memory, but vivid enough to carry some weight in Véronique's consciousness. The shot is an abstract, pulsing red intruded upon by a yellowish white moving image, which we soon surmise to be Weronika's obscured image at the moment of her death (synchronous with the actual point in the music that her passing occurred). The abstract functions as a mortal echo in Véronique's sympathetic soul.

Like Weronika, Véronique instinctively returns home after this quasi-amorous encounter over the telephone. She flies to her father for comfort, not because he can give her an answer to her nagging questions or fulfill her deepest desires, but because he provides a rootedness, a primary foundation for emotional and psychic stability. Her contemplative moment in front of

---

14. See Chapter 2 for a discussion of this scene. As mentioned in that discussion, this is the reprise of the same anxiety-ridden shot in *Decalogue V/Short Film about Killing*, as Piotr drags his scarf when going in to speak to the presiding judge in Jacek's capital murder case, which he has just lost.

the window, looking out on the countryside surrounding her home, reflects this assuredness.

Véronique declares immediately that she is in love with a man that she does not know. Her words to her father are the reverse of Weronika's claim: not that she had felt she was *not alone,* but that now she suddenly feels alone, and so she must bear the reverse burden of emptiness. The two women symbolize the two primary facets of spiritual need: the vacuum and the intuition of fulfillment undiscovered. Weronika's way of intuition was initiated by life; Véronique's intuition was awakened by death. Both women try to fill the nagging spiritual void with romance, assuming that the call of the question is the call of love. They both find romance wanting in this regard, as we see in the case of Véronique's mystery caller.

As she drives home from her father's house, the camera follows her, rooted in a graveyard, headstones passing in the foreground. The view from the dead land references Weronika, suggesting a presence that may persist from beyond.

Véronique is immediately confronted with the most cynical of deconstructions of the romantic ideal: a bitter divorce case in which she agrees to lie for the sake of her friend. Véronique's decision to perjure herself, even for the sake of her friend, is impulsive and strange. Perhaps she rationalizes it because the man did commit adultery numerous times. She casually drinks a glass of milk as she agrees to the plan. Kieślowski originally envisioned this scene as part of a large subplot that eventually had to be cut. He kept this scene because he wanted to "pull Véronique down to earth," and keep her from being conceived as only a hyperspiritualized character.[15] She is human like the rest of us, and, conversely, her presentiments could be our own.

A motivation here may be that Véronique has begun to identify romance with anonymity; from there it is a short jump to fabricating stories of routine sex with a man she hardly knows. Further evidence is her asking for detail on the man, particularly his most intimate traits and sexual performance ("I should know what a woman knows when she's had ... "). Véronique is naively utilizing this perjurous scenario to project the possibilities of her relationship with the mystery caller.

She backs out of this arrangement later, so perhaps we should infer it was all just an irrational burst of emotion amid her personal confusion.

---

15. Interview in Stok, *Kieślowski on Kieślowski,* 186.

So much about Kieślowski's characters is dependent upon inference. We will infer, in retrospect, that Alexandre overheard Véronique practicing the Van Budenmayer piece with her class. We infer that she has a weak heart. We infer that, despite her sweet, smiling looks, she is terribly confused. This dependence on inference can become confusing. The avoidance of Hollywood didacticism can sometimes result in an incomprehensible story with characters that appear strangely or even impossibly motivated. At the same time, Kieślowski constantly withholds expository information from us as a mirror of existential reality. We most often do not know what is truly happening within people. When we do find out, it carries the force of revelation.

The scene to follow shows her walking home, a sliver of light slipping between buildings, bathing her face in a warm glow. She stops, leans her head back, and basks in the radiance, like Weronika under the falling plaster, but with more fatigue and little joy. Moments like these are critical in Kieślowski's films, because they function without words but exude an extraordinary phenomenological impact: we *feel* the warmth and sympathize with her inner state and need for respite. The sun is not merely a thermal comfort, but also an index of a spiritual comfort, an experience larger than its denotative identity or physical function. The connection Kieślowski consistently explores is that of emotion and the physical world. Physical laws and properties are continually demonstrated and shown to be meaningful beyond themselves through the context of the character's inner life.

The string Véronique receives in the mail instantly reminds us of Weronika's broken music binder string. From our omniscient position, we are left to wonder if it is not some kind of warning from Véronique's doppelgänger, perhaps even a harbinger of death. In fact, the string has been sent by Alexandre, a reference to his own children's story and a clue for her to decipher. But is it only that? The pattern from this point on is a suggestion it may be both. Whereas the scientific explanation for the string is readily found, the timing of its arrival and its connection with Weronika's double (a connection only we, from a "divine," omniscient standpoint can make) suggest a primary ordinance behind the scientific explanation.

The next scene presents a similar scenario and suggests the idea more directly. A beautiful light flashes around Véronique's room, waking her from an afternoon rest. The source of this light is a boy with a mirror, or so we think at first. The boy disappears, but the light, mysteriously, remains for a brief time. I discussed this scene in Chapter 2, but a few more observations will serve here. First, this stands as another example in the recurring pattern of sleep and sign; often the metaphysical moments accompany the dream time, forcing a choice in interpretation: either the event is only a dream, or our dreamtime is the fertile ground where mystical happenings are given reign, a clue to other realities to which we are typically blind. Second, as the light illuminates a music folder just like Weronika's with the string attached to it, Véronique's iconic look at the camera suggests a break in the audience's distance from the scene. The suddenly animated, shifting camera suggests a presence above her. In my opinion, this is an example of Kieślowski's experiment with metaphysical style overreaching. It lacks the subtlety that pervades his later films. All the same, the metaphysical suggestion is undeniable and parallels Weronika's iconic look on the bus after gazing through her toy ball.

Like the Magi following the messianic star (alluded to in the opening of the film), Véronique reads the light as a sign, though she does not interpret it in any denotative sense. She immediately connects the string on the binder with the shoelace she had received and retrieves it from the garbage. After washing it, she toys with it over her cardiogram, a scene (discussed earlier in this chapter and in Chapter 2[16]) most powerful for its potent use both of abstract form and metaphorical power. The next scene yields another such image, that of Véronique's reflection looking back at her (a double) as she gazes in the bookshop window considering Alexandre's book.

The golden close-up of a teabag lazily spinning in the mug returns as one of Kieślowski's favorite images. The animation of the teabag seems almost self-generated, or, perhaps, divinely generated. It exudes a force that we do not often observe, though it may always be present. This shot is included in the long line of other close-ups on a glass; the cup of milk in *Decalogue I,* the glass of tea Dorota breaks in *Decalogue II,* and elsewhere. All of these images come at metaphysically significant points in the story, and this one is no exception. Having been given the spiritual sign, Véronique now embarks on an earnest search. The next shot shows her reading Alexandre's fairy tale, a story that rings all too true for her.

One small visual note: In a bit of graceful cinematic choreography, we watch Véronique roll on the bed toward us, rise, and look out the window at the postman. The curtain then closes the view. What is remarkable about this curtain is that Kieślowski demanded the assistant cameraman rack the

16. See Chapter 2 for a few still images from this shot.

focus to the fabric, and they hold on the curtain, in all its exquisite detail, a second longer than the average director or editor might. Lesser directors would simply use the curtain as a cutting point, never taking the time and effort to rack the focus to so near a foreground object, let alone light the curtain in a way that reveals its detail. Yet this detail was worthwhile to Kieślowski, and his editing gives us space to observe it. I do not believe the pattern of the curtain symbolizes anything in particular, but it is one more formal stroke in a series of abstract images, causing us to ponder form and what the experience of it might prompt within us.

Véronique's encounter with Jean-Pierre, her friend's divorcé, unnerves her. He knows she intends to lie about him in court, and he is clearly suicidal ("I'm just giving up," he says, throwing up his hands). This prompts another visit to her father, the tinkerer and inventor, who functions as her spiritual bedrock. She confesses to him a dream of a painting, a town with a church. The painting clearly is that of Weronika's father, but how she saw it is not clear even to her ("I must have dreamed it"). This very painting, replicated through Weronika's toy ball, recurs in her consciousness. Why? It is home for Weronika, and Véronique returns to her own home in search of it. Here is the call of the familiar place — the loved ones who form our primary social foundation.

The third package from Alexandre (the second being an empty cigar box, apparently related to the fairy tale, as Véronique clearly anticipated it) arrives at her father's house. It is the most important of the packages, because it contains the final clue to Alexandre's whereabouts, but it is also interesting because Véronique receives it here. Presumably Alexandre has discovered that she leaves the city on occasion and figured out who her father is, but the emotional significance of the parcel is that Alexandre's voice has intruded on her original home space. She does not play the tape for her father, nor does she remark on what it is; rather, she waits until she is in her own solitary space back in the city.

I discussed the formal qualities of sound in this scene in Chapter 2, but the narrative functions of this scene are no less important. A fragment of the haunting Van Budenmayer piece recurs on this tape, and it clearly catches Véronique's attention. The character of this sound is markedly different from the others in that it is the only sound not likely to be found in a "natural" city environment (which, we discover later, is a cafe in a train station). The possibility dangled before us is that Weronika (or some other power) is inserting herself into this recording. It is possible, of course, that

Alexandre merely edited in this fragment of music, having overheard it at Véronique's school, but that is only one of several possibilities. The mystical option seems as likely as the temporal, scientific explanation.

A brutal explosion ruptures the everyday ambience of the recording. Véronique rewinds the tape and plays it back, listening through the wail of an approaching ambulance, and then, as if sensing danger herself, sits upright and shouts, "Who's there?" She senses another presence in the apartment, but there are no clues here to Weronika's presence, except the slight shake of a handheld camera, a cinematic gesture that paradoxically embodies two mutually exclusive codes: the authenticity of the documentary and the gliding spirit-likeness of the supernatural. The temporal occurrences of the film seem to be regularly co-opted by spiritual forces, and we receive them as meaningful as intended. It occurs to Véronique to pick up a magnifying glass, and she holds it pensively (a return to her childhood image that initiated the film).

As we have seen in other films, Kieślowski returns to certain thematic elements: communication, mystery, technology (manifest in the headphones and remote control), trains, and car accidents. In many respects, these pedestrian, ambient noises illustrate the elements of Kieślowski's own life in a sort of auteurist audio-diary. The ambient nature of the sounds suggest his subconscious — a string of memories on tape. In the tradition of other auteurs, the media maker may, in this case, stand in for the director.

Magnifying glass in hand, Véronique dashes back to her father's house only to find him asleep. She examines the envelope that held the tape and inspects the stamp and postmark. The stamp, a ghostly image of a woman, marks Weronika's continual presence, competitive with all of Alexandre's machinations. While at the train station, she briefly makes eye contact with someone from Weronika's world (though Véronique hardly understands the significance, this woman does, because she was present at the meeting in which Weronika was awarded the soloist position). She follows Véronique with interest and reappears, still watching, a few scenes later. Her story only goes this far, though we can imagine it and place ourselves in her shoes: how many times have we seen a familiar face but not been able to place it? How many miraculous encounters have we had, only to write them off as coincidence?

Véronique meets Alexandre, after first balking at the chance, then seizing it. The remains of the destroyed car are continually seen through their interchange. One might read this as another harbinger of disaster, particularly if one sees Alexandre as a destructive force in Véronique's life. One might also see it as the ever-present danger that exists in relationships, a reminder of the risks that must be taken and the bitter consequences that may result. In either case, the conversation with Alexandre proves unnerving to Véronique; he suggests that his baiting her was, in fact, less romantic and more clinical: a research project for his fictional writing efforts aimed at projecting whether a woman might be drawn to an anonymous man simply through psychological suggestion. Véronique, of course, feels terribly used, and Alexandre's answer to her query only worsens the situation: "Why did you choose me?" After a pause, and a shamed look downward, he replies, "I don't know." She dashes away.

As she dashes out of the train station, she slips on the pavement, not unlike the previously mentioned falls of Weronika. She must not walk in those footsteps, and, perhaps, that is the entire point of Weronika's apparent intervention. Insdorf's interpretation is that Weronika is there to warn Véronique of the destructive influence of Alexandre. In my interpretation, this is partly the case. I am not sure Weronika is warning Véronique about Alexandre so much as she is revealing to her that the emptiness she experiences in her life runs far deeper than romantic love. The car accident cannot rationally have much to do with Weronika, but it may have something to do with God. The ironic mysteries of fate permeate Kieślowski's work, and this wouldn't be the first time one person's tragedy functioned as a redemptive act for someone else (consider the ending of *Red,* for instance). The destroyed car calls to mind the turn of the conscience that bears down upon Urszula in *No End,* as she narrowly avoids an accident herself because of her own stalled car.

The tables turn in the chase that ensues, however. As Alexandre desperately looks for her, she observes him through a colored-glass door. She watches him search for her (suddenly she is in the position of power), and she does a little "scientific" observation of her own. She witnesses him blow his nose, a mundane occurrence that marks a real person rather than the ridiculous persona Alexandre had staged earlier. She smiles slightly at this quotidian moment.

He catches her at the hotel and begs her forgiveness. "For what?" she asks, but Alexandre cannot produce an answer. Though his motives are hardly beyond dispute, the chase itself has clearly meant something to Véronique; the fact that he would pursue her so long and so passionately touches her. She allows him to rest in her hotel room. As he slumbers, exhausted from the running and the waiting in the train station (apparently having waited nearly two days for her), she notices the reflection of a nearby window, reminding her (no doubt) of the little boy's reflection transmitted into her room from another window some days ago. No doubt she misreads this as a sign of her assured destiny with Alexandre.

As he sleeps, Véronique gently removes his glasses from his hand. Why? We are not told, but the gesture continues the theme established in the beginning: Véronique's search for a new vision. The next scene shows her toying with the ring against her eye, just as Weronika did before her fatal performance. A shadow passes over ever so subtly but enough to get her attention. She looks around and above her, then drifts off to sleep. An interjected shot suggests a dream: the view of the Polish church from Weronika's bauble, stretched, inverted, and moving away. This is sampled from Weronika's fateful trip to Warsaw, of course, but it also ushers in an enormous amount of metaphysical connotation: transcendence, the spiritual world, and, perhaps, a church cemetery. When Alexandre wakes her, she speaks of a sheet falling down upon her (Weronika's shroud, we assume) as she was falling asleep (not after). This is the shadow and the first sense we have received that her spiritual sense has sharpened to the point that she recognizes a vision.

Alexandre responds with an immediate assertion of life: "I love you." As if to counter the looming face of death, she responds: "I love you." Upon declaring their affections, they ask questions of one another, and Véronique dumps her purse on the bed to initiate the "get to know me" session. Several things reveal themselves. They find among the pile a pair of glasses for which Véronique has been looking for for more than a year (a symbol of lost vision, or, rather, a different mode of vision). This is consistent with Véronique's increased spiritual sensitivity of late, and I am reminded of the anecdote of the great experimental filmmaker Stan Brakhage throwing his glasses away, refusing to submit to the 20/20 mandate for proper seeing. A quote from Brakhage seems applicable here as well:

> The ultimate searching visualization has been directed toward God out of the deepest possible human understanding that there can be no ultimate love where there is fear.[17]

---

17. Unfortunately, I cannot locate the original source of the eyeglasses anecdote. It may be apocryphal, but certainly it is not out of character with his ideas. The quote comes from a reprint of part of Brakhage's essay "Metaphors on Vision," in *The Avant-Garde Film:*

The toy ball, which Alexandre pretends to make disappear with some sleight of hand, is a denial of her microcosmic world more significant than he knows. He hides from her the divining tool, and a connection with Weronika.

They exchange a few potent thoughts. Alexandre asserts that he now knows why Véronique was the one he chose for his experiment, implying that, in fact, he realizes now he was in love with her. Véronique responds that she has known all along that he has been pursuing her, however clandestine his efforts. He is surprised at her powers of deduction, and she responds with a statement that most clearly shows the tangle of her spiritual intuition and her romantic pursuit:

> All my life I've felt I was in two places at the same time. Here and somewhere else. It's hard to explain. But I know . . . I always sense what I have to do.

Immediately after this statement, the clarity of her intuitive vision is questioned as Alexandre discovers "her" in the photograph on the square. Véronique sees her own photographic trace, but in someone else's coat. The psychic pressure of her dilemma overwhelms her. She falls on the bed, weeping; we are not told, explicitly, why she cries, but perhaps buried within deep sorrow is a deeper, spiritual root of sadness. Véronique's tears exude frustration, confusion, and fear, but also, perhaps, grief. Alexandre responds amorously, making love to her, and she desperately, passionately responds. We are reminded that the day one sees one's double is the beginning of the end, and Véronique's amorous response may be characterized as resistance to impending death.

Kieślowski's choice of the photographic trace carries with it the inscription of death that Roland Barthes so insightfully noted years ago:

> For Death must be somewhere in a society; if it is no longer (or less intensely) in religion, it must be elsewhere; perhaps in this image which produces Death while trying to preserve life. Contemporary with the withdrawal of rites, Photography may correspond to the intrusion, in our modern society, of an asymbolic Death, outside of religion, outside of ritual, a kind of abrupt dive into literal Death. . . . With the Photograph we enter into *flat Death.*[18]

A Reader of Theory and Criticism, ed. P. Adams Sitney (New York: Anthology Film Archives, 1987), 121.

18. Roland Barthes, *Camera Lucida: Reflections on Photography,* trans. Richard Howard (New York: Hill & Wang, 1981), 92.

Is not mediated culture a constant barrage of doppelgängers, reflections, and refractions? The photograph ontologically mediates the dead, and Véronique confronts her own corpse. Yet a hopeful interpretation may be that the very mediation of her doppelgänger prevents her sight of it from having a fatal effect. Weronika has seen her double in the flesh, Véronique beholds hers in the image. The deathly image is at once deathly and redemptive, inscribing and refiguring Weronika's passing as a Christological substitution on her behalf.

Indeed, the photograph here seems to bear spiritual significance. As their lovemaking swirls into a frenzied rush of various emotions (pleasure and tears), Véronique's view, pulsing in and out of focus, centers on the photograph of Weronika staring back at her and the toy ball rolling around next to it, stars swirling inside it. The scientific "document" and the mystical trace come together here, revealing the necessity of both for meaningful belief, and we return through these themes to the very first images of the film: an inverted, fantastic perspective on reality paired with an intensely analytic, microscopic, and scientific view through the magnifying glass.

Preisner/Van Budenmayer provides a musical bridge to the next scene, in which an overhead shot reveals Véronique awaking, as though from the dream she began in that hotel, but in a very different bed: a bachelor's mattress on a floor in Alexandre's apartment. Time has clearly passed. How much? We don't know, and the elision of time and space reflects the eternal flux that operates contrary to temporal chronology.

Véronique rises from the bed. The camera pans with her movement and slightly ahead. As though merging into her consciousness, the shot transforms into a rather intense POV shot, desperately wandering, searching through the apartment alone. An abandoned, snowy and flickering television (a perpetual Kieślowskian image of emptiness and abandonment) dominates the living room. Through Véronique's eyes (or are they Weronika's?), we move to the next room to discover Alexandre in his workshop. He has seized upon her story as inspiration for another fictional work — a parasitic artistic impulse that Bergman worried about in his films (particularly *Through a Glass Darkly*). She asks why he has made two dolls in her likeness, and he replies that they are easily damaged; there is more truth to that statement than he knows. With his help, she handles her own image in a frame packed with bewildering, even conflicting themes of control, identity, and will. The camera tilts down to reveal the other doll sprawled on the table in a deathly posture.

261

The crisis for Véronique is that the story Alexandre has relegated to fantasy is all too real and vexing for her. Alexandre's story tells of two women who are mystically connected; the entire time he reads, we never see him. He is bracketed from the equation, as if a commentary from beyond. The unwavering camera shows us Véronique's emotional face in relentless close-up. The story plunges her into a deep melancholy, and she leaves the room heavy hearted.

Alexandre, like the Judge in *Red,* is something of a pseudo-God: powerful and insightful, but ultimately shallow and inadequate for meeting genuine spiritual need. It is only natural that she would flee Alexandre and run home for the fourth time in this film.

Véronique's touching the tree (the final image in the French version of the film[19]) serves as another example of the nonverbal yet potent gesture in Kieślowski's cinema. As I have surveyed my students and numerous Kieślowski fans, the images most often remembered often include an expressive, close-up shot of the hand. In this case, we see a tender reconnection with home, as Kieślowski explained.[20]

Véronique's father, like Alexandre, works in his woodshop. Perhaps Alexandre's fashioning of her in his wood shop reminded her of the original woodworker who created her. Her flight from the artificial Véronique to the real, a relentless quest throughout her life, necessitates this return home. Her father, as if by instinct, spiritual calling, or both, raises his head. The edit to Véronique's hand on the tree solidifies the intuitive, familial connection between them. As only a father would, he asks her if she is cold and would like to come in. She runs to him, and the film ends with a remarkable double image of their embrace, the first sign of contentedness and resolution we have received, even amid the bifurcation of Véronique's world. The serene image expresses the symmetricality of our heroines and suggests they are beginning to find some peace.

There is a terrific amount of ambiguity in the last part of this film. Many, many things are left unexplained and/or unclear, and even Véronique's final emotional state is difficult to discern. This ambiguity, however, is something of a strength in Kieślowski's aesthetics, and the fact that he

---

19. Annette Insdorf, *Double Lives, Second Chances: The Cinema of Krzysztof Kieślowski* (New York: Hyperion, 1999), 135.

20. Kieślowski, as quoted in Hiroshi Takahashi, "Eyelashes Quiver in a Propeller's Breeze," in *Krzysztof Kieślowski: We Are What We've Absorbed* (Lódź, Poland: Camerimage, 2000), 6.

conceived numerous endings for this film (each varying in outcome) suggests the same determined, yet multiple potentialities that Kieślowski explored in *Blind Chance.*[21] We are products of fate, chance, *and* our choices. The resolution of the determinism versus free will debate may lie beyond this film, but Kieślowski's films enable us to distill the issues into meaningful, unforgettable moments of phenomenological intensity. Véronique's return home signals not a resolution of all her problems, but a need to find a solid place from which to renew the eternal search once more.

The Three Colors Trilogy

Just as the *Decalogue* builds its narratives around the themes of the Ten Commandments, the *Three Colors* trilogy utilizes the themes symbolized in the French flag (liberty, equality and fraternity) for stories of universal import. Like the *Decalogue,* they are not so much moral tales illustrating virtues, but stories that exemplify the inherent tensions these ideals generate as they clash with an all too imperfect universe. These themes embody not only French ideals, but also those of any democratic society. Having newly emerged from communism, they were, no doubt, of great interest to these Polish filmmakers, particularly as they sought to transcend local politics in their films. In these films, Kieślowski does not break stride in his metaphysical pursuit: "All three films are about people who have some sort of intuition. . . . "[22] Likewise, all three films end with a protagonist experiencing some sort of grace in their circumstance, weeping.

Blue (1993)

Synopsis: *Julie (Juliette Binoche) loses her husband, a famous composer, as well as her daughter in a car accident. She is the sole survivor. She attempts suicide in the hospital, but she cannot follow through. She elects to rid herself of all reminders of her past, sell her possessions, and clandestinely take up residence in a Paris apartment. Despite her best efforts, her past continues to creep in on her through reminders of her grief and publicity surrounding her husband. Two scandals emerge, the first being her husband's affair, and the second being the suggestion that Julie might have written her husband's music. Through various encounters with people from her past, such as her*

---

21. Originally, Kieślowski and Piesiewicz envisioned seventeen separate endings. See the interview with Stok, *Kieślowski on Kieślowski,* 187.

22. Ibid., 216.

husband's collaborator, Olivier (Benoit Regent), and new acquaintances in her present, Julie makes some decisions: she gives away her country home to her husband's mistress (now bearing his child) and endeavors to finish her husband's unfinished concerto for the Unification of Europe (the music that has haunted her ever since the accident). In the end, she finishes the musical work and, more importantly, reciprocates the love of Olivier. The final image shows her first tears since her family's funeral and an ambiguous expression on her face.

This film is an incarnation of grief: its unwieldiness, lulls, rhythms, frightening unpredictability, bursts of aggression, nebulous sense of time, and utter emptiness. The film is a requiem composed in images. The grief here is also a close cousin to the longing exhibited in *The Double Life of Véronique.* It is another experience of absence — a space in one's life vacated, a precious, foundational thing taken away. I know of no single film that so fully explores and articulates the dynamics of loss as *Blue.* It is a masterwork of phenomenological articulation. Kieślowski excels most when he speaks the language of *experience,* not words. The images are insightful, even devastating poetry, illuminating the many nuances of bereavement.

In this respect, this film stands as a reprise of *No End* nine crucial years later. Between *No End* (1984) and *Blue* (1993), Kieślowski ascended to international notoriety, solidly left behind the documentary form (his last documentary project being the short eighteen-minute *Seven Days a Week* in 1988), and, most importantly, witnessed the fall of communism in his country. The essentially desperate, pessimistic outlook in *No End* yields to a glimmer of hope, a hope for liberty from all sorts of personal bondage. Exterior wide shots filled with emptiness mark both films. Car accidents figure prominently in both stories. Both films feature a woman who has lost a husband and struggles with suicide. Both films feature strong Kieślowskian visuals (e.g., close-ups on hands), blue as a thematic color, striking abstract compositions, themes of grief and suicide, and a focused use of music. Most importantly, both films address the ultimate questions of existence and meaning and complement the metaphysical concerns with extraordinary formal strategies, surveying the liminal ground between immanent and transcendent.

Stylistically, *Blue* marks a high point for Kieślowski; the abstract style budding in his previous works and widely used in *Véronique* reaches a remarkable balance and maturity in this film. *Véronique* was not merely a whimsical stylistic experiment, but the building of a stylistic foundation. Sławomir Idziak returns for *Blue,* and his cinematography here carries as much power and genius as anything he had done previously with Kieślowski. He initiates what I would call a chromatic dialogue that characterizes the entire trilogy: the titular colors emerge as visual motifs of a polysemous nature. In this film, blue symbolizes all sorts of emotions and experiences, sometimes conflicting. Kieślowski's camera makes the colors into rich, intentional screens to receive our projected feelings.

The nearly wordless opening sequence to the film fully exhibits Kieślowski's mastery of film technique. The opening shot begins in black with gray vertical lines emerging slowly, accompanied by a nondescript soundtrack. As the camera pulls back and the sound of a car horn becomes prominent, we discover that we are looking at a car tire on a busy highway. We are traveling, but the abstract presentation has already told us that this will be no ordinary trip.[23]

No music is playing, but the genius of the sound design is its marvelous rhythm. All the natural sounds from each of the clips beat a consistent, steady time, not unlike the "fate" rhythms that characterize funeral dirges. The pulsating whir of the tires, the rush of lamp posts being passed, the ominous drip of fluid from a faulty brake line: all these rhythms form a continuous aural procession through the sequence and ultimately match the pace of Antoine's game with the stick and a wooden ball. At the very moment he wins the game, Julie loses: the car passes Antoine and smashes into a tree, unable to mitigate a proverbial turn in the road.

Engaging abstract visuals seamlessly accompany this richly textured soundscape. A child's hand, waving a blue candy wrapper in the wind, brings a flag to mind, but the image generates a surplus of meaning that cannot possibly be contained by mere metaphor. Anna, Julie's daughter, iconically stares at us through the back window of the sedan, flares and flashes of different shapes regularly gliding over her. Beautiful, mysterious distortions overlay her view of the road while in the tunnel (an important symbol in Kieślowski, as we have seen). As she runs for a roadside bathroom break, the dripping brake fluid figures prominently in the foreground. She returns to the car in the background, out of focus, and Kieślowski refuses to shift the focus from the ominous harbinger; Anna's form, spiritualized by abstraction, emerges as another harbinger simultaneously. Their car passes Antoine on the side of the road like a yellow-eyed ghost in the fog. We never see the point of impact, only hear its horrible sound as we read Antoine's shocked expression. The

---

23. See Chapter 2 for a few stills from this sequence.

sudden halt in the fate rhythm is terrifying, and we then see the car smashed into an ancient, immovable tree. A panicked dog dashes away, while sheets of paper fly from the car, and a lonely beach ball makes its tragic departure from its child owner, lazily rolling, as if cruelly unconcerned. Antoine slowly picks up his skateboard, then breaks into a desperate run to the scene. The wide shot yawns like a cold abyss of sky, one tree amid a vast plain, belittled in the bottom of the frame, the frigid blue heavens weighing down from above.[24]

Right away, the question of fate and its ironic contours raises its ugly visage. Why did they hit the one object amid that vast empty plain? Why does Antoine's success at the game (one attempt among, perhaps, hundreds) coincide with Julie's worst nightmare? What does one have to do with the other? Does one cause the other? Later we will learn that the car accident occurs between the repeated punch lines of a joke. Is this God's cruel joke? These questions will plague Julie throughout the film. Antoine himself will also wrestle with them as he discovers Julie's necklace at the scene and attempts to return this symbol of faith to her.[25] She is not able to receive it back so easily and leaves it with him. By film's end, he is wearing it, touching it, and contemplating it as he begins yet another day of his existence.

The semiotic polysemy of the abstract form emerges as its greatest strength in Kieślowski's skilled hand. Because of their epistemological properties, described in Chapter 2, the forms exude a primary aura, strongly suggesting the receiver think and process beyond the named and categorized world. Yet, on a mere semiotic level, they also create points of high irony, which Kieślowski sees as a primary characteristic of our existential struggle. The ironies outlined in the last paragraph continue in the following image, bridged to the opening sequence by the first of many fades to black. The new shot is difficult to label: a spidery, breezy form, both light and apparently soft, but also tentacled, like a predatory spider (after some time we guess the object is a down feather from the pillow Julie sleeps on). Like in the shot of dripping brake fluid, the focus does not shift as a blurry figure emerges from the background. As he stretches a hand to the camera, it enters the focal region, and he asks, "Are you able to talk?" The next shot, equally disorienting, shows the man's distorted reflection in Julie's eye, although we scarcely know at this point that the eye belongs

---

24. See Chapter 3 (discussion of *Blind Chance*) for a still image of this shot.
25. See Chapter 2 for a still image of this shot.

to Julie or where we are at all.[26] In concert with Julie's disorientation and shock-induced numbness, the abstract elements create psychological identification with her, but, as I have maintained, they do not simply do that. In the metaphysical context clearly laid in the opening sequence, the visuals direct the gaze of the audience beyond the temporal.

Julie's internal strain at the news of her daughter's death intensifies as she buries her head in her pillow. Her emotion climaxes poetically with the shattering of a window. Close inspection of the scene reveals it to be a glass of water thrown through a window, but a viewer in a natural viewing position would not identify these particulars. Rather, the shattering appears as a dynamic emotional extension of the previous shot, and the lull afterward reveals two worlds: a jagged, broken interior reflection and a cold, dark world beyond. Julie's suicide attempt follows.

The small television Olivier brings her gives her an absurd first image: skydivers falling through the air. As *Blue* goes on, the thrillseekers that show up on various televisions will stand as icons of free individuals defying death and danger. Their bodies, suspended in the air (often in slow motion), provide an echo of metaphysical weightlessness and freedom from temporal constraints.

The wide shot of Julie on her bed watching her family's televised funeral is difficult to identify, partly for its framing (the window, tinged purple by Idziak's filters, is dominant), and partly because she has pulled herself into a protective cocoon (or perhaps a tomb); no part of her is visible. A relentless extreme close-up then surveys her scars, bruises, and trembling lips. As she touches the screened image of her daughter's tiny casket, a tear escapes. Julie's reach for her little girl rends the heart, but it also continues Kieślowski's ongoing dialogue about the visual image and its mediation of the dead. In *Camera Buff*, it provides a living memory for Piotr; in *Blue*, what is lost in transmission stands for the vacancy in Julie's life. Her lips tighten, and, just as the man presiding mentions Patrice's new piece for Europe's Unification, she changes the channel. Her eye shifts to the camera. Like a cold, determined icon, skewed by an odd angle, her features threatening to break the claustrophobic frame, the lines of her face creating unnerving, almost-cubist distortions of her face (Fig. 52).

The establishing shot of the next scene is interesting in that it establishes the blue panes of glass that surround Julie. Again, most establishing shots

---

26. See Chapter 2 for still images from this sequence.

Fig. 52. The anguished icon in *Blue.*

are used as a tool for mapping the diegetic space and the character's position within it, but Julie is barely visible. Here, after numerous neglected
establishing shots, Kieślowski makes a point of establishing the blue panes
through not one, but two wide shots. As she rests, the music from the
funeral startles her from her slumber, and blue light floods the frame. This
will be the first of several intrusions into her psyche. In this case, as the
music thunders and the light blazes, she stares at the camera, drifting low
and side to side, staring back at her. Its movement and her fixed gaze suggest
a presence, though no presence can be accounted for. Like the intuitions
in *Véronique* or Urszula's sense of her husband in *No End,* Julie's daughter
will not abandon her psyche. In *Véronique* and *No End* these techniques were
much more concrete, suggestive of a real spiritual presence. In this film
they will come to less resemble a spirit, and more the shocking, relentless,
and unpredictable intrusion of memory and loss. As anyone who has lost
a loved one will testify, remembrance storms in suddenly, all at once, and
most unexpectedly.

In nearly every case, the blue lights that flood Julie can be diegetically
explained, as they are here by the blue panes of glass of the porch. However,
there will be one time when the light is not explained at all (to be discussed
later), a suggestion that more may be at work in the world than the laws
of physics and optics. This visionary episode will end with a fade to black,
a transitionary device that Kieślowski uses to articulate the slippage from
temporal consciousness to grieving consciousness and back again. Though
we are dealing with grief, the spiritual connotation is not completely absent;
perhaps Julie is retreading the ground of the "valley of the shadow of
death."[27] The television reporter has interrupted her moment in blue, and

27. Psalm 23:4.

here we get the first hint (from the woman's questions) that Julie may actually be a composer herself.

I mentioned that the colors are polysemous, and Kieślowski makes this a strength. At one time, the flood of blue can symbolize the call of liberty (i.e., liberty from grief and memory) as well as the persistence of sorrow ("the blues," various indicators of blue as a "cold" color, etc.). It no doubt symbolizes both these things and more. The moments of color function as a call to spiritual clarity, a time when the issues at hand must be reckoned in ultimate terms, as metaphysical questions crying for an answer. The abstract nature of the lights leads us in this direction, but it is only an arena for thought, not a dogmatic answer to any given question. It is this liminal, metaphysical zone that Julie will attempt to flee in futility. The real question in abstraction is not What does it signify? but How do I feel? In nearly every case the blue light can be explained scientifically, but it is presented phenomenologically (with explanations not easily available). The lights are a trace of the veritable myth, the old religion before modern demystification.

Julie is the first wealthy protagonist in all of Kieślowski's films, though Karol will attain wealth in the next film of the series, White. The emergence of capitalism in Kieślowski's homeland had some influence on these choices, and Kieślowski and Piesiewicz do not treat capitalism as an economic savior. In both cases, they move their characters away from materially focused lifestyles. For instance, Karol stages his own death for revenge on his wife, sacrificing his wealth to the cause. In Julie's case, her country estate is nothing short of stunning. The opulence of this location is no sooner absorbed then it is dismissed; Julie is selling everything and leaving. The home later becomes a very generous gift.

Her steely resolve only hardens as she moves around her home for the first time since the accident. She had her gardener clear out "the blue room" before her arrival, and we later deduce it belonged to her child. As she moves through it, one unavoidable trace of her daughter remains: a lamp with dangling blue crystals. Julie rips a strand from the lamp.

This marks the first in a chain of powerful gestures on Julie's part, unaccompanied by words. They serve as clues to the internal state behind her stony expression. Some of these moments prove to be Kieślowski's most memorable images. Rarely do I discuss Blue without someone mentioning the scene of Julie leaving the estate, dragging her knuckles along the wall. Likewise, the scene where Julie tests the piano lid support exhibits

Kieślowski's mastery of dynamics and his ability to place all the artistic potentialities in a given scene in service to the emotional needs of the moment. As Julie stands in the doorway to yet another room, the camera tilts slightly left in weighted harmony with the leaning books on the shelf in the background. The dynamics embody a force Julie cannot overcome, and she collapses left against the door frame. As she sits, thinking, blue flashes of light dance on her face. We don't know where they come from, and Kieślowski encourages us to reckon them as emotion made palpable. Olivier sees Julie, and we surmise that they have been in the same house this entire time, though they have not yet faced each other.[28] There is good reason for this: Olivier loves Julie and knows that Patrice, her husband, was not faithful to her. He carries a blue folder that holds correspondence and photos from the dead man. We learn later that Julie refused them. In retrospect, at the end of the film, Julie will see this as a defining, providential choice: had she taken the folder, she would have burned it and never discovered the affair.

Julie smiles wryly as the lawyer requests she tell him why she's selling everything. "No," is her simple reply. As he turns and leaves, the smile fades and the troubled look returns. The camera tilts to reveal blue crystals in her hand. She has been carrying them around since she yanked them away. Having borne this small burden for a time, she decides she can keep the lamp, and it is the only memento that shows up in her new apartment in Paris.

She discovers Marie, the housekeeper crying. "How can I forget?" the woman asks. Julie seeks her own answer to that rhetorical question. The fades to black ironically sum up both the effort to vacate memory and the constant reminder that emptiness, ironically, can be a haunting presence.

The abstract imagery has embued these first twenty minutes of the film with a metaphysical aura, reinforcing the idea that Julie's despair is as much a crisis of faith as anything else. The remarkable scene by the piano, where she first confronts a handwritten moment from the concerto, is no exception. As the close-up pans across the notes, the music plays, notes before and ahead obscured by an abstract blur. Only the present remains

---

28. The script suggests otherwise, stating that the desk Olivier cleans out is at the Academy of Music. It is not clear in the film that he is in a different building. Omitted establishing details can sometimes be confusing; like Tarkovsky, Kieślowski would sometimes eschew narrative clarity in favor of formal or emotional concerns.

in focus, moment by moment. The present is all that remains in clarity as she confronts her grief. All the while, a hollow, whistling wind pervades the soundtrack, diegetically strange but emotionally appropriate.[29] As the notes disappear, the music and wind continue, suggesting unrealized music to come. Her finger on the support of the piano lid poses a challenge to the limits of gravity, the physical laws of the universe, and the limits of her own volition. This is the same tempting of fate that Dorota exercises on her glass (*Decalogue II*) and Jacek with the rock on the overpass (*Decalogue V*). The crashing collapse of the lid tragically confirms to Julie that the world remains cruel and relentless. As she recovers from the violence of the moment, blue reflections from the pool outside (barely glimpsed in a shot or two) dance across her face.

The music continues to invade her emotional cocoon, just as it has twice already. In the copyist's office, it reappears as they look upon the score of the concerto Julie claimed did not exist. She throws it away. Her odyssey through self-inflicted amnesia has a winnowing effect, sifting out all that is not essential to her. In the end, her music and her daughter remain in her memory. Her realization of this fact leads to the two great redemptions in the story: her provision for Patrice's new child and her persistence in the final completion of the concerto with Olivier. In the case of the latter, she will achieve a partnership with a lover, something she could not achieve, apparently, with Patrice.

Like Véronique, she dumps out her purse — an emotional archeology of identity. Véronique discovers something more of who she is; in Julie's case, it is a revelation of everything she wishes to erase. The candy, complete with blue wrapper (the very kind that Anna held in the breeze at the opening of the film), provides a sensory link to her dead daughter. Her frenzied consumption of the candy embodies a desperate emotional pursuit, a visceral identification with her daughter. In the end it is hollow, of course, as the experience rings with absence. Grief and frustration poison every action.

As if to fill the sensory hole her husband once occupied, Julie invites Olivier over for sex (confirming he has always desired her). The motives

---

29. This is what Michael Chion calls "free counterpoint," like the example he gives from Tarkovsky's *Solaris,* where the movement of a character's frozen body is complemented by the sound of breaking glass (*Audio-Vision: Sound on Screen* [New York: Columbia University Press, 1990], 39). This is yet another example of Tarkovsky's influence on Kieślowski.

for this action are hidden, in large part because Julie barely understands them herself. She will confess later in the film that she loved her husband, and that he loved her; perhaps, like Urszula in *No End* and Karol in *White*, she has only realized this by way of his absence. Having sex with Olivier may be a dramatic way to test that love, that memory, while at the same time defiantly grasping after "liberty." Her motives may be complicated, confused, and impulsive, but her resolve, Olivier discovers, remains strong. Her marital bed is now stripped, white as a tomb. As Olivier enters, escaping the ominous storm raging outside, the framing places him in a tryptych of reflections, an expression, perhaps, of his own confusion about this summons and Julie's fragmented state of mind. The three reflections mark this as one of Kieślowski's liminal moments. The choice to pursue Julie romantically (or not) will be defining, and much of the rest of the film will hinge upon it. Julie immediately takes brutal command, demanding he strip, then reciprocates, so there is no doubt and no turning back.

As with Véronique, Weronika, and Urszula, the sex proves insufficient to fill the void. She awakens resentful, chastening him for idealizing her — indeed, for idealizing anything at all. Julie's world has no more room for ideals. She leaves her home deeply upset, dragging her knuckles on the wall masochistically, as though to assure herself that she can still feel emotion, even if it's pain.

This expressive, moving close-up is an unforgettable image of internal agony manifest, packed with extraordinary visceral power. Emma Wilson insightfully links this moment to a similar one in Alain Resnais' *Hiroshima, Mon Amour*, where the female protagonist scrapes her hands against the cellar walls in the wake of the loss of her German lover.[30] It is worth noting that Emmanuelle Riva, the primary actress in that film, plays Julie's mother in this one.

The recurring Kieślowskian image of the tunnel, an emergence from darkness, proves to be Julie's entrance into Paris, bearing with it all the existential strangeness that can accompany that experience. As if reborn into a new, anonymous existence, she appears somewhat bewildered at first, then carefully begins to make her way. Her aim: a place to live, registered under her maiden name, obscure, with no children in sight. In her new apartment she hangs the child's crystal lamp. She is compelled to touch it with her deeply wounded hand, covered in scabs. The moment is altogether

---

30. Wilson, *Memory and Survival*, 34.

poignant — a compassionate instance — and one feels Julie has hit some emotional seafloor after floating aimlessly for some time.

The first scene in the cafe demonstrates a novel approach to time consonant with the distortion of time that accompanies Julie's grief. Multiple "sheets" of time (to borrow a Deleuzean phrase) exist in the close-up image of the coffee; the image is a still life, but the music and shifting light animate it into something closer to time lapse, a rising and setting of the sun in one image. The framing of the image does not centralize any particular object but the liminal rim of the saucer.[31]

A fight erupts outside Julie's apartment. Just as Jacek ignored the fight in *A Short Film about Killing,* Julie does the same, but for different reasons. Jacek is calloused; Julie simply has no energy to help and no reserves to make the necessary sacrifice. She has nothing left within herself to give. The same feeling operates in her confrontation with her neighbor (who wants her to support the eviction of a loose-living tenant) and her lack of awareness of the old woman with the bottle at the recycling bin. After the crisis of the fight has passed, she assuages her guilt by belatedly emerging from her apartment. In an ironic twist, she finds herself in the position of the fugitive she failed to assist, locked out of her apartment with no safe haven.

This also places her, unwittingly, in the position of the voyeur. She witnesses her neighbors' infidelities (which will, in another ironic turn, gain her a friend). Also, on these steps, cut off from the comforts of her apartment (another cocoon), music returns as the persistent, invading force. The blue light appears when she closes her eyes and disappears when she opens them. This is the first example in which the blue light cannot be easily explained by any diegetic considerations.

As Antoine confronts her with her past in the cafe, the threat of void invades, expressed by the ominous fade to black. He returns a cross to her, which we first see in close-up, Julie out of focus in the background.[32] Julie asserts that nothing is important, not even this cross. This is the existential flip side to her statement to the realtor that she does nothing for a living. She refuses the cross and all it stands for. It is not merely a symbol of the faith, which Julie has lost, but a sign of sacrifice, a virtue she cannot muster.

---

31. See Chapter 2 for this still image.
32. See Chapter 2 for this still image.

As she floats in the swimming pool, in a fetal position, her hair floats abstractly in the water, much like that of the mother in Tarkovsky's *Mirror*. It expands and contracts in the liquid, a haunting image that appears both animate (the movement of the hair) and inanimate (Julie's lack of movement and breath). She hovers in this liminal state between death and life.

Her later conversation with her neighbor Lucille (Charlotte Very) provokes a conflict of emotions within her. Lucille is, in many ways, still a child, evident as she gaily pokes around Julie's apartment. Upon seeing the crystalline lamp, she remarks that she once had a lamp like it and often stared at it as a child. The film frames Julie's disturbed response dead-center, a framing that tends toward stasis and resembles the iconic. She carries flowers, an obvious allusion to her dead child's funeral, and the memory Lucille has inadvertently provoked flashes in painful streaks across her face. What is interesting here, however, is the turning point in Lucille's life. Julie has "shown her kindness" by not signing her eviction petition (though, in fact, Julie's refusal to sign came from her own insular instincts rather than benevolence). The unintended kindness leads to this moment wherein Lucille mirrors Julie's own child in some ways. The lamp is the touchstone for this analogue, but Julie comes to recognize other similarities (e.g., Lucille's father is something of a philanderer, we will learn). Julie feels compelled to care for her, but, in turn, Lucille also cares for Julie. They are two damaged souls, and Lucille's ability to remain cheerful and free appeals to Julie (though Lucille's own demons are revealed later).

Warped, shifting, and hazy, Julie's visage appears tormented. A second shot reveals this to be her reflection on the back of spoon in the same cafe where she met Antoine.[33] A flutist, whom she met before, plays a song very like what her husband (or she?) had written. A close-up of the sugar cube matches the tune, endowing it with dramatic significance, an abstract embodiment of melancholy.

The coffee creeps into the cube, as if an encroaching force, a personification of an inanimate object that marks Kieślowski's late style.[34] She asks the flutist if the music is his own; he calls it his invention. Coincidence? Perhaps. Kieślowski indicates that this is a universal gesture, indicating that people in different places think about the same things: "a sign of what unites

---

33. See Chapter 2 for a still image.
34. See Chapter 2 for a still image.

all men."[35] But the moment also serves to raise the question, once again, about Julie's authorship of the music. It could very well be that here, in this chance encounter with a street musician, Julie begins to consider laying claim to something in her old life once again: her music.

The tapestry of Julie's grief is multithreaded indeed. Not only does the music remind her of the calling of her identity, but the infant rats in her apartment appeal to her maternal instincts, even as they horrify her. As if in response, Julie returns to her own mother. As she speaks with her, a TV displays images of bungee jumpers, like the televised skydivers Julie first saw in the hospital. The images of freedom on the television form an emotional counterpoint to Julie and her mother's conversation. Clearly suffering from Alzheimer's (or some other disease affecting memory), her mother cannot keep Julie's identity straight. Struck with this tragedy, which also compounds her own recent tragedy, Julie attempts to reconstruct her impoverished identity by accounting all she has lost. She alludes to suicide overtly for the first time since the hospital. As she speaks, one particular shot frames her eyes, her mouth bracketed from us by the obstruction of her mother's head. In this one image, loss of memory renders speech insignificant, and Julie despairs.

All the while, men free-fall through the air, unencumbered by the earth and its gravitational burdens. The allusion is complex: the call of suicide (freedom from temporality) or perhaps the hopeful call of freedom, insisting on its existence and possibility. So far, Julie's self-imposed freedom from responsibility has proven not only ineffective, but a hellish nightmare of rootlessness and torture by memory. In some ways, her mother is more free for having lost that memory, but Julie has now utterly lost everything: a home, a family, a shared history. It is the antithesis to Véronique's flight home for comfort; Julie returns home only to find her home vacant of memory itself.

As she returns to the amniotic comforts of the pool, Julie's freedom again proves temporary. Lucille arrives and asks if she is crying. The music and atemporal invasion of black returns. Julie responds that it is just the water (a reprise of this ambiguous theme first seen at the end of *Decalogue I*). At this point, Kieślowski provides us with some comic relief (Lucille, Julie discovers, does not wear underwear), a winking nod to her freedom that amuses us but will also prove sobering in short time. As Lucille turns to

---

35. "Kieślowski's Cinema Lesson," *Blue* (DVD, Miramax, 2003).

leave, briefly flashing the camera, a parade of little girls arrives and jumps in the pool, at once reinforcing the tie between Lucille and childhood as well as a reminder to Julie (and to us) that the memory of her lost child will continue to invade her places of refuge.

As mentioned, Lucille helps Julie as a friend, most recently in the way she is cleaning up the carnage left by the cat Julie placed with the rats (and over which she feels guilty). Yet we discover in this next scene that Lucille also needs Julie for support. She wanders through her life as naively and childishly as she wandered through Julie's apartment. She may stand for her entire generation, a new manifestation of the "braless," sexually restless Anna in *Decalogue IV* and a marker of what might have happened to Anna had she not reached reconciliation with her father.

Idziak treats us to sumptuous, twinkling views of Paris as we hear a phone ringing. The call, a reach for human contact, could come from anyone. We do not know whose phone is ringing or who is calling, but we have been led to the moment by the narrative, the metaphysical context, in which people need to contact one another. It is only later revealed that Lucille is calling, waking Julie from her sleep. The source of Lucille's restlessness is to be revealed, and her general cheerfulness belied.

Lucille's father shows up at the strip club where Lucille dances. She is devastated and shaken. It is enough that Julie came to comfort her, she says, and we are struck with the fact that we know nothing about her mother. As she tells Julie about the upsetting incident, she perfunctorily arouses her performance partner, and the camera very deliberately pans back and forth between the two women, the lewd sexual performance in the background mediating (or coming between) the two women. The performance continually reminds us that we are in the museum of broken, twisted, empty desires. Julie even goes so far as to ask Lucille why she performs nude, to which she responds that she likes what she does and thinks everyone feels the same way deep down. This sudden confidence contradicts her recent upset, of course, and Julie does not appear particularly convinced. No doubt, she remembers her own frenzied sexual release with Olivier on the last night in her old home. One cannot amputate sexual desire from spiritual desire so easily.

In this same museum of desire, on a television, Julie witnesses her husband's lover for the first time. At once she is confronted with a side of her past reality she never knew as well as the realization that she did not effectively destroy the music she had set out to banish from her life (the publisher had kept a secret copy). As with so many other Kieślowskian moments, television is the mediator of this new knowledge, horrifying in all its starkness.

Olivier's decision to pursue the concert's completion is driven in large part by his frustration with Julie. After he had tracked her down in the cafe earlier, she had clearly communicated her determination to forget her past. In response, Olivier argues that his actions are designed to force Julie to reckon with her desires — to salvage them and reappropriate them, however painful: " . . . to make you say 'I want' or 'I don't want.' " In short, she must *communicate* and stop hiding.

Earlier, back at Olivier's apartment, a discussion of the concert ensues, and Julie pulls an old Bible off his shelf. The text for the concert is found there: an adaptation of St. Paul's ode to love in 1 Corinthians chapter 13. The chorus, sung in the original Greek, articulates many of the themes of the film, and the singing of it brings about the film's resolution. The text is worth considering here, because it delineates the great powers as well as the great difficulties and risks inherent in this, the greatest of all virtues. It is, in fact, the universal against which Julie has been struggling the entire film, and, in a miraculous paradox, may be the virtue that saves her:

> Though I speak with the tongue of angels, if I have not love, I am become as hollow brass. Though I have the gift of prophecy, and understand all mysteries, and all knowledge; and though I have enough faith to move the mightiest mountains, if I have not love, I am nothing. Love is patient, love is kind; it bears all things, it hopes all things. Love never fails. For prophecies shall fail, tongues shall cease, knowledge will wither away. And now shall abide faith, hope, and love; but the greatest of these is love.[36]

With classic Kieślowskian timing, Olivier asks her what she wants to do about the mistress. The music and black return (an invasion, but also a moment of decision), and the great tension hangs in Julie's conscience for the next few scenes. Her attempt to decide what she will do takes her to the courts, where (in a Kieślowskian wink) she walks in on Karol's divorce case in *White*. The connection is a small one, of course, but also posits the idea that Julie and Karol might have met, and might have found they had a lot in common had things been different.

The camera pans long and slow, as if in a funeral procession, across the stillness of the pool. After what seems like an eternity, Julie, having

---

36. Adaptation translated and printed in Geoff Andrew, *The "Three Colours" Trilogy* (London: BFI, 1998), 36.

tempted death yet again, pierces the water's surface, gasping for air. The next scene shows her returning to her mother, though no words mark this occasion. She simply observes her mother as she watches television, a scene of a tightrope walker ("floating" in the air, but precariously balanced on the liminal rope). Julie also finds herself in a liminal position, teetering between life and death, directly hinged to a moral decision. She leaves, an ambiguous expression on her face, that we will later realize is resolve.

"If I'd burned them, I'd never have known," she says to Olivier, understanding that the existence of her husband's blue file and its bitter secrets may contain a hidden grace. She begins an exciting session of composing with Olivier, steaming ahead on the completion of the concert. The allusion to Van Budenmayer, of course, gives Kieślowski yet another in-joke with his favorite film composer, Preisner. Marvelous moving close-ups of the music mark the acceleration of the effort. A very, very long wide shot chronicles their efforts, gradually slipping into an abstract loss of focus as they steadily move into the realm of inspiration. As per style, the abstraction also marks a metaphysical zone — in this case, the beginnings of Julie's healing.

In a spectacular redemptive act, a manifest love for her enemies, Julie yields her home, her very place of identity, to her husband's child and its mother, who betrayed her. Nothing in the scene, or in Juliette Binoche's performance, indicates that this is easy for Julie. On the contrary, the scene ends with an ambiguous expression that we have come to remember as pain lightly veiled. All the same, the good act is done.

Olivier insists that they both take credit for the music in a marvelous shot of his image doubled by his reflection on the piano lid. Julie must acknowledge herself as a composer and come forward, in a courageous step, with a publicly reconstituted identity. This new beginning is prefigured in Kieślowski's shooting; Julie's entire conversation about the matter is seen with her back turned toward the camera. It is not until the very end that she turns, revealing herself to our view and to the world. The gesture is an opening up, a new beginning, however painful. The final shot rises in a transcendent motion, up to the blue-crystalled lamp. We lose Julie's face in the jewels. It seems this chromatic source has been redeemed.

This transcendent suggestion initiates the remarkable final sequence. Beginning from black, the 1 Corinthians 13 chorus triumphantly thunders over a gliding, seamless, and nearly timeless revisitation of the characters in our play. All struggled for liberty in some way or another, and love is presented as a hopeful key to their situations, though easy sermonizing is hardly the case here, because many situations are unresolved. Julie and Olivier make love, her face pressed against a window that renders their forms abstract. The camera elides space to reveal Antoine awaking early, thoughtfully fingering the cross necklace Julie left with him; his story is left untold, but the suggestion is that all he witnessed opened deep questions within him, and this symbol of faith is providing, at the very least, a foundation on which to deal with them. Julie's mother is seen, staring at television, but also at us, as windows and reflections multiply her fractured self. Lucille is shown, sitting in the strip club, looking terribly sober and pensive. From the sex show of the club, a pan reveals new life arising in a sonogram, a child for Sandrine, Patrice's mistress. The camera pans to her face — an expression of wonder. Finally, we see a close-up on an eye, symmetrical to the eye that greeted us after the great catastrophe. This time another figure is reflected: Julie, with her naked back turned toward the subject. We do not know who possesses the eye; perhaps it is Olivier, perhaps God. Most likely, it is Julie, seeing her own image, turned away from herself (i.e., a selfless giving away) and now, for the first time, truly beholding herself with healing objectivity. The final close-up reveals her crying, facing the world through the window.

It is not easy to say exactly what Julie's expression means at this point, nor should it be. Grief is complex, and Kieślowski's film has taken us on an odyssey through its many dimensions. Something close to a smile approaches her lips near the end, and so we can believe that something positive has changed within her, but this is no storybook ending. The color blue creeps up from the bottom of the frame, an abstract rising screen coupled with the reflections of trees outside. The final cut to a vast screen of blue, over which the credits will appear, seals this ambiguity, and we should be grateful for it. The abstract color cannot dictate answers to us, but it can serve as a repository for our feelings, a screen onto which we can project our deepest needs and desires. The music continues to suggest, hopefully, that love is the key to freedom, even as the First Epistle of John says: "There is no fear in love; but perfect love casteth out fear. . . ."[37]

White (1993–1994)

SYNOPSIS: *Karol Karol (Zbigniew Zamachowski) is a Polish hairdresser, married to a beautiful French woman named Dominique (Julie Delpy). Unfortunately, he finds himself impotent, and his wife has decided to divorce him. Karol finds himself alone*

---

37. 1 John 4:18.

in Paris with no resources, because Dominique has vengefully conspired against him (canceled his credit cards, locked up his bank accounts, and even torched the beauty salon they owned together). Despairing and broke, he begs for money in the Paris subway, humming old Polish songs on his comb. A man named Mikołaj (Janusz Gajos) recognizes the tune and offers him an opportunity for money in Poland: he needs to kill someone who wishes to die but cannot bring himself or herself to commit suicide. After some debate, Karol agrees and devises a plan for Mikołaj to smuggle him back into Poland in a giant trunk. Unfortunately, the trunk is stolen in Poland, and Karol ends up barely surviving his encounter with the thieves. He reunites himself with his brother (Jerzy Stuhr), another hairdresser, and, through ingenuity, works his way into the Warsaw underworld. Though he is a peon in this shady environment, he is clever and uses his position to discover inside information on a real estate deal the mobsters hope to exploit. He immediately trumps them by buying a few plots throughout the coveted area and selling them back to them at a much higher price, to their chagrin. Through this deal, Karol ascends in stature and wealth and reunites with Mikołaj. It turns out Mikołaj himself was the subject of their suicidal arrangement earlier, but Karol has forced him to rethink his decision by deceptively pretending to kill him. The two men enter business, and Karol focuses his efforts on faking his own death and framing Dominique for it. In short, the plan works, and, at the same time, Karol's virility returns. In the end, he is broke again, supposedly dead, and visiting his wife in prison. She indicates her love for him and desire to remarry. He cries in happiness.

White is something of a departure from the tone and style of Kieślowski's other films. Most important in terms of this study, the use of abstraction is much more muted here than in any of the other post-Communist films. It is a comedy (albeit, a dark one), a genre in which Kieślowski never worked extensively. Comedic elements are prominent in only a few of his dramas (e.g., *Camera Buff*), and *Decalogue X* may be the only film that can rightly be called a comedy up to this point. The stylistic anomalies of *White* are best understood in light of the new demands of the comedic genre, Kieślowski's feelings on post-Communist Poland, and his dialogue with his older films.

The film is best understood, in my view, not as a realistic mimetic narrative, but as a cartoonish satire on contemporary materialism and the loss of traditional values. In terms of the comedic genre, the film bears the trappings of caricature, political satire, and, most explicitly, the farce. Oscar Brockett, in his classic text *History of the Theater,* describes the original farce of the European Middle Ages. I can think of no better description of *White*:

If the religious plays treat the triumph of virtue and the punishment of vice within an eternal order, the farces show imperfect humanity within the social order. Marital infidelity, quarreling, cheating, hypocrisy, and other human failings are the typical subjects. The clever man, even if a sinner, is usually the hero; the dupes deserve their fates because they are stupid or gullible. Sentiment is almost totally absent.[38]

Likewise, the difficult motivations and extreme actions of the characters are best explained when they are seen not as real people but as caricatures, players within that farcical, overblown capitalistic world. The critique running throughout the film is essentially political (i.e., money, power, and materialism in the crosshairs), without the zealotry, polemics, and self-assurance typical of that approach. In fact, I believe that Kieślowski was not really so much a Marxist as he was a smiling version of Aleksandr Solzhenitsyn (on this issue): critical of totalitarianism, but pessimistic about the negative effects of materialism inherent in contemporary capitalism.

Karol is an ordinary Pole in a bewildering new world. He comes home to Poland, just as Kieślowski returns to his homeland for a second and final time since the fall of communism. In *Véronique,* the concern was to reach out, a link between the Weronikas of Poland and the Véroniques of the Western world. In this film, however, Kieślowski faces his homeland straight on, targeting many issues that bothered him about Poland, before and after communism.

One major issue Kieślowski tackles is the definition of success. In general, "successful" people arrive at their position through intelligence and creativity tinged with a practical cutthroatedness. Even Karol must swindle the land deal and then employs his wealth to deceive and frame his own wife. Earlier Kieślowskian films dealt with the pre-Communist side of the success coin, that of aspiration. In this respect, several of Jerzy Stuhr's characters are examples of the man of ambition, foiled in the end. This is the theme in *Decalogue X,* in which he appears as Zbigniew Zamachowski's brother and the motivations are more banal (i.e., less about identity and calling and more about quick money and greed). That banality is seen again in *White* with the same ensemble: Zamachowski and Stuhr as brothers. In this particular case, Stuhr's character is not so tainted by greed or power factors, but he enables his brother's obsessions with them.

---

38. Oscar Brockett, *A History of the Theater,* 7th ed. (Boston: Allyn & Bacon, 1995), 107.

Other connections with Kieślowski's past films are easily spotted through-out. The eerie white, snow-covered fields (at once dead and beautiful, and prevalent in *The Scar*) return here. The ghostlike gas masks of *Camera Buff* make a reappearance (suggesting, perhaps, that things may still be just as frightening). One might also argue that the suicide in *No End* is reconsid-ered here, in a scene no less dramatic than that of its predecessor. In short, Kieślowski dialogues with his previous work throughout this film as some-thing of a retrospective in light of the dramatic changes in his homeland. Though he had publicly abandoned politics as uninteresting, political topics are revisited here in a comic fashion, as if to say that the issues deserve consideration and thought, but not so much hand-wringing as the more universal themes that drive his later dramas. Kieślowski is putting some matters to bed as he consciously moves on toward the final film of his career (*Red*).

The opening shot begins with a materialist allusion: a large trunk moving on a conveyor belt. It is worn but sturdy enough, and the substantial locks and latches, combined with the unwavering attention the camera gives it, suggest something valuable is inside. Karol turns out to be the precious cargo that, ironically, will be discarded as waste. This shot proves to be a flash-forward in the story. Indeed, much has been written about why Kieślowski would start this film in such a curious fashion, particularly since the transport to Poland does not prove to be any more crucial to the film's story than any other basic plot point. To my mind, Kieślowski begins the film with this image because of its thematic resonance: it establishes that materialism will be a topic of discussion throughout the film.[39] The suitcase also symbolizes Kieślowski's own return to Poland in a humorous fashion. One should remember that Kieślowski faced stern criticism from many Poles who felt he had abandoned them and the urgent political needs of the country.[40] Perhaps this scene is his wry, joking retort: he also must smuggle himself back into his homeland.

Kieślowski once commented that he envisioned Karol Karol (which may be translated as the Polish-equivalent of "Charlie Charlie") as a Chaplinesque

---

39. The genesis of this decision was more pragmatic. Kieślowski admits that the suitcase was added, to replace some beginning scenes that didn't work out the way he wished. "Kieślowski's Cinema Lesson," *White* (DVD, Miramax, 2003).

40. Janina Falkowska, "The Political in the Films of Andrzej Wajda and Krzysztof Kieślowski," *Cinema Journal* 34.2 (Winter 1995): 42.

character. The first present tense shot of the film, that of a man's feet, may be our first clue: a distinctive walk, well-worn shoes, not quite mimetic of the famous Tramp, but running in the same comedic mode. The feet pause in nervousness. Not only is Karol nervous about his court case, a summons instigated by his wife, but a couple is kissing passionately on the street, and he has reason to find this threatening. Further, he is a poor Pole in opulent Paris. Kieślowski himself notes that Karol even seems afraid of the passing cars.[41] The man is simply out of sorts.

We see several shots of Karol admiring the birds. The chromatic dialogue, via the color white, is then introduced in comic fashion: a bird defecates on Karol's shoulder. As Kieślowski says, "His candor toward nature betrayed him."[42] The bird reappears, however, in a more conciliatory (and nearly miraculous) way in the subway later. In dialectical fashion, the color white reappears in the courtroom within Karol's memory as a beautiful, dream-like reflection of their wedding day: Dominique's radiant, pale visage turns toward him smiling. The color swings back again to banality, however, in the form of a prominent white toilet (into which Karol vomits after publicly hearing that his wife no longer loves him). As in *Blue,* the thematic color does not carry any set meaning throughout the film, but serves as an emotional canvas onto which we will project various meanings derived from our interaction with the narrative. Edward Kłosiński's sturdy, realistic cinematography bears little resemblence to the adventurous formalism of Idziak or Sobociński (who lensed *Red*). I believe Kieślowski chose a less abstractly driven cinematographer because this satire is the earthiest of the three stories in the trilogy. The characters do not aspire to metaphysical heights, and the universal themes explored here tend to be negative: greed, exploitation, power, and revenge. In short, there is less abstraction because there is less transcendence. This lack of vision is deliberate on Kieślowski and Piesiewicz's part and consistent with their critique. In this narrative, the church is mentioned only in passing and relevant only in its proximity to a bunch of rip-off artists Mikołaj knows. The only religious image in the film, an actual icon, is used by Karol as a makeshift mirror by which he can style his hair. This image is the very antithesis of the icon's theological telos — the inverted perspective geared to drive the viewer inward, into the

41. "Kieślowski's Cinema Lesson," op. cit.
42. Ibid.

soul.[43] Karol is demonstrably more concerned with surface: that of the glass over the icon, as a reflective mirror, attendant to his exterior appearance.

During the trial, the need for Polish translation highlights the disconnect between Karol and his wife, though she clearly speaks some Polish. Dominique speaks French, as it is a French court, but Karol is placed in the defensive position of the foreigner and says so. In the middle of the trial, Julie (from *Blue*) enters and is told to leave, and we are left to wonder what a friendship between Julie and Karol might have been like: she wealthy, he poor, both betrayed by their spouses and suffering. Outside the court, Dominique unloads the suitcase (the very same trunk as opened the film) and waves goodbye, a gesture filled with cruel irony yet reprised lovingly at the film's end. Such symmetries mark Kieślowski's work to the end of his career.

"Enter your code, then press 'validate,' " the ATM says, as Karol attempts to withdraw funds. The larger meaning, of course, alludes to the dehumanizing effects of capitalism; Karol himself finds himself without "validity," both economically and existentially. The following scene makes it more personal; his ATM card is cut in half in a shot that exaggerates the size of those foreground shears (an image of emasculation, Insdorf observes[44]). Left shivering in the cold that night, he witnesses an old man attempting to place a bottle in a recycling bin. The effort is difficult, and Karol's face breaks into a wry smirk. There is something of a dirty joke here, but the joke is on Karol: that of the impotent phallus stuck in midcourse, unable to complete the job. Even as he amuses us, Kieślowski broadens the theme: impotence is, in its broadest and most literal sense, a lack of power. The old man lacks the physical strength; Karol lacks strength on nearly every level (sexual, sociological, economic, spiritual, etc.).

During their encounter and last (failed) sexual attempt in the salon, Dominique says that he does not understand her or realize her wants and needs of him. This is ironic, of course, as so many of Kieślowski's relationships are. The character's actions are diametrically opposed to what they truly

---

43. John Baggley, "Doors of Perception: Icons and Their Spiritual Significance" (London and Oxford: Mowbray, 1987), 80–81. Quoted in Angela Dalle Vacche, *Cinema and Painting* (Austin: University of Texas Press, 1996), 147. Also see the discussion of icons in Chapter 2.

44. From a lecture on *White,* Metropolitan Museum of Art, New York City, April 14, 2003.

desire. Dominique, in hopes of provoking a reaction from the "uncompre-
hending" Karol, lights the salon's curtains on fire and threatens to accuse
him of arson. Knowing he is at her mercy, he dashes away, frightened. Dominique's extreme actions seem bizarre; the actress playing her, Julie Delpy,
says that the character reminds her of a nigh-crazy cat she once had, in heat
and violent.[45]

Karol's fly is open, Mikołaj remarks. Every joke has a brutal edge to it, in
this case, a painful reminder of Karol's failed sexual attempt. Mikołaj recognized the Polish song Karol was playing on his comb ("The Last Sunday,"
a popular Polish song about doomed lovers, according to Insdorf[46]). Karol
gives him another — a military anthem delivered with delectable cynicism.
"I don't like it," Mikołaj remarks. The two men agree to share an illicit
bottle of whiskey together and talk. Mikołaj's card tricks reveal his memory
to be excellent, a liability in his case. During their conversation, a white
pigeon miraculously flies into the subway and lands near them. This surprises Karol, and he no doubt remembers his last encounter with a pigeon
outside the courthouse, but the white bird here functions as a sign of hope.
Mikołaj offers Karol a deal that will get him home to Poland.

"He has a wife, children, money . . . and wants to die?" Mikołaj is not
a caricature, but a touchstone to the spiritual destitution that can befall
any man or woman, as we witnessed in *Blue*. Material success very clearly
does not buy happiness. But, Kieślowski wryly observes, it might buy one
revenge.

The image of Brigitte Bardot introduces the idealized image of woman, a
mold into which Karol has placed Dominique. It is also worth mentioning
that the poster is for Godard's famous film *Le mépris,* the English title of
which is *Contempt.* The aptness of this allusion is strengthened by the sexual
taunting that is to follow, during Karol's phone call to Dominique with her
new lover present. Karol hangs up before Dominique's climax, as if to save
a bit of his dignity, but even his last two francs are stolen from him by the
phone. He angrily demands material recompense from the subway teller,
and the man begrudgingly complies. This restoration will be the first step
in a slow but deliberate process for Karol: his reconstitution and plan for
revenge.

45. "A Conversation with Julie Delpy on Kieślowski," *White* (DVD, Miramax, 2003).
46. Insdorf, *Double Lives,* 144.

He remarks that he has one thing to do before being shipped in the trunk to Poland: to steal something. Apparently, a bit of materialist therapy is in order. As usual, Kieślowski does not immediately tell us what Karol steals, but we soon learn that the coveted object is a plaster bust that enchanted Karol from its shop window. The visage is that of Dominique, or something close to it. He will steal it, and, likewise, attempt to possess her by force. Ironically, it is he who will be stolen in a short time.

We return to the opening sequence of the film, complemented by some additional, humorous images, such as the baggage handler's pain while hauling the trunk and its perilous ride atop the airport baggage tram. In the end, the trunk arrives in Warsaw, but the corrupt baggage handlers steal the trunk. After discovering Karol inside, they try to steal his two francs (which he desperately grabs back), and they beat him nearly senseless. He lifts his head to survey the sight, a snow-blanketed garbage dump. "Home at last," he remarks, and Preisner's music rushes in to highlight the sarcasm (a deliberate musical irony in the likeness of a piece by Chopin, a Polish nationalist hero[47]). Janina Falkowska points out that this is a direct reference to the final scene in Wajda's classic Polish film *Ashes and Diamonds,* in which the protagonist dies on a rubbish heap in liberated Socialist Poland in 1945. Karol is this character resurrected in a corrupt, capitalist Poland.[48]

"You bought a neon sign," Karol remarks as he collapses into his brother's arms. "This is Europe now," he replies, as if to say that gaudy advertising is synecdochic for the whole of European identity. During Karol's convalescence, he passes the time by repairing the bust he stole from the shop window. The duality is poignant: Karol, face battered and broken, attempts to piece together Dominique's shattered visage. This is the first suggestion that Karol's true subconscious desire is to piece the two of them together again.

By the river, Karol is ready to hurl his last French coin into the abyss, but it sticks to his hand through what Insdorf calls "metaphysical glue."[49] This is an apt description, in my judgment, as this miraculous, gravity-defying event marks a moment of inspiration for Karol. His face lights up with a

---

47. Interview with Zbigniew Preisner (Mark Russell and James Young, *Film Music* [Boston: Focal Press], 2000).

48. "*The Double Life of Véronique* and *Three Colours:* An Escape From Politics?" in *Lucid Dreams: The Films of Krzysztof Kieślowski,* ed. Paul Coates (Trowbridge, Wiltshire, England: Flicks Books, 1999), 150.

49. Insdorf, *Double Lives,* 160.

new thought, and the scene goes black. This is the visual converse of Julie's blackened memory intrusions. Here, Karol's mental state begins in black and emerges in a vision — a flash-forward to Dominique entering her hotel room — the beginning of a triumphant moment to come. This revelation is less transcendent vision or metaphysical intuition than the first vision of the possibilities of revenge. Kieślowski seems to be giving Karol a conditional destiny, and by breaking up the sequence into a series of flash-forwards, he offers Karol multiple opportunities to turn back. However, materialistic power (symbolized by the coin) will not leave him and will drive him to the end of a devilish plan.

Karol's introduction to the underworld is through a mobster counting money on his desk. Kieślowski typically avoids clichés, but here he seems to promote them for humor's sake. Karol manages to get a job as a guard for the man, and he is given a gun that shoots tear gas. The scene to follow is a marvelous bit of comedy; Karol swaggers around, posturing as a tough guy. It also suggests something of Poland's aspirations to be respected in a larger European context. As a Pole in France, Karol is impotent. On his home turf, he becomes quite powerful, even virile. Insdorf believes that Karol's eventual upward ascension could be a picture of the new Poland.[50] I agree, but this new generation also receives plenty of Kieślowskian criticism along the way.

Karol's new effort to learn French (by cassette) is at once a concerted attempt to combat his insecurity and a commentary on his inner thoughts: "Would that you had slept," "Would that I had left," "Would that I had pleased. . . . " (this convention was first tried by Kieślowski and Piesiewicz in *A Short Film about Love*). As the tape plays, he imagines himself kissing Dominique via the repaired bust.

The background behind Karol's ingenious swindle is that Ikea and Hartwig are two mega-corporations looking to take over peasant farm-land (another portrait of capitalism as an insatiable predator). As his plan shifts into gear, we are treated to a spin on Kieślowski's recurring communal image: two glasses in close-up, only this time they carry vodka, not tea. Karol suggests the old farmer satisfy himself with material goods: "Buy a car! A TV!" "What for? I never watch it. Always the same crap," the old man says, with some prodding from Kieślowski, it would seem. Lest we get comfortable with the materialist/capitalist critique, the old man's

---

50. From a lecture on *White,* op. cit.

alternative (which appeals to him) is to bury the money, an equally useless idea, unless one is paranoid of being robbed, as the old man clearly is. This is also an allusion to Christ's parable of the ten talents in which he suggests that burying the talents is a waste of resources.[51]

After Karol finds Mikołaj again and they restart their suicidal plan, a tiny, seemingly throwaway scene follows. It begins in close-up with the spinning of the French franc. A wider shot reveals Karol's face after stopping it. Nothing is said, but we read in his expression a look of resolve, however troubled. This talismanic moment, a consulting of the oracle, demonstrates a willingness on Karol's part to halt his plan, but the coin spells destiny as surely as the Judge's flip of the coin in *Red*. Indeed, the chance factor has been in dialectical tension with a certain predestined outcome throughout this film (from the God-like machinations of Karol manipulating his wife to the undeniable flash-forwards of Dominique in her Warsaw hotel room). His hesitancy is understandable, as his next step will require him to kill someone in the quest for money. We aren't sure exactly how his consultation with the coin turned out, because we do not know the terms in his mind, but another flash-forward to Dominique in her hotel room (a shot sequentially following the previously seen flash-forward) suggests progression in his mind and the abiding goal. He presses on with the plan.

The suicide scene and its consequent scene of boyish jubilation stand among the greatest dramatic moments in all of Kieślowski's films, simply for the perfection of dramatic timing they exhibit. When Mikołaj announces that he is the suicidal man, it is clear Karol has suspected this all along. Mikołaj forces the gun to his chest, and the suspense lingers: will he kill the only friend he has? The biblical maxim is turned around: "Greater love hath no man than this, that a man he lay down his life for his friend," Jesus once said.[52] As a show of "love," Karol must lay down his friend's life. The remarkable gamble Karol takes — and his true act of love — is to take Mikołaj to the liminal moment. This is the same limit that has been tested by numerous characters throughout Kieślowski's films: Dorota fingering the glass, Jacek fingering the rock, Julie nudging the piano lid support — all efforts aimed at finding the limit from which one can see more clearly. In all other cases they fall, but here, with the help of a friend, Mikołaj can be shown the edge of the cliff without tumbling over. With the first pistol

51. Matthew 25:15–30.
52. John 15:13.

shot, Mikołaj sags in extraordinary (and transcendent) slow motion. He hangs in liminal time, amputated from temporal chronos, a soul suspended in eternal space for a moment. Or so we all think. He collapses upon his friend and executioner, and after what seems to be an eternity, opens his eyes in the temporal world again.[53] Karol assures him that the next shot will not be a blank and asks him, yet again, if he is sure. Having seen the yawning abyss, Mikołaj no longer wants it. His existential dilemma has not changed, as their ensuing pedestrian conversation illustrates: "Mikołaj, we all have pain. . . . " "Yes, but I wanted less of it." Mikołaj gives Karol the money, and to his great relief, Karol has effectively gained all he needed and more.

The following scene, a quiet, luminescent winter pond (gorgeously photographed by Kłosiński) is suddenly energized by Preisner's romping tango and the sight of the two men dashing and sliding across the ice, liquor in hand, overcome with relief and sheer joy. We remember little Paweł in *Decalogue I,* and the tragic end to his love for the ice, but this story may function as something of Paweł's redemption. Both men collapse in happy exhaustion, and Mikołaj remarks that he feels like a kid again and that "everything seems possible." This same existential moment, a window of hope, glittering before other Kieślowskian characters (fleeting, as Piotr articulates in *Decalogue V* and *A Short Film about Killing*), manages to stay open here. The two men's happy faces, bathed in golden light, mark the central transcendent moment in this film, a welcome digression from the sarcastic, cynical tone that has marked the film throughout.

The thugs come after Karol, of course, and his airtight plan works: everything is willed to the church if he dies. From a more cynical point of view, one might say that one can count on the church to hang on to every square inch of Poland it can have. In either case, the gangsters are "screwed." Karol's carefully selected lots are all purchased by the gangsters (at 1,000 percent profit to Karol) over a handshake and the parting exchange: "You're a son of a bitch." "No, I just needed the money." This dichotomy rings with political critique as though Karol can claim that his actions do not demonstrate his true ideals and financial need suspends the ethical. But of

---

53. The beginning of this shot (the close-up of Mikołaj in a sitting position) has been slowed down as well, as careful inspection of the scene shows. Kieślowski clearly intended the time structures of the scene to move between normal and extranormal temporalities.

course, in this farcical comedy, the only people swindled are the swindlers, so all is well.

The following scene shows Mikołaj arriving at home with a Christmas tree mounted atop his modest car. "Shall I cut the engine, boss?" a gruff, moblike voice asks. Instead of an expected gangster reply, Karol remarks casually to keep the car warm (clearly asserting that he has enough money to burn gasoline, a coveted commodity in Poland).

Upon recruiting Mikołaj for his new company and wishing him a Merry Christmas, Karol witnesses a funeral. This scene not only demonstrates the sort of ironic synchronies that pervade the Kieślowskian universe (one man's moment of fortune is another's tragic end), but it also signals, in a straightforward way, that Karol's plan for revenge was not entirely clear until this point. The sight of the casket clearly sparks in him an idea.

The scene in the bare office is a comic version of Bednarz's tour of his new apartment in *The Scar*. The blank space signals a positive emptiness — a hopeful space begging for promising content. In Bednarz's case, it proves to be a substitute for home. In Karol's case, it is the reconstitution of a home he has lost. In both cases, however, the new dwelling turns out false. For Bednarz, the results are tragic and clear. In this film, Kieślowski signals this hollowness through comedy. The very next scene shows Karol making a flurry of business decisions as he walks through a giant warehouse, a ridiculous scenario (i.e., his instant business savvy, selling everything from food to electronics on the advice of experts). The next scene shows him building an actual lavish home for himself, and, in an equally ridiculous stroke, ordering the perimeter wall be torn down so that four small centimeters may be added to its depth, simply because someone nearby told him he should do so. Karol is the caricature of new capitalism: quick ascension with quick profits based on the beck and call of others. There is little sense of the whole, organic man, making life decisions on his own personal principles.

Karol awakes in the night dreaming of Dominique and attempts to contact her for the first time since that dreadful sexual taunting in Paris. She scarcely realizes it, but this is her final chance to avoid Karol's vengeance and accept his love (a paradoxical duality that is common enough in romance and caricatured throughout this film). She hangs up on him. The next scene shows him revising his will, leaving everything to his "ex-wife, Dominique." The incomparable Alexandr Bardini, playing the lawyer, pauses comically at the announcement. Dominique's name is not far from the French word *dominer* (meaning "to dominate"), and, thus far, she has lived up to her name. However, irony is a theme in all Kieślowskian films and it is most magnified here: by giving her everything, Karol will best steal everything from her, and so will dominate the dominator. So the final theme of the film, the French virtue of equality, will itself be ironically rendered here: an equality of misery and poverty, a getting even that leaves everyone broke.

Karol is clearly discontent. The flash of joy inherent in his quick rise to power still leaves him powerless in the face of his dreams of Dominique. He throws his plan into motion by having a clandestine meeting with Mikołaj outside, fearing the office has been bugged (a paranoia not unlike that of the old man from whom he first purchased the land). Mikołaj's bland acceptance of Karol's shocking news (that he will officially "die") highlights the grand reversal: a pseudo-death wrought by Karol upon Mikołaj produced a new approach to life; Mikołaj will now effect the same upon Karol, no questions asked. He flatly states that he does not want to know why Karol is executing this plan, most likely because he does know. His past experience has shown him that happiness cannot come through material means and that human desire, even in the face of death, is complex. He is an existentialist, and he is happy to return the existential favor to Karol — to facilitate a situation where he can choose his own convoluted fate.

Kieślowski's critique of soulless capitalism hits its apex in the purchase of the corpse ("These days you can buy anything," Karol's driver says). The dead man is discussed as a commodity, easily labeled and exchanged: a "Russian import." The driver asserts that things "couldn't be better" because the man is impossible to identify because of his crushed visage. All that is precious to our humanity is demeaned here: identity, thoughts, ideals, memories (all symbolized by the head). The corpse can be partially seen (a horror not unlike the corpse in *Decalogue III)*. This poor man is the quintessential pedestrian lost in the act of leaning his head out the train window. Why? To say goodbye to his family, perhaps? His story is not told, quite deliberately, as the man's commodification has rendered his memory irrelevant to his practical and economic value.

By this point, on the verge of sacrificing his fortune, it is clear that Karol has, parable-like, reached the end of his love for money. The cash is only as good as the vengeful power it bestows, and, as if to put to rest his financial ambitions, he buries his talismanic French franc with the corpse. It is fitting that a symbol of luck and chance also carries the connotation of unbridled capitalism. In this film, money rises far above its normal semiotic significance.

Like so many Kieślowskian women before her, Dominique understands something of her love for her husband in the face of his death. As if in comic dialogue with that motif, Kieślowski places Karol as a spy at his own funeral, gratified at his logistical achievement, but given pause at his wife's belated tears. The realization that she might, in fact, truly love him, throws him into conflict. He sighs and stares at the heavens.

Dominique's reaction upon seeing Karol in her bed is, of course, ridiculous. It is entirely unrealistic that she would not launch into an angry tirade at his manipulation of her. But this is not realistic drama; this is farce — an exaggeration intended to highlight certain truths that get buried under the realism of everyday life. The truth is Dominique loves him. She has always loved him. She needed him to be more self-assured, confident, and unsuspicious and to believe her when she claimed she loved him. A product of the West, she also needed a man with power. He is all these things now, having ascended and manipulated the game to the fullest extent. As she submits, almost comically helpless, to his romantic advance, they move to sex, and it is no coincidence that he is on top, a precise reversal of their previous coital attempt. He climaxes early (a potential disappointment for Dominique), but his renewed efforts on her behalf double his stature in her eyes. The fade to a celestial white at the point of climax is amusing, and for the first time brings the color white back to its original connotation: equality.

"You won't look at me?" she asks, and we shall soon discover why. When he does, he turns the conversation back toward competition ("You moaned louder than you did on the phone"). As her lithe, white body slumbers, beautifully entwined within the red sheets, Karol gets dressed. He picks up the phone and we wonder why. To call off the plan? The expression on his face as he hangs up the phone, gazing at his sleeping lover, suggests something of a pause in conscience. In a farcical turn, however, his face suddenly becomes mischievous, and a look at his watch and out the window suggests the plot is moving according to plan.

Just as she framed him for arson, falsely setting the police upon him, he cannot resist the vengeful symmetry. Her arrest for his murder forces her into despair, declaring him buried and dead, though she knows he is alive and has won the game. Her troubled expression is greeted by a reprise of the wedding scene, this time from her consciousness. All things being "equal," they are both united in the memory of what they have lost. A cut to Karol in close-up suggests his equal participation in this memory, and the return to the flashback extends it: to a wedding kiss between them. As Karol contemplates, he looks through his comb ("that once defined him," Insdorf observes[54]), another example of Kieślowskian characters attempting to see the world in a different way (one remembers Paweł's look through the electronic equipment at his father in *Decalogue I* and Filip's continual framing of the world with his fingers in *Camera Buff*). Karol's perspective is certainly changed now.

Why does he go forward with the plan? In typical Kieślowskian fashion, the motives are ambiguous and unexplained. In the original screenplay, Karol has second thoughts and desperately tries to halt his own plan, but Kieślowski cut this from the final film.[55] Perhaps Karol continues because he does not understand the full extent of his actions or motives. His mischievous look suggests that he is enjoying the cruel game, but perhaps he has abandoned himself to this happiness only because, once the trap has been sprung, there is no stopping it. His brother confirms, in the next scene, that to halt the plan would be to incriminate him, Mikołaj, the driver, and all the friends who helped him. Kieślowski suggests that Karol does not know, until the very end, that he really loves her.[56] For both Karol and Dominique, this realization only comes at the extreme, liminal edge, much like Mikołaj's experience.

Now, at the end of the game, Karol and Dominique are truly equal. Both have lost all the capital they have. Both have lost their public identities (hers by imprisonment and the surrender of her French passport, his by "death"). Kieślowski keeps the fairy-tale ending a possibility through the passing remark that the lawyer they have found for her "sees a light at the end of the tunnel." Indeed, a fairy-tale ending might not be inappropriate, as this highly unlikely story has ravished us with the negative, appealing to the darker sides of our humor and fantasies. Kieślowski once said:

> White is about equality understood as a contradiction. We understand the concept of "equality," that we all want to be equal. But I think this is absolutely not true. I don't think anybody really wants to be equal. Everybody wants to be more equal. There's a saying in Polish: There are those who are equal and those who are more equal.[57]

---

54. Insdorf, *Double Lives,* 163.

55. Krzysztof Kieślowski and Krzysztof Piesiewicz, *Three Colors Trilogy: Blue, White, Red* (London: Faber and Faber, 1998), 193–196.

56. Stok, *Kieślowski on Kieślowski,* 217.

57. Ibid.

The actual ending, however, is just as fanciful, humorous, and deeply sarcastic as the rest of the film.

Upon entering a mysterious place through metal doors (painted in striking, abstract brown and white stripes), Dominique and Karol see each other — she from the prison window, he from the prison yard via the very binoculars through which he saw her funeral tears. Their communication is through an intimate, nonverbal sign language, as the bars in front of Dominique roll out of focus (an image of happiness, Insdorf maintains[58]). Through a motion of handcuffs breaking, a person walking, and a wag of the finger, she suggests that she does not wish to escape. Rather, she still loves him, understands him, and wishes they be married again (through a gesture of a wedding ring on her finger). In short, she wishes to be bound in prison (temporarily?), so that she might be bound to him in marriage. The film ends with an extended close-up of Karol, deeply moved, tearful, and smiling. We do not know, at this point, how things will resolve between them. Even Preisner's score, ending the film on the sixth of the scale as opposed to the tonic, suggests a certain lack of resolution, and, for the characters, an open future. These characters will be seen again, however, at the end of the trilogy.

I interpret this scene as a farcical ending to a farcical journey. Through caricature, Kieślowski has examined and amplified the tensions inherent in all relationships: the need to give oneself while retaining one's identity, the need for trust to flow from security in one's self, the deep desire to love in extreme coupled with hate in the extreme upon failure. In the end, the sarcastic suggestion that one might achieve happiness and "equality" with one's mate through revenge, exploitation, manipulation, and loss of identity and liberty is to clearly assert the opposite: love cannot possibly flow from these things. What does it flow from? Well, that is a metaphysical question, and a winking Kieślowski leaves us to wonder as the credits roll.

Red (1994)

SYNOPSIS: *Valentine (Irène Jacob), a model in Geneva, has a jealous lover in England who is only heard, never seen in this film. She lives in an apartment above Café Joseph, which, we will learn, coincidentally, bears the name of the old man she will soon meet; this cafe c contains a slot machine, by which Valentine daily tests her fortunes. One day, when e accidentally strikes a dog with her car, her concern for the animal leads*

---

58. Fr   a lecture on *White,* op. cit.

her to its callous, mysterious owner, an old retired judge named Joseph Kern (Jean-Louis Trintignant). He is clearly bitter and disagreeable. Further encounters reveal him eavesdropping electronically on his neighbors. Despite her disgust, her relationship with him deepens, partly through circumstantial interactions, but mainly because of his remarkable understanding of her (including her fears for her brother Marc, a drug abuser). A secondary plotline follows the path of a young law student, Auguste (Jean-Pierre Lorit) who is trying to pass his bar exam, and his relationship with a woman named Karin (Frédérique Feder), who soon proves unfaithful to him. Remarkable coincidences abound in the film (e.g., Auguste drops a textbook in the street, and the page that is open upon its retrieval contains the answer to a key question on his exam). Some of these coincidences unite the plotlines of the different characters. More significantly, Auguste's plotline, in the end, proves to be a type of reincarnation of the Judge's life, lived decades before. As Valentine's feelings for the Judge shift from contempt to compassion, the Judge turns himself in to the authorities. In a tender conversation after Valentine's fashion show, the Judge reveals his own story to her: his love for a woman, her betrayal of him with another man, and his later dilemma of having to pronounce sentence on her lover. His disenchantment with the law and justice had spiraled into a general bitter skepticism. His insidious eavesdropping became a means of accessing truths to which he, as a judge, was not privy before. His affection for Valentine is obvious, and he tells her of a dream he had of her in which she was happy with a man beside her. Valentine, mistakenly assured by this, embarks upon a ferry trip to visit her lover. Disaster ensues, and only seven survivors remain: the barman of the ship, Stephen Killian; Julie and Olivier (from Blue*); Karol and Dominique (from* White*); and Valentine and Auguste. The film ends with the Judge staring out a broken window in his home, a solitary tear rolling down his cheek.*

In addition to declaring it his "most personal film,"[59] Kieślowski once said that *Red* is a film "in the conditional mood." As an example, he states that we cannot really be sure whether Auguste exists or whether he is a variation of the Judge's life forty years later. The heart of the film is about "whether people aren't, by chance, sometimes born at the wrong time."[60] In other interviews, Kieślowski stretches this conditionality even further, suggesting that, perhaps, the Judge himself does not really exist.[61] All this conditionality has led several critics to connect this film with Shakespeare's

---

59. Geoff Andrew, *The 'Three Colours' Trilogy* (London: BFI Publishing, 1998), 52.

60. Stok, *Kieślowski on Kieślowski,* 218.

61. Vincent Amiel and Michel Ciment, "Entretien avec Krzysztof Kieślowski: 'La fraternité existe dès que l'on est prêt à écouter l'autre,'" *Positif* 403 (September 1994): 28.

final work, *The Tempest*.[62] In that play, we see fantasy and reflexivity unite with dramatic action as Shakespeare gives us his subtle commentary on his career in artmaking through a fanciful story. The same interpretation may be applied here.

Kieślowski aligned himself with the Judge, saying "[T]o a great extent, he reflects my worldview. That's why I've often said that *Red* is very close to me." Yet, in the same interview, he added, "There is also this naive look that Valentine casts on people and things.... You could say that their opposing positions are mine." Irène Jacob, the actress who plays Valentine, aligns these positions with an interior struggle in the director: "How can the hopes of youth coexist with the experience of maturity?"[63] Indeed, that question had been asked by Kieślowski and Piesiewicz since their first collaboration, *No End*, where young Jacek becomes enchanted with a political movement for which his mother has no more stamina, physically or spiritually.

Given Kieślowski's self-alignment with the Judge, there is a strong case to be made that this film is, indeed, highly reflective of Kieślowski's life-long pursuit of metaphysics. The diegetic instances in the film point to larger cosmological issues, and Kieślowski, to the end, continued to "try to understand" the answers.[64] If *Véronique* tackled the issue of metaphysics and space (whether a unifying pan-spatial connection can exist between different souls), Kieślowski here approaches the metaphysical issue of time head on. In the divine economy, can the sins and injustices of history be redressed? As Kieślowski stated: "Has a mistake been committed some-where? And if it has, then is there anybody in a position to rectify it?"[65] In this film, Kieślowski drives harder than ever to the very core issue: the brokenness of reality and his desire for redemption.

Indeed, this story is no light fantasy. It is a dialogue between hopeful myth and the concrete, pedestrian world, where uncanny connections and occurrences form threads between characters who go to dance lessons, struggle with petty annoyances (like gum stuck in a front door lock), go

---

Cited in Paul Coates, "Kieślowski and the Antipolitics of Color: A Reading of the 'Three Colors' Trilogy," *Cinema Journal* 41.2 (Winter 2002): 62.

62. Wilson, *Memory and Survival,* 94–95; Andrew, *The 'Three Colours' Trilogy,* 60; Insdorf, *Double Lives,* 177.

63. Both citations are Insdorf's translations (ibid., 180) of *Krzysztof Kieślowski: Textes réunis et présentés par Vincent Amiel* (Paris: POSITIF/Jean-Michel Place, 1997), 146, 140.

64. Stok, *Kieślowski on Kieślowski,* 196.

65. Ibid., 220.

bowling, and so on. The concrete, immanental reality dialogues consistently with overarching metaphysical possibilities, and any accusation that the film is sentimental are quickly countered by the hard realism of tragedy. Valentine's brother is a drug addict. The Judge's neighbor, a closet homosexual with a family, seems surely doomed to misery (as the Judge predicts, "Sooner or later, he'll jump out a window"). On top of this, while the end of the film yields hope for all our characters (including the dramatis personae from the previous two films), it remains deeply tragic for everyone else. Kieślowski and Piesiewicz do not hide the ugly truth: our characters are the only survivors (save one) among more than 1,400 deaths. This staggering number cannot be dismissed lightly, and Kieślowski's daring to end his trilogy with such a massive tragedy deserves attention.

However, even this tragedy completes several thematic circles begun in early Kieślowskian films. Like the father in *Decalogue I*, the Judge has realized he cannot be God. In the former case, the realization is devastating. In this case, it is an enormous burden lifted from a very tired old man. The Judge's salvation is that, amid 1,400 deaths, there is a survivor for whom he cares deeply (and a resident hope, spoken by the wordless final image, that his own past mistakes may not be repeated). *Decalogue I* tells us the stories of the victims, and the iconic Madonna weeps in the end. *Red* is about the survivors, not just of this tragedy but of all the existential perils Kieślowski has ever addressed, and the Judge weeps in an equally iconic posture. The *Decalogue* grapples vigorously with absolute, universal questions. *Red* makes a gracious peace with the lack of answers, remaining hopeful at the end of a remarkable career.

This narrative is something of a veiled love story. It is not your typical May-December romance, but there is little doubt that the affection between Valentine and the Judge could have, under different circumstances, developed into passion. As it is, however, they develop something closer to a father-daughter relationship, and, in the vein of *Decalogue IV*, Kieślowski utilizes that familial romantic tension to interrogate the very definition of love (the bedrock beneath "fraternity") and search for something of an essence to this, the ultimate metaphysical concept. In numerous theologies, love is the premier virtue and the foundation for all others. Here we see that the entire trilogy has been built upon this concept. The liberty of *Blue* is posited to be the fruit of love, as demonstrated by the final sequence. The inverted approach to equality in *White* is shown to be the product of love's absence and its surprising reappearance the hope for the film's redemption. *Red*'s fraternity is revealed to be a path to a more far-reaching love, stretching beyond ordinary temporal friendship into the vast expanse of cosmological possibility.

Like *Véronique,* it is difficult to do this film justice on the printed page. So much of its import — indeed, its essence — lies in the phenomenological realm. The opening shot is the first example. A description can reveal something of the semiotic power in the image, but little of the experience Kieślowski has crafted through his abstraction of time and space. After a view of a telephone with a drink and Valentine's picture near it, the camera traces the electronic pulse of the call through the telephone cable. Cinematographer Piotr Sobociński filmed this sequence with a steadicam undercranking at three frames per second, resulting in a rocketlike pace upon playback. "We thought about using computers," he says, "but the scene had no life that way."[66] A certain organic root of the image is needed, even in the middle of this "impossible" spectacle, partly because the effect aims to describe a very real process.[67]

Abstract images pervade the sequence as metaphysical fingerprints, suggesting that the film we are about to see encompasses more than passing conversation. As the camera moves through myriad locations, we hear fragments of the numerous conversations the line carries. The image and sound embody one of Kieślowski's greatest themes: networks of communication, not simply technological, but existential. They also symbolize something deeper: a subterranean bedrock to human life, the search for which Kieślowski initiates at the beginning of this film. Kieślowski himself noted that all three films begin "in the basement of civilization, and of technology."[68]

Technology, for Kieślowski, is often synecdochic of his wider interest in human connectedness. Each of these conversations, Kieślowski reminds us continually, represents a reality: a very real world for someone. Just as he intended originally to pick a few stories out of a filled stadium of people as the genesis for the *Decalogue,* so Kieślowski is signaling to us that just a few stories are represented here. They are not more or less important than any

---

66. Stephen Pizzello, "Piotr Sobociński: *Red,*" *American Cinematographer* (June 1995): 73.

67. Close inspection of the film does suggests that one shot, the second one, intended to simulate a path through the internal wires of the telephone line, appears computer-generated after all.

68. "Kieślowski's Cinema Lesson," *White* (DVD, Miramax, 2003).

of the countless other stories he could have told. They exist to remind us that every life is fascinating and worthy of the telling, and that the narrative impulse is universal. In addition, the stories around us are intricately bound up in the stories of others. So complex is this existential matrix, that we may have connections, even vital connections, with people that surround us yet never make our acquaintance. At once the abiding concerns of *Blind Chance* return: possibility (the hope of miracle and revelation) and predestination (the suggestion that all our stories and their connections might bear the marks of ingenius design).

I have mentioned that technology is a theme for Kieślowski, and it is clear from this opening sequence that communication technology will play a vital role in the film. The hand we see dialing in the very first frame proves to be that of Michel, Valentine's boyfriend. This call and its subsequent, immediate redial are the first in several machinations of this controlling lover. Likewise, the embittered, technological intrusions of a cynical surveillant prove foundational for the story. Valentine's telephone discussions with her brother Marc (whom we never see) outline a tragic story, but visualization is denied. Valentine knows of the weather report girl, Karin, only through the Judge's illicit surveillance, though she has unknowingly seen Karin many times. Communication in the modern age encourages human interaction, but only of the partial, fragmented sort. The Judge's use of surveillance grants him insight into the darker corners of life that are hidden from us, but only at the expense of knowing these people in the flesh. One might argue that his assertion, "Here, at least, I know where the truth is," is, in fact, a more impoverished perspective on reality than he had before.

Kieślowski successfully transferred his documentary experience to the development of characters in *Red*. The dialogue in the beginning of the film is kept to a minimum. We do not *meet* the characters as much as we *observe* them in their respective environments and make our own conjectures about them as a result. Auguste keeps a slightly messy but charming apartment (he is a slightly messy but charming man). He plays with his dog (he is friendly and fun-loving). Later, he affectionately waves to his girlfriend (he is love-struck and vulnerable). In similar fashion, we learn that Valentine is cultured and professional, yet sweet, tender, and similarly vulnerable. Auguste tests the carrying strap on his books; they are secure (a small, but significant detail). Perhaps the most undervalued element in the scene, upon first viewing, is the poster on his wall. The image, that of a dancer extending gracefully backward, serves as a visual connection to Valentine (who will strike a nearly identical pose in her own dance class).[69] It is also worth noting that dancing itself incarnates the abstract. The dancer at once is immanent (a man or woman) and universal (a form that transcends himself or herself). Kieślowski's facination with dancers extends back to his days in the theater, his documentary *Seven Women of Different Ages* and scenes of dancers in *Personnel*.

Kieślowski loves these "links," not as cute connections between scenes, but rather, as expressions of the grand drama of unrealized relationships in the world, the thousands of "might have been" stories. These small links remind us that the world is sown with seeds of potential connection, and our lives are fundamentally shaped by our chance (or is it predestined?) nurturing of those we select. Bundled into these seemingly trivial events are a host of fundamental, important questions (free will vs. fate, the essence of a person, etc.).

The thematic color red is most prominent in this first sequence, culminating in the close-up of the Geneva switchboard light that rolls out of focus (an abstract telos) and ends the sequence. Like the other thematic colors, it will function here as a polysemous sign, closer to an abstract screen for the projection of emotion. The prominence of the color red in this film outweighs its counterparts in the other two chapters of the trilogy. The colors brown and orange (derivatives of red) abound as well, and the Swiss locale lends itself to the theme through its flag. Insdorf has remarked that the film is about isolation, and hence Switzerland, an island in the middle of Europe, seems appropriate.[70] To the extent that this is true, the film is also about the need to counter isolation through fraternity, and so the positive connotations of the color (love, signs of affection, etc.) will dialogue with its more negative associations (blood, for instance), mapping out the difficulties and possibilities of the ideal. The color more often appears in the mise-en-scène here than, say, through camera effects and filters. This may be seen as an attempt to more tightly weave the metaphysically suggestive abstract into the immanent fabric of the world. In addition, Sobociński

---

69. Indeed, a later shot shows the poster in close-up, with Auguste entering the frame in front of it, also in close-up. The connection between the man and the image is unmistakable. The same arched-back pose in the dance studio later precipitates Valentine seeing the Judge's story in the newspaper.

70. From a lecture at the Metropolitan Museum of Art, New York City, April 21, 2003.

took Vermeer as an inspiration and attempted to use primarily natural light, rather than manipulated artificial light sources.[71]

The audience truly does get a sense that it is passively observing these characters because they are introduced in fairly long takes. We see both Auguste and Valentine in their apartments. The camera is in wide shot and follows the characters as they move. The move to Valentine's apartment is particularly interesting in that the shot begins with Auguste walking out of his apartment. We see him walk down the street and cross it, and then the camera moves up to Valentine's window.[72] Still running, the camera cranes up into her window, where the phone is incessantly ringing. Valentine runs into the shot, answers the phone, and walks to the kitchen in the background. As the conversation progresses, she moves back again to the foreground, then moves across the apartment, the camera moving with her. Still running, the camera moves to a shot out the window, and Valentine moves into the frame to gaze at Auguste entering another building outside. The entire take is one minute, thirty-eight seconds long. In it, we have learned a great deal about this new character, all from observing a fairly typical ninety-eight seconds in this woman's life. Likewise, we have made a connection between her and Auguste (a theme that is crucial to the film).

The theoretical term for this shot is the *sequence shot* or the *plan sequence.* Over time, the term has broadened to encompass nearly every long shot that might have been visualized as several edited shots, but Kieślowski returns this long shot back to its original Bazinian connotation, a holistic approach to the world that Bazín noted in several important filmmakers, including Jean Renoir and Orson Welles[73] (whom Kieślowski greatly admired).

The crane shot into Véronique's window reveals a telephone table that also contains a red book (face down) and a half-eaten apple. Apart from their obvious contribution to the red theme, these items reveal something of her character (a certain restlessness that leaves many of her tasks incomplete). Her ensuing phone conversation with her boyfriend reveals his

---

71. Pizzello, "Piotr Sobociński," 70.

72. Pizzello writes that the shot was accomplished through the combination of a Technocrane and a dolly. (Ibid., 72–73). Says Sobociński: "We wanted to connect the outside world to our interior in a believable way, and we also wanted to establish the geography of the neighborhood.... [Valentine] and the younger judge in the film live very close together, but they never see each other. This move helped to convey their proximity."

73. André Bazín, *Jean Renoir* (New York: Touchstone, 1971), 64, 90.

mistrusting anticipation of infidelity. The sound of a helicopter (a foreshadowing of the rescue helicopter in the film's final moments) hangs over their
parting words: "I miss you."

Auguste picks up the phone. The opening sequence suggests it could
be Valentine, by intention or through a crossed wire. Instead, he connects
with his girlfriend, who runs the personal weather report service. The
next shot shows him departing, another sequence shot that places Auguste
and Valentine in the same frame. A series of sequences follow, many of
which function as expository for her character: she plays the lottery, goes
to a photo shoot, attends ballet class, drinks a sizable bottle of water, and
performs in a fashion show. Of all these sequences, only the photo shoot
and the fashion show are of any real consequence later. Most unimportant
to the plot is her ballet lesson. However, here again, Kieślowski allows the
audience to get to know Valentine by observing her relentlessly through an
extended stretch in the ballet and a long take watching her sloppily guzzle
the water after the lesson. This drinking shot appears unnecessary, except
that it is believable that Valentine would do such a thing. The water may be
a sign of innocence and purity, a connection that Fellini often made with
women in his films, but the phenomenology appears stronger than semiotics
here. We have witnessed a moment — perhaps not a pivotal moment, but
a true one.

During the fashion show, she stumbles slightly (very much like the
staggerings of Irène Jacob's other Kieślowskian characters, Weronika and
Véronique). After the fashion show, the stumble seems to signal a greater
accident ahead. Her trip across town is chronicled, in part, through an
extraordinary shot: a quasi-POV of the car, the red rear taillight dominant
in the right-hand side of the frame. We last saw a taillight image of this
magnitude in *Decalogue III* (which Sobociński also photographed). In that
film, the abstract marked a key moment in the drama: a frenzied car ride,
the outcome of which would be life or death. Here, the ride has a different
significance, but something no less spiritually momentous. Valentine pulls
up to an intersection that might be called *the* intersection for this film, the
sight of an enormous advertisement upon which her image will be mounted
(a detail not understood on first viewing, but clear in subsequent ones). As
she crosses the crosswalk, Auguste walks perpendicular to her, carrying his
books. After she passes, the strap securing his books breaks: a providential
moment on providential ground. Indeed, this whole film is characterized by
what Glenn Man calls "the aesthetics of intersection." Within this mosaic

of characters (and the camera's highlighting of their unknown proximity to each other) the film's structure reflects a "centralized enunciative authority."[74] Neither Man nor Kieślowski will name this authority as God, but the question as to whether it *is* God designing these intersections is constantly dangling over the narrative.

As Valentine drives, static squawks over her radio, and prominent abstract reflections play across her windshield. The static resembles the sounds of the Judge's electronic eavesdropping equipment. Perhaps this is the cause, perhaps it is mere chance or divine plan, but the resulting accident with his dog triggers Valentine's meeting with the old man. Just as the pigeon symbolized nature in *White,* Rita the German shepherd will stand for a teleology in the world, continually bringing Valentine back to the Judge. It is interesting how much time Kieślowski gives to this scene here. Kieślowski himself talked about the ruthlessness of editing — the need to trim away all but the essential material; in his mind, it was important that we see the slow registration of horror on Valentine's face and her very labored efforts to load the dog into the car. It says something of her compassion. The red bloodstains on her hands signal to us that the color itself will prove to be more than artifice; it is the dramatic canvas onto which all metaphysical issues will be painted.

As Valentine enters the Judge's house, Kieślowski treats us to the shot discussed in Chapter 2: that of her POV, which then morphs into a more objective profile. This scene was detailed in Chapter 2, but I should mention that the final profile here rhymes with the enormous advertisement that will haunt the primary traffic intersection of the film.

It is difficult to describe the mysterious feeling the Judge exudes, a mark of the wonderfully complex, nuanced performance of Jean-Louis Trintignant. We first see him with his back toward us and his head slumped in fatigue. From the state of the house and its abandoned rooms, it appears as if he might have been sitting there for decades. The disorted sounds of the radio suggest that perhaps he is dead (and, to a degree, he is, suspended in the half-life of isolation and one-way communication). Valentine's conversation with him angers her, not because he is a raving lunatic, but because he has a cold heart, dismissing his dog's welfare as unimportant. He mentions that Rita had run away the day before, making us wonder why she

---

74. From a paper, presented at the 2003 Society for Cinema and Media Studies conference, entitled "Realism in the Multi-Protagonist Film," 6, 9.

had. Valentine's acerbic quip, "If I ran over your daughter would you be so indifferent?" receives an unexpected, thoughtful reply: "I have no daughter, miss." The comment has cut deeper than she knows; the Judge's story will later reveal a betrayal by his wife that leaves him childless forever. Despite his apparent indifference and dismissal of her, he forcefully insists she leave the door open as she exits, another phrase laden with more meaning than it first appears. As she leaves, he watches her from the window.

In her next conversation with her boyfriend, she suggests to him that happenstance is never merely chance (i.e., their own chance meeting), and perhaps, even now, she suspects that the accident with the dog is significant. Her reaction to the name Marc in the vet's office certainly suggests she is looking for significance, jumping at her brother's name (though we do not understand this yet). Her boyfriend, on the other hand, is cynical, suspicious, and looking for betrayal.

The scene with the photographer reveals a number of interesting and important things. First, the seemingly banal idea of a bubble gum advertisement becomes a wider metaphor: "the breath of life." This advertising slogan, pretentious to the point of insult, does inform the narrative here. Valentine will become an invigorating force in the life of the Judge — a pleasant breeze blowing through his dusty, decrepit house. She will also be one of the few people at the film's end still living. When asked if she will be recognized in the ad, Valentine's response suggests that she has a lack of true friends. The photographer attempts to seduce her, turning out the light and asking her what she is thinking, just as he manipulated her thoughts during the photo shoot earlier (encouraging her to look sad). These artificial emotional machinations on his part do not move her, and she rebuffs him. She seeks a genuine connection, one that engages her free choice yet also bears the marks of a certain predestination, a relationship that is meant to be.

The next morning Valentine begins her routine again. The newspaper this day bears bad tidings, though Kieślowski does not give us the details of this troublesome news. As Auguste recedes with his dog into his apartment, the camera racks focus to Valentine's hand in the foreground pulling the slot machine; the chain of circumstance is more labyrinthine than she knows, and the weight of this pull heavier than she can conceive. The machine has been called the "one-armed bandit," and here it yields fortune (at a price). The scales of good and bad must be balanced, in Valentine's experience ("I think I know why I won"). The coins are deposited into a large jar holding her other fortunes, as if to save them for emergencies. We learn that the paper carries a picture of her brother, though it is still not clear why her reaction is so negative. We later deduce that her brother's picture accompanies a story on drugs in Switzerland, and her winnings at the slot machine are part of a fatalistic mode in the film that Insdorf calls "compensatory."[75]

The escapades of the dog, Rita, provide welcome comic relief at this point, but also function like a magnet (not unlike the magnetic force holding the coin to Karol's hand in *White*), drawing Valentine toward her destiny. The dog does return to the Judge, and upon finding her again, the Judge urges Valentine to call the dog ("She is yours," he says). Rita, tellingly, stays put, looking back and forth between the two people, as if to draw them together. Valentine discovers that the money she received at home via anonymous delivery was from the Judge to cover the veterinary bills. She is stunned that he had found her address. "That was easy," he asserts, adding to the impression that the Judge may, in fact, possess some extraordinary powers. She insists on returning the excess money, and the Judge asks her to wait while he retrieves some change in the house. He does not come back out for some time, precipitating Valentine's second entrance into the domicile.

This little scene may seem obvious, but in fact there is a very subtle form of dramatic tension going on. The idea of debt becomes the moral burden shifting between them. Valentine wants no extra generosity from the Judge, in part, because she is distressed at his lack of investment in his dog. The Judge does not insist on the extra money, but, instead, uses the exchange as a lure into his home. At this point in the film, the audience has no idea what the Judge is up to, why he is acting so strangely, or why he so nonchalantly accepts Valentine's acid barbs (e.g., she suggests he stop breathing; never breaking stride he responds, "Good idea"). There is an element of suspense as Valentine finally enters the house, and the POV shot (a horror movie code for impending danger) supports the idea.

But the horror here is metaphysical and moral, not physical. Disembodied voices play throughout the house, talking of bodies and sexual longing. The Judge, who apparently wished her to discover his clandestine activities, callously remarks that Valentine cut off the conversation just as things were getting interesting. Why the Judge wishes to be exposed in his eavesdropping

---

75. Metropolitan Museum of Art lecture, op. cit.

is unknown and only grows more complex as the film moves along. At first, it appears he takes pleasure in shocking her and witnessing her reactions to his loathsome activities. Then it appears he is attempting to use these shocks to read her soul — to diabolically cross-examine her on her views of human nature (Hannibal Lecter–like), including her own motivations for not telling the truth to the man next door. Finally, as the film nears a conclusion and their friendship begins to bloom, it appears that the Judge needed to be caught in order to save himself from self-destruction.

As a matter of justice, before Valentine marches over to tell the neighbor he is being spied upon, the Judge points to her remaining thirty francs (the money he owes her). The thirty francs may be seen as a modern manifestation of the thirty pieces of silver for which Judas betrayed Christ — the Judge's attempt to rid himself of his guilty gains. (As an in-joke, the money sits upon a Van Budenmayer record jacket, the film composer Zbigniew Preisner's alter ego). The challenge to turn him in is issued by the Judge himself. Valentine, upon realizing the little girl's knowledge of the neighbor's affair has vastly amplified the ramifications of any disclosure, cannot bring herself to follow through. Instead, she turns upon the Judge, asking him to stop his aural peep show. "I've done it all my life," he responds, and he reveals that he was once a judge (as he callously and contemptuously spills hot water on his floor — a wasting of the communal image of tea in the Kieślowskian lexicon). In many respects, from that bench, he was constantly listening in on people's private affairs as a witness to their personal crises and society's perpetual decay. Ironically, he often did not know enough, however, to give his judgments the moral force of the truth. The approximatory nature of human judgment became frustrating to him. "I don't know if I was on the good side or the bad side. Here, at least, I know where the truth is."

In many respects, this film is about that wider issue: the search for truth and its terrible pitfalls. One needs a sort of faith to weather the agnostic storm. Valentine, symbolizing love via her namesake saint, suggests that faith is also a matter of action — a reaching out amid the meaninglessness. The Judge's face, behind the glass of his window as he watches Valentine march back from the neighbor's house, suggests a type of imprisonment, a self-induced isolation that allows him to see and hear all, but touch no one. That glass will be proverbially and literally shattered.

In his relentless cross-examination of her, he suggests that the motivations for moral action are just as suspect as the motivations for illicit activity.

("Did you feel remorse, or were you afraid to do harm?" The paradox that one must sometimes do harm, for the greater good, is a continual burr to him.) Motivations remain complex and often self-interested. In the end, he asserts that it does not matter, because sooner or later that situation next door will erupt into chaos. "What can we do about it?" he asks, a question that he, as a failed judge (in his estimation), has no doubt asked himself thousands of times. The Judge resorts to cynicism and personal amusement as he watches the world burn around him. His forceful assessment of the situation gives Valentine great pause, forcing her thoughts to a boy she knows, who the careful viewer will understand to be her brother. The Judge is equally perceptive, having guessed much of the story from his read of Valentine's reactions, her aggression toward the drug dealer, and her misplaced newspaper article. Her brother, Marc, discovered he was not his father's son when he was fifteen years old, a revelation that spawned years of self-destruction and family tension. The young girl in the next house gives Valentine pause precisely because her life is another manifestation of this destructive pattern of a parent's sins being visited upon a child. A certain paralysis develops in this scenario. At the very moment that she makes this connection between the young girl and her own brother, the Judge asks her to be still. In an eerie moment of prescience, he states, "The light is beautiful."

As if at his command, sunlight breaks through the clouds and fills the room with light. The effect is difficult to describe. On one level, the light is a metaphor for the resident, abiding hope that if beauty still exists in the world, grace may also exist. This is offset by the sense that the Judge has some apparent causal relationship to the light. The camera cranes upward in a transcendent, God's-eye gesture. At this very moment, a bodiless voice comes over the sound system. "Personal weather reports," Auguste's girlfriend answers the phone, and we hear her meteorological advice to a traveler. Kieślowski's transformation of such a modern, pedestrian thing as a personal weather report service into a transcendent metaphor is the hallmark of his style. These metaphors will not work without visual support, and it is precisely the nonverbal epistemological weight that the images carry that create the metaphor's foundation. A personal weather report indeed; can one predict the storminess in one's life? It is precisely the surprise of the "weather" in our everyday experience that reminds us of the need for something greater than ourselves.

The sun disappears just before the next call from Auguste. As the two discuss their lovemaking of the night before, Valentine covers her ears, attempting to act ethically in the situation (or, as the Judge suggested in the earlier scenario, acting in self-interest, fear, or possibly jealousy). The Judge is playing a new role and raises his finger in prediction before Auguste speaks. His God-like omniscience blends with an image of chance as he flips a coin in concert with the woman's coin. He winces at the result, and her voice confirms it: tails, meaning the two will go bowling together tonight.

It seems the Judge does not cause the future, but has developed a strong acuity for its probabilities. As the conversation finishes, the Judge asks her if she listened at all, and her negative response is coupled with yet another reflection of Valentine's face in the glass of a nearby picture (one of many multiplied images of her in the Judge's house). She is a divided, unsettled person, but the reflection also suggests potentiality: the idea that she might become a new person, in this case, *with* a new person; at the same time, she may also be the woman of the past the Judge never met (as he suggests later). The Judge matter-of-factly asserts that Auguste has not met the right woman yet. The Judge may know a lot of evil things, but this is the first suggestion (a revelation even to him, perhaps) that he may see projections of grace in the future as well (the relationship of Valentine and Auguste). When asked how he knows Auguste is misguided, the Judge does not claim intuition, but observation; his is a rigorous and jaded sense, rather than a mystical premonition. He is, overall, pessimistic, much as Kieślowski confessed himself to be. "I've got an increasingly strong feeling that all we really care about is ourselves," he once said.[76] Perhaps Valentine is a manifestation of his great hope that he might be wrong about that. The ensuing conversation here seems to indicate so. It may also explain why the Judge, in a later conversation, urges Valentine to simply "be," so that this hope may not cease to exist.

The next subject of the Judge's observation is a drug dealer. He utilizes this scenario to provoke Valentine's capacity for hatred and vengeance. Having read the article on her brother, he has guessed her sensitivity on the drug issue and proves correct in his anticipation that she will lash out ("You deserve to die," she tells the man). "What did I do?" she says to herself somewhat regretfully after making the call. The Judge encourages her on, giving her the man's number, and suggesting that she be bitter like himself.

---

76. Stok, *Kieślowski on Kieślowski,* 217.

The Judge has said to her, "What can we do about it?" and that question hangs over the fourth overheard conversation: an old woman manipulating her daughter to come see her through feigned needs. Kieślowski and Piesiewicz carefully structured this remarkable episode at the Judge's house around four conversations. Voices without bodies suggest a sort of universality. They move through four scenarios; the first addresses a form of desire (and betrayal), the second discusses love and sex ("romantic," the Judge says), the third illustrates a clear-cut case of wrongdoing, and the fourth represents a conventional family drama about a mother and daughter. Each of these dramas, with the exception of the third, contains sympathetic appeal as well as grounds for punishment. The conversations illustrate the tangle of good and evil in the world in all sorts of characters. Amid all this overwhelming complexity, even Valentine's "judgment" in the third case strikes her as hollow. Each scenario appeals to a different sensibility in Valentine (the first to her idealization of privacy, the second to her need for romance, the third to her bitterness about her brother, and the fourth to her compassion). In every case, the Judge seeks to complicate her ideals on these topics — to throw her into an ethical tailspin and see if she can retain her identity (her compassionate essence). He sarcastically suggests she do the old woman's errands (alluded to in the fourth phone call), implicitly suggesting that she cannot possibly solve all the problems in the world, and that her little acts of kindness are, most likely, self-perpetuating mechanisms of comfort, a balm for her conscience rather than a consistent, efficacious application of an ideal.

The Judge is fascinated by this paralysis and the question of human motivation in general. Like Alexandre in *The Double Life of Véronique,* he manipulates to observe reactions in human subjects. Whereas Alexandre initiated his experiment for his own curiosity's sake (as well as physical attraction), the Judge is repeating an experiment he has long exercised as a contemptible mode of self-assurance — a self-congratulatory affirmation of his own nihilistic cynicism. Valentine is but one more helpless human pointlessly treading water in the existential sea. The questions he asks Valentine and his manipulation of her all aim to show her the complexity of her actions and motivations. She is forced to admit that, perhaps, she acted in self-interest (at least partly), both in her hesitancy with the neighbor and in her rescue of Rita. He even demystifies the story of the old woman needing errands done, suggesting the she has a history of lying about her needs as a means to manipulate her daughter into seeing her. Valentine acknowledges that this may be true, at least partially, but she insists that the Judge is wrong about human nature. People are not bad, she avows, and asserts that she can only feel pity for him before she leaves.

Valentine's arguments fall flat in the face of the Judge's interrogation, but clearly her compassion, turned upon him in the end, strikes him in an unexpected way. The term *theodicy* has been used to describe an argument for God's goodness even in the presence of evil. Though in no way theologically explicit, Valentine's character is something of a living theodicy, particularly if coupled with the "miraculous" synchronies of the film. The film might seem essentially humanistic and nonreligious, but Kieślowski does not simply neuter the religious mystery; he leaves the door open for divine action and probes the shaky foundations of a humanistic ethical system. It is precisely because the Judge is right about human nature that humanistic moral systems will not work. In short, they posit ideals that cannot be fulfilled because they make false assumptions about the inherent goodness of the human person. On the other hand, Valentine exists to show the Judge that his experience may be general but not absolute. Goodness exists in the world, and, wherever it comes from, it should become the telos of one's efforts. To deny it philosophically is, in actuality, an axiological cop-out.

The theme music of the film plays in a minor key as Valentine drives home. The images are multiple and abstract, the most remarkable being the contrary movements of the road in front and the reflection of the road behind in the rearview mirror, suggesting a multiplicity of place and direction. In short, it is abstract, eternal geography, and Valentine's drive follows a very disturbing moment for her spiritually.[77] All of her values have been shaken to the core, and the most painful parts of her life have been dredged up in the Judge's home courtroom. Her insecurity and loneliness reflect themselves in her rootless, winding, seemingly directionless drive.

Kieślowski traces her arrival home with her passing by Auguste, who fruitlessly endeavors to return to his apartment in time to receive a phone call (from Karin, we assume). He calls her back, and the line is busy. Kieślowski is constantly vexing us with the existential scenario: should we be suspicious when a lover's line is busy? Perhaps so; perhaps not. In the case of Valentine's boyfriend, he should not, and we despise him for his suspicion. In this case, Auguste does not appear bothered by the busy signal, but he well should be (we later discover).

---

77. See Chapter 2 for a still image from this shot.

The next shot reveals Valentine dialing (suggesting a yet-unrealized telephonic connection between them). The phone call is a reverse lie of the fourth call in the Judge's home. The old woman claimed to be unwell, when she was (at least on the physical level). In this case, Marc insists he is well, but the conversation reveals quite the opposite. He abruptly ends it, and Valentine longs for comfort from her boyfriend, Michel.

The photographer Jacques invites her bowling, the very social outing at which Auguste is to meet his girlfriend (though Valentine does not know this, since her ears were covered). The remarkable shot of the bowling ball creates a strong, vibrant impression of red movement contrasting with the light tan floor below it. This vibrancy, inherent in the red of the ball, the red sweater Valentine wears, and numerous other items, darkens as the camera tracks several lanes over to a haunting still life: a red-and-white crushed cigarette package (the Marlboros we have come to associate with Auguste) and a shattered beer glass (an image of brokenness that will resonate both positively and negatively in the Judge's house later). This is the aftermath of a connection missed, not simply between Valentine and Auguste, but between Auguste and his girlfriend, with whom he apparently never connected at the bowling alley. They will reunite for a few more scenes, but disaster is close.

We witness the slow ascension (from the underworld?) of a van equipped with flashing lights and a revolving electronic receiving dish. The music stops suddenly, and only the grind of the vehicle can be heard. Kieślowski amplifies the sobriety of the moment through cuts of open, unpopulated spaces: the drug dealer's backyard (reflections of the flashing lights subtly glimmering off the windows of that house) and a shot of the Judge's property, the van slowly entering the frame and coming to rest there.

Auguste passes his exams, aided by the open page of the book dropped in the street. His girlfriend presents him with a gift of a fountain pen (exactly like the Judge's broken one). As he wonders what his first signed judgment will be, we see the Judge facing his neighbors outside the courtroom for his eavesdropping hearing. In addition to the awkwardness of this encounter, Auguste's girlfriend meets another man here (another of the Judge's victims). In a sense, the Judge has brought them together.

Valentine's headphones in the record store cut her off from Auguste and his girlfriend listening behind her, a new manifestation of her covered ears when overhearing their previous conversation. The music is by Van Budenmayer (the soundtrack from *Decalogue IX*), which continues the in-joke, but also suggests that Valentine is thinking about the old Judge and attempting to forge a connection with him (assuming she saw the Van Budenmayer record in his home).

Valentine, for the first time, is invited into the Judge's house (not manipulated). As she closes the door behind her, she notices the sun dropping behind a mountain — an echo of their previous meeting and a reminder of the literal ray of hope present at that occasion. The Judge has turned himself in because she asked him too, he says. She had appealed to his pity by telling him Rita was pregnant, and now the dog has delivered. The seven puppies, Insdorf maintains, correspond to the seven survivors at the end of the film.[78] The young lives are, indeed, a symbol of new life and, for the Judge, something of an ironic rebirth. Further, they are the redemption of the infant rats that Julie has killed (at the cost of her conscience) in *Blue*.

The conversation that ensues is strange in some respects, and the editing is somewhat choppy, in synchrony with the fits and starts of the Judge's behavior. The Judge asserts that he turned himself in to see what she would do, and his gestures as he talks suggest something like a sexual advance. Valentine clearly backs away a step but ultimately holds her ground. It is as if she realizes that this is the end of the bravado and manipulative conversation from him. He is finally coming to terms with himself and, perhaps, his past. One line appears aggressive, only to be followed with a pitiable statement. He finally sits down with her and asks her to smile for him. This incredibly manipulative gesture may, in fact, be the opposite of the machinations of the photographer (who asked her to be sad), but it is manipulation all the same. Valentine's great virtue, however, is that she recognizes this manipulation as an expression of need. After thought, she yields a smile, however bashful.

The Judge tells her that the day she left crying was the day he began writing his penitent letters. "The fountain pen I'd used all my life was out of ink," he says proverbially, and as he continues with the story, the camera races backward and into a side room, rushing on a dilapidated billiard table with a giant broken jar on it. This is a forceful image, punctuating their conversation with a dramatic sweep of intensity and power, but it ultimately remains enigmatic. In the original script, the allusion becomes only a bit more clear through the Judge's story (excised from the film):

---

78. From a lecture at the Metropolitan Museum of Art, op. cit.

I used to spend hours playing billiards at one time. I wasn't much good. Once I took a clumsy shot. The ball fell off the table straight into a large glass. We couldn't get it out. And I had to break the glass. . . .[79]

The import of this story is that it directly follows the Judge's observation that Valentine was at the bowling alley at the same time as Auguste. We know from the previous scene that Auguste's presence was symbolized by broken glass. The roundness of the billiard balls and the sharp glass edges link Auguste with the Judge and also look forward, imagistically, to the stones and broken windows the Judge's neighbors give him.

However, with the script's words excised, these connections are difficult to make. Kieślowski's reasons for leaving the shot in remain his own, but I conjecture that the strength of the image has more to do with form and experience than metaphor. In many ways, this shot is typical of the Kieślowskian style, which prizes experience over clarity. We must respond to it intuitively as a rush to broken glass and all it might typify. We have no obvious metaphorical connection (brokenness as good? Brokenness as bad? A "break through" or "shattering"?); we must simply fold it into the emotion of the moment. It functions like a visual surge of adrenaline at the high point of the Judge's life story.

The conversation turns toward Auguste and his girlfriend, and the Judge says the relationship is nearly over. Visibly angry, Valentine walks across the room and turns in accusation ("Did you provoke it?" she asks). As she speaks, the wide shot reveals them, a strong vertical line (a bookcase) dividing them (much like a shot out of an Antonioni film). The Judge confesses that, in a way, he has provoked it through his eavesdropping and trial.

Their conversation continues into the evening as darkness falls. She feels guilty about abandoning her mother and brother at the height of their troubles to go to England to visit Michel. The Judge speaks as if omniscient: "Leave; it's your destiny." She wishes she could help her brother, and he suggests that she "be." That is it. Existence. To be is the best remedy. It is also the one request Witek had of God in *Blind Chance,* and, perhaps, Valentine is the Judge's first indication that, in fact, He might "be."

The Judge announces that on this very day (his birthday) thirty-five years earlier he rendered one of his first judgments (and we are mindful that today is the commencement of Auguste's first case). The Judge acquitted a man

79. Kieślowski and Piesiewicz, *Three Colours Trilogy,* 261.

that he now says was guilty. The bulb burns out on the lamp between them, and the Judge replaces it with one from above. The light bursts onto the dark scene, emblazoning Valentine's face with oppressive light. The shade restores a balance and a warm reddish tone.[80] Kieślowski seems to be suggesting here that the hard truth, such as that gained by surveillance, can be too difficult to process, but darkness is no acceptable alternative. The diffuse light is best, and the Judge's slow revelation of his own story to Valentine (a process that will take several days to complete) illustrates the point. One is reminded of the poem (#1129) by Emily Dickinson:

> Tell all the Truth but tell it slant —
> Success in Circuit lies
> Too bright for our infirm Delight
> The Truth's superb surprise
> As Lightning to the Children eased
> With explanation kind
> The Truth must dazzle gradually
> Or every man be blind —

Valentine believes that the Judge's acquittal was necessary, in that, in the end, the man went on to live a happy life (a providential view). The Judge speaks about how many others he could have acquitted, even if guilty, in order to "save them." She toasts him (the return of the Kieślowskian communal drink image), asserting she would like him to be her Judge if ever she were in court. He asserts that she will never be in court: "Justice does not deal with the innocent." He has never been sure of anyone else's innocence, and this is why he obeyed her. Cut directly against this statement is a startling moment of judgment: a rock through the window. Even this image, broken glass and a collection of stones on the piano, will be redeemed as a symbol of grace. Those who live in glass houses should not throw stones, the Judge has learned over his lifetime, and he keeps the rocks as a reminder; in his neighbors' place, he asserts, he would kill, steal, and lie.

The Judge is a God figure in many respects, and his powers reflect Kieślowski's God-like powers to manipulate the filmic image, but the thrust of the film is the Judge's lifelong realization that he is *not* God and cannot possibly know the truth or significance of everything. His surveillance has been a blatant attempt to be God (the original temptation of humankind, according to Genesis[81]). He wants to know the absolute truth — to make

---

80. See Chapter 2 for still images from this scene.
81. Genesis 3:4.

absolutely correct judgments; ironically, the more he learns, the more difficult he finds the judgments to be (does one turn the adulterous man in, to the peril of his family?). To believe in one's ability to know what is true and what is not seems to him a "lack of modesty." "Vanity?" Valentine suggests, alluding directly to the biblical book of Ecclesiastes. He agrees. His intuition that the ferry is her destiny is shaken, as he considers for a moment that he may very well have sent Valentine unknowingly to her death. When she emerges with Auguste, he is given a picture of grace. He cannot control the future, but perhaps something (or Someone) else does.

When asked if he has ever loved someone, he states flatly that the day before he had dreamed of her, old and happy. Though she doubtless understands that he is projecting her back into his past (what might have been different, had they loved one another), she forces him to turn it into a kindness to her: "Do your dreams ever come true?" He refuses to answer directly, though his statement may, in fact, suggest the affirmative: "It's been years since I dreamed something nice."

By this point, it is clear that several parallels exist between Auguste and the Judge. These similarities continue to emerge until it becomes clear that Auguste, in fact, is tracing the Judge's life over again. He repeats the tragedies in the Judge's story, but the end of the story incarnates Werner's hope in *Blind Chance* that the younger generation will do better than his own. The two generations here are another manifestation of that film's three possibilities. Auguste's reckless trip to his girlfriend's apartment is paired with a close-up on the slot machine of the cafe (the good fortune of three cherries functioning as counterpoint to his bad fortune), and he eventually ascends (ironically by way of a garbage container) to his girlfriend's window (stumbling on the way, just as Valentine stumbled out of the Judge's apartment earlier, in spiritual distress). The window before him shows an empty room (her office) with ominous weather patterns playing over the computer (a foreshadowing he does not yet understand). The second window reveals his worst nightmare: her naked body copulating with another man. He arrives home in the morning, leaving his headlights on and his car battery to die, a parallel with the Judge's car, which rejuvenates for Valentine. Auguste pursues his girlfriend even on her date with the other man. Whereas he ultimately hides from her, the Judge does not, calling her weather service the next day for a report on the English Channel. It is then that she reveals her yachting trip (she had been looking at pictures of a sailboat on her date with the other man). She implies that she may go even further and, perhaps, not come back (she is closing up her business).

Auguste abandons his dog in despair by Lake Geneva, the very lake we have seen countless times as Valentine has ascended to the Judge's home and Auguste to his girlfriend's apartment. As we have seen, he is not the first judge to abandon his dog, the devoted creature dependent upon him. A later scene reveals that he returned for it, as he carries it on the ferry.

"We told you not to smile!" the producer of the fashion show says in stark contrast to the Judge's request of Valentine in his home. At this point, however, we are left to wonder if she will go on at all, as a passing wardrobe rack runs over her toe. Will she stumble again as she walks the platform? She does not, though her focus is clearly on the audience, searching. Just as a stumble carries a broader, metaphysical meaning, her search is not simply for the Judge. She is searching, period. The abstract flashes of cameras pop amid the inky blackness, and Valentine must wonder to herself if all is not vanity as the Judge affirmed. The show itself, a pageant of red, signals an emotional moment for Valentine as well. She is clearly sad afterward, staring at herself. The show, a display of her beauty, doubtless rings hollow in the face of Michel's lack of true love for her. As she prepares to leave, she sees the Judge amid the theater seats, a lone figure waving, engaging her, in a sea of red.

The Judge's first trip out, in what must have been many years, places him in the path of the enormous advertisement bearing Valentine's picture, and the slogan "The Breath of Life."[82] The significance for the Judge is obvious. After the show, their ensuing conversation proves to be the key unlocking all the synchronies and parallelisms of the film. The Judge tells several stories that directly parallel Auguste's life (the falling book, the betrayal of his blond love, etc.), and the Judge's sense of destiny has, no doubt, been building as he has discovered these details via his eavesdropping.

It also poses the question of whether history holds hidden graces, redemptions, and corrections that we cannot fully perceive. The Judge affirms that his dream will come true for Valentine (that she will be old, happy, and with a companion), but he does not know who the man will be. When asked who he is, he humbly replies: "A retired judge." This is true in many

---

82. The French text for this chewing gum advertisement is "En toute circonstance, Fraicheur de vivre," which could be translated, "In every occasion, the freshness of being alive."

ways, as he has stopped judging people and stopped trying to find out the truth about them. Like Véronique, Weronika, and so many Kieślowskian characters before her, Valentine testifies to the feeling that something important, but little understood, is happening around her. The Judge offers no interpretations or refutations. He simply extends his hand, a human touch they have not experienced between them.

The storm interrupts them, and the Judge's expression shows concern (a premonition) as Valentine struggles with the doors of the theater, swallowed up in the white of the curtain (not unlike the foam of the ocean). They retreat from the storm over some coffee. Kieślowski gives us one last communal image, a close-up of the two friends' cups together, the liquid gently rocking inside (cut with the sound of the doors being closed). The movement is slow, indeed, slowed down, and the next cut reveals the Judge holding his cup. This intervening, nearly abstract shot of the cups in a sea of background red, signals a timeless, metaphysically laden moment.

Valentine demonstrates insight of her own as she spells out for the Judge the major events of his story. In this touching conversation, Kieślowski seems to be asserting that Valentine's charity may be no less miraculous than the synchronies and uncanny twists of fate that have pervaded this film.

As the Judge speaks of seeing his wife in bed with a man named Hugo Holbling, an unexplained loud sound startles us all, Valentine included. This device fits the tension of the moment, but the sound itself is unidentified (we assume it is a swinging door from the storm or the dropping of a metal pail from the housekeeper); it fits the pattern of the bracket, encouraging emotional perception before identification. This is one among many creative uses of sound in this film, some of which were discussed in Chapter 2. Off-screen sounds have been common, primarily as diegetic harbingers of the film's catastrophic ending. Helicopters punctuate the soundtrack at odd times. A foghorn interrupts Valentine's photo shoot. In addition, the conversations between the Judge and Valentine often lapse into silence — an eerie, mysterious stillness that exudes mystery.[83] One gets the impression that the cosmos accompanies this drama and steers it.

They part the theater with a semitouch, their hands abstractly close-up, separated only by the glass of the car window. This marvelous cinematic

---

83. See interview with sound mixer William Flageollet in "Insights into Red," *Red* (DVD, Miramax, 2003).

gesture communicates so much more than simple character and plot resolution. The abstract nature of the shot amplifies the significance of it,
suggesting love of the highest, metaphysical order. The hand gesture is
even more significant in light of the fact that the Judge asked to see her
ferry ticket shortly before, as if he sensed something to come. At the same
time, the glass symbolizes a barrier: a romantic connection reached for, but
impossible.[84]

As he leaves, Valentine sees an old woman struggling to put a bottle in the
recycling bin. Unlike Julie and Karol, who failed charity in their encounters
with this situation, Valentine moves to help her. It is not only the redemption
of this motif of the trilogy but also of the fourth dilemma posited in the
Judge's house, the helping of the elderly woman who wished to see her
daughter. The glass shatters as it hits the bottom of the bin. Kieślowski,
when asked about the motif, replied: "All I want to do is remind us that
someday we might be too old to get a bottle into a recycling bin."[85] The
sound of breaking glass also redeems the shattered windows of the Judge's
house.

On the ferry, it is revealed that Auguste and Valentine ride together,
unaware of each other. It is possible that Auguste is following in the Judge's
footsteps, "crossing the Channel" in obsessive pursuit of his lover, who is
yachting nearby. The hull of the ship closes in a magnificent shot revealing,
only through a tiny crack, a ferry (swallowed in blackness). An equally
astonishing shot follows, that of Valentine's face, suddenly wrinkling and
collapsing; our initial perception of the image is revised as we see the image
is actually the removal of the advertisement. A mighty storm rolls through
Geneva, upsetting a lone glass of tea on the Judge's billiard table, spilling it
(and we worry this is a rupturing of their communion).

The Judge has clearly changed. He lovingly pets one of the puppies,
collaring it and setting it aside for Valentine upon her return. The storm
has passed, and a glorious morning shines through as he goes to fetch
his paper. The newspaper reveals the tragedy on the Channel, from which
only seven passengers have escaped. We are left to wonder, will this be yet
another Kieślowskian irony in which good fortune is coupled with disaster?
The Judge anxiously watches the news report on the television (brought
him by Valentine's brother, Marc). The cause of the accident is unknown

---

84. See Chapter 2 for a still image.
85. Insdorf, *Double Lives*, 181.

(steeping it in metaphysical mystery, not unlike the breaking of the ice in *Decalogue I*). We are told that, in addition to the ferry, a yacht carrying two people has also sunk; those aboard are missing (undoubtedly Auguste's girlfriend and her new love). Kieślowski spares us nothing, showing news pictures of dead bodies sliding down the side of the capsized ferry.

The survivors number seven, a perfect number in the Jewish biblical tradition. Stephen Killian (the ferry barkeep) is the only survivor with whom we are not familiar, but perhaps his story could be another film. Julie (from *Blue*) is shown, as are Karol and Dominique from *White* and then Olivier from *Blue*. Perhaps it is not prudent to read too much into these stories. (Why are Julie and Olivier not announced together? Why are Karol and Dominique on this ship? Has Dominique been released, or are they escaping together?) The questions remain, as do the questions surrounding Valentine and Auguste's future together (this shot is the first time they have made eye contact in the film). The freeze frame creates an astonishing visual parallel to the advertisement, the picture in which she expressed fear under the title "The Breath of Life." Never has the slogan been more appropriate, and the red jacket of a rescue worker forms the abstract red background that unifies the film and suggests the metaphysical order of things (beyond mere chance).[86]

Kieślowski then presents us with one of the most resonant images in all his career. The Judge, weeping for the first time, stands staring through the broken glass of his home. His iconic look engages us, incorporating us into the drama we have witnessed, insisting we engage with the image and consider all we have seen. I am hesitant to interpret the image too much, because, like so many images in the film, it loses something in the telling. All the same, we see the Judge has broken through in some way; the stones of judgment have, ironically, created a way of redemption. His gaze exudes mystery of a higher order than anything we have seen so far. The icon, this transcendent visual form, utilized for hundreds of years in the Christian church and so consistently by Kieślowski, leads us to the final image, a return to the freeze frame of Valentine in close-up. The breath of life.

---

86. The inspiration for this idea came from Sobociński (Pizzello, "Piotr Sobociński," 71–72).

Afterword

T he French critic Vincent Amiel shares my admiration for the final image of the judge in *Red*,[1] but for slightly different reasons. Amiel sees the broken window as an image of surrender, a symbol of the end of Kieślowski's career, and his efforts to make the cinema represent the real.

> In all other aesthetics, the journey of Kieślowski is of the same nature as that of a Fellini or of a Resnais throughout their filmography: from realism to artifice, of the will to testify to the affirmation of an arbitrary subjectivity. . . . All the mediations are contested [in *Red*]: the telephone, the recordings, the incessant screens formed by the windows between the looks, between the lights, between the hands that lay one on another. . . . And the judge, in the last scene, sees life at last through a broken window . . . *Red* marks in this way the end of the representation, but also, logically, the end of the cinema of Kieślowski. . . . Few artists have pushed to such heights of lucidity as well as honesty.[2]

Indeed, Kieślowski himself, in an interview with Geoff Andrew, affirmed that his retirement was partly influenced by his frustration with film's materiality, its helplessness "when it comes to describing the soul." At the very same time, Kieślowski also admitted, in his own self-effacing way, that he may have developed some "tricks" for escaping film's literalism in his last few films. He also testified to something of a "transcendent optimism" in these efforts.[3]

Undoubtedly, Amiel is correct in the sense that *Red* articulates the constant difficulty of transcendence, yet I hope that my analysis has shown that

---

1. See Chapter 2 for a still image of this shot.

2. Vincent Amiel, "Kieślowski et la méfiance du visible," in *Krzysztof Kieślowski,* ed. Vincent Amiel (Paris: Jean-Michel Place, 1997), 15. My thanks to Linnea Leonard Kickasola for this translation.

3. Geoff Andrew, *The 'Three Colours' Trilogy* (London: BFI Publishing, 1999), 82.

Kieślowski's style demarcated that liminal ground in a powerful fashion, beyond mere "tricks." The image of the judge behind the broken window is less an image of surrender than it is a suggestion that transcendence (and redemption) remains the essential possibility. This is the hope for Joseph Kern, the life-scarred, penitent Judge, and for all of us.

The New Trilogy

A year after Kieślowski's death, *Dialog* magazine printed the script for the inaugural effort in a new trilogy, consisting of the films *Paradise, Hell,* and *Purgatory.* Whereas the latter two films were to be written by Kieślowski's longtime collaborator, Krzysztof Piesiewicz, the script for *Heaven* had been completed largely by Piesiewicz and Kieślowski before his death. The lingering question was, of course, Who will direct? Many critics, including myself, reacted with great skepticism to the choice of the young German director Tom Tykwer, whose first film. *Run, Lola, Run,* bore some thematic resemblances to Kieślowski, but had little in common stylistically with him. As entertaining as *Lola* was, it did not approach the ingenious craftsmanship or philosophical depth that even the most humble Kieślowski films consistently showed, in my opinion. However, in *Heaven* (2002), Tykwer showed more sensitivity to Kieślowski's material than I expected. Wisely, he did not attempt to imitate the late director's style directly, but he did manage to incorporate abstraction in a subtle, complementary way that did not strike me as derivative or ostentatious. In short, the rich material, full of Kieślowskian synchronies, uncanny circumstances, spiritual crisis, and metaphysical suggestion, lends itself to abstraction, and Tykwer employed his own style in a way that respected what Kieślowski was trying to accomplish. I do not believe the film ultimately ascends to the artistic heights of Kieślowski's work, but it remains a worthy effort all the same. The final shot of the film is a particularly suggestive view of an ascending helicopter that transforms into a wondrous abstract image of transcendence, much as Kieślowski had described it in the script.[4]

---

4. Paul Coates translates: "The helicopter, still visible for a moment, melts into the sky. The light beneath it now looks like one of the stars hung high above the people looking upwards" (*Lucid Dreams: The Films of Krzysztof Kieślowski* [Trowbridge, Wiltshire, England: Flicks Books, 1999]), 13.

The story of *Heaven* follows Philippa, a woman who attempts to bomb the office of a drug runner, but ends up accidentally killing innocent people instead. Remembering the burning anger Valentine reserved for the drug dealer in *Red*, we might see Philippa as an amplification of this idea. Philippa (wonderfully acted by Cate Blanchett) is horrified to discover her reckless mistake, and, after her arrest, a police stenographer named Filippo (played by Giovanni Ribisi) senses her remorse, falls in love with her, and engineers her escape. The rest of the film traces their run from the law, the deepening of their amorous relationship, and the discovery of their uncanny similarities. It is clear, by the film's transcendentally suggestive conclusion, that the story has taken on a mythic quality.

Hell and *Purgatory* were the second and final films of the proposed trilogy that never made it past the treatment stage during Kieślowski's life. At the time of this writing, both projects are still in development. *Hell* lives up to its title, telling the story of a man falsely accused of child abuse, who returns to his home after imprisonment, only to find his family has become a disaster. He commits suicide, and the rest of the film traces the results of this devastating chain of events through the adult lives of the man's three children. Paul Coates notes that many Kieślowskian themes return, including telephones as markers of the loss of communication in the characters' lives.[5] The story of *Purgatory* largely remains a mystery at the time of this writing, but centers on a woman "whose reporter husband dies in Kosovo during the war."[6] Piesiewicz stated, in an interview with Annette Insdorf, that all these later scripts contained an unusual amount of individual descriptions of images.[7] In my opinion, we have yet to see a filmmaker who will be able to do them justice; Kieślowski simply cannot be replaced.

A Final Word

In an interview with Paul Coates, Kieślowski said:

> ... I make films for people like me, people who are open to sitting down and having a chat, reflecting together, sharing. In other words, I think that,

---

5. Ibid., 12–14.

6. "Heaven Can't Wait," *The Guardian* (online version), May 24, 2002, http://film.guardian.co.uk/interview/interviewpages/0,6737,720934,00.html (accessed July 24, 2003).

7. Interview with Annette Insdorf, Harold Lloyd Master Seminar, American Film Institute, September 25, 2000.

if I share the film with the viewer, the viewer will share its reception with me — which means that there is a certain balance and justice about the matter. I tell him a story and expect him not only to hear it out, but also to enter into some kind of a relationship with it. And, in order for him to be able to do so, the story I tell him must leave him a certain amount of space and freedom to interpret or take it — or certain parts of it — one way or another. I've always thought this and still do today.[8]

I have attempted to give my own side of my virtual conversation with Kieślowski, and only regret that I was never able to make it actual. My own interpretation of his films sees his images as liminal, tracing the threshold of mystery in our human experience. Kieślowski flatly denied overt religious undertones to the word *mystery* in relation to his work, but at the same time he acknowledged "certain religious questions" posed in his films, arising from "the existential questions."[9] In short, Kieślowski saw reality as shot through with metaphysical possibilities. Mystery is

> purely and simply the mystery we actually face every day. The mystery of life, of death, of what follows death, what preceded life: the general mystery of our presence in the world at this particular time, in this particular social, political, personal and familial context, and any other context you might think of. . . . [B]ut I think that there is a point at which all these little mysteries come together like droplets of mercury to form a larger question about the meaning of life, about our presence here, what in fact went before and what will come after, whether there is someone who controls all this, or whether it all depends on our own reason or on someone or something else. That mystery is there all the time.[10]

In the end, Kieślowski's work is about the meanings we search for and occasionally find, folded within these mysteries. The sheer lucidity of his work, the resonance of his images, and the integrity of his spiritual search amount to the fulfillment of what George Steiner describes as the liminal telos of all great art:

> Why should there be art, why poetic creation? . . . The teeming prodigality of the phenomenal world, its inexhaustible deployment ("thereness") of sensory, communicative energies and forms is such as to saturate even the hungriest appetite for perception, even the most ample capacities for reception. The colours, metamorphic shapes and sonorities of the actual exceed immeasurably human capacities for registration and response. The animate logic of congruent symmetries, of organic motifs in the human body, is of

---

8. Coates, *Lucid Dreams,* 162.
9. Ibid., 167.
10. Ibid.

a designate wonder — a wonder of design as we see it in [Leonardo da Vinci's] famous icon of frontal and cosmic man — such as to overwhelm understanding. And it is in this tensed caesura between analytic intelligibility and perception, when cognition holds its breath, that our sense of being is host to beauty. Why, then, art, why the created realm of fiction? . . . [T]here is aesthetic creation because there is *creation*.[11]

---

11. George Steiner, *Real Presences* (Chicago: University of Chicago Press, 1989), 200–201.

Index